Kentucky Bluegrass
Country

Lynwood Montell, General Editor

FOLKLIFE IN THE SOUTH SERIES

Kentucky Bluegrass Country

R. Gerald Alvey

WITH A FOREWORD BY *Thomas D. Clark*

University Press of Mississippi Jackson and London

Copyright © 1992 by University Press of Mississippi
Manufactured in the United States of America

95 94 93 92   4 3 2 1

The paper in this book meets the guidelines for
permanence and durability of the Committee on
Production Guidelines for Book Longevity of the
Council on Library Resources.

Library of Congress Cataloging-in-Publication Data

Alvey, R. Gerald, 1935–
    Kentucky bluegrass country / R. Gerald Alvey;
with a foreword by Thomas D. Clark.
      p. cm. — (Folklife in the South series)
    Includes bibliographical references and index.
    ISBN 0-87805-510-X (alk. paper).
    ISBN 0-87805-544-4 (pbk. alk. paper)
    1. Kentucky—Social life and customs. I. Title.
II. Series.
F451.A68 1992   91-48029
976.9'3—dc20   CIP

British Library Cataloging-in-Publication data available

For Donna
my beloved wife

Contents

Folklife, a familiar concept in European scholarship for over a century, is the sum of a community's traditional forms of expression and behavior. It has claimed the attention of American folklorists since the 1950s. Each volume in the Folklife in the South Series focuses on the shared traditions that link people with their past and provide meaning and continuity for them in the present, and sets these traditions in the social contexts in which they flourish. Prepared by recognized scholars in various academic disciplines, these volumes are designed to be read separately. Each contains a vivid description of the traditional cultural elements—ethnic and mainstream, rural and urban—of a geographic area that, in concert with other recognizable southern regions, lend a unique interpretation to the complex social structure of the South.

Kentucky Bluegrass Country, the second in the Folklife in the South Series, is the best description by far ever written about Kentucky Bluegrass traditions. Richly imbued with history, this exemplary and definitive study examines the Bluegrass horse world, the traditions associated with tobacco and bourbon, the codes of the hunt, gambling and dueling customs, vernacular architecture, and regional foodways. *Kentucky Bluegrass Country* is unique among folklife studies for the attention it gives to the folk traditions of the well-to-do residents of the region.

William Lynwood Montell
SERIES EDITOR

The Bluegrass Region of Kentucky is a land set apart by geographers, historians, and the folkways of its inhabitants. At times it is difficult to separate fact from folklore and legend. There seems not to exist a clear documentary record as to who first proclaimed the land of the Bluegrass a western Eden. There is no mystery, however, about it being the magic lodestone, which early drew all sorts of adventurers, speculators, empire builders, and common footsore emigrants to it. First there were the Indians of several layers of culture who littered the land with their artifacts. They came from north and south to hunt, but not to establish their villages. The caneland was to them a great animal preserve, so much so that the Iroquois gave it the name Kentucky, or Land of Tomorrow.

In 1750 it was indeed the land of tomorrow for English and colonial American speculative companies. In April of that year the Loyal Land Company of Charlottesville, Virginia, sent Dr. Thomas Walker and a party of explorers west to spy out the land and to establish tomahawk claims to it. That party stopped just short of the Bluegrass, but it did open the great gateway, the Cumberland Gap. The next year the rival British Ohio Land Company sent Christopher Gist west to explore the fabled caneland, and he too failed to reach the Bluegrass, but left a journal of his experiences in a rough country.

The way was opened, and the time was rapidly approaching when long hunters and aimless wanderers would finally enter the Bluegrass Region. Buffalo and Indian trails already led from one salt lick to another or crossed the Region. By 1775 the Bluegrass canelands were no longer shrouded in Indian and long-hunter lore, even to European cartographers.

Once settlers drifted into the Bluegrass area and erected forts, blockhouses, and homes, and carved out farms, the land became fabulously productive. In hyperbole Sam Meredith, a friend of John Breckinridge, quoted the Baptist minister Lewis Craig as describing Heaven as "a Kentucky of a place." Meredith told Breckinridge that the land was so fertile that anyone desiring to create a numerous family quickly should move to the Bluegrass. He said, "Female animals of every sort are very prolific, it's frequent for ewes to bear three lambs at a time, & women & cows to have twins at a time."

The legend of fabulously fertile land nurtured legends and myths of equal fecundity. When Daniel Boone's trailbreaking party in 1775 at last cleared the barrier of the mountainous wilderness and stood in the saddle of the last land gap, they gazed into the hazy distance of cane and saw a herd of buffalo loping leisurely to cover. Young Felix Walker exclaimed in ecstasy that they had at last reached the Promised Land. Before them rolled the southern meadowlands of present-day Madison County, which in unbelievably short time would give rise to one of America's most self-satisfied societies.

There sprang up in the Region almost overnight farmsteads and family seats. What had been struggling yeoman farmers back on the exhausted soils of Virginia now became Kentucky country squires laying claims to broad acres in the valleys of the Kentucky, Hickman Creek, the Elkhorn forks, and along the Licking. Not only did farms or plantations come into existence almost within half a decade, so did a Kentucky panoply of heroes, great and small. Old land scouts and hunters like Daniel Boone, Simon Kenton, the McAfee Brothers, James Harrod, Michael Stoner, Richard Callaway, and the others were quickly succeeded by the Shelbys, Browns, Prestons, Clays, Harts, and Nicholases, who became political leaders and landed gentry.

Almost before the last Indian raid, which stormed Little Mount and Bryan's Station, and rendered the bloody thunderclap at the Lower Blue Licks, the raw frontier era was over in much of the Bluegrass. Rapidly "Old" Fayette County was subdivided and resubdivided into Bourbon, Woodford, Clark, Jessamine, and a part of Franklin counties. Along with the establishment of new county boundaries, there arose Georgian colonial family seats, which quickly reflected the impact of the land on the folkways of life. The fields and meadows returned rich bounties of field crops and of prime livestock.

The new Kentucky squire, like Henry Clay who had ridden over the lonely Wilderness Road on his way from the Slashes of Virginia, dreamed of the day when they would establish a new regional aristocracy of the land. They dreamed not only of creating a Kentucky gentry, but one in essence like that of rural England.

Prof. R. Gerald Alvey has produced a capital study, which gives full exposure to the folkways of the Kentucky Bluegrass. He has pursued his subject up many a byway of human occupation and the making of social adjustments in a strong and impelling natural environment. Here he presents a skillful blend of fact and fiction, and a keen sense of the realities of history itself. Always Bluegrass Kentuckians have lived at two, if not three, levels of history in the Region. The elevated level of fertile and productive land formed a firm basis for the creation of a colorful and romantic island in North America.

At an early date Bluegrass Kentucky became a major region of visitation for both European and domestic travelers. For Europeans on the "grand tour," Kentucky was the place to view the snaggletooth American frontiersman on his own rude doorstep. The only part of Kentucky the querulous visitors ever saw was along the Maysville Road to Lexington, and from Lexington to Louisville and a rejoining with the Ohio River. Many of their ephemeral impressions of the people, their habits, culture, or lack of it, and their views about things in general were gathered in the Bluegrass. The travelers saw only Bluegrass Kentuckians and those along the Ohio. Their associations with the people were fleeting and superficial.

Thomas Ashe, the notorious Irish liar, visited Kentucky on a so-called scientific visit. He left behind him a storm of denunciation and legends that would not die. He described a Bluegrass cavern of immense dimension, and traces of a lost race of men and their culture. Christian Schultze followed hard on Ashe's trail, denouncing him at every bend of the Ohio. To many of the visitors the Kentucky personality epitomized that of all frontier America. Thomas Hamilton on a visit to America in search of the truth about the Republic touched Kentucky at Louisville. He declared the natives the Irish of America, and the only Americans who could understand a joke. It was too bad that Hamilton was unable to visit Henry Clay at his Ashland estate as he had planned to do. Maybe he could have tested Clay to see if he could understand a joke.

Whether or not the Bluegrass Kentuckians were the Irish of America would have been furiously disputed by many of them. They could, however, enjoy a good yarn. They loved to spin yarns almost endlessly. Even more, they cherished the symbols of their land and culture. There was the everlasting stillhouse on the bank of a limestone creek, which produced liquor from the local grain and creek water and had a distinctive character. It was said that local gaugers developed such a discriminating taste for Bluegrass whiskey that they could tell on which side of the Kentucky River it was distilled.

The history of the first "stilling" of Kentucky bourbon is shrouded in myth, not so much as to its making, but who first distilled it. It sounds quaint to lay it on the Baptist preacher Elijah Craig. He was said to have been led from the narrow path of sobriety by the fertile land along the middle fork of Elkhorn Creek. No matter its origin, bourbon whiskey and Kentucky are all but synonymous.

How could the Bluegrass have bourbon without having Kentucky Colonels to quaff it? There may be a document somewhere, probably folded up as backing for an ancestor's portrait, that proves who the individual was who was first anointed "colonel" without being bloodied in battle, or who grew a mustache and goatee to honor the title. The historical record is mute on the subject. Colonels in the late nineteenth century and the first part of this one were honorary members of the governor's staff and wore fancy official uniforms to grace His Excellency. There was the story of a Lexington Colonel who went to a Main Street clothing store and got himself regally fitted in the official fancy suiting of the office. It was adorned with enough brass buttons to stagger an entire regiment, looped diagonally across the Colonel's bulging abdomen was a golden sash, and chained at the waist was a sword and scabbard. All of this rigging was topped off with a broadbrim Confederate gray hat. He strode down South Limestone Street to his home and knocked on the door. A child greeted him, and the Colonel asked if his mother was at home. The child ran through the house calling, "Mama, there's a man at the door who talks like Papa but looks like God."

The Colonels no longer look like God. There are so many of them the Governor would have difficulty finding a field big enough for them all to muster, and they have become only God's children with their commissions displayed on filling-station walls, over mountain mantel pieces, and in pine-paneled dens.

The land of the Bluegrass was created as much for animals as for people. Once buffalo, those great natural topographers, tramped out trails from grazing grounds to salt licks, and to the mountain passes and stream crossings. After the pioneers entered the great meadow of the Bluegrass, it would have been sacrilegious to have had available such bountiful grazing lands and not to have bred livestock of comparable quality. The horse, both beast of burden and sporting animal, has ever been a revered creature in the Bluegrass. Over two centuries a genealogist could possibly have better luck tracing the lineage of a Thoroughbred stallion than that of its owner. To have a touch of the blood of such sires as Grey Eagle, American Eclipse, Boston, Lexington, and later, Man O'War, Polynesian, or Whirlaway is comparable to human descent from Isaac Shelby, Daniel Boone, John Brown, Kentucky's first senator, or Henry Clay.

Few regional American communities have so many physical symbols, folkways, embroidered myths and legends as Bluegrass Kentucky. This is especially true of the sporting horse industry. It would be hard to visualize a Central Kentucky horse farm without at least a short span of rock fence, a long front of white board fencing, and hardwood paneled stables. The square cupola is as much a fixture of a horse barn as the stable cat and manure fork. One expects a lantern to flash a warning from these sentinels and horsemen dashing forth to warn of a calamity to come.

Professor Alvey has created an exciting book, which searches every alleyway of Bluegrass life, real and imagined. He has drawn into a unified text a clear concept of the concentric worlds that whirl around in the Bluegrass constellation. Of all the books written about horses in Kentucky, none gives such a clear picture of the workaday affairs behind the white plank fences and in the paneled barns of the horse farms. The breeding of Thoroughbred and Standardbred horses is a full story within itself, a story which the author handles with clear precision.

There have been, from the beginning of settlement of the Bluegrass Region, worlds within worlds, often with one having little knowledge of the other. Here are centered the golden Burley tobacco world with its emerald fields, staunch old weathered barns, and sprawling sales floors, a world which has generated its own rich folklore and legend. There is no more certain harbinger of spring than the long canvas-shrouded tobacco beds, which, like mushrooms, pop up overnight. Growing Burley tobacco is a "fifteen month a year" activity, and one crop is hardly sold before the next one is cast. From the purchase of seed to harvest, there is the routine of setting plants, cultivating, deworming, topping, cutting, barning, and stripping. In no spot in Kentucky, except the corridor of a rural courthouse, have more yarns been spun, more foxes run, more girls courted, more squirrels killed, and more liquor drunk than in an overheated Bluegrass tobacco stripping room in November each year.

Whirling around in its own particular Bluegrass orbit is the world of academia with its own folk characters and ways, always including the glittering sideshows of athletic events. Sometimes one wonders whether or not the central purpose of higher education in the Bluegrass is not to create an institutional excuse for supporting winning athletic teams. In season and out, college athletics, along with horse racing and a little cockfighting on the side, keeps the Region constantly astir with celebrations, which range from the tailgate pregame parties of the commoners to the pre-Derby extravaganzas of competing hostesses. All of these things keep up the swirl of the folk world of the Bluegrass, and all of them produce their folk characters, rich and poor, their folkways, and veil the real life of the Region beneath a pleasant gossamer of legend and myth.

Professor Alvey has written a book which for decades has cried out to be written. He has been diligent in his searches of a complex divergency of sources of information. He not only has written factually of life in the Region, but he demonstrates a clear understanding of the nuances of fact and legend by which Bluegrass Kentuckians have ever lived. The author has successfully created in this book a perceptive study of man's adaptations to the land and its mores, often in a colorful manner, and never in an entirely dull one. Not since James Lane Allen published his *Blue Grass Region of Kentucky* has this island of distinctive provincial American folk culture been treated in so competent a fashion.

The Bluegrass Region of Kentucky, since the day that brown tribesman chipped the first flint artifact along what is now the Mount Horeb Pike, down to the most recent Hamburg Place and Greentree Farm pre-Derby party or the last tailgate roundup, has drawn people to it from far and near. A barely literate Fayette County jailer once observed that he was geographically an ignorant man, but he knew full well the world is round because every so-and-so who ever left the Bluegrass always came back. Professor Alvey, in this book, has prepared them a clear folk map to guide them in their return to a comfortable world of culture and ways which they cherish. He has given literary perpetuity to that great mass of human experiences and regional manners and color that so often falls through the cracks of more formal historical presentation.

Thomas D. Clark
Lexington, Kentucky

This book constitutes a survey of the typical or dominant forms of folk culture found in the Bluegrass Region of Kentucky. Though not an exhaustive study, which would fill several volumes, this work concentrates upon those basic forms of Bluegrass folklife that exist in discernible *patterns*, ones that residents of the Bluegrass themselves recognize as contributing to the Region's distinctive character.

Most scholars agree that the Bluegrass Region has more or less natural—geographic and geological—boundaries, and that there is an "outer" and an "inner" Bluegrass; the Inner Bluegrass especially is a clearly defined geographic area with its own ecosystem. Culture, however, is another matter. People, not geography, create culture, and because people do not necessarily confine themselves by natural boundaries, culture often defies natural physiographic divisions.

Although this survey discusses Bluegrass folk culture in general, it concentrates upon the forms of culture typical of the Inner Bluegrass, especially the counties of Bourbon, Boyle, Clark, Fayette, Franklin, Jessamine, Mercer, Scott, and Woodford. It is in those counties that the cultural characteristics are most prevalent, characteristics that residents and nonresidents alike usually associate with the Bluegrass.

Three cultural systems operate in modern American society: folk, popular, and elite. This survey concentrates on Bluegrass folk culture, but it sometimes brings in popular and elite culture issues, since all three affect each other. Elite culture is learned primarily from formal, institutionalized, academic, official or legal or governmental sources; thus, elite culture is "establishment" culture. By contrast, popular culture is for the public—the crowd, the consumer. Popular culture is essentially mass media culture, learned from TV, movies, advertisements. Folk culture consists of those aspects of our lives learned from those closest to us—from family, friends, peers, and other intimates in an informal, nonacademic, noninstitutionalized, unofficial context. Folk culture is local traditional culture at the grass roots level.

Don Yoder, the dean of American folklife scholars, defines folklife studies as

a total scholarly concentration on the folk-levels of a . . . regional culture. In brief, folklife studies involves the analysis of a folk–culture in its entirety. . . . Folk

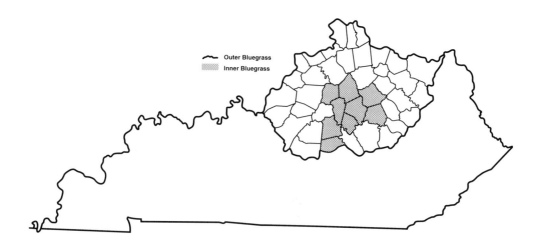

Map showing approxi-
mate boundaries of Inner
and Outer Bluegrass
and the nine counties
featured in this study
(Map by University of
Kentucky Cartography
Lab)

culture is traditional culture, bound by tradition and transmitted by tradition, and is basically (although not exclusively) rural and pre–industrial. Obviously it is the opposite of the mass-produced, mechanized, popular culture of the twentieth century.

In that respect, Kentucky might be seen as a natural "living laboratory" for the study of her folklife traditions, for her natural boundaries—the Ohio and Mississippi rivers and the Appalachian Mountains—have helped to keep her to herself. Her folklife traditions have been created and perpetuated—have *become* traditions—to a large degree because of the geographic uniqueness of Kentucky and especially the Bluegrass Region. As Tom Clark, the preeminent Kentucky historian, writes: "Geography determined the nature of the society and economy which would come to exist in all of Kentucky, particularly in the Bluegrass." Coupled with this relative geographic separation was a desire on the part of many early Kentuckians to remain separate, apart, even isolated, different—and proud of it. Even today Kentuckians have to a large degree maintained their cultural distinctiveness. Kentucky journalist M. B. Morton claims Kentuckians are torn between their "natural kindliness" and "intense partisanship," and as a consequence have become a "curious combina-tion of tolerance and intolerance." He writes:

There are no other people just like Kentuckians. They approach you differently. It is easy to make a friend or an enemy of a Kentuckian, and you must be either one or the other. There is no middle ground. They are a generous and a hospitable people, romantic and sentimental, they are proud of their reputation as judges of female loveliness, fine horses, and Kentucky whisky. They cannot help loving Kentucky women and Kentucky horses. Many of them are quite fond of draw poker. But candor compels the statement that thousands of Kentuckians never saw a race horse, played a game of chance, or took a drink of whisky. Yet Kentucky is the home of the Thoroughbred and Kentucky Bourbon....

This does not mean that all Kentuckians, or even all residents of the Bluegrass, are culturally homogeneous. Just as there is no such thing as a "typical" American, there is no such thing as a "typical" Bluegrass Kentuckian. In fact, considering that they are predominantly WASP, Kentuckians manifest great cultural diversity. Nevertheless, the Bluegrass, upon analysis, does reveal many identifiable cultural *patterns*. These, and many other folk cultural characteristics of Bluegrass residents are discussed throughout this study.

However, some folklife traditions found in the Bluegrass are not discussed here. For example, many people in the Bluegrass engage in folk crafts—quilting, wood carving, pottery, or the making of folk musical instruments, and so on—but such activities are neither unique to the Region nor by any means typify it. In addition, all sorts of oral folklore, including folksongs and musical traditions, and especially folk stories, are not treated separately.

Bluegrass residents—and Kentuckians in general—are addicted to storytelling, many being expert raconteurs, and folk stories on all sorts of topics and events are legion. Ask a Kentuckian a question, and he will likely as not tell you a story, the assumption being that imbedded in the story is an appropriate answer to your question. Thus, folktales are discussed in relation to other topics and activities, as they occur in the natural context of Bluegrass daily life.

"Bluegrass" music, on the other hand, has little connection with the Bluegrass Region. In the 1940s and 1950s, the style of music called Bluegrass began to be widely popularized by Bill Monroe and the Bluegrass Boys, the name of his band; it was so–called presumably because Monroe is from Kentucky—but Western Kentucky, not the Bluegrass Region—and because the name had appeal and recognition as the state's nickname. So Monroe's form of music quickly came to be known as Bluegrass music, although it is in essence derived from the Nashville and Grand Old Opry experience. Bluegrass music is, of course, played in the Bluegrass Region, and in recent years there has been an annual gathering—primarily of out–of–state musicians and aficionados—called the Festival of the Bluegrass. Aside from such incidental connections, Bluegrass music itself has little to do with the Region, and is therefore not included in this study.

Chief among the readily recognized and widespread folk traditions unique to the Bluegrass are the following cultural areas, discussed at length in this survey: traditional architectural forms on the Bluegrass landscape and traditions surrounding them (including black–white relationships, which are also discussed in relation to other pertinent topics); tobacco folk culture and its traditions; whiskey folk culture and its traditions; gambling traditions; dueling and traditions of violence; outdoor traditions, including hunting, fishing, and foxhunting; parties and other social and convivial folk traditions, including traditional gathering places; and, a very prominent Bluegrass tradition, folk foodways.

To many residents, however, the Bluegrass means, above all else, horses. Indeed, the love of horses traditionally has been a hallmark of all Kentuckians. There is an old saying: "If a man does not like horses, no matter where he happened to be born, he is not a Kentuckian." Lexington, the heart of the Bluegrass, has more monuments to horses than to people, and entire subdivisions and innumerable streets are named either after horses or horse interests. Kentucky's auto license plate displays a mare and her foal and is emblazoned with the proud epithet "The Bluegrass State." In some way horse interests and horse activities affect everyone in the Region and have, from the days of the first settlement, largely typified the Bluegrass, both in the eyes of fellow Kentuckians and the world.

Yet, raising horses in the Bluegrass is not merely a typical activity. Rather, there exists a "horse world" in the Bluegrass, which constitutes an enduring and complex folk culture; though, as notes Tom Clark, it is primarily a culture of the socioeconomic elite.

The horse world of the Bluegrass lives apart. The course of its life is guided by its own folk mores, an unorthodox kind of economics, and its peculiar needs are served as they arise. This landed island even exerts its peculiar pressures on its counties, and upon Frankfort. Horsemen use their own semantics [a distinct vernacular is a sure sign of a viable folk culture], and an outsider can commit no greater folly than to misuse their terms. To live and thrive in the horsy community offers social prestige, but demands a sizable backlog of ready cash to do so successfully. To be a really big horseman, breeding and racing glamorous stakes winners, necessitates phenomenal expenditures . . . so much in fact that since 1880 fewer native sons have been able to stand the gaff.

Most Bluegrass residents, of whatever socioeconomic status, readily recognize that the gentry have a traditional way of life, and they often refer to that wealthy sociocultural group with the generic folk term "the horsey set." It is often said in jest, but also with some envy, and sometimes even pride—pride in living in a Region where that way of life enjoys world renown, even though it has severely restricted membership and esoteric activities and traditions. Thus, the horse world, its history, culture, and influence, is central to an understanding of the Bluegrass.

By focusing upon the folk traditions of the Bluegrass horse world and its gentleman farmers, this study breaks with the conventional approach of most folklife studies, which seldom concern themselves with traditions of the socioeconomic elite. Many persons erroneously assign folk culture exclusively to the lower economic strata and automatically equate elite culture with affluence and social prestige. Some folklorists have even argued that folk culture is the sole province of the destitute and "the proletariat." Have–nots do possess an extensive folk culture, and they are represented in this survey, but they are not alone. All people have folk culture, and possession of wealth, position, and familiarity with elite taste does not preclude a traditional folk culture as well. The same folklorists, for example, who argue for a "proletariat" folk are quick to admit that there is an ongoing, viable folk culture of University faculty— one of the world's *most* culturally elite groups. Yet, faculty are not usually members of the social elite—not, for example, in the social register—nor are they often members of the economic elite, as average academic salaries will verify. To some extent, wealth and social position are antagonistic to folk traditions, but hardly ever to the point of completely eradicating them; moreover, new and different folk traditions always accompany each social or monetary level.

So although it is true that, as the socioeconomic elite, Bluegrass gentry usually have more ready access to, have been more influenced by, and perhaps have more appreciation of elite culture than the average nongentry Bluegrass resident, that fact does not automatically negate the influence of folk culture in their lives. As Wm. Hugh Jansen, a folklorist who resided in the Bluegrass for over thirty years, noted: "Too often folklore is considered the property of the underprivileged or of those isolated from the main trends of civilization." To illustrate, he cited the Bluegrass horse world's traditions, which he said embraced "the very rich, the poor, the aristocrats, members of the international set, poorly paid workers, and . . . curious . . . onlookers." In sum, social and economic status do not *necessarily* correlate with cultural orientation; and all people have folklore, no matter their social or economic class—including Bluegrass gentry.

Because, as folklife scholars are fond of saying, "Nothing less than the whole of the past is needed to understand the present," Part I of this work is an historical and folkloristic analysis of the social, cultural, and demographic influences that have shaped the Bluegrass. It is against that background that the other parts of this study should be viewed. Part II concerns itself with material culture—the tangible products created by a folk way of life. Because they are the most obvious folklife forms on the landscape, the many types of Bluegrass folk architecture are surveyed, including their builders and functions, as well as influences on them and resulting from them. In Part III the array of Bluegrass customs and other traditions listed above—those that best represent the Region—are presented in their historical contexts, with particular attention to traditions of Bluegrass gentleman farmers.

The Lay of the Land, and the People Who Walk on It

Limestone, "Blue" Grass, Boone, and Folk Worldview

The distinctive character of the Inner Bluegrass Region of Kentucky is revealed in pastoral scenes reminiscent of Christmas cards and pictorial calendars. Gently undulating pastures, beautifully expansive and graceful, are criss-crossed by black or white plank fences, or handmade limestone walls—called fences in Kentucky—beyond which are silhouetted tobacco or horse barns and other outbuildings, all in service to the main dwelling. Some of these homes are grand, some modest, and many are still functional nearly two hundred years after they were built.

The Bluegrass is indeed one of the world's more splendid examples of the beauty and ideals of a pastoral way of life. The late Colonel Phil T. Chinn, lifelong admirer of the Bluegrass, succinctly summarized his feelings about it: "It is unforgettable to see such beauty. Wouldn't it be hell, sir, to die and leave it?" Lexington lawyer and journalist J. Soule Smith was reconciled to dying by the thought of being buried in his beloved Bluegrass, so his spirit would be able to contemplate its glories eternally. Even nonnatives praise the Region's beauty. At the turn of the century, a circuit judge wrote: "When God made the picturesque valleys of Southwest Virginia, He was just practicing for the Bluegrass country."

Contemporary folk sayings continue this tradition of praise. People today still say that "heaven must be a Bluegrass of a place." Near Harrodsburg, which was the first white settlement in the Bluegrass, is the town of McAfee, named for the McAfee brothers who held a 1,000-acre preemption and surveyed it in 1773. When he first saw the area, Robert McAfee declared he had arrived at Eldorado—a local name for McAfee right up to modern times. Many early settlers from Virginia held this Eldorado concept of the Bluegrass. Felix Walker, one of Daniel Boone's companions, was so moved by his first sight of these lovely lands that he kissed the soil, and later wrote: "We felt ourselves as passengers through a wilderness just arrived at the fields of Elysium, or at a garden where there was no forbidden fruit." Many people still invoke that idyllic

Garden of Eden metaphor. Woodford countians have a saying that carries the idea still further: "If the Bluegrass is the country's garden spot, then Woodford County is its asparagus bed." In the same vein, other Bluegrass residents and even visitors refer to it as a modern-day Promised Land.

Many of the laudatory, often romantic, and even chauvinistic early descriptions of the Bluegrass were carried to outsiders by visitors to the Region. John Filson, who, following a trip in 1784, wrote Kentucky's first travelogue, called the area "the best tract of land in North America, and probably the world." Gilbert Imlay, like Filson a native of New Jersey, wrote a widely read description of the Region that was so tainted with romantic and chauvinistic comments that it is considered unreliable by some historians. Hyperbolic accounts of the Bluegrass were spread first by adventurers and hunters, and later through the stories of traveling journalists, businessmen, and other outsiders, not the least of whom were the riverboatmen, often loud, boisterous, drunken braggarts. Some of these storytellers had an ulterior motive in writing such transports: they were trying to lure settlers to the Region and sell them land. Curiously, many Kentuckians themselves believe these stereotypes.

Most stereotypes are, to some extent, condensations of prevalent folk notions and beliefs (and, often, a lot of wishful thinking), and whether they are founded in fact or fancy has little effect upon their acceptance and distribution. Such stereotypical views of the Bluegrass have become widely held folk beliefs, which are reflected in many stories and sayings. These illustrate and support a folk worldview of the Edenic qualities of the Bluegrass.

Yet, this Eden of the West stereotype fails to consider the often harsh and demanding experiences encountered by early settlers. They had to "solve" the so-called Indian problem—that is, displace them—and they had to "tame" the land to make it fit for permanent white habitation. The area was in many places so heavily forested that a settlers' joke held that three months chopping could scarcely make a "small sunlight hole in the woods."

The cane in the Bluegrass (*Arundinaria gigantea*, sometimes called American bamboo) was so thick and tall—in places as high as twenty feet and often two inches thick—that it was nearly impenetrable. A legend relates that in the 1770s two men were hunting separately, near what is now North Middletown. Each thought he was the only white man in the area, so when they heard one another through the thick canebrakes, each surmised an Indian was stalking him. After dodging one another for three days, they finally met. Elated and relieved to discover that neither was an Indian, they threw their arms around each other and embraced.

(Embracing is not at all common among male Kentuckians, even to this day, and it is probably this unusual aspect of the legend that lends it credibility.) Originally the cane was widespread throughout the entire Bluegrass, surrounding the sites of Harrodsburg and Georgetown, but by 1799 it was cleared, to the extent that it no longer presented a threat to farmers. The laborious efforts of these pioneers and subsequent settlers so "manicured" the area that today it resembles an immense pasture or garden. Little exaggeration is involved in such statements as this by Tom Clark: "Perhaps there is not on the earth a naturally richer country than the area of sixteen hundred square miles of which Lexington is the center. . . ."

LIMESTONE AND BLUE GRASS

Lying beneath the gently undulating pastures of the Bluegrass is limestone—in places, 25,000 feet thick—and this, some say, gives the soil of the Region its great virtues as grazing land for horses and other livestock. The mineral-rich soil produces grass that builds the bones and muscle of champions.

With unabashed geographic and geological determinism, Charles Dudley Warner claimed that the physical attractiveness and well-being of humans and animals alike, and even the culture of Bluegrass residents, derives from the Region's physical properties. He asserted that the fine horses, excellent cattle, and even "the stature of the men, and the beauty of the women" and their "social and moral" disposition and "graciousness of life" could be attributed to the Bluegrass Region's soil. Others who agreed even cited a nineteenth century study by the U.S. Army that provided the physical measurements of more than one million "white men" from the United States, Canada, Britain, Ireland, Germany, and Scandinavia, and revealed that the 50,333 men from Kentucky and Tennessee exceeded all the others "in average height, weight, and in their proportion of tall men, and their weight to the cubic inch." Aside from their obviously romantic and deterministic orientation, such sentiments reveal something of the folk worldview of many Bluegrass natives and admirers.

In support of that worldview, a number of beliefs, sayings, and stories contend, often humorously, that Bluegrass culture is to be found only within the specific geological perimeters of the Bluegrass itself. Warner says that he has "no doubt that there is a distinct variety of woman known as the blue-grass girl." As proof, he relates this story told to him by a Kentucky geologist who was exploring the Region with a fellow geologist, a non-Kentuckian:

As they approached the blue-grass region from the southward they were carefully examining the rock formations and studying the surface indications, which are usually marked on the border line, to determine exactly where the peculiar limestone formation began. Indications, however, were wanting. Suddenly... [the Kentucky] geologist looked up the road and exclaimed:

"We are in the blue-grass region now."

"How do you know?" asked the other.

"Why there is a blue-grass girl."

There was no mistaking the neat dress, the style, the rounded contours, the gracious personage. A few steps farther on the geologists found the outcropping of the blue limestone.

A more modern example of this Bluegrass worldview is a saying often emblazoned on bumper stickers, license plate frames, and tourist bric-a-brac: "Kentucky the Bluegrass State, Home of Beautiful Women, Fast Horses, and Good Whiskey" (sometimes the adjectives are reversed to yield "Beautiful Horses, Fast Women..."). Again reflecting geographic and geological determinism, Ulric Bell, among others, attributes these supposed Bluegrass characteristics to the limestone-enriched soil, maintaining, "If women are the prettiest, horses the swiftest and liquor the fieriest in Kentucky, it must be because of the soil."

The Famous Blue Grass Geology and geography obviously play a crucial role in the development and distribution of Bluegrass culture, but that fact should not be interpreted as geographic or geological determinism. Geologists say that the Bluegrass Region includes rocks of Ordovician, Silurian, and Devonian ages, and that its outer boundaries are marked by resistant limestones of Mississippian age. Folk culture boundaries in the Region closely align—are in places even congruent— with geological/geographical boundaries.

Some say that the limestone underlying the lush pastures—which in turn have permitted the evolution of successful farms, an affluent lifestyle, and accompanying culture—is itself also responsible for the claim that the famous grass grown in those pastures is "blue." There is great controversy over the blue grass and its origin—and the origins of the belief in its blueness. Like all such controversies, this one has generated many stories and folk beliefs and explanations.

The grass is, in fact, not blue but green, and a vibrant green at that, even greener than many other grasses. However, a bluish vein does run through the limestone nourishing those verdant pastures, and this sometimes lends the limestone a blue tinge. Thus, some people believe that it is the constantly decomposing "blue" limestone that grows "blue" grass. Yet, elsewhere limestone-enriched soils produce abundant grasses, none of which have been labeled "blue." Moreover, a prevalent folk belief is that Kentucky bluegrass cannot be transplanted to other areas. "Farmers of other parts of the country have eagerly sought the seed of the 'true Kentucky blue grass,' " writes Dr. Robert Peter, "but they have found that, unless their soils and other local conditions are congenial to the highest development of this grass, they fail to obtain the results which it gives in the Blue Limestone Region of Kentucky."

A box of bluegrass seed was once presented to Queen Marie of Romania by a Bluegrass lady, evidently the ultimate gift. Printed on the box were excerpts from a famous speech on grass, given by John J. Ingalls, from 1873 to 1891 a United States Senator from Kansas. "Grass," said Senator Ingalls, "is the forgiveness of nature." He then launched into a long orotund eulogy on bluegrass. Following is a portion of Ingalls' remarks:

One grass differs from another grass in glory. One is vulgar and another patrician. There are grades in its vegetable nobility. But the king of them all, with genuine blue blood, is bluegrass. Why it is called blue, save that it is most vividly and intensely green, is inexplicable; but had its unknown priest baptized it with all the hues of the prism, he would not have changed its hereditary title to imperial superiority, over all its humbler kin.

There is a portion of Kentucky known as the "Blue Grass Region," and it is safe to say that it has been the arena of the most magnificent intellectual and physical development that has been witnessed among men or animals upon the American continent, or perhaps upon the whole face of the world. In corroboration of this belief, it is necessary only to mention Henry Clay, the orator, and the horse, Lexington, both peerless, electric, immortal. The ennobling love of the horse has extended to all other races of animals. The reflex of this solicitude appears in the muscular, athletic vigor of the men, and the voluptuous beauty of the women who inhabit this favored land. Palaces, temples, forests, peaceful institutions, social order, spring like exhalations from the congenial soil.

All these marvels are attributable as directly to the potential influence of bluegrass as day and night to the revolution of the earth. Eradicate it, substitute for it the scrawny herbage of impoverished barrens, and in a single generation man and beast would alike degenerate into a common decay. . . .

Though blatantly chauvinistic and reeking of romantic geological and geographic determinism, Ingalls' eloquent tribute poignantly reveals aspects of the Bluegrass folk worldview. Ever since it was first delivered, Bluegrass residents, in their fervor to proclaim the gospel of Bluegrass the Beautiful, have circulated copies of Ingalls' paean far and wide. The quote above was taken from one such copy given to me by a Bluegrass resident.

The process of circulating such statements, stories, or whatever, is a traditional method of sharing, preserving, and perpetuating topics of common interest among people who participate in the same culture. Because they were delivered as an official address while he was a member of the Senate, Ingalls' words were originally a part of elite culture. Shortly thereafter, this address was printed in various newspapers, and thus became a part of popular culture. However, when Bluegrass residents heard about, or read, Ingalls' laudatory remarks, they immediately repeated them, paraphrased them, and copied them to share with everyone. That different versions of Ingalls' tribute exist is one of the hallmarks of the traditional folkloric mode of perpetuating such information. By participating in that process, Bluegrass people made his words traditional, and therefore their own.

Such traditional processes often constitute the only opportunity the average person has to participate in demonstrations of shared beliefs and values. For the average person, it is a way to express cultural cohesion, proclaim allegiance and solidarity, and philosophize from and about a common worldview. Although Ingalls' fustian oratory, and Bluegrass residents' use of it, reveals much about Bluegrass culture, it provides little scientific explanation of the grass called blue.

Kentucky bluegrass belongs to the family of grasses called Gramineae, and the genus *Poa;* the strain in Kentucky is *Poa pratensis*, which has long narrow leaves, grows 18–24 inches tall, or even higher under favorable conditions, spreads via underground rhizomes, resulting in a strong root system and dense sod, and can regenerate itself for years without reseeding. Some Bluegrass farms have maintained the same stand of bluegrass for 100 years. One authority is convinced that the use of the term "bluegrass" to describe Kentucky's *Poa pratensis* derives from *Poa compressa*, otherwise known as Canada bluegrass, which does have bluish-green blades and is therefore the original "blue" grass; *Poa pratensis*, however, is considered a superior grass. Some contend it appears blue when in full bloom and producing seed.

In the past, bluegrass seed has been an important cash crop—in 1939, Bourbon County was the largest bluegrass seed market in the world—but in more recent years sales have declined—from 21 million pounds in 1912 to just 200,000 pounds in 1970. It is ironic that today the Bluegrass Region produces no certified bluegrass seed for the commercial market, principally because the crop is no longer economically feasible; today most certified bluegrass seed is grown in western states. In earlier days, harvesting the seed was a picturesque, labor intensive activity commonly seen on Bluegrass farms. The seed was usually harvested with a mule-drawn stripper, one man driving the mule while another sat in the stripper box; others bagged the seeds for market. The seeds—so tiny that a pound contains over two million—are harvested at full bloom, after

which the grass is usually cut and livestock put out to graze the pastures; consequently, the period during which *Poa pratensis* casts a bluish aura is, at best, fleeting and elusive.

Harvesting bluegrass seed, Fayette County, early twentieth century (Photo courtesy of Kentucky Historical Society)

Elusive also are documented data concerning the date and manner in which *Poa pratensis* was first introduced to Kentucky's limestone-fertile soils. However, a number of folk legends supposedly explain its arrival.

WHITE INVASION OF THE BLUEGRASS

Early explorers of the Inner Bluegrass were avid hunters and trappers, as were several tribes of Native Americans, none of whom established year-round extensive permanent villages in the area; instead, the Region was used as a great hunting preserve. Over many generations competing tribes fought for territorial hunting rights in this game-rich savanna, and in later years the tribes had to fight the invading white man as well. As a result of all this warring a Cherokee chief named Dragging Canoe prophesied at the Treaty of Sycamore Shoals in 1775 that the area would become known as the "dark and bloody ground," an epithet that on occasion is evoked even today; however, the original meaning of the name of the Cherokee term Anglicized into "Kentucky" was "great meadowland," a description that fits the Bluegrass Region rather than the Commonwealth. The native tribes maintained that "the ghosts and specters of the dead nations roamed eternally" in what is now the Inner Bluegrass, and consequently, they believed that the entire Region was unholy and dangerous for all men. These beliefs, some contend, were purposely propagated by the Indians to frighten potential intruders away from their hunting grounds. Some people today believe that the damp night air of the Region is unhealthy, some even say "poison"—and indeed, the Bluegrass has an extremely high incidence of respiratory disease. So perhaps the tribes' reluctance to live in the Region, for whatever reason, made sense.

Nevertheless, the native tribes could do little to stem the tide of settlers. For a while, the tribes continued to hunt in the Region. The abundant game, including buffalo, turkey, deer, and bear, could easily be taken, often by stalking them through the huge canebrakes that virtually covered the land. Unfortunately, incessant and wanton white hunting practices too often decimated game; as happened later in the West, white men killed game for sport and left the carcasses lying with only the hide and perhaps a haunch carried off for use. As early as 1775, hunters complained that game had been hunted so relentlessly that they had to go as far as thirty miles before spotting any. One group of long hunters from the Carolinas—so-called because such hunting trips were necessarily of unusually long duration—had their cache of deerskins stolen and in exasperation carved on a tree "2,300 deerskins lost, ruination, by God."*

Settlers   Following the long hunters and the adventurers came the settlers. As early as 1775 livestock had been introduced into Kentucky to compete with the game, and by the close of the eighteenth century, the land was cleared. The combination of the wanton slaughter by white hunters and the influx of white settlers and their black slaves and their livestock into the Region was naturally viewed as an invasion by the tribes, and they retaliated in a series of raids. The Bluegrass is riddled

*Carvings on trees, called dendroglyphs, have for ages constituted a rudimentary form of folk expression and communication, and they were common in the early exploration and settlement of the Bluegrass. This particular dendroglyph tells us several things: (1) a few men unconscionably slaughtered 2,300 deer; (2) theft apparently was a problem even on the frontier; (3) the ability to vent rage, according to psychiatrists and psychologists, is cathartic, so the carving served as a form of do-it-yourself psychotherapy, as well as a warning to others; (4) men either cursed God, blaming him for their misfortune, or used his name to emphasize their rage—an attitude toward the divinity that would not be acceptable in most theologies.

with legends of settlers' encounters, many disastrous, with the Indians. (One historian claims that in the decade 1776–1786 over 850 settlers were killed by Indians.) Of this period, Clark McMeekin writes: "Every [Kentucky] family treasures handed-down stories of Great-grandfather's bravery or Aunt Fronnie's outwitting of the red varmints, passed on from generation to generation, and happily set down, now and then, in diary or journal."

Many early settlers did indeed consider the Shawnee and Cherokee to be "varmints" fit only to be killed or run off; however, their stories about Indians may also document the evolution of other historical matters. One legend claims that Kentucky's capitol city of Frankfort was so named because a pioneer named Stephen Frank was killed by Indians while fording (therefore "Frank's ford") the Kentucky River nearby. Another legend contends that early hunters and trappers gave some *Poa pratensis* seed to Indians to plant near buffalo traces or close to salt licks to encourage game. Folklorists believe that most folk legends contain at least a kernel of fact. If this legend were true, the *Poa pratensis* would have spread out from these areas of early planting and eventually covered the whole Region. However, the four most persistent bluegrass-origin legends are all from Clark County.

ORIGIN STORIES OF THE GRASS CALLED BLUE

In his 1769 trip to Kentucky, Daniel Boone was supposedly accompanied by an Englishman and his wife, who carried, tied up in the corner of her handkerchief, some grass seeds from England. She planted them in her garden at Boonesborough, but when the grass threatened to overrun the area, she pulled it up and tossed it over the fence, where it took root and spread. A more detailed version maintains that one Dr. Martin purchased a bushel of the seed from the English woman, paying $2.25 for it, and thus introduced bluegrass to the state.

A second story attributes the introduction of bluegrass to one Thomas Goff, who lived in Clark County in the early nineteenth century. Goff regularly drove his cattle to market to locations in the East, and during one of these trips he supposedly found *Poa pratensis* growing somewhere near the Blue Ridge Mountains; with his pocket knife he cut a section of its sod, took it back home with him, and cultivated it in his garden. The Goff origin story is confirmed by a man named Sam McElwain, who was born and raised next to the Goff farm and claimed that this discovery took place about the time of his own birth (1807). McElwain recalled hearing many people tell the story, especially around his father's blacksmith shop (a typical center for story swapping). "After I was old enough to remember," McElwain wrote, "the grass was sparsely scattered through the neighborhood, having followed the course of a creek running by the Goff farm, and as it took root and formed tufts of sod, the seed were gathered and sown each year, till when I left there, at the age of seventeen, the farms in the community were generally well set with it."

Another version of this legend claims that Goff brought the bluegrass "in a thimble from England" and also introduced the first timothy to the area via "a thimble of timothy from Virginia, which he planted." Still another version claims that it was Goff's son Elisha who first sowed timothy and red clover in Kentucky.

A third bluegrass-origin story credits one Ebenezer Chorn with spreading bluegrass throughout the Region. Chorn was an immigrant from Virginia, who in about 1790 bought a farm in the Big Stoner Settlement, near what is now the Clark and Montgomery County line. Captain Buford Allen Tracy, a descendant of one of the original members of the settlement (called locally Tracy Settlement), recorded this version in his memoirs, written about 1890:

The first bluegrass ever seen in Kentucky was found growing around an old deer lick about three miles north of Ebenezer Chorn's . . . near the banks of the creek which derived its name from that spot, "Grassy Lick." There was not more than an acre or so of this grass, but it grew thick and luxuriantly and from this patch of grass Mr. Chorn stripped seed with his fingers and sowed it upon his farm. His efforts to grow this grass was [sic] a success from the start. Many others tried to grow it again and again but without success, so that it became the popular opinion of settlers that this much desired grass would not grow anywhere except upon Ebenezer Chorn's land. People often came from quite a distance to see this wonderful grass and to learn what they could about it and then ride on to the old deer lick to see it in its original state and if possible procure some of the seed or roots.

However, wary of the skepticism with which this story might be received, Tracy added: "What we have written is no doubt the true origin of Kentucky blue grass, at least as far as the Big Stoner Settlement is concerned and there we leave it."

Two additional legendary anecdotes, also from Clark County, maintain that bluegrass was not introduced until either 1785 or 1800, in the Strode's Creek area by either John Constant or Robert Cunningham, who got the seed from the Potomac River area. A third fragment claims bluegrass derived its name from a Pennsylvanian named Blue, who first called attention to *Poa pratensis* growing in the area.

A final legend is told by Lucien Beckner, also of Clark County, in his 1932 paper about Eskippakithiki, the last Indian village in Kentucky. In this legend it was John Findley who unwittingly carried the bluegrass seed into Kentucky. Apparently an accomplished raconteur, Findley enticed Boone with his tales (probably *tall* ones) about the Bluegrass and later guided him into Kentucky. Findley was a Presbyterian Irishman from Pennsylvania, Boone's home state, and like Boone, an adventurer. According to the legend, in the fall of 1752 (another version says 1751), Findley, with four white servants and various trade goods, went down the Ohio from Pennsylvania to Big Bone Lick (now in Boone County). Here he encountered a party of Shawnee, who invited him to their home at Eskippakithiki. When Findley reached the Indian village, he unpacked his goods to trade with them. According to the story, Findley had packed his trade goods with hay made of English grass (presumably *Poa pratensis*), the seeds for which had been imported from England. When he threw his packing aside on the rich soil at Eskippakithiki, it germinated and spread, and was thus the first bluegrass to grow in Kentucky. The story of Findley's visit to Eskippakithiki was later recounted by Daniel Boone, who told it to his nephew, Daniel Bryan, who in turn related it to Dr. Lynam C. Draper.

The legend goes on to claim that when permanent settlers came to Kentucky, some twenty-five years later, the only bluegrass to be found was at Grassy Lick in Montgomery County and at Indian Old Fields, the current name for Eskippakithiki (near modern Kiddville). This area actually lies outside the easily detectable natural geological boundary of the Inner Bluegrass, a fact perhaps recognized by the Shawnee, who observed their taboo against residing within the Region.

Legendary Kentuckians It is interesting to note that all these stories place the origin of bluegrass in approximately the same general area, the last two legends locating it near Grassy Lick. These accounts may have some basis in documentable fact, but the evidence is not conclusive.

The first legend is primarily about Boone and his settlement at Boonesborough, and instead of offering much insight into the origin of bluegrass, it serves chiefly to add to the formidable stature of Boone himself. This is one of the primary functions of such legendary material: to elevate historical personages and their exploits to superhuman levels. One such Bluegrass frontiersman was Benjamin Logan, after whom Logan's Fort (near modern Stanford) was named. Logan, a giant of a man, was famed for a 200–mile run through canebrakes and forest to obtain help for his small stockade, besieged by the Shawnee in 1777. Men like Logan, of great physical stature or heroic abilities or uncanny luck, were made even greater through the traditional legendary process. Although his legendary fame, unlike Boone's, remained local, historian

R. S. Cotterill calls Logan, "the most heroic figure that ever trod Kentucky soil." Marshall Fishwick sees Boone as "the American Moses, who led us into the Promised Land," and says Boone's importance "in the history of American [folk] heroes and symbols can hardly be overstated."

Four other Bluegrass legends about Boone are noteworthy. One relates that in 1770 Boone and some compatriots from the Yadkin Country of North Carolina camped near Eskippakithiki on a creek, where they hastily built a temporary lean-to as shelter from a fierce storm. To occupy their time they read from a copy of *Gulliver's Travels*, which one in the company had carried with him. From that experience, they named the creek "Lulbegrud," derived from one of the names in Swift's novel. This legend is apparently accurate for on September 15, 1796, Boone made a legal deposition wherein he documented his account of the naming of the creek. The story also serves to correct the mistaken belief that all early Kentucky settlers were illiterates.

In 1776, Boone's daughter Jemima and two other girls were captured near Boonesborough by Indians, who grabbed their drifting canoe. Boone and a party of men from the fort rescued them within three days, a rescue that had an interesting romantic aspect: three of Boone's men were the girls' suitors, and later became their husbands. Boone himself was captured in 1778 and lived among the Shawnee for six months before he could escape. The Shawnee, because they respected him, adopted Boone, and supposedly gave him the sobriquet "Big Turtle," possibly as a humorous reflection of his short height and girth.

A final legend describes how Boone, on his second trip to Kentucky, first saw the Bluegrass from a hill, which he supposedly named Pilot Knob. Now famous, the hill is located in Powell County, not far from Indian Old Fields. What Boone actually saw, however, was not the rolling Inner Bluegrass, but the relatively flat area of Indian Old Fields.

In folk history, "facts" can vary considerably from one version to another. In illustration of this, one local historian, obviously relying too heavily upon traditional lore, within the space of twenty pages claims three different dates for Boone's climbing Pilot Knob: by himself in 1741, with Findley in 1759, and again with Findley in 1775. The two later dates are certainly possible, but considering that Boone is thought to have been born circa 1734, it would have been a remarkable feat indeed for him to have climbed Pilot Knob in 1741, legendary prowess or no.

Like all information in oral circulation for any length of time, legendary data are subject to lapse of memory or purposeful modification for any number of personal reasons—religious taboos, ego enhancement, or simply to make a better story—and consequently details often vary from one version of the legend to the other. For this reason, most historians are extremely cautious about accepting the accuracy of such stories. Nevertheless, legendary material has been shown time and again to contain at least a modicum of fact. In these Boone legends we do have some acceptable evidence—like the names "Lulbegrud Creek" and "Pilot Knob," both still in use. The legends of how they came to be named are by no means unconvincing.

At least one aspect of these legends appears to be supported even by scientific evidence: Kentucky bluegrass evidently did originate in England, where the common name for it was "smooth meadow grass." No doubt it was brought here by early settlers, but by whom and whether on purpose or by accident remain topics for speculation and further investigation. As is often the case, when scientific evidence is not available, colorful folk explanations fill the void. However, the belief that the grass came from England does agree with the demographic evidence that English and Scotch–Irish settlers were in the majority in the early development of the Bluegrass. Many of the early immigrants of English ancestry came from Virginia, of which Kentucky was a part prior to 1790.

Demographics, Stereotypes, and the Formation of Bluegrass Culture

Prior to the great influx of Virginians through the Cumberland Gap, which began around 1780, Kentucky contained only a few hundred white men, mostly adventurers and hunters. Occasionally the cabin of hardy pioneers, like Daniel and Rebecca Boone, could be found at the tiny stations dotting the Bluegrass landscape. These early settlers came primarily from Virginia, Maryland, North Carolina, and Pennsylvania (Boone himself was born near Reading, Pennsylvania, and migrated to North Carolina at age 16). Many came to Kentucky chiefly for the love of adventure. Attesting to their devil-may-care attitude is a legend about Boone. While hunting, a small band of men, led by James Knox, heard

not far away in the forest a voice raised in what was probably meant to be song. Cautiously approaching, they saw a white man stretched ... on the ground singing with the full strength of a pair of lungs which had evidently been fashioned for other purposes. It was Daniel Boone, who with rare recklessness was giving himself up to the pleasure of his own music in entire forgetfulness of Indians and all things hostile.

Another version of this story maintains that it was Boone's old Yadkin friend Gaspar Mansker who was startled by hearing Boone, a considerable distance from any fort, singing to his dogs in the woods. Believing the noise to be from Indians, Mansker was creeping up to shoot them when he discovered it was his old friend Boone.

Nearly all of such early Kentucky settlement was in the Bluegrass, in forts such as Harrodstown (settled by Virginians) and Boonesborough (settled by North Carolinians). Most men were engaged either in hunting or raising Indian corn, primarily the former, for, as Richard Henderson, a friend of Boone's, complained, "Many of the settlers were idle and worthless, having come to Kentucky merely that they might go back home and boast of their journey."

Such early pioneers were soon supplanted by an influx of settlers streaming through the Cumberland Gap in the decades between 1780 and 1800. As Bourbon County historian H. E. Everman notes: "Like many another wilderness . . . [the Bluegrass] first beckoned the hunter, then the pastoralist, and finally the farmer." Similarly, Kentucky cultural geographer Karl Raitz lists four groups of settlers coming to the Bluegrass at different times and for somewhat different reasons.

The first were adventurous hunters and trappers escaping the responsibilities of sedentary life in Virginia and North Carolina. They intermixed with a second group, the Indian fighters and surveyors who opened the country to permanent white settlement. . . . A third group, the dirt farmers, were the first to occupy and farm the land in significant numbers. The farmers, often squatters on Indian or Federal lands, managed a meager subsistence by raising Indian corn and garden crops and by hunting. . . . The farmers were then joined by a fourth group, planters migrating to Kentucky from The Tidewater and Piedmont country of Maryland, Virginia, and the Carolinas. The planters . . . members of the landed aristocracy of the East . . . had the greatest impact on the future character of the region because they . . . brought their culture . . . controlled large blocks of the most productive land and were politically active and dominant from the beginning.

Few movements of population in America have compared in magnitude with this flow. Passage of liberal Virginia land laws, in 1776 and again in 1779, spurred new settlers into crossing the mountains into what was then Kentucky County of Virginia. Though a few stopped and settled in the mountains along the trails leading to the meadows of central Kentucky, most continued to the Bluegrass. Indeed, historians have likened pioneer Kentucky to a wheel, with the Bluegrass the hub and the roads leading to it the spokes. The population leaped from a few hundred before 1780 to over 100,000 in 1792, and was composed of mainly rural communities with no town of more than 1,000 people; at that time, no other state had experienced such rapid growth.

Among these newcomers to the Bluegrass were men and women of diverse social, economic, and educational circumstances—backwoodsmen, farmers, traders, artisans, scholars, professional men, aristocrats, slaves, and bondsmen. Some of the young families came highly pedigreed, but many did not. They were both foreigners—English, Scots, Scotch-Irish, Irish, and a few Germans and French Huguenots newly arrived from Europe—and second and third generation Virginians, Carolinians, Marylanders, and Pennsylvanians. Many of the original founders of Lexington, at the heart of the Inner Bluegrass, were of English, Scots, and Scotch-Irish ancestry, who had been living on the fringes of Western Pennsylvania and Virginia for several generations. In spite of this "mixing bowl" of people, however, it was Virginia that played the most significant role in molding the economic and social institutions, the character and the worldview of the new Bluegrass inhabitants. Virginia influence prevailed primarily because the wealth and intellectual and political leadership of the new society was dominated by the Virginia gentry and soon-to-be gentry, who had brought to the Bluegrass their slaves, their thoroughbred animals, and their rural, patrician way of life.

STEREOTYPES AND DISTINCTION

With the subjugation of the Indian, thus affording a relative degree of safety for inhabitants of the Bluegrass, came not only an increasing influx of pioneers but also a steady trickle of visitors and travelers from the East and even Great Britain, curious about this new Eden of the West. English and Scotch-Irish gentry had brought with them a predilection for culture and education, and Lexington, as the only major cultural center west of the Alleghenies, was viewed by travelers as the Athens of the West. Like earlier sojourners, a number of these guests chose to publish their impressions of the Bluegrass and especially the character of its people. Not surprisingly, several such treatises strayed substantially from the truth. One popular folk stereotype portrayed Kentuckians, according to the famous boast, as "half-horse and half-alligator"—crude and violent backwoods bullies, brawlers, and braggarts who drank and gambled with inordinate passion, and who, as Irishman Thomas Ashe wrote, were a "fallen people living atop an older Indian civilization over which they had made little improvement." Concurring with this negative appraisal, Captain Thomas Hamilton scurrilously slandered both Irishmen and Kentuckians, calling Kentuckians "the Irish of America." Hamilton asserted: "They have all that levity of character, that subjection of the moral to the convivial, that buoyance of spirit, that jocular ferocity, that ardour, both of attachment and of hatred, which distinguishes the natives of the Emerald Isle."

The Colonel   Somewhat later a second, equally simplistic folk stereotype portrayed the typical Bluegrass Kentuckian as gentleman farmer, a goateed colonel sipping mint juleps in a rocking chair on the veranda; or a courageous and noble young blade astride a magnificent steed, and his counterpart, the Bluegrass belle, coquetting about in her crinolines. Reflecting this aspect of Bluegrass character is William H. Townsend, in his Introduction to *Bluegrass Houses and Their Traditions:* "And so ... this impulsive, sprightly people wrought mightily in public affairs, loved fiercely, entertained graciously and lavishly, drank prodigiously, fought common enemies and each other gallantly—even joyously, and died bravely." Such folk appraisals of the Bluegrass character often attributed such heroic, gentlemanly, and cultured qualities to its Virginia and English bloodlines, as did Harvard Dean Nathaniel Shaler, embellished by James Lane Allen:

In Kentucky...we shall find nearly pure English blood. It is, moreover, the largest body of pure English folk that has, speaking generally, been separated from the mother-country for two hundred years. They, the blue-grass Kentuckians, are the descendants of those hardy, high-spirited, picked Englishmen, largely of the squire and yeoman class, whose absorbing passion was not religious disputation, nor the intellectual purpose of founding a State, but the ownership of land and the pursuits and pleasures of rural life, close to the rich soil, and full of its strength and sunlight. They have to this day, in a degree perhaps equalled by no others living, the race qualities of their English ancestry and the tastes and habitudes of their forefathers.

These stereotypes did reflect at least *some* Bluegrass character traits, but the average central Kentuckian would not have recognized himself in such characterizations. Shaler did, however, identify a prevailing feature of the bluegrass character—a preoccupation and an identification with the land and with life on the land.

Love of Land   An early satire enumerating the pocket contents of a "typical" Kentuckian listed "a precis of a law-suit intended to de-fraud his neighbor of his land." In fact, it was true that pioneer Kentuckians, whether of aristocratic blue blood or merely plebeian red blood, came to the Bluegrass because they wanted land. Tom Clark observes:

In early Kentucky towns and cities were no more than gathering places for expatriate farmers and a few tradesmen and professional people. They all looked to the countryside rather than within themselves for economic strength. The Bluegrass was one of the few places in this country where farmers were as much or more sophisticated than were their small-town neighbors. It was here that the all-absorbing agrarian tradition of Kentucky was to flourish, and to help shape both the Kentucky personality and the attitude of the people toward the world about them.

Clark McMeekin notes that "the traditional Kentuckian is, deep-down, a country boy, for Kentucky is a country state rather than a town one." Tom Clark also points out that the great men of nineteenth-century Kentucky were primarily men from farm backgrounds. Consider master statesman Henry Clay. Clark contends that "many of the etchings of Clay show his Ashland estate in the background, not to emphasize its magnificence but to imply that Clay was a son of the soil." The land has marked the Bluegrass Kentuckian intimately and personally, as Clark has noted: "His folk mores are those of the land, so are his idioms and figures of speech, the tone of his voice, and his mental responses. He feels most comfortable with this heritage. It is the source of his humor, his pathos, and his solace." As a result, many common attributes of early Bluegrass character can be traced to man's relationship with the land.

Individuality   The ability to be self-sufficient, which in turn encouraged the development of individuality, was an essential characteristic of the early Bluegrass Kentuckian; it must be remembered that Kentuckians so valued their independence and individuality that many strongly resisted efforts to join the Union. The settler wanted to be left to live his own life. As James G. Leyburn notes, the pioneer objected to paying taxes to support "a section of the country whose life and folkways were not his; he looked forward to the development of his own region. . . . He was, like all normal men, self-seeking."

Moderating these character traits, however, was the necessity, or the predilection, for common endeavors: house raisings and warmings, land clearings, rolling of logs and splitting of rails, and similar communal efforts. Helping neighbors was different from contributing to the distant state capitol. Similarly, the occasional opportunity for communal play was a welcome respite from the peril and toil and loneliness of pioneer life. Early historian Mann Butler remarked: "Every young man I know has a horse, a gun, and a violin." A colorful and stereotypical exaggeration rather than historical fact, this statement nonetheless lists the major devices of folk entertainment for the day. The violin provided music for dancing parties; the gun was used for various hunting and shooting matches; and the horse—a source of special love and pride even for Bluegrass pioneers—provided opportunity for spirited races.

Accompanying such sporting activities was a great deal of bragging and drinking and betting and sometimes a no-holds-barred fistfight. Such instances of uninhibited revelry eventually gave rise to the characterization of the Kentuckian, in contemporary terms, as "hard-living." Old Hickory (Andrew Jackson) is quoted as saying: "I have never seen a Kentuckian without a gun, a bottle of whiskey, and pack of cards in my life." While a resident in Lexington, Amos Kendall, the Postmaster General during Jackson's presidency, wrote: "I think I have learned the way to be popular in Kentucky. . . drink whiskey and talk loud with the fullest confidence and you will hardly fail of being called a clever fellow."

Extremes and Contrasts   The frontier did not attract mild-mannered, reticent men and women, rather young men and young families who had the strength and passion to endure the hostilities and unrelenting physical drudgery of the wilderness. Bluegrass Kentuckians worked hard and played hard. They were never a lukewarm people, but a people of extremes and contrasts. Clark McMeekin's popular history of the Commonwealth claims: "Kentucky's story is always full of contradictions, warm hearts and hot heads, gentleness and violence, hard drinkin' and rigid teetotalism, erudition and illiteracy, outstanding statesmanship and the stuffed ballot box, the sharpest sort of horse trading and the most openhanded hospitality." A nineteenth century Scot, Charles Augustus Murray, compared Ohio people with Kentuckians by saying that Kentuckians appeared to possess greater faults and greater merits than their northern neighbors: "Their moral features were distinctive," Murray wrote, "they were frank, hospitable, rough, overbearing, and inclined to bragging. They had a strange affinity for gambling and horse racing." A notable wit once quipped that Kentuckians are "just like other folks, only more so;" they "never do things by halves." The poem "In Kentucky," much beloved by Kentuckians, illustrates the point with superlatives; the final stanza is probably recognized by every Bluegrass resident:

> The song birds are the sweetest
> > In Kentucky;
> The thoroughbreds are fleetest
> > In Kentucky;
> Mountains tower proudest,
> Thunder peals the loudest,
> The landscape is the grandest
> And politics—the damndest
> > In Kentucky.

Thomas Clark notes that "Bluegrass literature is fairly sprinkled with 'first' and 'biggest' things. Achievements and possessions often became only comparatively important. A good horse, a beautiful daughter, a faithful wife, had only limited significance. Only the 'best' was worth possessing."

Bluegrass Kentuckians are loyal to their state, but to many "Kentucky" simply means *my* neighborhood, *my* hometown, and especially *my* county. Like many rural people, many Bluegrass residents identify principally with a given *county*. It is a widespread Kentucky tradition to "stay put," and in the Bluegrass, many natives live out their lives in close proximity to where they were born. In fact, 100 years after Kentucky became a state, fewer than one half of 1 percent of its populace were *not* native Kentuckians. Living together for generations often encouraged hospitable relationships.

In fact, generous hospitality is perhaps one of the more cherished traditions of the Bluegrass. As Tom Clark notes, in pioneer Kentucky, no matter how poor the host, visitors were always welcomed:

Acceptance of the stranger at the door was an expression of genuine hospitality without offering assurances of either sophistication or refinement. The stranger was crowded in at the table to partake of whatever came from the pot, and he was bedded down on the floor amidst a host of tossing children. This kind of hospitality was . . . a Kentucky pride. Kentuckians have often extended themselves to take in company when there was scarcely enough food or floor space to go around.

Later, among affluent Bluegrass farmers and planters, hospitality was accorded on a grander scale. Visitors were always welcome, with or without invitations. "Guests drove up unannounced," wrote J. Winston Coleman, Jr., "sent their horses to the stables, had their portmanteaus and trunks carried into the manor house and lingered for weeks." On occasion some stayed for years. Even today, the cordiality and generosity of the Region is remarked upon by visitors.

A Distinctive Character   Throughout the 1800s, Kentucky society developed an increasingly variegated public character, created by growing disparities in wealth, position, and education, and in the possession of land, upon which all other attributes rested. Although many a Bluegrass gentleman based his bid for social distinction upon his Virginia lineage—for a Kentuckian, especially one from Central Kentucky, ancestral origin in Virginia was construed as linkage with nobility—Kentuckians were not clones of the aristocratic Virginians. When Henry Clay, dubbed the Cock of Kentucky by John Randolph, returned East to Congress, he personified his lusty young state, whose inhabitants had replaced Virginia propriety with Kentucky pride and presumptuousness.

Though the gentry should not be used to typify the Region, the Bluegrass does possess a distinctive culture of affluent neopatricians. However, other recognizable cultures also exist, such as white working class culture and black culture. These will be discussed throughout this survey.

BLACKS IN THE BLUEGRASS

No cultural discussion of the Bluegrass could be complete without recognition of the role played by black Americans in early Kentucky history. The first blacks to enter Kentucky were probably brought by members of Boone's 1775 trailblazing party; indeed, two slaves were killed by the Shawnee in a raid on Boone's camp. A legend of the Thomas Goff family (not recorded in print until 1923) relates the experiences of a black cook, owned by Goff, who accompanied his master, Boone, and others on a hunting expedition. The group was surprised by a roving band of hostile Indians who—perhaps having never seen a black man before—pursued the cook "with savage fierceness," ignoring the white men. Goff and his companions escaped and made their way to Boonesborough, but the frightened cook, in his headlong flight, became separated from the group. Somehow he outdistanced his pursuers and wandered in the wilderness until he finally made his way back to Virginia. Needless to say, the man never wanted to return to Kentucky, and Goff allowed him to remain behind in the Old Dominion.

As early as 1777, when the first census of Harrodstown was taken, nineteen out of a total population of 198 were slaves, seven of whom were children under the age of ten. By 1790 the population of Kentucky had grown to 73,000, of whom 12,430 were slaves. Many of the slaves proved to be excellent frontiersmen; they cleared and helped to develop vast areas of central Kentucky, chopping down the cane and heavy timber, helping build the forts and cabins, planting the crops, and performing the countless laborious chores needed to provide shelter, sustenance, and some comfort in the wilderness.

Throughout the first half of the 1790s small bands of roving Indians continued to harass Bluegrass settlers, and in 1793 during the last major raid, an old slave named Rosa, belonging to one Samuel Tribble, proved herself a heroine. Tribble was absent from his home, leaving his wife and Aunt Rosa behind to protect the homestead. Awakened during the night by a great commotion in the barnyard, the two women, armed with a pair of heavy fire tongs, ventured forth to investigate. Fortunately, the cause of the uproar was not Indians but a wolf intent upon reaching a young calf confined in a rail pen. Slipping up behind the wolf, intrepid Aunt Rosa laid the fire tongs across her shoulder, took deliberate aim, breathed a prayer, and brought the tongs crashing down on the wolf's head. That was the end of the marauding animal.

Aunt Rosa and Mrs. Tribble were sterling examples of the nameless heroines, black and white, of Kentucky pioneer society—women who bore children, cared for the sick, buried the dead, comforted the living, helped build and outfit cabins, fed and clothed their families, plowed the fields, fought the Indians, and made do with what was available.

During the same raid in which Aunt Rosa distinguished herself, Morgan's Station was attacked and its inhabitants killed or captured. According to legend, only one old slave escaped. The night before the attack, he had seen a crow light on one of the buildings, and, believing this to be an omen of approaching danger, he refused to sleep inside the fort. Hiding outside, he escaped, saved by a folk superstition.

In the years to follow, many more blacks were brought into the Bluegrass, usually as slaves, and primarily by planters from slaveholding states such as Maryland and, of course, Virginia. Three out of four Kentuckians owned no slaves at all. Among those who did, the great majority held fewer than five, and some families owned only one or two. However, large-scale farmers, especially those involved in the production of hemp, owned dozens. Very little tobacco was grown until after the Civil War, and hemp constituted the largest and most important antebellum crop. Because hemp cultivation and processing was so labor intensive—the historian of the Kentucky hemp industry, James F. Hopkins, wrote that hemp was "sowed by hand, cut by hand, and broken by hand" —and because it was a year-round process, it was economically advantageous to own large numbers of slaves. In fact, as Hopkins observed, "Without hemp, slavery might not have flourished in Kentucky."

Slaves were also used in many other capacities in the early Bluegrass. In addition to cultivating hemp, they toiled in the production of what tobacco was grown—not the White Burley for which Kentucky is famous today, but the "dark-fired" variety widely grown in Virginia—worked the grain fields, and processed maple sugar and molasses. They cared for growing herds of livestock—cattle, sheep, hogs, mules, and especially horses, and it was in the role of horse trainers, handlers, and grooms that they demonstrated a special aptitude, as attested by the diary of a Bluegrass Confederate wife who said that their "servant" Durastus was "the most trusted with the horses." They also worked in mills and shops, and they assisted many white families with commercial and domestic duties.

On the large farms the slaves were roughly divided into two groups: the field hands who lived in rows of cabins called the quarters and the domestic servants who usually resided in more comfortable houses near the mansion or big house. The latter cared for the master and his family and generally enjoyed a more congenial lifestyle than did the field workers; domestic slaves often ate the same food as was served at the master's table and wore the cast-off clothes of their owners, or their children. Indeed, in the homes of the wealthier landowners, J. Winston Coleman, Jr. notes that:

House servants were all-important.... Some of the richer families had a head butler, usually an aged Negro major-domo with a "biled" shirt and correct dresscoat who, in his bearing toward guests, was the paragon of civility and politeness. To him was entrusted that all-important duty of mixing and serving the frosted mint juleps in the finely wrought coin-silver cups. It was freely conceded among those whose opinions were respected in such matters, that not even Henry Clay's Charles could mix a mint julep like Robert Todd's Nelson.

Though slavery itself was an official, legal institution—and therefore a product of elite culture—many of the attitudes, customs, and activities associated with it were folk cultural in nature. In antebellum years, when the number of slaves a family owned indicated its social position, many Bluegrass slave owners clung to the delusion that the Negro was actually better off as a slave than as a free man. They reasoned that slavery in Kentucky was a domestic institution—that is, slaves were often inherited or born into a family and considered members of the family circle rather than chattel property—and they viewed Kentucky slavery as the mildest of any Southern state. Consequently, many Bluegrass residents considered it a bitter irony that Harriet Beecher Stowe should utilize a Kentucky setting for *Uncle Tom's Cabin,* her exposé of the cruelty and inhumanity of slavery.

Stowe scathingly attacked one of the most odious aspects of Kentucky slavery: the tacitly approved practice of selling "excess" Bluegrass slaves to the Deep South, which gave rise to the common American expression "sold down the river." In the thirty years before the Civil War, the shipping of slaves to the South became as common as the sale of livestock. An owner could keep unruly or "uppity" blacks in line with the terrible threat, "Behave or I'll sell you south." One slave, a carpenter by trade, was so terrified of being sold South and separated from his family that he cut off his own hand, and thus rendered himself "worthless." The prospect of separation made slave marriages so precarious that it was a common practice of slave preachers, such as Lexington's Lincoln Farrell, to include in the ceremony the phrase "until death or distance do thee part."

No critic of slavery was more vociferous than Cassius Marcellus Clay, son of a prominent Bluegrass slave owner, who in the mid 1840s published a weekly emancipationist newsletter in Lexington, a bastion of proslavery sympathizers. Appropriately called the "Lion of White Hall," Clay was never a man of moderation or tact. Rather than employing diplomacy to persuade his neighbors of the evils of slavery, he virtually invited them to do battle by fortifying his newspaper office with rifles, a stand of lances, black powder bombs, and a small cannon. Confrontation was averted only when Clay became ill, and a proslavery mob simply packed up his press and type and sent them to Cincinnati—less than one hundred miles northeast of Lexington, but considered an "Eastern city" and, to the Bluegrass mind, a different world.

Freedmen   Not all blacks in the Bluegrass were slaves, of course; and the number of free blacks steadily increased during the antebellum years, although their numbers remained minuscule in comparison to the slave population and to the numbers of whites. Free blacks followed various trades, most of them considered to be folk occupations: barbers, carpenters, millers, farmers, stonemasons, shoemakers, painters, blacksmiths, horse trainers, and silversmiths. One of the more distasteful requirements of slavery laws forced some free blacks themselves to own slaves. If a free black's spouse or children were still owned by a white family, the only certain way to be united was to buy them legally. Once purchased, most remained legal slaves to their black family owner because it was too expensive to free them legally and the slave-owner arrangement provided a degree of protection from whites. Black owner-ship of slaves produced some curious situations. For example, because a slave's owner was required by law to know the whereabouts of a slave at all times, one free black woman who had purchased her husband from a white family had to provide him a pass, indicating his destination and time of return, whenever he went out at night.

These free blacks provided much of the leadership in the black communities after the Civil War. Not surprisingly, many whites resented them. This antagonism, coupled with a stubborn allegiance to the ideals of the defeated Confederacy and an adamantly independent nature, led many Bluegrass slavery sympathizers to oppose the 15th Amendment, which gave blacks the right to vote. To circumvent black voting, whites resorted to several devious shenanigans, described in *The Louisville Courier-Journal:*

Paris and Nicholasville redrew their boundaries, placing black neighborhoods outside the city. . . . In Danville, where residents had to own property to vote, a group of clever Democrats sold 4-inch-wide slivers of land to white farmers in the outlying county so they could qualify to vote. . . . Lexington moved its vote up a month so it would fall before the amendment's proclamation. Then it extended the terms of city fathers to postpone the inevitable black vote. . . . Such resistance was confined to only a small number of Kentucky communities. Most counties readily accepted the first black vote, partly because blacks were such a small minority that they posed no threat. Blacks accounted for only about 20 percent of the state's population, and half lived in only eight counties [most of them in the Bluegrass, where black population comprised almost 50 percent]. . . . Although some cities continued to use poll taxes to keep blacks from voting, measures such as literacy tests, which long endured in the Deep South, never gained a foothold in Kentucky.

(As for the 13th Amendment, which abolished slavery itself, Kentucky finally did ratify it, over 100 years later—in 1976.)

Unfortunately, black emancipation and subsequent suffrage only in-creased the animosity from lower socioeconomic whites, many of Irish and Scotch-Irish descent, who felt threatened by black competition for employment.

THE SCOTCH-IRISH

Even a superficial survey of early Bluegrass surnames would quickly reveal the presence of Irish and particularly Scotch-Irish families. (The

Scotch-Irish were not people of Scotch and Irish descent but Protestant Scots from the north of Ireland, where they had been relocated in the early 1600s—Orangemen, in fact.) For example, John Findley, who explored Kentucky in 1767 and whose stories inspired Daniel Boone to accompany him on a 1769 expedition, was a North Carolinian of Scotch-Irish descent. The first survey on the Kentucky River was conducted by the McAfee brothers of Virginia in 1773, when they marked off approximately 600 acres in the Frankfort area. Lexington received its name in 1775—in honor of Lexington, Massachusetts, where the Revolution began—from a group of frontiersmen led by Pennsylvanian William McConnell. His party included John McClelland, founder of McClelland's Station (now Georgetown) and the first person to bring horses and cattle into Kentucky. Early Kentucky Indian fighter and folk hero Simon Kenton was the son of an obscure Irish immigrant. The founder of the Transylvania Company, Richard Henderson, was born in Virginia of Scotch-Irish parentage and moved to North Carolina at age ten. The names of the myriad stations dotting the Bluegrass landscape further reflected the extent of Irish and Scotch-Irish settlement. Bearers of Irish and Scotch-Irish names such as Clark, Brown, Breckinridge, Butler, Campbell, Bullitt, Wallace, Robertson, Preston, Todd, Rice, McKee, and others reached greater prominence in the Bluegrass than they ever achieved in their native lands.

When the Irish and Scotch-Irish first began arriving in the American colonies, they were regarded simply as "Irish." Indeed, Bluegrass people were often derogatorily labeled "the Irish of Kentucky" by the populace of other states. It is difficult to determine precisely the numbers and relative proportions of Protestant and Catholic Irish who came to the colonies, and later to Kentucky, although on the Bluegrass frontier, at least, the Scotch-Irish predominated. As Kerby A. Miller notes, the lower ranks of both Protestants and Catholics, especially in the 18th century, shared numerous folk culture characteristics: "localism and familism; Celtic customs and superstitions; low rates of formal religious observance; an overfondness of whiskey; and strong emphasis on economic security and communal solidarity." The great majority of these immigrants were of humble origin, smallholders or tenant farmers, laborers, artisans, or cottier–weavers; indeed, the first spinning wheel in Kentucky was brought to Franklin County by Ann McGinty who produced a kind of linsey-woolsey out of nettles and buffalo wool. Some came individually as indentured servants, unable to afford ship passage any other way. More came in family, or even communal, groups, and in some cases entire villages emigrated together. In general, regardless of their socioeconomic status, what these immigrants sought in America was independence, and the satisfaction and rewards of being a landowning farmer or self-employed artisan. Many believed they could realize their dreams in Kentucky's Eden of the West, which was portrayed as an agrarian paradise. One Ulster-American wrote, "a fellow that will put his hand to anything . . . can get work . . . seven days in the week & can earn a Dollar every day he sees" in the Bluegrass.

The Scotch-Irish especially took to frontier life with gusto, and by 1790 perhaps half or more of the settlers beyond the Appalachians—"the Men of the Western Waters,"* as they called themselves—were of Scotch-Irish descent. These pioneers flowed into the Bluegrass from Pennsylvania, Virginia, and North Carolina—some 300,000 by 1800. In the more settled East their reputation for contentiousness, turbulence, and pugnacity had sometimes alienated them from the more established populaces, but in the Bluegrass wilderness such attributes enhanced the likelihood of survival.

Some of these Scotch–Irish and Irish migrants stopped before reaching the Bluegrass and planted roots in the hills, mountains, and rough areas to the north, to the east, and to the south of the Bluegrass. Subsequently they spawned generations of children, many of whom found it more economically advantageous to move to the Bluegrass or at least to the Outer Bluegrass. Many were probably poor to begin with and settled in impoverished areas, and thus created pockets of poverty, many of which still exist.

However, the predominant, influential socioeconomic class in the Inner Bluegrass has always been well–to–do white farmers, many of them modern day "Kentucky Colonels" who, though not of the Colonel Sanders stereotype, are admittedly fond of titles. "Any title, earned or complimentary," writes Clark McMeekin, "is . . . [a Kentuckian's] for life. The accusation that all Kentuckians are Colonels is an exaggeration. *Nearly* all are, thanks to obliging governors."

A NEW VINTAGE COLONEL

In contrast to the stereotypically portrayed Kentucky colonel—with mustache and goatee, white frock coat, planter's broad-brimmed hat, gold-headed cane, and the inevitable mint julep—is a more realistic representative of the Bluegrass gentleman farmer: "Squire" J. Winston Coleman, Jr. A descendant of Virginia emigrants of the 1790s, the Squire operated his ancestral farm which was situated two miles north of Lexington and was a part of the original Coleman tract purchased in

---

*They called themselves this because at that time everything beyond the Alleghenies was considered "the West," and the early settlers felt as free as the waters that flowed there.

1810 by Winston's great-grandfather. Coleman called himself "a plain dirt farmer," and devoted himself to raising tobacco, wheat, corn, oats, alfalfa and red clover hay, white-faced Herefords, sheep, hogs, and even hemp (during World War II). He wrote numerous books and articles about Kentucky history and in 1952 was inducted into the American Antiquarian Society, at that time the only Kentuckian so honored, and one of only a very few in the South. In addition, he amassed one of the largest private collections of Kentuckiana in the Commonwealth and earned for himself the reputation as a host extraordinaire.

A 1941 article by Clement Eaton, "Kentucky Colonel—New Vintage," provides a sketch of Coleman that could describe any number of other Bluegrass gentleman farmers:

The Squire of Winburn Farm . . . was a robust gentleman of early middle age, with a frank, sun-tanned countenance, and a hearty voice. His coat was off, his belt was loose, and his shirt open at the throat. . . . Around his farm are the luxurious estates where the Kentucky thoroughbred horses and their long-legged colts graze. . . . [The Squire] does not attempt to breed race horses, for he says it is the quickest way "to break" a gentleman of moderate means. . . . Nevertheless, he delights in horse-flesh and is proud of the Kentucky racers. He escorts . . . friends to these "show places" and jokes with the old Negroes who display the retired horses of the turf. . . . He enjoys the independence and peace of mind of a country gentleman. No Southerner could be more hospitable. . . . The food that he serves his guests is grown largely on his own farm. . . . When he makes a mint julep, he steps outside his door and pulls a sprig of mint from the bank of the stream by the spring house. He serves his delicious concoction from coin silver cups that his grandfather Coleman drank from, and he gleefully shows you how worn are the edges of the spoon, with which his "grandpappy" stirred his juleps.

Eaton's "new vintage" Colonel was an informal and unpretentious man, who often directed a gentle joke at those who follow "the fox and hound in fancy costumes." For Eaton, however, a more appealing facet of Coleman's personality was his tranquil philosophy of enjoying life: an "appreciation of leisure, to use for culture and the enjoyment of good companionship"—a philosophy shared by many Bluegrass gentry.

Although this is an accurate representation of a typical way of life for a number of Bluegrass residents of the antebellum period and during the first half of this century, today that way of life, and the new vintage Colonel depicted by Coleman's admirers, is slowly, and perhaps irreversibly, fading.

Unlike the Virginia practice of primogeniture—which is a primary reason Virginia's younger sons left for Kentucky—throughout the Bluegrass the custom of gavelkind (inherited from England) has been followed, which divides the family estate among the children at the demise of the father. Thus, land holdings in the Bluegrass have continually dwindled in size. Moreover, today much of the beautiful Bluegrass has been chopped up into all sorts and sizes of subdivisions, ranging from trailer parks, to pretentious minitracts of one-half to five acres, to developments with homes in the $200,000–$1 million range. In 1967, Coleman's Winburn Farm itself was turned into a subdivision. Also continually subjected to the merciless appetite of "developers" and their bulldozers are large sections of Bluegrass farm land sacrificed to industrial uses, including the gigantic Toyota plant in Scott County. A famous horse farm plans to convert a huge section of its land into a regional shopping mall, and, unfortunately, even the University of Kentucky plans to allow commercial interests to develop a large research complex on its beautiful Coldstream Farm, which for years has been devoted to agricultural research.

Where large tracts of Bluegrass pasture land have remained intact, it has been through their purchase by primarily absentee-owners, who turn the land into huge Thoroughbred (and livestock) farms. Such investments have been not only profitable tax shelters, but landowners also often obtain both entry into the social network of the original old-line Bluegrass aristocracy and a setting in which dignitaries from around the world can be graciously entertained "country style." It is even possible to turn an actual profit from the farming and the horse breeding and racing aspects of the estate. Where the land is still owned by descendants of original Bluegrass settlers, the owners are predominantly farmers; many, like Coleman, do not raise Thoroughbreds. However, few of these contemporary "Kentucky Colonels" can afford either the pursuit of scholarly endeavors or the leisurely lifestyle enjoyed by Eaton's "congenial Squire."

It is ultimately the limestone underlying those gently rolling pastures that has allowed some Inner Bluegrass landed gentry, ever since they settled in the area, to enjoy an affluent country gentleman lifestyle supported by livestock farming—and for some, Thoroughbred and Standardbred horse breeding—and grain and tobacco (or, previously, hemp) raising. Not only do such activities flourish on limestone-enriched bluegrass, they also are precisely the sort of country gentleman, semirural farming operations conducive to the neopatrician, quasi-aristocratic way of life preferred by many Bluegrass landed gentry. Limestone provides calcium and other minerals, via the bluegrass and the innumerable limestone-fed springs and streams, to build strong bones and healthy livestock. Some observers maintain that the exemplary livestock found in the Bluegrass simply could not be created or perpetuated outside the Region. When moved to Pennsylvania or other Eastern states, these chauvinists maintain, Bluegrass livestock undergo a change in bone and musculature that, by the end of a few generations, has created an inferior breed of animals. In this view, excellence has less to do with bloodlines than with environment, reflecting the prevalent folk belief that excellent bloodlines only realize their full potential in the Bluegrass. However, as Karl Raitz notes, when tested, the soils of some Bluegrass horse farms are "strongly acid, low in organic material, and not naturally fertile;" moreover, the Region's horse farms spend millions annually for custom-manufactured feeds and imported hay. Raitz suggests, therefore, that the idea that the Region's limestone is responsible for its immaculate livestock is in some cases more folk belief than reality. Rather, Raitz contends that the proliferation of gentleman farms in the Bluegrass was as much the result of Tidewater migrants transplanting their aristocratic lifestyle and plantation agriculture to the Region as it was to the composition of Bluegrass soil.

In any case, the quality of Bluegrass livestock is renowned throughout the world. Whether it be Thoroughbred horses winning races or various other champion livestock winning ribbons at worldwide shows, Bluegrass born and bred livestock are exemplary of their species.

In 1815 at the Sandersville farm near Lexington, Bluegrass farmers held the first agricultural fair west of the Alleghenies. (It was also the second in the nation, the only earlier one having been held in 1811 in Berkshire, Massachusetts.) Admission was free, and as prizes Lexingtonians donated fifteen or more silver cups to be awarded by the five judges, chosen from Frankfort, Woodford County, Lexington, Clark County, and Bath County (the only county not in the Inner Bluegrass). In 1816 an agricultural society was formed. By 1856 a typical Bluegrass fair in Bourbon County judged silverware, needlework, garden vegetables, dairy products, preserves, pickles and jellies, mules, jackasses and jennets, chickens, ducks, long-wool sheep, hogs, fat cattle, oxen, milk cows, Merino sheep, Durham cattle, draft horses, saddle horses, and, of course, Thoroughbreds.

Today the excellence of Bluegrass livestock is often enjoyed by tourists, who often spend days simply driving around the Region's farms admiring the beauty of Bluegrass pastures—which in the nineteenth century were called "grazing parks"—populated with herds of carefreely cavorting horses, languishly grazing cattle, or other immaculate purebred livestock.

THE OTHER KENTUCKY

These beautiful farms that so obviously proclaim affluent Bluegrass folk culture are located almost exclusively within the confines of the Inner Bluegrass. As soon as one leaves the undulating limestone-based pastures, the changes in economic, and attending sociocultural, realities are blatantly apparent. Not long after it became firmly entrenched, the culture of the Inner Bluegrass gentry incorporated an elitist folk worldview of their own culture and the limestone-based Region in which it flourished. That worldview, while principally ascribing laudatory attributes to the Bluegrass and its way of life, also contained negative appraisals and attitudes about the rest of Kentucky. Tom Clark notes that from the beginning,

prosperous farmers and merchants of the central counties held the important national and state offices, imported purebred livestock, exhibited their animals and produce at fairs, and were visited by foreign traders. . . . There were, however, two Kentuckys. . . . That part of the Kentucky population settled in outlying areas clearly fell into the social and political category of the "great common people." Their churches were more primitive, their schools were late in being organized, no important press spoke for them, and no major political leadership sprang from their ranks. In the isolated areas circling the central counties humanity was willing to accept the fortunes of life as they unfolded, to cling to . . . old ways, and to block changes by creating stubborn barriers of social inertia.

Furthermore, Clark states: "If you could take a knife and run it around the outer Bluegrass, the inner Bluegrass would have to sustain it and support it." Such views are maintained even today, not only by Bluegrass residents but also by some outside the Region.

The sociocultural and economic differences are especially noticeable in those Inner Bluegrass counties that border to the south and east of the Region. For example, the area north and west of Winchester, seat of Clark County, is geologically and culturally within the boundaries of the Inner Bluegrass. To the south and east of Winchester, however, rolling Bluegrass changes to knobby hills and steep gullies. This change is so marked that the Appalachian Regional Commission regards Appalachia as beginning in Clark County. Not only is it rather easy for outsiders to recognize the existence of "two Kentuckys," most Kentuckians themselves are only too aware of such social, economic, and cultural divisions. After a recent report on the television program "48 Hours" which depicted lifestyles of eastern Kentucky's impoverished lower class, Kentuckians across the Commonwealth were shamed and angered. A teacher from eastern Kentucky commented: "The thing that has upset the politicians so much is that now the entire country knows, 'Yes, there are two Kentucky's'. . . . If you doubt this, drive past Winchester. . . ." Another eastern Kentucky native lamented "the difference between west-of-Winchester and east-of-Winchester," claiming that it is "almost like there are two different states under the heading of one." In Clark

County, then, is a good illustration that—at least as far as the Bluegrass is concerned—geology, geography, economics, and sociocultural and even political aspects of life tend to be more or less congruent.

Historically, it is on the Bluegrass farms that the different socioeconomic classes have come together. For it was (and to considerable extent still is) on the landed gentry's farms that many from the lower socioeconomic strata found work. To the farms first came blacks—primarily because of their race and slavery's rules of segregation—and other have-nots, such as Irish immigrants. Later, they were joined by relocated subsistence farmers, and later still by laid-off loggers and coalminers—many from outlying areas, primarily eastern Kentucky, and many of them Scotch-Irish in descent. They brought little with them but their labor and their folk skills, but with these they helped transform the Bluegrass into its manorial splendor. They farmed the land and cared for the livestock—and often for the owner and his family as well. They helped build the houses, the barns and other outbuildings, and, not least of all, the Bluegrass stone fences—many of which structures are fine examples of folk tradition.

The landscape created by the Bluegrass aristocrats and their slaves and other laborers from lower socioeconomic groups eventually became one of engaging beauty, reminiscent of the tranquil green perfection of an English countryside, from which many of the gentry traced their lineage. Describing a typical Bluegrass scene, a surprised visitor, journeying for the first time from Cincinnati to Lexington in 1834, wrote:

The soil is of the richest kind, and the improvements superior to any that I have seen in any part of the United States. I had long been aware of the high character claimed for the country around Lexington; but, prepared as I was to behold a region rich in attractive scenery, and highly embellished by the hand of art, I was agreeably surprised in finding that it surpassed my anticipations. The dwellings are all commodious and comfortable, and the most of them very far superior to those usually inhabited by farmers. Many of them are surrounded by gardens and pleasure-grounds, adorned with trees and shrubs in the most tasteful manner; and the eye is continually regaled with a beautiful variety of rural embellishment. There is something substantial as well as elegant in the residence of a farmer of this part of Kentucky; a combination of taste, neatness, comfort, and abundance. . . . Every foot of ground has been adorned or rendered fruitful. The woodland pastures, which are peculiar to this section of country, are remarkably beautiful. . . .

That lovely limestone-based and forested meadowland that gave rise to agrarian affluence and its attendant culture also provided the materials with which those "embellishments" the traveler noted were constructed. Today, many of those folk artifacts remain on the Bluegrass landscape.

Folk Patterns and Material Culture Forms on the Bluegrass Landscape

Fences

Perhaps no other material culture forms are as widespread throughout the Inner Bluegrass as the two dominant kinds of fences: limestone and wooden plank. Serving to enclose the pastures and paddocks, or to mark boundaries, these fences trail alongside narrow picturesque roadways, many of which date to wagon and stagecoach days, or even to when they were nothing more than buffalo traces. The older of the two, in harmony with the landscape upon which it is placed, is the stone fence. The surviving stone fences constitute only a fraction of what once was probably the most extensive network of quarried stone fences in the world. The remnants of this network are still the largest collection of stone fences in the United States.

Until recently this network was thought by scholars to have been constructed entirely by slaves, but research by Karl Raitz and Carolyn Murray Wooley has revealed that the Bluegrass stone fence was originally the work of white craftsmen, who brought the craft from their ancestral homelands. Moreover, the slowly evolving creation of the Region's stone fences can be seen as an index for the social, cultural, and economic evolution of the Bluegrass itself.

SPLIT-RAIL FENCE TO QUARRIED STONE

During the settlement period, fences, like nearly all other structures, were made of wood, the most readily available material. Trees, which had to be felled for farming, were split lengthwise into long sections or "rails." "An accomplished woodsman could split . . . seventy-five ordinary rails per day," writes Lloyd G. Lee, "but only about forty tough locust rails [the favorite for split-rail fences], which were normally cut in lengths from twelve to fourteen feet." A split-rail fence was also called a "worm" or "snake" fence, and Bourbon County's *Kentuckian-Citizen* noted that it was "almost exclusively used . . . for division fencing for a hundred years. It was built V-shape, and when staked and ridered was quite strong and durable." However, because they could be rather easily taken apart, rail fences were sometimes the objects of Halloween pranks; in Boyle County one year some boys dismantled a fence and built a

40-foot high tower with the rails. No original Bluegrass rail fence still exists, to my knowledge, but records, sketches, and even photos help document their distribution.

Soon, however, trees suitable for fencing were not as plentiful, and in the settled areas new laws required that livestock be securely contained, or the straying animal's owner could be substantially fined. Strays were such a problem that some drastic solutions were attempted. In Bourbon County, a "stray pen" was built adjacent to the court house, so that it would be handy for farmers looking for their animals, and it remained in use for years despite the smells and noises. To solve the problem permanently, Bluegrass farmers, like their ancestors in Britain and Ulster who had faced the same problem generations before, looked to the plentiful stone underlying the land as a source for more secure and permanent fencing material.

STONE FENCES

Some Bluegrass farmers no doubt still retained the folk knowledge of how to build stone fences, and some of the more prominent immigrants may have brought skilled masons with them. Records reveal that stone masonry was a favorite folk occupation, and the early stone fences—the earliest being in Harrodsburg in 1777 and at that time called a stone wall—were obviously constructed by people with knowledge of the craft as practiced in Ulster and Britain. In both places, the stone walls—called dykes in Scotland and in the north of Ireland and England—are markedly similar to early Kentucky stone fences. Moreover, other early Bluegrass stone structures such as cellars, mills, houses, and even jails, often found in areas with early stone fences, have been shown to be of British and Ulster craftsmanship. So the demographic evidence supports Raitz and Wooley in their contention that the earliest Bluegrass stone fences were probably constructed by British and Scotch–Irish craftsmen. These masons may, nonetheless, have supervised laborers—such as black slaves or even other whites—doing the heavy work.

The Irish and the Germans Many of these white laborers were Irish immigrants. Although a small minority in the early settlement of the Region, the Irish flooded into the Bluegrass in the wake of the terrible Irish Potato Famine of the 1840s and 1850s. They found work building the old Kentucky Central Railroad and constructing turnpikes. Some Irish were working on Bluegrass roads as early as the 1830s, and by the 1850s, when Kentucky roads were being surfaced with stone, or macadamized, it was natural that the Irish should be hired to quarry the stone from outcroppings alongside the right of way and then to construct the turnpikes. A few Irish were sufficiently skilled masons to build retaining walls, bridges, and abutments. In 1850, of 117 turnpike workers in Bourbon County, 113 were Irish, while thirteen Irish were skilled free lance masons. Since the turnpikes naturally bordered their property, Bluegrass landowners observed the Irish masons' skills and often hired them to build or repair stone fences on their estates. The Irish were familiar with such construction, an ancient folk craft in Ireland. Much of the common labor carried out under the direction of the Irish masons was done by unskilled Irish, who broke up large rocks with knapping hammers. On the estates, however, they were usually assisted by the landowners' slaves. Laboring side by side, the free Irish and the black slaves were both poorer than church mice and precariously tottered on the lowest rungs of the socioeconomic Bluegrass ladder.

In some areas of the Bluegrass, the Irish masons were also assisted by German laborers, mostly on the railroad and turnpikes but to some extent even on the stone fences. In Bourbon County, so many Germans concentrated in one area that its local nickname was "Old Dutch Settlement," and Boyle County had its Little Austria, Woodford County its Little Germany, and Clark County its Germantown. Germans came chiefly to escape compulsory military service or in the wake of the 1848 upheavals in Europe.

Both Irish and Germans were much resented by earlier arrivals. They were willing to work for pittance wages—what the railroads and turnpike companies paid. A few were qualified to enter a profession or trade. In either case, they were thought to be taking jobs from native–born Americans. If they were Roman Catholics, they were regarded with suspicion and bigotry; indeed, some German and Irish Catholics were stoned in Frankfort when they tried to vote.

The native whites frequently slandered these newcomers with negative stereotypes, especially the Irish. Local newspapers called attention to what they saw as Irish-instigated "problems," always referring to them— as whites did with blacks—as stereotyped nameless entities: "the" Irish (as in "the" black); or "Irishman dies" (as in "slave dies"). The folk image of Irish laborers usually emphasized whiskey. Some Irish turnpikers were paid with room and board, a small wage, and a set amount of liquor, and the local assumption was that they cared most for the jiggers. Irish laborers, it was claimed, would leave a job enmasse if another employer offered six jiggers of whiskey instead of four. If Irish masons had actually consumed as much liquor as the stereotype portrayed, it is a wonder that the stone fences were ever built or followed a straight line.

Nonetheless, Irish immigrants stayed the course and helped to build the roads, the railroads, Bluegrass stone fences, and other structures.

Gradually these immigrants acquired legal citizenship; for example, in nineteenth century Bourbon County, of the 155 naturalized citizens, nearly half were Irish. Many of the Irish and German immigrants were buried in the Old Dutch Graveyard in Paris, the seat of Bourbon County.

After the Civil War, the numbers of Irish masons dwindled, as free blacks, capitalizing on the experience gained while building fences as slaves, adopted the craft. White native Kentuckians, no doubt also trained by Irish masons, competed with the Irish as well. For instance, as early as 1870 in Bourbon County, there were seven native white and four black masons competing with a diminishing number of thirty-six Irish masons. Such competition did not go unresented, but now the shoe was on the other foot: the Irish, slowly being edged out by the freed blacks, were the new haters. Poignantly reflecting this situation is an 1904 anecdote about a local town character in Georgetown who was an Irish mason called Old Fitz. Sixty years old, with badly stooped shoulders and hair as white as cotton, Old Fitz was nonetheless a fine rock-fence builder. On Court Day, however, he habitually got "tanked up" on Kentucky whiskey and would wander into someone's back yard where he would lie around all day mumbling to himself, "Dom the niggers." This hatred was reciprocated by blacks who called the Irish "white niggers." Even before the Civil War, antagonism between the groups had been established by some slaveholders, who believed their Negroes to be more valuable than "Paddies" and therefore spared their blacks by hiring the Irish for the most dangerous and unhealthy jobs. Not unnaturally, when the Civil War broke out, many Southern Irish favored States' Rights and denounced "the Yanks" as "dirty nigger lovers." After the War, the pattern of replacing Irish masons with natives, white and black, continued, so that by 1910 in Bourbon County, masons numbered twenty-three black, seven native white, but only one Irish. Today, the majority of Bluegrass fence masons are white but not Irish.

Dry Stack Fences   The early stone fences constructed by the British and Ulstermen and later by the Irish and black masons were predominantly a dry-laid level-coursed type, sometimes called a dry stack fence, an ancient form of construction. Remnants of these dry stack fences are still found around paddocks, pastures, barnyards, gardens, and fields, and especially marking property lines. Those built at the same time as the turnpikes follow road frontage. Ordinarily, a Bluegrass stone fence is not called a wall, but there are exceptions: an 1863 Woodford County estate was named Stonewall after the outstanding stone "wall" bordering its property. Technically, a stone fence differs from a rock fence. Stones for a rock fence are placed "as is" and are not altered whatsoever, whereas stones for a stone fence are somewhat shaped by the

Typical Bluegrass scene showing traditional dry-stack stone fence and black four-plank wooden fence (Photo by author)

mason. In the speech patterns of the Bluegrass, however, the terms are interchangeable.

A dry stack fence was usually constructed as follows. On a sunken foundation of the largest stones available—always wider than the fence—a two-course, double-faced fence was erected. The mason shaped the stones and laid them in, largest at the bottom, smaller as the courses rose to the top, and longest side toward the inside of the fence. A dry stack fence was built slightly hollow. The two separate fence courses were made to lean in slightly (called battering), so that between the two vertical courses, on the hollow inside, the long stones formed an irregular surface. This created stability and allowed rainwater to drain toward the inside and out the bottom, thus avoiding damage from freezing and thawing. Stability was also achieved by lapping every stone—one over two, and two over one—thus avoiding vertical joints, and by using tie rocks which run crosswise through the fence, thus tying the two separate vertical courses together, from the face of one to the face of the other. These tie rocks were spaced about 4 to 6 feet apart and placed 1 and 2 feet from the ground; in some cases the tie rocks protruded from the otherwise flat plane of the fence face, usually only on the inside.

The irregular cavity in the fence hollow, between the two courses, was then filled with small fragments of rock (called spalls) chipped away by the mason in the shaping process; ideally, the spalls would be tamped down or otherwise made solid, but sometimes they were simply dumped in until they reached the desired level. The fence was then capped with rocks spanning the entire width, tying the two courses together and creating a more stable structure. The cap stones, sometimes a bit wider than the stones in the top regular course, were laid as level as possible to provide a secure base for the coping stones. Ideally, coping stones were the same shape, but somewhat smaller than cap stones, and were placed on the cap stones at a slight angle, longest and heaviest edge down. If the fence was on an incline, as was often the case, the tops of the coping rocks were slanted downhill, so that gravity assisted in securing them in place. Although the primary function of the coping stones was to create stability, they also served, with their jagged edges pointing upward, to dissuade livestock from testing whether the grass was greener on the other side of the fence and to discourage trespassers. Most of the dry stack fences have both cap and coping stones, and they are not only the oldest and—many believe—best fence type, but the sort most often found in the Bluegrass—until suburbanization and other "developments" began to encroach on the beautiful farmland, forcing a change in fencing traditions.

Edge Fences   A dry-laid edge fence—the second oldest type Bluegrass stone fence—was less complicated and less costly to construct than a dry stack fence and consequently was erected on less valuable land. Usually it was found in low-lying wet areas or on steep terrain, such as along the Athens-Boonesborough Road or Irish Ridge in western Mercer County, which was settled by Irish Catholics in the 1840s; remnants of edge fences are still found there today.

Unlike the level-course stack fences, which were built mostly of quarried stone, edge fences were constructed from loose field stones gathered in preparing the fields for crops or pasture, which were then, without benefit of a footing, simply set directly on the ground on their edges. The largest stones were placed on the bottom, side by side. Successively smaller stones were used for the other courses, thus creating battered sides. The stones were simply jammed and wedged, edges down, between the protruding tops of the stones in each lower course. Sometimes large tie rocks were laid flat on top of the stones in the last course. In essence, an edge fence is an entire fence treated like courses of coping with large tie rocks on top. Since they were erected in relatively

Stone "edge" fence on hilly terrain, Athens-Boonesborough Road (Photo by Jerry Schureman)

poor areas, most edge fences in the Bluegrass were probably do-it-yourself projects, no doubt modeled after similar fences in Britain and Ireland.

Mortared Fences and Stiles   Built exclusively in modern times and still being erected today, mortared fences of quarried, shaped stone (sometimes recycled from partially demolished or relocated older fences) are constructed almost invariably as decorative embellishments to horse farms and other rural and suburban Bluegrass real estate. Set into concrete footings, mortared fences display cut-stone faces, but their cores are of concrete, and they usually lack such good masonry practices as tie rocks and cap courses. Their courses are often laid against the grain, and their coping rocks are usually filled with spalls and then topped with cement.

Because the use of mortar permits creativity, masons have decorated these fences by arranging vertical stones in a variety of coursing patterns, many of which have already become traditional motifs: "random ashlar," "two to one," "flag pattern," and so on. Many of these fences are pretentious, some even with castellated copings, and although many were built to simulate the older dry stack fences, the mortar always reveals that they are imitations.

Some of the mortared and dry stack fences had stiles. These were usually created by placing unusually long stones through the fence so that they protruded on both sides to form steps to the top where the coping rocks were replaced with a flat rock to form the topmost step. If the fence crossed water, a culvert was left for small streams or a simple bridge was built. If a stream crossed a property line, it was often spanned by arches of various sorts, sometimes built as part of the fence. Underneath the arch a hanging grill was usually suspended (many are still used) to control debris, prevent damming, and preclude passage of horses and other livestock to another's property.

Destruction of Stone Fences   Only a meager 5 to 10 percent of these old stone fences still exist. What happened to the other 90 to 95 percent? Scholars have very little reliable information on this question, but through anecdotal oral history and other data gathered by Raitz and Wooley, a number of reasons for their disappearance can be conjectured.

Some of the oldest fences may have been torn down and broken up for material to surface roads in the 1820s to 1840s. Most principal roads were surfaced with limestone aggregate in those days and, to facilitate turnpike development, laws were passed enabling workers to gather rocks from land adjoining the right of way. The turnpike law also stipulated a 30-foot width, so existing fences may have been torn down to comply. Because some fences were not built as well as others, and all required (and still do require) constant attention and repair, some farmers probably had them removed to save the time, trouble, and increasing costs of maintenance. In addition, some farmers may have been forced to remove stone fences as a result of changes in size and type of agricultural machinery when farming methods changed, requiring both larger fields and more space to maneuver. During the Depression, Civilian Conservation Corps crews, in their campaigns to improve soil and fertility in marginal farming areas, probably tore down some fences as well; in places there still exist huge piles of stones attesting to CCC activity. In some modern development, as constructing a new shopping center, bulldozers have been known to bury stone fences by simply cutting a large trench in the ground, pushing the fence into it, and covering it over.

Such myopic and expedient—but hardly necessary—destruction of historical treasures is a disaster that continues to this day. For several years, opposing forces have argued over the proposal to widen the two-lane Paris Pike between Paris and Lexington—a road steeped in history.* The Pike courses by some of the more beautiful and representa-

---

*Many Bluegrass roads are called "pikes," because they were at one time toll roads; most were privately owned, and a traveler paid to have the "pike" "turned"—that is, the bar or gate lifted—before he could proceed down the road.

tive farms (horse and other) in the Bluegrass Region, and along it are located lengthy stretches of some exquisite old stone fences, which surely would have to be taken down. Bluegrass scholar Dr. Mary Wharton believes that on this twelve-mile pike is located the highest concentration of historic horse farms perhaps in the world; it may also contain the highest concentration of stone fences left in the Bluegrass. Raitz wrote in 1980:

Aesthetic and functional value of the stone fences will be given consideration by the State Highway Department in their evaluation of the new [Paris Pike] right-of-way. It remains to be seen, however, how many of the farm owners would reconstruct their fences, because it is estimated that a wet wall fence would cost well over $13,000 per mile to rebuild.

Today, of course, it would cost even more, and even as this is being written the current governor has announced his support of the proposal to "improve" the road, though much of the opposition is from the farmers who own the land and the fences.

In modern times, some farmers have dismantled stone fences to sell to developers to create stone veneer houses (and even a few churches), many of which can be seen throughout the labyrinth of subdivisions now covering much of the Bluegrass. Some present-day horse farms and other suburban residents also buy stones from demolished fences and use them either to create various ornamental objects, or to erect entirely new stone fences—but ones that bear little resemblance to the British and Irish folk masons' original creations.

PLANK FENCES

Also built exclusively in modern times is the traditional four-plank wooden fence, usually solid oak or oak planks on locust posts. Although plank fences in no way resemble the stone fences, they very often join them or even stand one in back of the other. These fences, surrounding large horse farms and gentleman farms, are ubiquitous on the Inner Bluegrass landscape, and consequently are today a more typical culture form than the older stone fences. The plank fence, whitewashed with a lime solution, had become an emblem of the Bluegrass by the end of the nineteenth century. Until the last two decades, when black paint suddenly became popular, nearly all such fences, mile after mile of them, were painted white. Writing in 1955, Bradley Smith observed that tourists "to the Bluegrass are awed by the incredible mileage of clean white fences that are repainted every spring," and noted that "Mereworth Farm is unique because it has the only black fences in the countryside." Today, short of conducting an actual count, it would be difficult to estimate which is more prevalent, the white or the black plank fence.

Wooden fences—their ideal form, color, type, size, kind of woods, durability, construction techniques and materials, and safety—constitute topics for a great deal of speculation and discussion among Bluegrass denizens, and even some controversy. Some horse breeders adamantly maintain that the traditional white plank fence is not only more aesthetically pleasing but, more importantly, it is safer for the costly horses (some worth millions of dollars), because they can see the white fence more easily in the dark. Others consider such ideas to be unfounded and point out that the black asphalt/creosote paint put on the wood has to be repainted only every four to five years compared to annually or at the most every two to three years for white paint, and thus costs less to maintain. Moreover, they claim, black fencing is just as picturesque as white, and perhaps more so.

Current average initial cost for black fencing is about $44 per 16-foot panel installed, 330 panels per mile. Thus a mile of fencing, which is the way many Bluegrass farms calculate it, costs $14,000-$15,000. Some black fences cost even more: at $4.75 per foot plus $1.50 for painting, a total of $33,000 per mile. Some white fences can run as high as $77 per 16-foot panel, or over $25,000 per mile. In either case, on many horse farms, even where there is an older stone fence, a four-plank wood fence, white or black, is often erected on the *inside* (pasture side) of the stone fence to protect valuable horses from the sharp edges of the stones. Though a few farmers prefer a design in their wooden fences, the most common is the traditional plain four–plank basic folk construction, either white or black.

NEW TYPES OF FENCE

Some recent innovations have been made in fencing. Claiborne Farm, one of the preeminent horse farms in the Bluegrass, pioneered a new type of diamond-mesh wire fencing, sometimes called V-mesh, trade-named Keep-Safe. Claiborne is a large farm; it has about 3,500 acres, twenty-seven miles of roads, forty-four barns, thirty-two homes for employees, three larger homes for the owner's family, forty-seven licensed vehicles, twenty-five tractors, 161 employees, and requires about $7.2 million annually to operate; the farm also has about ninety-seven miles of fencing. The farm maintains literally hundreds of horses, many valued at millions of dollars—Claiborne was home to the late Triple Crown winner (1973) Secretariat—and the safety of these animals is a primary concern. Because there is always the risk of a horse impaling himself on a splinter of plank fence, Claiborne decided to use the diamond-mesh wire, which is flexible and gives way if a horse runs into it. The wire is put up in sections between two wooden posts, framed by one wooden board at the top, but the largest surface area is wire. The cost of installing diamond mesh approximates that of four-plank wood: $230 per 165 feet for the wire plus wooden posts and wooden top boards, but maintenance costs are much less. The wire, as well as the wooden parts, are all painted with a new black acrylic which does not fade, turn, or mildew as does the old asphalt.

The Blood Horse magazine—published and widely read in the Bluegrass— now advertises a new fence made to resemble the traditional four-plank wooden fence. Designed of maintenance-free polymer, it requires no paint and supposedly will not crack, splinter, or rot. Whether Bluegrass farmers will adopt it remains to be seen.

GATES

The traditional gate for Bluegrass fences is variously known as the Kentucky Gate, the patent gate, the easy gate, or—because it does not require one to dismount a horse or get out of a vehicle—the lazy gate. Invented at the close of the Civil War and originally called the Lincoln Automatic Gate, it is opened and closed by means of two long arms, one extended in the air on each side of the gate. Dangling from the ends of these arms is usually a cord, rope, piece of leather, or a long wooden handle. To pass, one simply reaches out from the vehicle or horse, and pulls down on the handle or rope, etc., attached to the arm, thus opening the gate; to close it after passing through, one pulls down on the handle attached to the arm on the other side.

These gates, for years manufactured in Fayette County, have been sold all over the world. Passing through these gates and beyond the fences, one finds an assortment of houses, barns, and other structures built in traditional forms.

CHAPTER 4

Antebellum Folk Houses

LOG CONSTRUCTION

Just as the first fences were of split-rail, made from available timber, many of the first roofed structures were also constructed of logs, chinked with rock and mortar. Log construction was introduced to the New World by immigrant Scandinavians settling along the Delaware River in the first half of the seventeenth century. Log construction in this country was always a frontier phenomenon and, as there was no British prototype, was not used by early New England and Virginia colonists. German immigrants, however, were familiar with such construction and quickly adopted the log medium, erecting log structures in Maryland, Virginia, North Carolina, and especially Pennsylvania, where many of them settled. Their Scotch–Irish neighbors readily relinquished their own traditional stone and mud construction when they realized the practicability of building with logs on the forested frontier, and they added to the basic construction technique their own traditional expertise in stone work.

These assimilated traditions of log and stone construction were then brought to the Bluegrass in the late eighteenth century, and soon the chinked-log house became the universal dwelling place of the frontier, eventually adopted even by the Indian. Considering that, of Kentucky's 25,715,840 acres, 24,230,000 were covered with about seventy species of virgin timber, much of which had to be cleared for settlement and farming, log construction proved to be the most practical method to provide shelter. Favorite timber trees for this purpose were blue ash, black walnut, white oak, and honey locust.

Some of the first log cabins—usually a single–pen, "pen" meaning a small four-sided enclosure—were erected inside a large fortified area such as Harrodstown (now called Harrodsburg), the oldest town in Kentucky and the Bluegrass.★

★The Bluegrass is fortunate to have a number of outdoor folk museums, modeled after the prototype in Skansen, Sweden, which not only preserve and/or re-create the original structures but also endeavor to provide visitors with an authentic representation of pioneer life, offering demonstrations of various arts and crafts and activities. Both Harrodsburg and Boonesborough are among these restored outdoor museums, as well as Pleasant Hill at Shakertown, Waveland in Fayette County, and Danville's Constitution Square, which has a

The majority of early cabins, however, were built outside the confines of such protective stockades, often near the numerous streams or salt springs (called "licks" by pioneers because wild animals came there to lick up the salt). The site of the first log house at what would become Lexington was chosen for its proximity to springs, and what is now Nicholasville, in Jessamine County, was established because of its proximity to four major springs and streams. A local legend, retold by Maude Ward Lafferty, claims that Jessamine County itself

was named for a lovely girl, Jessamine Douglas, the only county which memorializes a woman, though many...lost their lives in the settlement of the state. The father of...young Jessamine built his cabin home at the head of the pretty creek which flows through the county into the Kentucky River, and one day when the lovely girl was seated on a rock beside the stream...an Indian spied her and sent his tomahawk...through her brain. The stream was named Jessamine Creek; and the county...was named for the stream.

A major Bluegrass spring in Georgetown was the site of the town's first cabin, built in 1775 and called McClelland's Fort. The cabin was built at what is now called Royal Spring—also known locally as Big Spring—which remains to this day the main source of water for Georgetown, producing a million gallons per day. Another delightful spring, this one at Harrodsburg, became nationally famous in the nineteenth century as a spa. It was named Graham Springs, but visitors affectionately called it White Sulphur of Kentucky.

Many early outlying log homes were built close to the numerous stockades or "stations" that popped up like mushrooms in the early Bluegrass settlement process. For years after the settlement era *any* cabin in the Bluegrass was called a station, and the term is still used for shopping centers and so on occupying the site of an original log cabin station. Log structures dotted the Bluegrass for years, but from 1810 to 1860 the landscape gradually filled up with houses, mills, turnpikes, distilleries, farm buildings, and warehouses.

The form of the earliest type cabin, of unhewn logs, was by definition a one-room dwelling, usually square—for example, fourteen by fourteen feet or sixteen by sixteen feet—or rectangular (perhaps sixteen by eighteen feet or sixteen by twenty feet), one story high or one-and-a-half (ground floor plus loft). The logs that made up the walls were interlocked with crude saddle notching. Most lacked even a fireplace or chimney, but some had a stone fireplace surmounted by a chimney of small logs, lined

---

replica of its first meeting house, jail, courthouse, and post office. Harrodsburg offers the best examples of the types of early log cabins built, as many were, inside the larger fortified enclosure; one, legend says, was built by Daniel Boone, but scholars still debate this.

with hardened mud. The cabin floor was dirt; the roof was covered with split shingles or shakes, made by using a froe to split a short seasoned log into relatively thin slices. These were placed in overlapping rows on the roof and held in place either by logs overlaid at strategic intervals, or by laying long thin poles or saplings across the shakes from gable end to gable end and then either tying the poles down or tying weights on their ends. The last row of shakes at the ridge of the roof protruded above the ridge line to shelter the join from the weather. A widespread folk belief maintained that shakes must be put on only when the moon was waning (or "shrinking") or they would warp, turning the ends up and allowing weather to enter the house.

Hewn-Log Houses   Because the unhewn-log cabin was often meant to be temporary, usually constructed of unseasoned timbers, no known Bluegrass examples of it have survived. However, numerous examples of the larger, more permanent log house are still extant. Constructed of seasoned timbers, carefully squared with a broadax, these houses were better able to withstand the ravages of weather and insects. Log ends were held in place at the corners by various patterns of notching, the two most common being the half dovetail (favored by Carolina settlers) and V notching (favored by Virginians). The logs were placed on a loose, unmortared foundation of stacked limestone rocks, which often allowed snakes to enter—at times even into the house or loft area. The single-pen floor plan was elaborated in several ways. There often was a small "pigeon" loft, where the youngest children slept and which permitted some storage. On the rafters above the loft, green beans, fruits, and even meats were hung up to dry. In some log houses, access to the loft was by ladder, but most had enclosed or "boxed in" narrow stairs (an architectural form dating from medieval times), usually positioned in a corner on the wall opposite the fireplace; the space under the steps served as a small closet, usually the only one in the house.

Floors were made of puncheon, timbers smoothed and placed with the flat side up. Later, thick wooden slabs, dressed down with an adze, replaced puncheon floors, and later still, when sawmills were available, plank flooring was used. Puncheon and slab floors were usually of ash and sometimes oak, while milled flooring was ash, oak, or poplar; pine flooring was rare in the Bluegrass, but a few examples of cherry flooring (and even logs) were discovered in 1820s cabins. The Bluegrass house-wife of the era prided herself on having "sparkling white" floors, scrubbed so on hands and knees with homemade lye soap and/or sand, using corn shucks as rags. Floors were fastened with treenails (pronounced trunnels), wooden spars or pegs fashioned by hand with a knife, usually made of pin oak but some in more elaborate houses were of black walnut. Roofs were still made of shakes but, as blacksmithing had become available, they were kept in place with nails individually fashioned by hand at the smithy's.

To minimize the danger of fire, the kitchen was often built as a separate log pen, usually with a small chimney (a common arrangement in Virginia and throughout the South). This detached kitchen was sometimes connected to the main dwelling by a roofed passageway, creating what moderns call a breezeway. In these improved hewn-log houses, the chimney was usually made of stone, but in a few instances (usually in towns) of homemade bricks.

At least one early extant Scott County farmhouse combines living quarters with a lean-to at the rear for livestock. People and animals sheltered under one roof was an ancient architectural arrangement common in Ulster and Ireland. This allowed the family to tend to its animals without venturing outside during inclement weather. Some scholars maintain that this arrangement was duplicated in America only infrequently, and indeed I know of only the Scott County example in the Bluegrass. Of course, a lean-to had many other uses; in one of the oldest log houses in Clark County, the lean-to served as a blacksmith's shop.

To withstand possible attack, a few hewn-log houses were built like forts. Innes' Station in Franklin County, a two-story double log house (it burned in 1961), was said to have had portholes for guns in the gable ends of the second story. If this was true, the Station was no doubt used to fend off the 1792 Indian assault, but some scholars believe that such claims about gunports are merely products of legendary exaggeration. The Marshall family house, called Buck Pond, a huge two-story log house in Woodford County built in 1784 by Thomas Marshall, father of the renowned Chief Justice, could certainly have served as a fort; it was constructed with enough gigantic oak timbers that, if dismantled and sawed into modern lumber, would almost build a village.

In most Bluegrass log houses, the floor plan and the masonry work were basically Scotch–Irish and English in origin, and the external chimney of English design, but other features and construction techniques, including notching, average cabin height, and rafters that butted against the roof ridge, were predominantly German characteristics.

Scholars debate the settlement era sources of these architectural forms. Some assert that, in spite of the infiltration of Scotch-Irish, German, and other influences, Kentucky developments were simply westward projections of Virginia institutions. George W. Ranck, Lexington's early historian, called Lexington of 1793 "a perfect type of the Virginia towns of that period." Other scholars maintain that the Scotch-Irish, though they borrowed the log medium and German construction techniques, built houses whose floor plans resembled those of typical Ulster farmhouses. Some even contend that the entire layout of the early Bluegrass farmsteads were designed primarily from Scotch-Irish models.

COMMON FOLK HOUSING TYPES

Pioneers usually modified a hewn-log house by either stacking the pens to create two stories or by adding pens to either end or as ells. The most common forms that evolved from such modifications are called double-pen, dogtrot, saddlebag, I-house, and hall-and-parlor house.

Double-Pen Houses   The one-story double-pen was no doubt the most expedient way for settlers to add space for growing families. The second pen was added to the first pen at the gable end opposite the chimney. The dimensions of both pens were usually the same, though only one had a chimney. Often the two pens had no interior door from one pen to the other, but all had two external front doors. Like many single-pen houses, many double-pens had an ell or perhaps a T extending at the rear, often a lean-to but sometimes a smaller pen connected to the main pen by a breezeway. Though it lacks an addition, there is an outstanding example of a double-pen log house, called the Crittenden cabin, on the grounds of the Methodist Home in Woodford County.

Saddlebag House   Though some scholars maintain that the saddlebag house was rare in the Bluegrass, Langsam and Johnson's recent survey of historic architecture in Bourbon County states: "The second most common form of log construction in the county was the saddlebag type.... Thirteen were recorded in the county." The saddle-bag house consists of two log pens, roughly equal in size, built around a huge central chimney. An early settler, in this case a gentryman, wrote in a letter that his saddlebag house, intended as a temporary residence, was "28 by 16 feet with a chimney in the middle having two fireplaces to each room ... our dining room is 16 by 12 feet and our chamber is two feet narrower." Since the saddlebag was originally an English-Pennsylvania type, it may have been brought to the Bluegrass by Pennsylvania settlers.

Dogtrot House   Another form of two separate pens is the dogtrot (or 'possum trot) house, usually a one-story structure. The dogtrot's two pens, usually equal size, were separated by a wide, open, central breezeway allowing passage from front to back (thus "dogtrot"). The entire structure was covered by a common roof so that the dogtrot was very like the single pen with separate pen for a kitchen. In the dogtrot, however, the separate kitchen pen was usually placed away from the main

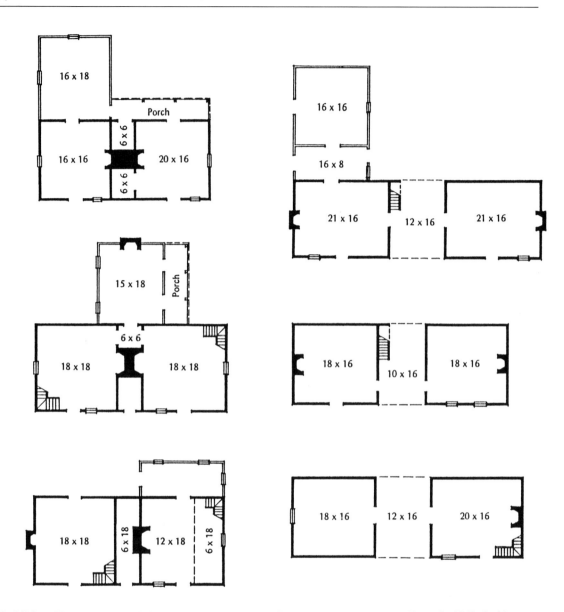

Saddlebag Houses (From William Lynwood Montell and Michael Lynn Morse, *Kentucky Folk Architecture*, courtesy of University Press of Kentucky)

Dog Trot Houses (From *Kentucky Folk Architecture*, courtesy of University Press of Kentucky)

house. Each of the separate pens had its own gable end stone chimney, and each had its own centered side door facing the dogtrot. However, both pens could—but usually only one did, and rarely at that—have another door facing the front of the house.

The pen containing the kitchen was seldom used solely as a kitchen, but also for storage and even family activities. The dogtrot area allowed night air to circulate around each separate pen and, since it was shaded by the roof, was a delightful place to sit on hot days, or to wash dishes or clothes or even oneself. Music playing, storytelling, and even dancing took place in the dogtrot area. In the winter, the open dogtrot usually served as a sort of natural refrigerator for food storage. To protect food from roving animals or the family dogs, it was often placed in a wooden or wire cage raised to near the ceiling by a rope and pulley. Eventually, when it no longer served a purpose to be left open, the breezeway or dogtrot area of many of these houses was closed in.

THE FIRST "GRAND" HOUSES

With the influx of planters from Virginia, the Carolinas, and Maryland, who were accustomed to and could afford elaborate dwellings, Bluegrass houses began to change from "humble" to "grand." The I–house became one of the first "grand" houses, sometimes even pretentious (as when adorned with gingerbread), widely constructed in the Bluegrass.

The I-House   The two-story I-house was named by cultural geographer Fred Kniffen, who believed that three states whose names begin with I—Indiana, Iowa, and Illinois—were in some way a matrix for the type. However, this two-story central-passage structure was a favorite house form throughout the American countryside, including the South. I-house popularity probably reached its zenith during the nineteenth century and the type is widely distributed throughout the Bluegrass today. The I-house is eminently livable and simple in form. Sometimes called a "two over two" house, it is two rooms wide, two rooms high, and one room deep. There is usually a central hallway, a borrowing from the Georgian house, both downstairs and upstairs. Rear additions in the form of an ell or T are common, and porches across both the front and side are popular.

Such houses, some of log construction though later covered with weatherboarding, are among the oldest in the Bluegrass. I-houses with a two-story portico were also introduced at an early date. Typical of rural Southern antebellum homes, such I-houses were much in vogue with smaller Kentucky farmers who wanted to emulate the aristocratic lifestyles of the big planters in their Georgian and Greek Revival mansions.

The I-house came to symbolize social position, prestige, and economic affluence, especially in the rural Bluegrass. It was often built on a prominent knoll to display its stylish features. Easily embellished with moldings and other ornamentations, Bluegrass I-houses were dressed up with all sorts of fashionable facades. Italianate, for example, so captured

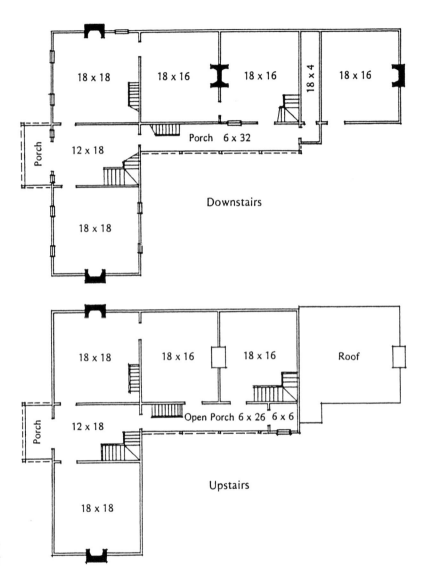

I-Houses (From *Kentucky Folk Architecture*, courtesy of University Press of Kentucky)

the fancy of Clark Countians that it became the most faddish facade in the area.

Most Bluegrass I-houses were of frame or brick construction, and a few of stone. Those originally built of logs have been sided with weatherboard, and because many have a portico and other exterior embellishments, their basic form is often obscured. Yet, the basic I-house has proved to be one of the more stable, enduring, and unaltered of all folk house forms. For example, throughout the nineteenth century in Clark County, it was not only the most popular but also the least modified house form built. Many Bluegrass I-houses are still standing.

There is an unaltered, unadorned 1800 brick I-house on Claiborne Farm, now used as a guest house. One fine brick I-house in Lexington became notorious because its owner, Lewis C. Robards, the town's leading "nigger trader," used it as a warehouse for his "choice stock" of female slaves.*

Central-Passage and Hall-and-Parlor Forms Because of its basic form—two stories high, one room deep, two rooms wide, usually with central hall—the I-house can also be called a central-passage house. Unfortunately, the term central passage has been used erroneously to refer to the hall-and-parlor house. The hall-and-parlor form, said to have evolved from a medieval English prototype, is basically a two front-room floor plan, in which the larger of the two rooms was called a hall, and the smaller room a parlor. Since we no longer call a main room of a house a hall, the term hall-and-parlor house is misleading. The hall-and-parlor house form is not a central-passage house because it has no central hallway. Like the I-house, the hall-and-parlor is a frequently encountered form in the Bluegrass, found in log, frame, stone, and brick houses of almost any style.

The *true* central-passage house, a much more recent form, has a genuine separate hall. The front door opens into an enclosed central passageway, off which doors lead to two separate rooms. Many central-passage houses—if they are two stories high and one room deep—are I-houses. Other central-passage houses—that are not I-houses—may be one story or a story and a half; if they have two stories, they must be two or more rooms deep. Most hall-and-parlor, and I-houses and other central-passage houses alike, have external chimneys centered at both gable ends. On others, the chimneys are placed closer together straddling the ridgeline of the roof.

BRICK, STONE, AND FRAME

Log houses and other structures continued to be built commonly until the Civil War, but after 1800 people more and more turned to frame, brick, and stone for their homes. One scholar maintains that it was the use of brick that signified Kentucky's advancement beyond pioneer days.

---

*A "nigger trader" was widely despised in the Bluegrass as a vulgar upstart, engaged in an infamous business. Yet, Robards prospered. His "choice stock" consisted primarily of what were known as "fancy girls"—beautiful black girls sold to white men to use as mistresses. Like New Orleans, Lexington was a favorite resort for wealthy men whose licentiousness was indulged without racial prejudice.

The new houses were also larger and no longer functioned solely as shelter.

According to visitors to early Lexington, log houses disappeared between 1797 and 1816. If not demolished, they were at least hidden behind a facade or siding. Whereas Lexington of the 1780s was a cluster of about fifty log houses, and only scant frame construction, in 1806 the town contained 104 brick, ten stone, and 187 frame and log houses, the majority of log apparently covered with wooden siding.

Brick quickly became the building material of choice, particularly in towns where trees were no longer easily accessible and brick plants were established. Not only was brick readily available and comparatively easy to work with, it also required little maintenance, and—probably of most importance—houses of brick conveyed a positive image of their owners, whereas log houses generally conveyed a somewhat negative one. However, it must be remembered that some log houses were relatively elaborate or could be modified into the new styles: Greek Revival, Federal, Gothic, and later Victorian. In addition, both the form and construction of many log houses—though of folk provenance—were relatively sophisticated, thus log construction did not *necessarily* imply poverty. For many settlers, log construction was merely an alternative, familiar, and traditional medium.

In contrast to the towns, building with logs continued for years in the countryside. In Clark County, for instance, the decade 1830-40 was a peak period for log construction. The early Bluegrass reflected a cultural lag between town and country, and upper and lower classes. As soon as an area developed to town size, residents quickly demonstrated their preferences for the "better" things in life, including housing, which became one of the more obvious ways to indicate socioeconomic status and various pretensions. The houses of well-to-do Bluegrass townsfolk differentiated them sharply from what Bourbon County historian H. E. Everman calls "the other side"—the laboring classes and members of ethnic enclaves that began to appear after the Civil War. Like their city cousins, rural gentry began to crave more luxurious living space than the old log structures permitted. At this time many houses of Bluegrass gentry began to exhibit architectural characteristics that became typical of the South: symmetrical disposition of structures; classical frontal porticos; wide central halls; open two-story galleries; and detached service buildings.

Some of those "detached service buildings" housed slaves and were called simply the quarters. Most were log houses, a few of brick or stone, a very few of frame. Some, even of wood, are still standing. A slave cabin was usually a simple square or nearly square structure with small windows, small chimney and fireplace (it was not unusual for the cabin to have no fireplace at all), and a dirt floor. In the rural Bluegrass, slave quarters were usually located behind the main house, doors facing the main back door. In towns, slave quarters were established either behind the house or opening onto a side alley. Some slave houses, especially on rural estates, were double-pen log cabins, or, if constructured of brick or stone, they might be designed to accommodate several families. Slaves were also kept in the big house, usually in the attic or the basement, where some houses had partitioned—often locked or barred—slave quarters. In a few places slaves were kept in a shed or barn. It has also been theorized that so-called travelers' rooms, which were located in service areas or above the detached (usually brick) kitchen, may actually have been part of the servants' quarters.

Many such homes of the gentry, though they were usually built of brick and embellished with fashionable facades, were nevertheless built according to a traditional floor plan. Even those not based on a folk form often used other traditional concepts, such as the detached kitchen. With their fine houses, many of which would be the envy of elegant people in *any* part of the country, the well-to-do of the Bluegrass probably hoped to dispel the negative stereotype of frontier Kentuckians: rowdy, uncultured, violent, drunken profilgates, living in log cabin squalor. James Lane Allen's comments are to the point:

The beginnings of Kentucky life represented not simply a slow development from the rudest pioneer conditions, but also a direct and immediate implantation of the best of long-established social forms [from Virginia]. And in no wise did the latter embody itself more persuasively and lastingly than in the building of costly homes.

Indeed, most brick houses were built by the well-to-do, and as one traveled out from Lexington and the surrounding towns, the number of brick houses decreased in direct proportion to the diminishing Inner Bluegrass topography. In the countryside, antebellum Bluegrass gentry had their houses built from materials on their own land, including bricks. The homemade bricks in some early Bluegrass brick houses are imprinted with the footprints of deer, foxes, raccoons, and other animals, which ran across the bricks in the fields where they were laid out to dry. Oakland in Fayette County, now called Pebblebrook, an early (ca. 1820) rural brick home, has many such footprint bricks.

THE STONE HOUSE

Stone houses, unlike brick, were evidently few in number. In 1806, of the 301 houses in Lexington, only ten were stone. Although some stone houses were contemporaneous with early log dwellings, relatively few were constructed during the pioneer period. Rather, stone, the Region's most logical building material, appears to have been used principally for building mills, bridges, spring houses, and foundations and chimneys of timber houses. Despite this, the Bluegrass contains more folk houses of stone than any other area in the Upland South, and the Region is noted for them. Especially noteworthy are the magnificent stone structures built (the earliest dated 1809) by the Shakers at Pleasant Hill, their community in Mercer County.

The William Crow house near Danville is thought to be the first (1783) stone house in the Commonwealth, and the General John Payne house (1790) in Scott County and Welcome Hall (ca. 1789–1792) in Woodford County are other very early examples of the Bluegrass "stone age." Welcome Hall, owned by the same family since 1816 and now on the National Register, is also an excellent example of early self-sufficiency, for on its grounds were a mill, a distillery, orchards, icehouse, dairy, smokehouse, and, of course, slave quarters—for those who did all of the work necessary to keep Welcome Hall self-sufficient. A second self-sufficient Bluegrass estate, with stone house and numerous outbuildings still intact, is Cave Spring, built in the 1790s. Of this establishment Richard DeCamp, executive director of the Lexington-Fayette County Historic Commission, says:

Probably no other farm complex in Kentucky has as many original buildings demonstrating the self-sufficiency of early farms as Cave Spring. Here one can find an early sequence of log, stone, and brick construction.... [It includes a] large stone kitchen with a traveler's [or sometimes called the stranger's] room above ... connected to the main house by a covered, open-sided dogtrot that was enclosed about 1800 to make a dining room. In 1968, a stone wing was added to the north end ... to accommodate a master-bedroom suite. During the period 1784–1800, ancillary buildings also were constructed.... In a fine state of repair are the smokehouse ... hemp house, a brick cabin, a log house, and ... icehouse.

Tradition maintains that some stone houses were built with small windows as defense against attack; Harkaway (1780s) in Bourbon County is an example, and the oldest house in Clark County, the John Martin house, had walls 28 inches thick and was referred to as "the old stone house with portholes." Many rural stone houses were built near the numerous streams and creeks, such as the Grimes house and mill; the house, sitting considerably above the mill and stream, is considered by architectural historian Clay Lancaster as "the finest stone house existing in Fayette County."

Near the streams, builders had relatively easy access to the sort of Bluegrass limestone commonly called Kentucky marble, which was cut

Grimes House, showing "Kentucky marble" laid in Flemish Bond (Photo by Jerry Schureman)

and shaped in large blocks for house construction; many stone houses were built from stone quarried on the owner's estate. Several types of construction-quality limestone exist in the Inner Bluegrass, so the masons created stone houses that vary considerably in both color and texture, but as a rule only white limestone was given the name Kentucky marble. Kentucky marble is laid on a number of Bluegrass stone houses in a perfectly smooth and even fashion to resemble the elegant Flemish bond found so often in brick houses; such an accomplishment with the heavy, cumbersome limestone is testimony to the ingenuity and expertise of the masons.

One of the more noteworthy of the early builders was John Metcalfe, an accomplished mason, who built a number of stone houses in Flemish bond. An example is Mount Lebanon in Bourbon County, which, with its ell, is also an example of the Kentucky L-shaped house. Metcalfe's brother Thomas helped him and was also an expert mason—so expert that he was nicknamed Old Stonehammer. He built a number of impressive stone houses and other structures, including the oldest extant courthouse in Kentucky, in Green County, and the Old Governor's Mansion in Frankfort. Old Stonehammer earned such a reputation that he became the state's tenth governor, and later served in the U.S. Senate. A number of Bluegrass stone houses are believed to have been built by the Metcalfes, and their skills were so highly valued that even when the builder of a stone house is not conclusively documented, folk tradition often credits the Metcalfes with its construction; such is the case with Warwick (1799), called the most "advanced" example of the craft of stonemasonry in Scott County.

A number of interesting legends are told about some early stonemasons. One describes a Scott County contest for masons to determine who could build the most beautiful chimney, and when the judges refused to decide between the two finalists, they split the prize money. Another concerns an early (1812) stone I-house under construction. The masons, usually diligent and consistent, one day simply failed to show up for work; the owners eventually discovered that they had left to fight in the War of 1812.

As in Lexington, other Bluegrass areas experienced only a short span of stone construction. Early stone houses in Clark County, for example, were built primarily during the decade 1800–10. Jessamine County has sixteen extant early stone structures, all apparently built before 1815. Bourbon County has documented twenty-eight stone houses, two churches, a distillery warehouse, a commercial structure, and a large springhouse, all of stone. The situation is similar throughout the Region. Perhaps there are proportionately few stone houses in the Bluegrass because, as one study suggests, brick, made and fired locally and easily managed, supplanted limestone in the 1790s, for stone was certainly harder both to prepare and handle than was brick.

Many early stone houses utilized the same house forms as did log-pen construction, such as hall-and-parlor and central-passage plans. Most were two-story or one-and-a-half story, and displayed Federal or Georgian facades. The hall-and-parlor form could be used for both small and large houses, but central-passage plans, the I-house, and L-shape houses were usually chosen for large families. Unlike nearly all other domestic architecture in the Bluegrass, stone houses tended to retain their original appearance; of course, some stone houses were embellished with facades, particularly Georgian and Federal styles, but most resisted the Greek and Gothic Revivals, Italianate, etc., which appeared just before the Civil War.

The Frame House   Sawmills appeared quite early in the Bluegrass—some even changed ownership in the mid-1790s—and consequently some frame houses were constructed by early settlers. A few used the "log frame" or "braced frame" method modeled after the ancient English "half timber" forms. Massive timbers of hewn logs were shaped into frames, braced by diagonal pieces, and joined at the corners to form a skeleton house. Spaces between the timbers were filled with nogging— mud, brick, or a mixture of the two—and then sheathed with weatherboarding. Before the advent of water-powered (later steam-powered) sawmills, planks were sometimes sawed out by hand using a special "pit saw," which had handles at both ends. A hole was dug in the ground deep enough for a man to stand erect in, and a log was rolled over the hole; then one man stood in the hole and another on the ground, and the two pulled the saw up and down between them until they had sawed out a plank. The man in the hole wore a huge broad-brimmed hat to keep sawdust out of his eyes.* Not many planks were obtained by this laborious method, certainly not enough to weatherboard† many houses. Thus, most frame housing was built after powered sawmills were introduced. An excellent example of an early weatherboarded log house is the Adam Rankin house, thought to be one of the oldest houses (built ca. 1784) in Lexington.

The proliferation of frame houses was accompanied by an increasing number of building specialists, called by various terms: "house-joiner," "house wright," "house carpenter," or "undertaker of buildings." In essence, these craftsmen were the first Bluegrass architects and contractors. Many had their own shops, and although most relied somewhat upon popular plan books, they also continued to build in traditional forms. Many frame houses in the Bluegrass used the hall-and-parlor floor plan, a central-passage plan (often the I-house), or the two-pen plan common to log houses, with two front entrances.

So many of these hall-and-parlor houses, I-houses and other central-passage houses eventually acquired an attached ell that they gave rise to a common vernacular* form which incorporated an ell into the traditional floor plan. In this plan, the ell extends from the *front* of the house (most ell additions extend at the rear). The most popular form was the gable-facing I-house, so called because the house was turned 90 degrees on its axis causing one gable end to face the street and thus reduce street frontage. Clark McMeekin notes that many of these L-shaped houses were "made of hand-fired brick of a soft brown-rose color, sometimes painted white or saffron or the ubiquitous freight-train red." Though in Kentucky most were built in the postbellum era, they first appeared in the late antebellum period, and are today common throughout the Bluegrass. As is the case with many houses in the Region, many of these old L-shaped houses are known by the names of families who lived in them for generations. As McMeekin notes, a visitor might be directed to

*A good example of this ingenious technique is displayed at the annual Forkland Heritage Festival in Boyle County.

†The term "weatherboard" is of English derivation, and its widespread use in the Bluegrass as the term for wooden siding, rather than "clapboard," which is of German derivation, indicates the dominance of English (by way of Virginia) cultural patterns in the Region.

*"Vernacular" refers to popular as well as folk forms, or hybrids of the two.

the old McAfee place, across from the Crittenden's, though no one of either name has lived there for years. Also associated with many such Bluegrass homes are a number of long-standing traditions and illuminating folktales, ranging from infamous slavery events, murders, and other atrocities, to eccentric doings, to endearing and touching activities of their owners.

LEGENDS OF BLUEGRASS HOUSES

One such tale, of a self-made man, concerns Scotch-Irishman John Scott who came to Jessamine County from Virginia in the 1780s. He carried his entire fortune—two shillings and ninepence—in his pocket. Thence forward, he signed his name "John 2/9 Scott" and was known in the Bluegrass as 2/9 Scott. As a soldier in the Indian wars, he was granted some land and through hard work prospered and increased his holdings by several thousand acres; he shipped his farm goods to New Orleans on flatboats and then, as was the custom for a number of Bluegrass farmers, *walked* back to the Bluegrass with his profits. As one of the area's wealthiest men, Scott built a stone house—unique for the 1790s—and left his four children great parcels of land. In 1840 one of his sons built a brick I-house with a massive Greek Revival facade.

Another widely circulated story revolves around Bourbon County's The Grange, an excellent example of an early Federal brick. In antebellum days it was home to Edward Stone, Bourbon County's only slave trader. Notorious for his cruelty, Stone kept slaves in his cellars; his business practices are described by J. Winston Coleman, Jr.:

[Stone] engaged in . . . trade as early as 1816, buying slaves of both sexes, stowing them in his . . . cellar in irons, then dressing them in good cloth, daubing grey hair with shoe black, rubbing oil on their dusky faces to give a "sleek healthy color" . . . then starting down river.

During his last such trip (1826), his slaves, having suffered beyond endurance, revolted and killed Stone as he was transporting seventy-seven of them on a boat to be sold South. A Lexington paper applauded the slaves' action, calling it "a just murder of a nefarious slave trader."

Certainly one of the more treasured early Bluegrass brick homes is Hopemont, the Hunt-Morgan house, home of John Wesley Hunt, thought to be Kentucky's first millionaire. He married the niece of Francis Scott Key, author of our national anthem, and became the grandfather of General John Hunt Morgan ("Thunderbolt of the Confederacy"), who led many successful guerrilla raids against Union forces. While being chased by Yankees after one such raid, Morgan—this is the story as I have heard it—galloped to Lexington on Black Bess, his famous mare, rode her up to his house and through the front door, and, without dismounting, leaned over and kissed his mother. As he was riding the mare out the back door he called to his mother to prepare his dinner for he would return shortly. The house does have an unusually large modified Federal style front entrance, so the story may be true.

Near Lexington, Eothan, now called Malvern Hill, was once the home of Confederate Colonel Redd, who for years after the war wore his full-dress uniform, rode his favorite charger, and shrieked blood-curdling rebel yells at every opportunity.

A stately late Georgian brick house, which is today a state shrine, is Frankfort's Liberty Hall. Legend claims the house was designed by Thomas Jefferson, who was the friend of John Brown, the original owner and first U.S. senator from Kentucky. Visited by numerous dignitaries, including four presidents and the Marquis de Lafayette, Liberty Hall has generated a number of legends about ghosts. Brown's wife's aunt, a Mrs. Varick, died just three days after arriving at Liberty Hall, following an eight-hundred-mile journey on horseback to console her niece when the Brown's eight-year-old daughter died of typhoid fever. Mrs. Varick's ghost, called the Gray Lady because of her gray silk dress, has been seen numerous times by different people, often sitting in a chair sewing or coming down the stairs or in the garden where Mrs. Varick is buried; and sometimes she is seen with a little girl beside her, reputedly the ghost of the Brown child. Many of the usual ghostly phenomena are present— empty rocking chairs rock, and other objects move apparently for no reason; sounds are heard, such as footsteps and the rustling of the Gray Lady's silk dress, and so on. Moreover, this ghost has even been photographed (or so it is claimed) and the photograph is available for viewing. Another curious happening is the discovery, by one of the employees at the house, of three gold bracelets lying on the tea table in the room where the Gray Lady is most often seen. Since they were not part of the house collection, which has been catalogued, the bracelets were taken to a jeweler, who verified that they were made in New York, Mrs. Varick's home, during the period of her untimely death.

No legendary deaths are associated with Mount Brilliant near Lexington, but it was the scene of a violent 1843 episode that nearly resulted in the death of Cassius M. Clay, the abolitionist and one of the Bluegrass area's more colorful sons. He fought a man from New Orleans, who boasted of never having lost any of his more than forty fights. The event still lives in folk legend, as related by Richard S. DeCamp:

Meetings and barbecues were often held at Mount Brilliant. It was at a political rally here in the summer of 1843 that Cassius M. Clay...had his famous encounter with Samuel Brown from New Orleans. The story is told that while

Clay was heckling a speaker, he was knocked down from behind by Brown. While drawing his famous bowie knife, Clay was shot from arm's length. Clay would have been shot in the heart except that the bullet was deflected by the scabbard of his knife, leaving only a red spot on his chest. Enraged, Clay cut off Brown's ear, gouged out one of his eyes, split his head open, and threw him over the fence. . . . Both men lived. Cassius Clay was tried for mayhem and defended in court by his cousin Henry Clay, who based his legal argument on the premise that Cassius was only acting in the manner befitting a Kentuckian. The jury agreed with the persuasive attorney.

Another Clay legend began at White Hall, the venerable old fire-brand's estate. Cassius had an abiding interest in women and in 1849, at the age of eighty-four, he married Dora Richardson, the fifteen-year-old daughter of a tenant farmer. This so shocked local sensibilities that the sheriff and a seven-man posse descended on White Hall for the purpose of rescuing Dora from what was considered an immoral situation. Apparently warned of the approaching posse, Cassius stood waiting on the piazza: one of his cannon was loaded with fragments of chain, broken horseshoes, and nails; his bowie knife was strapped across his chest, his Winchester in his hand, and the revolver that President Lincoln had given him, in his holster. William Townsend describes what happened next:

Nobody knew who fired first, but at least sixteen bullet holes still remain in that front door and the piazza columns. The old general fired his cannon and knocked down the tree the sheriff was behind. He emptied his rifle and then charged down the steps with his pistol in one hand and bowie knife in the other.

The posse wisely fled, and the sheriff wrote out his report to the judge:

Judge we went out to White Hall, but we didn't do no good. It was a mistake to go out there with only seven men. Judge, the old General was awful mad. He got to cussing and shooting and we had to shoot back. I thought we hit him two or three times, but don't guess we did—he didn't act like it. We came out right good considering. I'm having some misery from two splinters of wood in my side. Dick Collier was hurt a little when his shirt-tail and britches were shot off by a piece of horseshoe and nails that came out of that old cannon. Have you seen Jack. He wrenched his neck and shoulder when his horse throwed him as we were getting away. Judge, I think you'll have to go to Frankfort to see Brown (John Young Brown who was governor). If he would send Captain Longmeyer up here with two [cannon] . . . he could divide his men and send some with the cannon around to the front of the house—but not too close—and the others around through the corn field and up by the cabins and . . . springhouse to the back porch. I think this might do it.

Legend relates the tragic history of Castleton, an imposing brick edifice on an estate recognized as a preeminent breeder of Standardbred horses. Originally built in the late eighteenth century by Virginia immigrant John Breckinridge, who became United States senator and attorney general under Thomas Jefferson, the estate was first called Cabell's Dale to honor Breckinridge's wife, Mary Cabell. (After Breckinridge's death, his daughter Mary Ann inherited part of the estate and married David Castleman, who built the house Castleton for her in 1806.) Undoubtedly Breckinridge and his wife enjoyed a marvelous marriage, for when he died unexpectedly, she was prostrate with grief. Until the day of her death fifty years later, she wore a widow's mourning cap and was called Grandma Black Cap by the family. To compound the widow's loss, a few months after her husband's death she lost her sight, and it was a family saying that Grandma Black Cap cried her eyes out. It is also said of Castleton that during the Civil War the family hid its strong box of valuables under the front steps to conceal it from marauders.

Style and Form   The adoption of brick as a building material and the arrival of Georgian and late Federal architecture—nonfolk *styles*—did not necessarily decrease the use of traditional house *forms*.⋆ For instance, in Bourbon County most Federal brick houses were built on a central-passage plan, with hall-and-parlor forms a distant second. Most houses were built single pile—that is, one room deep; and if two stories high, they were I-houses. In essence, then, the Federal style hall-and-parlor house is basically a folk form with a nonfolk style, the combining of folk form and nonfolk style being a common practice. In addition to the hall-and-parlor plan, many two-story Bluegrass houses were constructed according to the I-house floor plan, and embellished with Georgian, Federal, Greek and Gothic Revival, Italianate, and even Victorian and Colonial Revival facades.

An excellent example of this mixing of folk and nonfolk architectural aspects is Mount Brilliant, the scene of Cassius Clay's fight with Brown. Built in 1792 on land granted by Thomas Jefferson to Virginian William Russell, who named it after the estate of his friend Patrick Henry, this handsome mansion now has nine bays and four rooms across the front and is porticoed with massive Doric columns of Greek Revival style. As early as 1807 the house was likened to the elegant country estates of the

---

⋆"Style" and "form" denote different architectural concepts. Style usually refers to the exterior design—type and placement of windows and doors, trim characteristics—and interior embellishments, such as reeded woodwork. Form refers to the basic layout or floor plan and, to some extent, to construction aspects of the house.

well-to-do in the French countryside by Fortescue Cuming in his *Sketches of a Tour to the Western Country*, and the mansion has historically typified the graciousness of the Bluegrass. Notwithstanding such praise and reverence, or the mansion's elegant facade, the basic floor plan of Mount Brilliant, as originally built by Russell, is the traditional I-house! The original structure forms the nucleus of the main house and has been somewhat swallowed up by additions and embellishments. As illustrated in Mount Brilliant, it was a Bluegrass custom to build a newer structure around an older house, thus incorporating the older form as the core part of the modern house.

Another example of incorporating an older traditional house into a newer shell is seen in Faywood, so-called because it straddles the Fayette-Woodford county line. For some years Faywood stood vacant, possibly because it is supposedly haunted by the ghost of a woman who committed suicide there in 1932. In any event, the huge Colonial style mansion—seventeen rooms, eight and one-half baths—was built around a log dogtrot. Thus one cannot always identify a folk-form house simply by looking at facades because most of them constitute either elite or pop-culture embellishments.

Life on the Antebellum Estate   Most of the early brick and stone houses in the Bluegrass were, of course, the houses of the landed gentry, many of them slave owners. The slaves not only made possible an elegant antebellum lifestyle for their masters, but also affected the way of life of nearly everyone in the Bluegrass before and after the Civil War. The gentry's way of life, affluent though it was, and made possible largely through the institution of slavery, constituted nonetheless basically a folk, self-sufficient manner of living. That lifestyle was often symbolized in their houses, and is romantically described by Squire Coleman:

On a well-established Kentucky plantation, or farm . . . was to be found the mansion, or big house, of the master, usually located some distance from the road in a grove of beautiful trees. In a detached group at the rear of the manor house were the slave cabins, usually constructed of logs, but often of stone or brick. These were familiarly known as the "quarters." Not far distant were to be found the coach-house, the stables or barns for the carriage or riding horses, the hemp-house, the ice-house, weaving and spinning room, smoke-house, wash room, dairy, stone spring-house, blacksmith and carpenter shops.

Sustaining the plantation was a self-perpetuating retinue of slaves: blacksmiths, carpenters, cobblers, weavers and other folk artisans, gardeners, washer women, seamstresses, nurses and other house servants, and general farm hands. Presiding over this virtual village were the master and mistress. She, in the words of Squire Coleman, in addition to mothering her own children as well as supervising all children on the farm,

carried all the keys, directed the household routine and all the various domestic industries, served as head nurse, and taught morals and religion by precept and example.

The master's concern was chiefly with his crops and his livestock. He laid the plans, guessed the weather, ordered the work and saw to its performance. He went out early and returned late. . . . Yet he found time for visits to the county seat on court days, visits to the "watering-places" during the hot summer months, took time for politics and enjoyed sports and social affairs. The one big item in the lives of . . . ante-bellum Kentucky planters was their inherent and abiding love of hospitality upon a large scale. . . . The Kentucky planter was a kind of feudal lord over his house, his family, his plantation and his black people. Money invested in the purchase of a man or woman brought the solution of the owner's labor problem; it obviated re-hire, as possession extended over the life of the slave, and brought natural increment as it vested the owner with title to all the slave's offspring. Once a man had a force of slaves equal to the needs of his plantation, his labor problem seemed not only to be solved temporarily, it seemed solved for all time, for the supply, which involved only a moderate investment, was self-perpetuating. . . . It was in this environment of lavish nature, prodigal outlay, [and] ample hospitality . . . that the folks in the big house lived and enjoyed life in . . . colorful and romantic . . . ante-bellum Kentucky.

Then came the Civil War.

Postbellum Vernacular House Forms and Folk Patterns of Residence

The Civil War brought radical, sometimes violent, changes to Bluegrass life. The traditional antebellum Bluegrass way of life was forever altered. Raiding parties of both Confederate and Federal forces, as well as deserters, wreaked havoc. Rebels plundered the properties of Union sympathizers, and Union soldiers commandeered anything they wanted, particularly from citizens deemed "disloyal," which included many Bluegrass landed gentry. Many estates were ransacked, some houses were actually destroyed, and horses and other livestock were often stolen or commandeered. With their men away at war,* and slaves freed or fled, many Bluegrass wives, struggling to keep the estate functional and solvent, simply found the task insurmountable. By the fall of 1864 plantations were overrun with weeds, fields lay idle, and farming tools rotted or rusted where they lay. Returning from the war, many planters, often penniless and lacking slave labor, found it impossible to restore their ruined estates. Such severe losses were never overcome by many Bluegrass plantations.

In the years surrounding the war, Bluegrass blacks—who discovered that freedom often proved to be considerably less than they had imagined in their hopes, prayers, and dreams—shifted residence, and moved to nearby towns or to other parts of Kentucky, thus creating different patterns of life for both whites and blacks. These new patterns, in turn, called for new patterns of architecture. Black migration also resulted in the establishment of ethnic enclaves, and many of their accompanying architectural forms remain to this day.

---

*Although Kentucky never seceded, her population was split in loyalties, the Bluegrass being predominately pro-Confederate. Kentucky supplied over 30,000 men to the Confederacy, many of them Bluegrass sons.

POSTWAR VERNACULAR ARCHITECTURE

If an owner was able to refurbish or replace his house, he usually yielded to the popular fashions of the day instead of attempting to re-create the former style or form. The Civil War, then, brought to an end the substantial architecture that had heretofore symbolized Bluegrass culture. In its place was introduced a new architecture vaguely referred to as Victorian. It is a favorite and widespread—even national—style, but not considered folk. However, some folk house forms did proliferate after the war.

THE SHOTGUN HOUSE

Located almost exclusively in towns and invariably in lower class neighborhoods (often black enclaves) is the dwelling known by its folk name, the shotgun house. Constructed usually in frame (though some brick ones exist), the shotgun house is one story high, one room wide, and usually three or four rooms deep. The gable ends of the roof face the front and rear of the house, opposite that of most other folk types. The front door, which might or might not be centered, is aligned with the interior doors, so that if all doors were open one could see through to the backyard. (A resident of a shotgun told me, "You can shoot a shotgun straight through it." Hence the name.)* The house, therefore, is straight and narrow, and usually has one or more squatty ridgeline chimneys which serve as flues for free-standing stoves. They often have additions such as a small "settin'" porch or rooms added to the back end to make them even longer, or sometimes in the T or L form. Some have lean-to sheds.

The shotgun house has been shown to be an adaptation of an African prototype to American uses, and relatively elegant examples have been found in the Deep South, especially New Orleans. In more recent times it is commonly found in ghetto areas throughout the South. In the late nineteenth century, mass-produced shotgun-house "kits" were offered by commercial lumber mills.

In the Bluegrass, following the pattern in other parts of the South, the shotgun house was used primarily by blacks and others—such as Irish—on the lower ends of the socioeconomic scale. Because the house type was quite narrow, two or even three of them could be placed on the

---

*Folklorist John M. Vlach has researched the shotgun thoroughly and concludes that its Anglicized name derives from the African word "to-gun," which means "place of assembly."

same width lot used for one normal-width house. In Frankfort, distillery employees and other working class families occupied a variety of small frame houses, including the shotgun, as described by Carl E. Kramer:

Particularly popular were the T-plan and shotgun styles, which generally were characterized by a standard floor plan but differentiated by a rich variety of exterior ornamentation. Aesthetically, the importance of such vernacular dwellings derives not from their style but from the rhythm and continuity of scale which result from the frequency and regularity of their distribution around the neighborhood.

POSTBELLEUM BLACK RESIDENTIAL PATTERNS

Before the war, slaves in many Bluegrass towns, especially Lexington, were often housed, as were their rural counterparts, behind their owners' houses. For example, Raitz's 1980 description of Lexington's black settlement pattern states:

Most of the city's blacks live in residential clusters, many of which were established before the end of the Civil War. Domestic servants or slaves were often housed across the back alley from the owner's home, which faced a main thoroughfare or fronted on a fashionable court. Multiple alinements of back alley houses along a block or series of blocks created small enclaves of Black residents which were often not large enough to be a viable neighborhood, with a church and a shop or two, but rather were dependent on other Black neighborhoods for services and salvation.

Some of the more wealthy Lexington slave holders, writes Raitz, "built their mansions facing fashionable Broadway Avenue and housed . . . slaves along the back alley and Kenton Street. The . . . high density of the dwellings is maintained in part by building houses in the narrow 'shotgun' style." Similar early black residential patterns also existed in other Bluegrass towns, such as Georgetown, where the double shotgun house was an important local variant.

After the war, many such areas became, or bordered on, black ghettoes, particularly when rural freedmen moved to town, and naturally preferred to settle in the vicinity of their city cousins. Today many of those peripheral back-street areas, particularly in Lexington, are also occupied by poor whites, most of them migrants from poverty pockets in rural areas, in search of jobs in the city. The towns in the Bluegrass, however, never did experience an influx of blacks from the Deep South, who moved to the North after the war, nor was the population of Bluegrass blacks increased to any great extent by the large migrations, especially since the 1930s, of Deep South blacks seeking jobs in Northern cities.

Most blacks in the Bluegrass are descendants of the slaves who helped build the Eden of the West, and they inherited from their slave forebears a wide array of folk traditions. Many of these traditions are still functional today, including residential patterns and architecture. In fact, like their former masters' lives (though for quite different reasons and on a different level), the daily lives of most freedmen adhered to traditional patterns. They had little, if any, formal education and were not permitted to participate in civic affairs (both elite culture activities), and they had little money with which to engage in what little popular culture existed. So they lived by the traditions they had always known.

After the war many Bluegrass gentry retained some of their former slaves as paid employees; the 1870 Scott County census, for example, revealed that many blacks were considered members of white households. Still, many runaway slaves and freedmen migrated to other areas. Both Woodford and Scott County lost more than 2,000 black residents in the 1860s. In 1865 some blacks left the Region via free railroad passes, nicknamed Palmer's passes, since they were provided by U.S. Army General Palmer. Also, during and immediately following the war, violence at the hands of the Ku Klux Klan and other white "regulator" groups no doubt prompted many black citizens to flee to Northern cities. Later, during the so-called Kansas Fever of 1877, black population declines occurred in the Bluegrass when innumerable black families bought "emigrant tickets" for eleven dollars and departed for Nicodemus, Kansas, a town established by blacks from Kentucky and Tennessee. Many of the rural freedmen, however, moved to Bluegrass towns, such as Frankfort or Lexington, where black relatives or acquaintances already lived and worked and where Freedman's Bureaus had been established to help newly freed blacks obtain jobs and locate housing. So many rural blacks moved to Lexington that by 1870 its black population swelled to 50 percent of the total.

Like most Kentuckians, however, many blacks preferred to stay close to their birthplaces. Charles Hicks, a local black folk historian from Georgetown, estimates:

[Approximately] 65–70 percent of Georgetown black people are somewhat related and they're all real clannish; when the slaves was freed most came here to town or went to Frankfort or Winchester or Lexington, *but that's as far as most would go;* so a lot of black people all over this here area are related, or at least they know each other.

Unfortunately, most Bluegrass rural freedmen were poorly prepared for life in town, as noted by Tom Clark:

In the vigorous campaign to secure freedom for the Negro slave, the crusaders, as crusaders have nearly always done, forgot to be concerned with the problems of fitting the ex-slave into a newly established Southern economic system.... [Blacks were] freed from the old slave quarters; they had gained the right of assembling, of reading and writing, and of traveling when and where they pleased, but they had not gained economic freedom. They were transplanted from a system of chattel enslavement to one of economic servitude.

When the newly freed slaves moved to town, the free blacks already there had enormous advantages.

Even before the war some free blacks resided in the Bluegrass. In the late eighteenth century, for example, Bourbon County's best-known tavern keeper was Ready Money Jack, a free black who kept an inn near Millersburg. Bluegrass towns were especially attractive to free blacks; over 600 resided in Lexington by 1858. Although some rented or erected shanties on squatter's land, a number of these free blacks owned small houses. They had either saved enough money to buy a small piece of property or, on rare occasion had, at the death of their owner (or free relative), inherited, along with their freedom, enough to buy a small parcel of land. These parcels of land lay sometimes in the back of a wealthy estate or on the alleys or side streets of an affluent neighborhood, where the former slave often worked as a domestic servant.*

Too, a small number of free blacks in Bluegrass towns worked as laborers or factory workers, or mastered some craft: silversmiths, blacksmiths, carpenters, barbers, millers, shoemakers, wagoners, bricklayers, stone cutters, iron workers, and post and railers—skills that are often passed down in families, and in some cases are still practiced today. Even in the settlement era some blacks had gained wide recognition for specialized skills. For example, A. Goff Bedford describes a slave called

Edmond Stonestreet, owned by a family of that name...[as] Winchester's only dentist. He pulled teeth and was under continual demand. Legend has it that Henry Clay travelled all the way from Washington to Winchester for Edmond's help. He made no effort to make artificial teeth. Between times, he made boots and shoes.

Some conscientious Bluegrass slaveowners took pains to see that slaves they intended to manumit were trained in some craft before they were given their freedom.

Postwar Black Ghettoes   When emancipated blacks from both town and rural areas were either forced or chose to relocate, they

---

*Much antebellum free-black housing was racially integrated; free blacks shared neighborhoods with poor whites, and slaves were forced by the system to live with white masters.

often moved to urban areas where free blacks had already established something of a black neighborhood. Sometimes free blacks divided their property with relatives; sometimes freed relatives or friends simply moved in with the free blacks. Some were eventually able to buy property of their own so that, although in the immediate postwar period it was common to find two or more families living under one roof, within twenty years many families had been able to establish homes of their own. Thus free blacks played a significant role in the relocation of newly emancipated blacks—even before, but especially during and after, the war. In fact, it has been theorized that leaders of black communities had, for the most part, been free before the Civil War.

Unfortunately, many rural blacks had no benefactors in urban free-black communities. In some towns they erected squatter shanties on so-called worthless land just outside the town limits. In other towns, such as Lexington, the Region's first slum lords exploited the sudden demand for places to live by hastily building small shacks on the outskirts of town. In the summer of 1865 they began renting these shacks to freedmen. The impelling motive of most such developers was to make as much money from as little land as possible. The narrower form of the shotgun house was used to maximize housing density; and garden space, front yards, playgrounds, and even necessary living space were severely limited. This was the first stage in the process of altering the racially integrated antebellum residential pattern and the beginning of black folk neighborhoods—the ghettoes we know today.

The second stage of this development began when white landowners partitioned their property and offered the new lots for sale. Soon these subdivisions became enclaves, crowded all-black neighborhoods. Some modern Lexington blacks believe that whites of that era, not wanting blacks to own property, spread hate propaganda and employed fear tactics to prevent them from settling in densely populated town clusters. Indeed, it was the white consensus that blacks would be better off in the country. Writing around the turn of the century, B. O. Gaines, a Scott County local historian, contrasted the lives of city and rural blacks in favor of the country, concluding that city life led to laziness, crime, and destitution, whereas, "If the Negro could be gotten into the country and kept there, he would do better. He would command respect, become a land owner and lay a good foundation upon which to build his future."

Still, black neighborhoods continued to grow, and many freedmen who had been employed by their former owners and had continued to reside on their employers' property moved out to join the other free blacks in the burgeoning new all-black communities. By 1880 Georgetown's blacks had ceased to live within their former owners' homes and preferred the densely populated black neighborhoods. In Lexington, black land ownership steadily increased from 1865 to 1879. Free blacks owned seventy-three lots in 1865—this was before slavery was abolished in Kentucky—and by 1879 that number ballooned to 666 city lots, a pattern proportionately similar to other Bluegrass towns. Even so, by 1880 the majority of Lexington's blacks still owned little property and supported themselves with menial jobs. Neighborhoods were becoming segregated. The old quarter of town was home to most of the whites and a sprinkling of blacks, while the newer areas contained a majority of the black population but only a very few whites.

As Lexington expanded, white housing was built out and around these black neighborhoods; encircled with no room for expansion, they became enclaved folk ghettoes, a pattern followed in most Bluegrass towns. A 1977 assessment of such black neighborhoods commented that many "remain today, anachronistic in plan and purpose and replete with poverty, undernutrition, crime, and poor sanitation." Thus, some scholars maintain that the creation of most Bluegrass segregated neighborhoods was not due to race prejudice or discrimination, but to a failure to provide blacks with the educational and economic opportunities which would enable them to join the mainstream of Bluegrass society.

In summation, black segregated neighborhoods were a result of several "impersonal" circumstances: (1) newly freed blacks crowded into the towns in such numbers that there simply was no room for them in existing areas; (2) to accommodate these newcomers, most of whom were uneducated and able to secure only menial jobs, inexpensive residential areas were developed on the then outskirts of towns; (3) some of these clusters of drab shanties developed into full-fledged black ghettoes; (4) white housing eventually encircled black areas or simply avoided them as undesirable.

Undesirable they certainly were: poorly drained lowland areas or steeply pitched hill districts; noise-and-dirt-ridden streets along the railroad tracks; sections of town near the public dump or the cemetery— wherever white people did not particularly care to live became ghettoes for the freedmen. By World War I the development of most black neighborhoods was almost complete.

THE RISE OF NEIGHBORHOODS

Railroad Influence   Most railroads* were located on land considered worthless and/or unfit for habitation except by the lower classes,

---

*Railroads actually created some Bluegrass towns, as did the confluence of waterways or buffalo traces in pioneer times. Just as Athens (pronounced locally A-Thens) was originally called Cross Plains, because it was located at the intersection of two buffalo traces, so

Lexington "shotgun" houses on "wrong side of the tracks" (Photo by Jerry Schureman)

particularly black people. In view of the economic expansion and affluence that the railroads brought to communities, this was ironic, but then the people who benefited most from railroads seldom lived near them. Eventually, the railroads affected residential patterns throughout communities, as the tracks came to symbolize—and often literally divided—broad social, economic, and cultural sections of towns. In addition to the tracks themselves, identifiable patterns of living and architecture divided the areas. Bordering the tracks were shanties, tarpaper shacks, shotguns, kit-built T-plans, and other cheap housing, as well as establishments catering to unsavory diversions—gambling houses, taverns, houses of prostitution.

The land immediately adjoining the railroad and extending a few blocks from it was given the folk designation "wrong side of the tracks." Because black people were often forced to live in or close to these poorer areas, the term was especially applied to black neighborhoods. Today, whether or not the part of town considered to be undesirable is actually set apart by railroad tracks, most people nonetheless perceive their town

Midway (so named because it is halfway between Lexington and Frankfort) owes its existence to the old Lexington and Ohio Railroad, which ran down the middle of the town's principal street; originally, all the town's streets were named after Railroad officials. (Midway, incidentally, is thought to have more structures on the National Register of Historic Places than any other community in the Commonwealth.)

to be divided between a "wrong side" and a "right side." More often than not the "wrong side" is primarily, or even limited to, black neighborhoods, although poor white sections can also be included.

Thomas D. Clark, in discussing Southern folk culture in general, notes that "the southern rural way of life included social classes with subtle boundaries." In the Bluegrass such boundaries are often not very subtle. The derogatory expressions "wrong side of town" and "wrong side of the tracks" are still in use today, and a family about to settle in a Bluegrass town is often advised to be certain they locate on the right side.

An anecdote, still told in Winchester, reveals the social and cultural importance placed upon those notions of residence. Before the railroads came to Winchester, residential patterns were not so firmly divided, and stylish houses were scattered all over the town. ("Grand" houses can still be seen on the "wrong" side of town.) One well-liked man, owner of a "grand" brick house before the railroad arrived, enjoyed socializing and was invited to parties all over town. Then, the railroad arrived and people began to attach the associated notions of wrong/right side of town to residence. His stylish brick house was suddenly on the "wrong" side of town; people stopped asking him to parties. After much concern and dismay he finally coaxed his best friend (who lived on the "right" side) to tell him why he was no longer invited to social gatherings. When his friend confided that he lived on the "wrong" side of town, he protested that he had always lived there, and that his house was even more costly and elegant than his friend's. That did not matter, his friend explained. "It's on the wrong side of town, and that's all there is to it." The man then sold his house and bought a much inferior, more humble house, but on the "right" side of town, and soon he was once more invited to social functions.

Today in Clark County folk patterns and divisions still exist, as it does in most Bluegrass towns, but in new forms. Before the Interstates were built, old Kentucky Highway 15, through Hazard toward Lexington, was the primary route out of the Appalachians, and Winchester was the first Bluegrass town reached on that road by the thousands of Eastern Kentuckians migrating to richer pastures. Many chose to settle in Winchester, and their poorer descendants still live on the "wrong side" of that town, especially on the "wrong side" of the railroad tracks and in eastern Clark County, all of which makes the area an interesting example of sociocultural adaptation, acculturation, change, and culture clash. In Winchester and other Bluegrass towns, "wrong side" residents cram narrow house trailers into crowded pockets, the way shotguns were jammed into "wrong side" areas in post-Civil War days.

An interesting story is told of such an area in Danville, ironically now occupied by the historic Constitution Square Park. The tale claims that in this vicinity was once a brothel known as the Heifer House, the front porch of which was dynamited by some drunks who were rejected by the madam because of their condition.

The Craw   Some historians believe the term "wrong side of the tracks" actually originated in one black/white ghetto called Craw in the Bluegrass town of Frankfort. Like many other ghettoized black and poor-white areas, Craw began on worthless land—in Craw's case the northern section of Frankfort known as Crawdad Country, Crawfish Bottom, or simply the Bottoms or the Craw. This was a wetland area of stagnant ponds, where cattails and mosquitos thrived and regularly recurring floods would leave crayfish stranded by the hundreds. After the penitentiary was established in 1799, relatives of inmates moved to Frankfort to be close to the prison, and since they were usually indigent, they settled in Craw, the area no one else wanted, and built shacks. After the incarcerated family member's release, many families simply remained in Craw. In a short time the Craw became a haven for vagrants and other undesirables, who ran bootleg bars and brothels, engaged in cock fights and other modes of gambling, and delighted in a wide range of other unsavory activities. Eventually residents of the area came to be called crawbats. Once the railroad reached Frankfort, it served to separate Craw from the rest of the city still further, and it is thought that this was when the term "wrong side of the tracks" was first used.

After the Civil War, Frankfort's black population exploded, increasing in the decade 1860–1870 by 82.1 percent, and many moved to Craw, the cheapest land available. Thus, between 1865 and 1880 innumerable small frame houses sprang up in Craw, most rented to blacks, but others to poor whites, thereby establishing an early integrated Bluegrass neighborhood. Then in the mid-twentieth century Urban Renewal focused on Craw. The result is described by Carl E. Kramer:

To most civic leaders and city officials . . . [the Craw] was an unmitigated slum, a collection of "rickety, leaky and insanitary houses, cottages, hovels and shacks which more or less kept the rain off the city's most badly housed . . . community." Proponents of the project viewed Craw as "a hotbed of vice and corruption" populated by a "rough class of people, who didn't mind killing or being killed." To much of the city's white middle class the area was symbolized by such hangouts as the Blue Moon, the Tiptoe Inn, and the Peach Tree Inn, where prostution and gambling were rampant. Long-time politicians paid homage to the "King of Craw," the neighborhood boss who controlled bootlegging and gambling and whose legendary ability to turn out the vote could swing an election to his chosen candidate.

Residents of Craw were no less aware of the neighborhood's seamy side. They lived with it every day. But most of the citizens were peaceful, law-abiding people who managed to develop a sense of community and even a fondness for the place. No doubt it was a community forged at least partially out of the realization of a common predicament, where poor blacks [about 50 percent of the population] and whites made a virtue of necessity. As one former resident recalled, "the people in Craw formed a bond of togetherness that has not been equalled before or since.... We lived together, played together, fought with one another, cried together and all other things that make people close." Strengthening the bond was a shared perception that Craw was exploited by "city fathers ... [who wanted to make sure] high society would not be disturbed." In the final analysis, though, togetherness ... was not sufficient to prevent the neighborhood's destruction.

Today Craw no longer exists as a neighborhood. Rather, standing on its site is the pretentious Capital Plaza Towers complex, which contains government offices, a hotel, banks and other businesses, all in an upscale shopping/office complex, in any part of which the average self-respecting "crawbat" would undoubtedly feel out of place.

The Craw example of segregating poor, and especially black, neighborhoods, is similar to the situation in most Bluegrass counties. In Versailles (pronounced locally Vur-Sails), seat of Woodford County, residents generally agree that no well-defined "wrong" side of town exists "mainly because black communities have historically been situated outside the city limits." Some do admit, however, that there are a few "poor white trash" sections. According to realtors, however, the entire southern half of Woodford is the "wrong" side of the county, although this is apparently not for racial reasons but because of property values. Two residents also described an area that, like Frankfort's ghetto, was named after the lowly crayfish:

There's an old "Huntertown" that used to be a black area but it doesn't even exist now, but there's still a "Huntertown Road," and it used to be called "Crayfish Lane!" That's because it was in the poorest section of the county; it was so poor that ... it was the only road into town that wasn't a toll road.

Expanding Black Neighborhoods   Today Woodford County's black communities of Jacksontown and Russelltown both lie outside the city limits of Versailles, and similar, more or less segregated, areas exist in other Bluegrass towns. In Paris and Danville some locals refer to the black area, as they do in other towns, as Colored Town. Black sections in some areas are still occasionally referred to by the even more derogatory designation Nigger Town, though that term is heard everywhere less and less today. Many black people in Paris call their own neighborhood by their own folk term, "over the hill." In Winchester the "official" name for the black ghetto is Poynterville but blacks and whites alike call it Bucktown. In Nicholasville a lifelong white resident in his seventies declared he had *never* been across Main Street into the east-side black neighborhood called Herveytown (after the man who owned most of the property there).

In their migration to Bluegrass towns blacks were assisted by abolitionists and others as they attempted to establish themselves as free, responsible citizens; some of these benefactors donated land, or sold it at low prices, to the freedmen. A prime example is Pralltown in Lexington, now in the immediate vicinity of the University of Kentucky. A 1975 academic study of Pralltown proposed to replace the original wood frame shotgun houses with equally narrow modern "garden houses" that could be situated on the 24–25 foot lots. That plan has not materialized, however. Other older black neighborhoods in Lexington were known by their folk names: Kinkeadtown, Smithtown, Davis Bottom, Goodloetown, Gunntown, Adamstown, Taylortown, Brucetown, and Sprucetown (often called Chicago Bottoms by residents).

In addition to their housing forms and folk names, such neighborhoods are often *themselves, in their entirety,* folk areas; although most such enclaves are originally products of socioeconomic disparities, once established they usually become cohesive sociocultural entities. In contrast to today's homogenized, prefabricated, bland, developer-created subdivisions, such folk neighborhoods as Pralltown—and even Craw—are of, by, and for the people who live there. Such neighborhoods have their own distinct personality, one that reflects the values and worldview of their residents—just as the residential patterns of the landed gentry reveal much about their lives.

Most modern subdivisions say little about their residents; rather, such nonresident-derived developments reflect the supposed values and hyped products that popular culture advertisements have led us to believe we want, and which elite and popular culture developers, planners, and architects who design and sell such places are all too eager to provide, for high profits. Such Bluegrass-roots neighborhoods as Pralltown, as well as other folk residential patterns, reveal much more about the social, cultural, and economic history and current lives of any region's peoples than do most glitzy, modern, planned-for-high-profit developments.

An excellent modern example of a black neighborhood folk celebration is the annual Labor Day event in Winchester. As long as anyone can remember, says a seventy-eight-year-old white resident, "Labor Day has been turned over to the black people. It's their day to celebrate, and they have a big parade downtown and everybody goes down to see it; it's really a big thing." Blacks themselves view the entire three-day holiday as their special time; as one lady said of the upcoming Labor Day celebra-

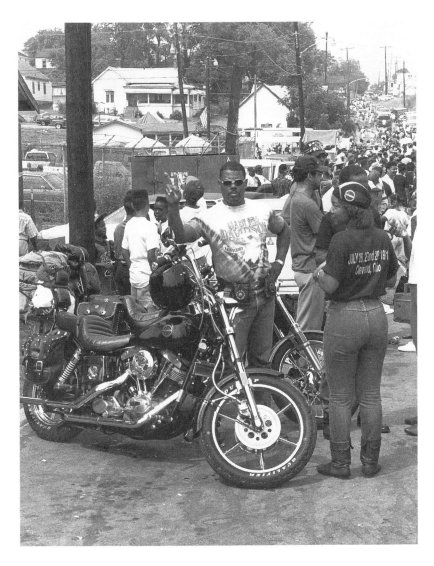

Participants fill the main drag of "Bucktown" during Winchester's black Labor Day weekend celebration, 1991 (Photo by author)

tion, "You all remember now, it's black weekend." The weekend serves as a general homecoming, and celebrations of all sorts and at all socioeconomic levels of the black community are practically nonstop from Friday afternoon until after the parade is over on Labor Day afternoon. The main drag of the black community, called Bucktown, is jammed with hundreds of people, and not just locals but black people from nearby communities, who come to join the celebration. In fact, many former residents return just for this event, some coming from as far away as Chicago, Cleveland, St. Louis, and even California. The parade begins and ends in Bucktown, after winding its way through the downtown area and down Main Street, and features beauty queens, scholastic achievers, and others honored by the black community; it also has musicians and street dancers and motorcyclists, and is sometimes joined by members of the local black motorcycle club, the Ebony Riders. The Labor Day celebration constitutes an eloquent testimony to the contributions of black citizens to the town and also serves to reaffirm that Bucktown,* as a black neighborhood, is an integral part of the community. This traditional "black weekend" event is a prime example of a Bluegrass-roots folk celebration.

Poor-White Ghettoes   In addition to the many black neighborhoods in the Bluegrass, the Region also contains several poor-white enclaves, the majority of which reflect a pattern similar to early German and Irish settlement. Most of the trailer parks in "wrong side" areas, for example, are populated by poor whites. As with black ghettoes, these too are often given derogatory labels. Clark County has Hungry Holler and Rat Row, both on the supposed "wrong side" of town, but Lexington's Irishtown is perhaps the epitome of all such enclaves. In earlier years, many poor-white areas were occupied by German immigrants, but these people and their descendants managed to advance economically and thus moved out and blended in with other whites. The same was not always true of the Irish, and hence Lexington still has its Irishtown.

What came to be called Irishtown was first known as the Town of Manchester, laid out in 1812 on 40 acres of low-lying land on the outskirts of Lexington by an eastern businessman, James Prentiss, who came to the Bluegrass to raise Merino sheep and to exploit the boom in land speculation and new business development. In addition to his farm in the area, Prentiss built the Lexington Manufactory, which was run by steam power and produced woolen goods—particularly cassimeres—and all kinds of paper. However, in 1818 all of Prentiss's businesses failed, and new owners converted the property to a distillery, which operated successfully into the twentieth century. Other factories were soon located in and near Manchester, and they drew laborers to the area, nearly all poor whites. When great numbers of Irish fleeing the Potato Famine arrived in the Bluegrass in the 1840s, many of them settled in Manchester and went to work building the railroads and working in the factories; it was then that locals began referring to the area as Irishtown. In fact, Pine Street—from High Street to Manchester Street—was once called Irish Street. Though many of the Irish eventually left the area—in 1908

---

*The main drag of Bucktown is also where black males congregate in the early morning hours in hopes that a farmer or other employer (almost always white) will drive by looking for laborers for temporary or seasonal work; such traditional, informal labor markets are usually located in or near a black neighborhood, and are found in many Bluegrass towns, including Lexington.

supposedly only a single Irish family remained—and many of the present-day residents are migrants from the poor mountainous areas of eastern Kentucky, the folk name Irishtown has proved to be indelible.

Adjoining Irishtown is another low-lying section first called Davis Bottom, now Davistown, populated by blacks. A 1980 study revealed that unemployment in these neighborhoods was nearly 40 percent, with the incomes of 90 percent of Irishtown residents and 99 percent of Davistown residents being "very low." In recent years government efforts have been made to replace the older housing, mostly shotguns, in the two neighborhoods with modern apartments, yet such efforts are often resisted by the residents. As residents said in 1983 upon being evicted, "You can't fight the government. . . . If I could stay here, I wouldn't move. . . . You put your whole life in one house. I raised my children here, my grandchildren. . . . I hate to see the old people hurt. . . . It's just like tearing my heart. . . ." In fact, one eighty-one-year-old lady suffered a heart attack and died from the effort to move her from her lifelong home to "improve" her life.

Most outsiders fail to realize that such a neighborhood constitutes a folk society with its own distinct culture, which may include values difficult for strangers to understand. The pastor of a mission in Davistown perceptively declares:

These people have a culture of their own. People outside place a great importance on education, . . . career, success and moving up. Most people here don't value those things at all. But they'll drop anything for the family. It may not always look like it, but let there be a crisis and they're all together. And they value their turf—even though they don't own it.

The uprooting and destruction of folk societies such as Irishtown and Davistown serve as eloquent testimony to the constant conflicts between elite (official, governmental) culture or popular (commercial and business interests) culture, and folk (unofficial, informal, do-it-yourself) culture. Such conflicts occur at all levels of society, but most often affect the socioeconomic lower strata most severely. *Any* people, anywhere, who are culturally "different" are often attacked by those who fear or dislike those differences; such is the stuff of prejudice and stereotypes of all sorts. People in Irishtown-Davistown and other such Bluegrass neighborhoods, including black neighborhoods, are viewed not only as "different," but their way of life is looked upon as something shameful, a way of life most other Bluegrass residents would like to forget or ignore. For instance, an old saying among Lexington's middle and upper classes, still sometimes heard, is "Lord, she's so bad lookin' she looks like she came out of Irishtown." Other sayings have slandered Bluegrass Irish over the years: an "Irish kiss" meant a slap on the face; and the "Irish Social

Club" referred to the local police court, where loafers went as a form of entertainment to observe Irish and others receive "justice." Despite being the objects of such derision, the Irish nonetheless have maintained their dignity. As one Irishtown resident says, "Some people talk to you like you ought to be ashamed of it [living in Irishtown]. 'Are you still living down *there?*' [acquaintances say] Well, I'm not a bit ashamed. . . . It's not where you live, it's who you are." Unfortunately, outsiders often fail to recognize the truth embodied in this lady's statement, and instead hold people who live in such places as Irishtown in contempt simply because they are poor, live in shotgun houses, and have a different worldview. Though the Irishtown of today is but a remnant of the original neighborhood, and though housing projects and modern houses have been built, often by charitable concerns, some Irishtown streets nonetheless are still lined with shotgun houses and other folk architectural forms.

CHANGES IN THE RURAL BLUEGRASS

Although the shotgun house was the predominant form in postbellum urban ghettoes, it was never used extensively in rural Bluegrass settings. Rather, the rural poor adopted other residential patterns, some of which were provided for them.

As described earlier, the war permanently altered the social, economic, and cultural way of life of the Bluegrass gentry. Their estates were in disrepair; livestock had been run off, commandeered, stolen, or killed; crops had been neither planted nor harvested. They, of course, no longer had slaves, and many desperately lacked capital. These conditions were exacerbated by the nationwide financial crisis of 1873; as a result, many estates were never restored to their antebellum prime, and a number were sold to pay creditors. It was during this era, especially in the 1870s, that wealthy interests in the East started taking advantage of the financial distress in the Bluegrass and purchased large estates, turning many of them into the horse farms for which the Region is justifiably famous. This pattern of out-of-state ownership has been perpetuated to this day.

Nevertheless, some original estate owners managed to retain their cherished Bluegrass homes. Those who did prosper accepted the new state of affairs and found equally new solutions. Without slaves, and because many blacks, now free, had moved to the towns, labor was the gentry's most immediate problem; drastic solutions were attempted, as noted by Karl Raitz:

The shortage of labor. . . was so critical that at one point a widespread campaign was launched to encourage foreign laborers, including Chinese coolies, to settle in central Kentucky. Efforts were also made to induce landless whites from other states to come to the Bluegrass and work as tenants.

Black Hamlets To solve this labor shortage, the gentry and horse farm owners endeavored to attract those blacks who wished to remain in the country or were unable to find work in the towns. In 1869 they even set up an employment agency in Lexington to assist freedmen who wanted jobs on the estates, and many returned to their old occupations, but now as paid employees. To house these new black workers, some estate owners adopted a new approach to black residential patterns. Whereas in slavery they were housed directly behind the big house, they now were moved all the way out to the very edge of estate property, in what would become a patterned system of black folk hamlets dotting the Bluegrass landscape. A precedent had been established for this pattern some years before the war when four black hamlets were begun by former slaves who had inherited their freedom and a small parcel of estate land at the death of their masters; the original founders of these nascent hamlets subsequently subdivided their parcels of land among their children and other relatives. So, after the war, when the estates wanted to hire freedmen, they followed the pattern of the four existing hamlets, as described by Karl Raitz:

Tracts of ten to twenty acres were divided into lots of a quarter acre to five acres, and the land was given or sold at a modest price to the Negroes. They were also assisted in building a house, often a carpenter's-plan cabin with three rooms and an attic. Water was supplied by a community well and . . . rainwater from the roof of the house. The remainder of the lot was planted in garden crops, and often small sheds or barns were built to house swine and chickens.

This arrangement was satisfactory to the estate owners. They paid only a small wage for laborers and were no longer responsible for the upkeep and the well-being of the Negroes. When they needed labor it was readily available at the "freetown" [the folk name for these black hamlets]. . . . Negroes were again dependent on estate owners, but they thought the arrangement was agreeable despite the restricting conditions.

Not all of the Negro hamlets were established by benevolent owners. . . . Three hamlets . . . were created when white entrepreneurs purchased parcels of farm property from destitute farmers and divided the land into lots, selling them exclusively to Negroes. [Too, some hamlets were created when abandoned property was taken over by blacks, others were founded under unique circumstances, and a few have unknown origins].

Thus, although the vast majority of rural blacks migrated elsewhere, especially to Bluegrass towns, enough blacks remained in the hamlets to provide some labor for the estates.

Today, many of these Bluegrass rural black hamlets still exist, though their populations are slowly declining, and most of the black residents no longer work for the estates. Instead, like other working-class Bluegrass residents, black or white, they commute to jobs in the surrounding towns. Some, however, live as close to a subsistence way of life as is possible in modern times, and that subsistence pattern follows a long-standing tradition begun by their ancestors. When estate owners lost their farms to creditors, the freedmen were left without work and were forced to exist primarily on their garden produce. Today, many people in the hamlets still carry on subsistence traditions. Many have turned their plots into miniature farms, with large gardens, chickens, and perhaps a garbage-fed sow, and some families raise tobacco as a cash crop. Some larger hamlets even have a church and some sort of small grocery nearby, though most lack these amenities. None are incorporated or would qualify as a town, but they are prime examples of black rural Bluegrass-roots folklife at its best. Although contemporary large estates no longer depend upon these black hamlets for a labor force, the reliable labor they supplied during the postwar decades might well have saved the Bluegrass and its present-day way of life, both social and agricultural.

New Crops and a New Configuration for the Estates

The creation of these hamlets also helped to alter the typical layout of the Bluegrass estates. No longer did the majority resemble the romantic antebellum scene: a century-old manor house, its walls encroached by wildflowers and vines, standing amid knee-deep bluegrass, surrounded by post-and-rail fencing, paddocks, springhouses and other picturesque outbuildings, the slave quarters to the rear. Rather, former slaves' cabins were now razed and the configuration of much of the estate was altered to accommodate changes in farm operation. Burley tobacco began to replace both hemp and dark-fired tobacco as the major cash crop; other estates were converted exclusively to horse farms, usually by wealthy new owners from the East.

White Tenant Labor   Not all postbellum Bluegrass estates fit this pattern; nor did they all create black hamlets on the periphery of their property. Instead, they depended upon white tenant labor. Some estates, sold to pay debts, were chopped up into smaller acreage and converted to working livestock, grain, and tobacco farms by the new owners, who also relied upon white tenant labor. This spread of white tenancy after the Civil War was caused by the loss of rural black labor to the towns and the resultant encouragement of landless whites, both from other regions of Kentucky and from neighboring states, to relocate to the Bluegrass. During this period the Burley tobacco industry was growing,

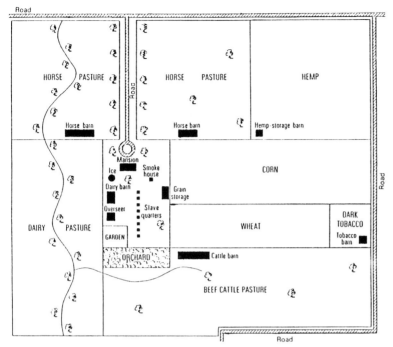

Antebellum Bluegrass Estate

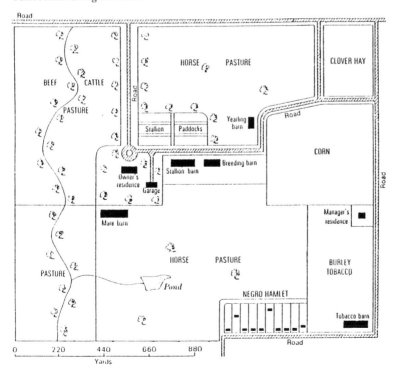

Postbellum Bluegrass Estate

Typical Layout of Antebellum and Post-bellum Bluegrass Estates (From Peter C. Smith and Karl B. Raitz, "Negro Hamlets and Agricultural Estates in Kentucky's Inner Bluegrass," courtesy of *The Geographical Review*) and the white tenant was soon considered the most trustworthy "hand" with tobacco, a belief still prevalent and probably stemming from postwar discrimination against freedmen. Thus, many farmers who either had no access to or preferred not to rely upon labor from the black hamlets, instead established accommodations on their property for the white tenant laborers. If they agreed to raise tobacco and a few other crops, and assist with other general farm duties, tenants were usually provided a house and garden—most often a fenced-off plot in a less attractive area of the estate situated discreetly apart from the main house.

Tobacco was raised on "shares," meaning profits would be divided, usually equally, by tenant and owner. This arrangement was so successful that by 1900, one out of three Kentucky farmers were white tenants, far outnumbering blacks. Southern tenancy, wherever it was instituted, tended to replace the old economic system of slave-master, but white tenants were often even poorer than the former slaves, and, just as they had with blacks, many Bluegrass residents harbored a negative perception of them. They were considered "shiftless and lazy" and were given derogatory labels such as "poor white trash." However, tenantry in the Bluegrass never reached the same proportions as elsewhere in Kentucky.

The Tenant House   As the tenant system spread in the late nineteenth century, a distinct house form evolved. It has been appropriately dubbed the tenant house by Kentucky folklorist Lynwood Montell:

The tenant house . . . is generally a story-and-a-half tall, is almost always framed and covered with weatherboards, has two front doors [a very low front porch, covered by the extended sloping roof], and possesses a small, central chimney which serves as a double flue for stoves located in each of the two front rooms. . . . The two rooms across the front almost always function as a parlor and a guest bedroom. The kitchen and dining area are located in a rear addition; sleeping quarters are upstairs. Late nineteenth century examples were constructed with T or ell additions; but the more recent flimsy, "shack" variety of the tenant house contains a lean-to shed addition tacked onto the back. . . .

Just as white tenancy replaced slavery, so the tenant house replaced the slave quarters. The floor plan is often the hall-and-parlor or a modified version of it. The tenant house is widespread across Kentucky and the Bluegrass countryside, and found in even small towns and cities, usually in poorer or "wrong side" neighborhoods. In rural Bluegrass areas the tenant house is nearly always situated alone on a fenced-off plot, and it is seldom found in clusters—unlike the shotgun. Some scholars postulate that the tenant house—primarily because of its central, squatty chimney and two front doors—is related to the saddlebag, but it is also possible that it derives from the double-pen log house, which also had two front doors. In any event, some interesting folk patterns concern the two front doors of the tenant house.

Some tenant house residents conjecture that the two front doors served as a ventilation system by creating a draft throughout the whole house when, along with the rear kitchen door, both front doors were opened. Other residents believe the house was designed with the two front doors because many tenants had large families and the two doors allowed the house to be somewhat divided into male and female areas for the children. Large families necessarily tended to designate one front room as a bedroom, to which a private door was especially important since it permitted one to slip outside to the privy without passing through the rest of the house. In any event, the two front doors on such an otherwise plain, small, and uncomplicated house form remain a puzzle to scholars.

Indeed, it seems to baffle the tenants themselves. Many do not use both doors and have adopted various folk techniques to make it obvious to a visitor which door is really *not* a door. In towns they may place the mailbox next to the *real* door—an option not always available to rural tenants. Other residents place porch furniture, or even a swing, directly in front of the nondoor, or they maintain the old custom of keeping washers or refrigerators, or even a living room couch, on the front porch, situated in front of the nondoor. In some instances, boxes, jars, lard cans, and even bundles of roofing shingles may be stacked in front of the nondoor, or placed in such a way that the message is plain: "This is not a door, even though it looks like one."

Few tenant houses are located on the elegant "gentleman farms" or on the majority of horse farms; rather, they are nearly always found alone on an unpretentious family farm raising livestock, grain, and/or tobacco. In contrast, upscale farms, especially horse farms—if they have workers' houses at all—sometimes locate them in lots along a road that borders the estate—very much like the black hamlets of postbellum days. However, these workers' houses are usually of somewhat better quality and design than the two-front-door tenant house, but are nevertheless usually rubber-stamp copies of each other and located well away from the main house.

CHAPTER 6

The Bluegrass Gentleman Farm and Other Rural Folk Patterns

Kentucky cultural geographer Karl Raitz has studied what he calls the "gentleman farms" of the Inner Bluegrass. Not all of these upscale farms are horse farms, notes Raitz, and thus "the customary use of 'horse farm' as a surrogate is invalid because all farms which keep horses are not gentleman farms and not all gentleman farms have horses." Such gentleman farms exist in various cultural pockets of America, but as Raitz observes, "Kentucky's Inner Bluegrass has the most extensive development and the richest tradition, with its roots in the cavalier culture of antebellum Virginia."

SMALL-SCALE FARMING

Gentleman farms must be differentiated from the dozens of small-scale Bluegrass farms which raise cattle or horses commercially. Owners of such farms conduct their operations, usually with a limited capital investment, for profit. They may raise purebred cattle or Thoroughbred or Standardbred horses, though they are more likely to specialize in popular pleasure horse breeds such as Morgan, Arabian, and Tennessee Walker. Aesthetics are relatively unimportant: stables, barns and other farm buildings are strictly utilitarian, and pastures lack the manicured look of gentleman farms.

In addition to these specialized farms, and the family working farms discussed earlier, are what Bluegrass residents refer to as baby farms—a residential pattern of low density "short commute" fringe areas near towns. Most baby farms are from five to sixty acres, and, if farmed at all, usually by a neighbor; the tobacco allotment is ordinarily rented out and the land left in pasture, with a sizable area devoted to expansive yard and garden. Owners of many baby farms endeavor to imitate the larger gentleman farms by installing four-plank fencing with pillared entrances and by erecting oversize houses with columned facades. Like an increasing number of Bluegrass rural residents, baby farmers nearly always commute to a job in the city, where many are upper-middle income middle-management ("yuppies"). A few baby farmers are retirees.

Also well represented in the Bluegrass is another type of farm—small (hundred-plus acres) and semiproductive, increasingly run by a part-time farmer. He usually commutes to a city job, because, although his farm, unlike the baby farm, is intended eventually to be his major source of income, he finds it impossible for the present to live entirely on its profits.

Some of these part-time farmers live on their land in trailers. Often they come from other areas of the Commonwealth and may have grown up on a farm. As adults they moved to the Bluegrass for work, often in a factory, and after saving enough money, they bought a small-acreage Bluegrass farm, often unimproved except perhaps for a tobacco barn. Because most are only shoestring-financed, to be able to work the farm (usually only tobacco is raised) and enjoy it more easily, they set up a trailer, usually close to the barn, and live there until they can build a permanent home, often on the same site the trailer occupies. This trailer-barn arrangement is seen throughout the Bluegrass. In fact, this pattern is a modern equivalent to the early settlers' custom of living in a temporary log house until the big house was built. The obvious difference is that the early gentry had the wherewithal to build their permanent homes, they simply needed time, but many modern part-time farmers *never* save enough to build a house and therefore live in their trailers indefinitely.

Consequently, many such trailers show evidence of do-it-yourself endeavors to make the trailer into a real home. Most have removed the trailer's wheels and secured the shell in place, often adding wooden porches. Some owners undertake minor landscaping and make an effort to create a yard. Some attach—and it is a certain indicator of permanency—an external brick fireplace to the trailer. The ultimate indicator of permanency, however, is to build a house shell, usually frame, around the entire trailer, a pattern becoming popular in the Bluegrass. This can be viewed as the contemporary equivalent of the earlier practice of building a more elaborate house around a core folk form, discussed earlier. A large number of rural trailer parks (sixty-three by a 1980 count)—much more upscale than the trailer pockets on the "wrong side" of many towns—are also found in the Bluegrass, some called Such-and-Such Estates. Residents of these trailer "estates" also modify their mass-produced dwelling units to make them "home"—porches and patios, landscaping and flower and vegetable gardens, yard ornaments, bird houses, etc. Trailers are also used on family farms as "weaning" homes for sons by placing them on that section of the farm they will eventually inherit. The future heir then usually lives in the trailer with his bride until they either have enough money to construct a permanent house or the expansion of their family forces them to borrow. Farm economics are so difficult that, even though he is an heir, the son, like some part-time farmers, often must remain in the trailer for years.

THE GENTLEMAN FARM

Despite the many small-scale farms in the Region, it is the gentleman farm that symbolizes the Bluegrass. Nearly all owners of such estates are independently wealthy and run their farms as an avocation or hobby, or as a tax advantage. Often the farm is an ongoing experiment, an investment in plant breeding or breeding fine livestock—usually for show, for sale, and for racing. Some owners of these gentleman farms are actual descendants of the original gentry from Virginia or Maryland, who first established estates in the Bluegrass. Other estates are owned by out-of-state interests who, in addition to the above uses, enjoy their Bluegrass farms as refuges from the cities and as rural social "places." (Many have additional "places" in New York, France, Bermuda, or other wealthy enclaves.) Still others are owned by affluent Kentucky businessmen and professional people who live on their farms and enjoy them for the breeding activity and the prestige and social life they generate. To be a Bluegrass gentleman farmer is to be, most often, a celebrity and part of an old-line "squirearchy." That prestige and social activity is international in scope, as illustrated by frequent visits of celebrities from around the world, including England's Queen Elizabeth who, because of her passion for horses, has several times visited Bluegrass horse farms and been the guest of their gentleman-farmer owners.

Most of these idyllic farms are quite large, ranging from hundreds to thousands of beautiful acres; they are also very expensive—land runs to thousands of dollars per acre, and annual operating costs are in the high six figures. Usually anywhere from twenty to a hundred, or even more, employees are needed to manage the extensive operation. The landscape itself reflects the aesthetics of the gentleman farmer, as noted by Raitz:

Ostentation is rarely garish. . . . The gentleman farmer creates or makes over his rural world to conform with his image of what is ideal in the rural environment. It is this parkland farmscape which the city tourist . . . finds so magnetic. From the earliest spring blossoms . . . through the last . . . tones of autumn, the . . . farmroads around Lexington are covered each Sunday afternoon with lines of kid-filled station wagons which trundle along at a snail's-pace while the occupants drink in the sights [a longstanding Bluegrass phenomenon].

Many of the Bluegrass gentleman farms are in contiguous clusters north and west of Lexington, toward Paris, Georgetown, Midway, Versailles, Nicholasville, Harrodsburg, and Frankfort, with a smaller representation near Danville. Many that still have an antebellum heritage are located either along or just off the roads that run like spokes of a wheel from Lexington to the nearby county seats.

Eight Characteristics

In his survey of over 200 gentleman farms, Raitz has identified eight definitive characteristics. Notwithstanding the fact that they are wealthy, elite estates, these gentleman farms typify a folk culture, following tacitly approved, communally adhered to, recurrent, esoteric, and traditional patterns. They seem to Kentucky, and perhaps to the world, to be unique to the Region, for, as Raitz notes, outside the confines of the Inner Bluegrass "Gentleman farms were not to be found."

The first and most constant of the eight folk characteristics is the vast manicured and well maintained "farmscape." A very small percentage of the total acreage is under crop cultivation; instead, pastures are rendered by constant care and cultivated coaxing into a parklike perfection—a tradition begun with the "grazing parks" of earlier times.

Of the seven remaining characteristics, three are found on more than 95 percent of gentleman farms: fences, livestock, and driveways. It is on these farms that the Region's best old stone fences and either black or white four-plank wooden fences line literally miles of Edenic grandeur. Claiborne Farm, discussed earlier, has ninety-seven miles of fencing. In fact, on many farms, even the stately old trees, many of them hardwood, whether in numerous clumps or as solitary sentinels, are boxed-in with wooden fences to protect them from livestock and to protect the costly livestock from rubbing themselves raw on the trees. On those gentleman farms that raise horses, separate double-fenced paddocks are always used for the stallions, to protect the mares from the stallions and to protect the stallions from each other. This double fencing creates aisles between paddocks, through which a stallion can be safely led to and from his stable. One black groom, who has worked at Darby Dan Farm for over thirty years in charge of the stallions says, "If ever two of them stallions get in there [the same paddock] together I'm just going home." The stallions would fight so fiercely, he says, that it would be dangerous to try to separate them. Mares, foals, and yearlings, on the other hand, are grouped in large pastures.

Presence of expensive purebred livestock constitutes the second of the three characteristics found on more than 95 percent of gentleman farms. Thoroughbred horses predominate overall, but Standardbreds or Saddlebreds are raised on some gentleman farms and purebred cattle on others; however, it is rare for any one farm to raise more than one kind of animal. Common, less attractive animals such as hogs or chickens are rarely seen, and mixed breeds of anything are frowned upon. However, some farms buy cattle in the spring to graze the summer pastures and then sell them for a profit in the fall, and some farms add the final touch to the parklike environment by keeping beautiful swans and ducks gliding over their tranquil, shimmering ponds, and even peacocks which promenade around as proudly as the farm's owner.

The third characteristic seen on more than 95 percent of these farms is a distinctive, but nonetheless traditionally patterned driveway, purposely planned to meander and wind through tree-lined, shrubbed, and flowered beauty before it arrives at the main house. Moreover, most gentleman farms have miles (some over twenty miles) of picturesque roads, a luxury not seen on family working farms, since it takes up valuable, productive land. On gentleman farms such private roads further adorn the landscape and permit easy, leisurely passage to and from the various parts of the estate for workers, vets, clients with mares to breed, and even on occasion, the owner.

The remaining four folk characteristics are: elaborate entranceway (on 93 percent of the farms); elegant residence (also on 93 percent); employee residences (on 78 percent of the farms); and farm color scheme (at 58 percent, the weakest identifying characteristic of these farms).

On many family working farms in the Bluegrass a weathered, usually unnamed, mailbox, often bent and crumpled or even full of bullet holes, is the only indication that the farm lies just off the main road, often on a gravel lane. In stark contrast, gentleman-farm mailboxes—if present at all, for mail is often delivered elsewhere—are often encapsulated in a massive stone or brick pillar. In addition, nearly all gentleman farms feature a highly formal entrance, including an immaculate stone or brick fence, or sometimes a wooden one, gracefully curving along both sides of the paved driveway and abutting on pylons at both ends, of which the center two often support an elaborate ornamental gate. Usually one or more of the pylons contains a plaque emblazoned with the farm's, and sometimes its owner's, name, and often a sign directing business deliveries to the service gate, or announcing that the farm is private and/or does not conduct tours, etc. For many years the sign at the entrance to Dixiana Farm read:

Nothing but a good race horse wanted. Agents for the sale of books, patent medicines, sewing machines, wheat farms, and especially lightning rods, not admitted. Visitors who come to my house are always welcome.

Entrance to Calumet
Farm, Fayette County
(Photo by author)

Such pillared entrances constitute a folk tradition dating to ancient times, prototypes of which can be seen all over rural (and even urban) Britain and Ireland. Another venerable folk symbol, this one having its roots in early Americana, often adorns the entrance to these farms: the pylons are topped with an iron or cast masonry eagle, an emblem of good fortune.*

The main house approached by way of this grand entranceway is always large and elegant. Raitz describes it:

The model residence features the Greek Revival architecture popular in the antebellum South. Classic Greek pillars reach two stories to a pediment-roofed porch. The brick or stone walls are inset with large windows. Elaborate cornice work is topped with a slate or copper roof. Several corbeled fireplace chimneys complete the silhouette.

Employee residences, on the other hand, are small; some farms simply house employees in mobile homes. Usually, employee houses, especially

*Eagles nesting on one's property in antebellum days was believed to bring good luck in racing.

the frame rubber-stamp copies, are painted in the same color scheme, often the racing colors of the estate. On some estates these colors mark everything belonging to the estate, including vehicles and outbuildings. In fact, farm employees are sometimes outfitted in quasi-uniforms in the farm's racing colors, including pants, shirt with name badge, jacket, and baseball cap, all often emblazoned with the farm's name—a modern Bluegrass version of a folk costume.

BLUEGRASS OUTBUILDINGS

The two most frequently seen and most culturally significant outbuildings in the Bluegrass are tobacco barns and horse barns. In their array of outbuildings, some of the horse farms, especially those devoted to race horses, often have neither tobacco barns nor other crop or livestock barns; they rent out their tobacco allotment and buy hay and other feeds, which are stored in various horse barns.

Horse Barns   The modern Thoroughbred farm typically has a number of specialized outbuildings: stallion barn; breeding barn (usually called breeding "shed," and sometimes attached to one end of the stallion barn); foaling barn; filly barn; colt barn; training barn; and a number of brood mare barns, plus equipment sheds and a maintenance shop. Like the employees' houses, outbuildings sometimes have the same color scheme, often the estate's racing colors—Claiborne Farm's Wheatland Yellow, for example, is patented by Porter Paints. A number of the older horse barns are converted transverse-crib tobacco barns (wooden) and as such do not have outside stall doors; but some of the more modern barns (concrete block) do have outside stall doors or are built U-shape, like the yearling barns on Claiborne Farm; the number of stalls run from two to twenty-three, and stall size is usually twelve feet square to sixteen feet square. A number of horse barns have been designed by world-class architects, such as the Normandy barn, described by Bluegrass scholar Dr. Mary Wharton:

[It was] designed by the famous Philadelphia architect, Horace Trumbauer... and completed in 1933. Patterned after barns in Normandy, it has wooden stalls arranged in an "L" with a round clocktower in the angle. True to Normandy superstition, it has ceramic cats and other animals climbing on the slate roof, and storks (it is a foaling barn) and other birds perched on gables, cupolas, and dormers.

In earlier days, some Bluegrass horse barns were so elaborate and luxurious they were described as "palaces" or "cathedrals;" some even had stained glass windows and seating areas where visitors scrutinized horses paraded before them. That tradition has continued and a number of today's Bluegrass horse barns are so elaborate as to defy the category "barn." As Dr. Wharton notes:

Architectural styles in Bluegrass horse barns have paralleled to some extent period styles in residential architecture. Early ones were rectangular, plain, staunch, and sturdy, and some plain ones continued to be built later. However, when residences bore a profusion of Victorian embellishments, the accompanying barns and carriage houses often had irregular roof lines, varying floor plans, brackets, arches, and an almost ubiquitous cupola.... At the turn of the century several barns followed a cathedral-like plan having a clerestory and a lower section along the sides containing the stalls. One of these was an 80-stall barn for mares and foals at Patchen Wilkes Farm, said to be the largest horse barn in the country.

Bluegrass horse barns have also followed the folk trends in use of construction materials, some having been built originally of log, then frame, and brick, and a few even of stone, the best early example of which was built in the 1790s on Colonel Robert Sander's farm. (This is the same farm on which the Bluegrass' first agricultural fair was held.) That historic stone horse barn was recently dismantled and then reconstructed elsewhere as a modern office for Kentuckiana Farms. Today, while a few barns are simple prefabricated products of metal construction, the more substantial, more attractive, and more traditional horse barns are built either of frame or—because fire is an abiding concern—fireproof concrete block, or a combination. In addition, some are still built of brick and/or stone.

In recent years the creation and development of the Kentucky Horse Park, just outside Lexington, has provided a model working example of the Bluegrass horse farm. The park functions as an outdoor museum and is the only such facility in the country, serving to illustrate to visitors the entire world of the horse and related way of life. Each year it attracts many thousands of visitors, and a full schedule of national and even international equine events fills the annual calendar.

Although some horse-farm outbuildings are unique and therefore not of folk origins, many continue the traditional Bluegrass designs, often featuring traditional cupolas, several in a row atop the larger barns, and dormers. In addition to the constant transverse-crib gabled-end form, many horse barns also have a side entrance, also usually gabled and, as with the gabled ends, sometimes featuring Palladian windows. Many horse barns, in fact, are modern adaptations of traditional transverse-crib barns which, however used or in whatever modified form, are ubiquitous on the Bluegrass landscape. Today, if not used as horse barns, most serve as tobacco barns.

Tobacco Barns During the Civil War era, when slaves were fleeing the rural Bluegrass, hemp farming—once the Region's most labor intensive and profitable farm product—was being replaced with White Burley tobacco. Too, transportation improvements during the era enabled farmers to carry tobacco to market more easily, making it not only a more profitable crop, but also one that required less labor than hemp. Tobacco farming came to be, and still is, the single most profitable and most widely found cash crop across Kentucky. Consequently, the ubiquitous silhouette of the transverse-crib tobacco barn stands today as perhaps the single most typical of all the Region's outbuildings.

The typical Bluegrass transverse-crib tobacco barn is of frame construction and almost invariably painted black. There are a number of theories about the derivation of this traditional barn, including the possibility that it is a modification of the English flat barn, with racks to hold the sticks of curing tobacco and sides constructed with movable panels so that they can be opened for air circulation during the curing process. It is equally credible that it evolved as a hybrid form by combining the four-crib log barn with the drive-through-center log corn crib. The basic transverse-crib barn, no matter its special uses or modifications, has a driveway running from gable end to gable end, with partitions (or "cribs") of whatever sort running along both sides of the driveway. Hay is sometimes stored in a loft, tossed there from wagons in the barn's driveway.

Transverse-crib barns modified for horses utilize more elaborate and substantial construction materials and stylistic features than do those housing tobacco. Unlike the horse barns, tobacco barns are never ornate, but frugally built of plain lumber, and have fewer "cribs" or stalls. In addition, the sides of most Bluegrass tobacco barns have hinged vertical sections running from the foundation to just below the eaves; usually one or two boards wide, they are regularly spaced along the entire length of both sides of the barn. When opened periodically during the curing process, these hinged sections allow air to circulate and thus control moisture and heat and permit ventilation of the curing tobacco. Most tobacco barns also have roof ventilators, either built into the ridgeline of the roof (usually tin), or evenly spaced capped tube vents along the length of the ridgeline.

Tobacco barns are usually referred to by their number of "bents," a folk term for the evenly spaced interior partitions between the barn's vertical posts. Thus a tobacco barn can be a "five bent" or a "seven

Typical transverse-crib tobacco barn with attached stripping shed (Photo by Jerry Schureman)

bent" barn, the more bents the larger the barn. Inside, curing tobacco is hung from long sticks above the barn's driveway and cribs. An elaborate, tiered superstructure of specially placed boards or beams runs the entire length of the barn and extends up to the loft floor, and here the tobacco sticks are hung, several rows across. The transverse-crib barn was possibly first modified for tobacco in the Chesapeake and Tidewater Regions; consequently some scholars call this barn type the Chesapeake air-cured tobacco barn, or the Maryland tobacco barn; and barns from those areas no doubt supplied ideas to Bluegrass tobacco farmers for their version of this folk barn type. A considerable number of the Bluegrass version of these tobacco barns have additional "wings" extending to one or both sides, creating more storage space either to hang tobacco or, more commonly, for farm tractors and other equipment. A high percentage of Bluegrass tobacco barns, especially those having only one added wing or no wings at all, also have an attached "stripping shed," either a pitched-roof lean-to or a flat roof rectangular frame box. The shed nearly always has a flue for a space heater since the tobacco is stripped from its stalks during late fall and early winter in preparation for the sales, which are usually completed in January. Though there are other historic Bluegrass outbuildings, the transverse-crib barn, whether used for horses or tobacco, is the most typical folk form, both historically and today.

Mills, Taverns, and Churches on the Historic Bluegrass Landscape

EARLY MILLS

Soon after the appearance of the earliest homes, mills of various kinds were constructed, the most numerous being gristmills for grinding corn (and later wheat and barley) into meal and flour for the settlers. Although prior to 1780 few mill sites existed—only nine or ten are mentioned in the minutes of the Virginia Land Court from October 12, 1779, to April 26, 1780—the decades of the 1780s and 1790s witnessed the construction of so many new mills that one local historian described the phenomenon as "mill mania." A gristmill was needed every few miles; a farmer had to be able to carry his grain to the mill, have it ground, and return home before dark. The earliest mills were operated with horse power, and these were quickly replaced by the more efficient water mills constructed on the numerous streams winding through the Bluegrass.

A permit to construct a water mill had to be acquired from the county court, and because the mill required a dam, which in turn would flood the surrounding land and springs belonging perhaps to a neighbor, receiving such permission could be a contentious affair. This damage to adjacent property was assessed by a local jury, which then determined an appropriate recompense to be paid by the would-be mill operator(s). In July, 1788, an applicant for a mill right had, as members of his jury, Bluegrass luminaries Daniel Boone and Simon Kenton.

Materials for the construction of these early mills, which were normally built using some combination of wood and stone or brick, were readily available. Structures could be two- or even three-stories high; foundations usually consisted of unmortared stone quarried from nearby limestone ledges, and the upper one or two stories were most often of wood, a variation of which can be seen in the Xalapa Farm Mill on Stoner Creek. Following the pattern of houses, the wood portions of the early mills were of log, and a bit later, of frame. Some mills were built entirely of stone or Kentucky marble—such as DeGaris Mill near Georgetown, razed around 1912, and the three-story Martin-Holder-Bush Mill in Clark County, built in the 1780s but now reduced to a deserted ruin. A few mills were constructed of brick; Flournoy's Mill in Scott County was considered an excellent example of early industrial architecture, but in 1979 it, too, was unfortunately demolished.

Erected in 1803, a famous old Bluegrass stone mill, Grimes Mill on Boone Creek, still stands; the Kentucky marble for this magnificent stone structure was cut by Peter Paul, an Irish stonemason living in Lexington. It is a massive two-and-one-half story building of quarried Boone Creek stone, except for its framed gables. After it ceased operating as a mill, Grimes became in 1928 the clubhouse for the Iroquois Hunt Club and center for its activities. Although the original wooden mill wheel is gone, a nineteenth-century iron wheel is still in place in the lower floor of the building. The quarry that provided the stone for Grimes Mill—called appropriately the Grimes Mill Quarry—also produced the Kentucky marble for the Daniel Boone and Henry Clay monuments (in Frankfort and Lexington, respectively) and for the fluted columns and pediment of the Old Capitol in Frankfort. Structures built of this material continue to be in perfect condition.

The massive structural timbers of the more substantial mills, often made of hand-hewn walnut, were particularly beautiful, as attested by the still surviving Grimes Mill. The gears and machinery of these mills were also of wood, most often well-seasoned, hand-hewn oak or hickory. The millstones, a bit more difficult to acquire and certainly more arduous to transport, were either imported from France or England, or cut from local quarries. In 1796, for example, the best French burr millstones were advertised in the Lexington *Kentucky Gazette*, and somewhat later, in 1809, stones from the Red and Laurel rivers were offered. When possible, the stones were transported by water, since heavily loaded wagons, even when pulled by six-horse teams, often sank to their hubcaps in the mire of muddy roads.

Mills were often erected adjacent to these roadways, as poor as they were, to facilitate their construction and entice customers to their doors. If a road was not already present when a mill was erected, it was quickly built. Historical records show roads being frequently routed from or to specific mills; indeed numerous roads, or pikes, adopted the names of the mills they serviced: Garrard's Mill Road and Ruddle's Mill Road in Bourbon County; Glass Mill Road in Jessamine; Lemon's Mill Pike in Scott; and Wade's Mill Road in Clark are but a few such examples. Although the mills themselves have disappeared into the oblivion of history, the road names persist. So vital were mills to a community that it was the custom for a mill-bound farmer to receive free passage on the toll roads. It is said that some farmers abused this custom by carrying bags of bran around with them, pretending they were grist. Every early family had its own handmade meal sacks to carry corn to the mill and bring meal back; these were usually made from strong, tightly woven material so the meal would not leak out; many were brightly colored, red or blue, some with stripes; when they became too thin to use as meal sacks, they became towels.

Mills as Social Centers   Visits to the mills involved not only chores and business transactions but also folk recreation. Fishing was popular around mill dams, where the fish evidently "bit well." One early patron of Clark County's first mill, erected around 1785, regularly carried home fifty to sixty pounds of fish. Catches are considerably smaller today, but fishing around dams is still a popular pastime. A gristmill also tended to attract a blacksmith shop, perhaps a country store, maybe even a tavern or small inn. Thus mills became social centers as well as places of business, and visits to them were relished in the same way as Court Day or modern livestock auctions. Lemon's Mill in Scott County became famous for its location and the many public events held nearby: political gatherings, militia musters, and picnics. Describing the everyday mill atmosphere, Bourbon County local historian Edna Talbot Whitley recounts:

While the first comer's corn was being ground it gave the later arrivals a chance to exchange news items of happenings in the neighborhood. Births . . . marriages, illnesses, and deaths [were] seldom reported in newspapers. Sooner or later the discussions explored world affairs, state and local politics. Fine stock was . . . exhibited . . . and farm practices . . . compared.

In some neighborhoods things occasionally got out of hand while the miller was attending to duties. Several times the members of the Cooper's Run Baptist congregation remonstrated with brother Alexander Ogle about the behavior of persons around his mill. Finally in August 1812, he issued a warning through the Western Citizen telling trespassers who rendezvoused at the mill to plan to stay away. He notified slaves not to come without the lawful written permission of their masters, adding there was no need to apply to him, anymore, to pull teeth. Evidently this was their threadbare excuse for coming. No doubt the fish bit well when approached from his dam, and while waiting his turn one could always be assured of a large and lively company on the acre legally set apart as a mill lot.

Today, nearly all of these mills lie in ruin or have been totally destroyed. Fire was an omnipresent danger; in 1810 Bourbon County imposed a $2 fine on anyone who carried a fire to within 20 yards of a mill. However, most of the old mills disappeared because of disuse and neglect; a crumbling wall, an old stone dam, a solitary stone chimney, or an occasional grinding stone or mill wheel are all that survive as reminders of most Central Kentucky mills. The Bluegrass does have one working mill, the Weisenberger Mill in Scott County, operated by Phil Weisenberger. The present mill was built in 1913 after operations had been moved from a nearby mill site that had been established in 1865 by Weisenberger's great-great-great grandfather; indeed, the millstone standing before the present entrance was relocated from the original mill, as were others forming part of a yard wall around a house above the mill. Power for the milling process is now provided by a water-powered turbine wheel. Open to visitors, the Weisenberger Mill produces a regular run of flour as well as prepackaged, prepared mixes of Bluegrass food specialties such as hush puppies, cornbread, biscuits, seasoned flours, and pancakes.

An example of a steam-powered gristmill is preserved and featured at the annual Forkland Community Heritage Festival, which is the best example of a grassroots, truly authentic folk festival in the Bluegrass. All participants must either live in the community or trace their roots to it; no outside vendors are allowed to participate. Each festival display is staffed by local, unpaid residents of the community, many of whom are still actively engaged in the continuing traditions represented at the festival. This concerted effort of the Forkland Community creates a living museum of the entire range of folk traditions, artifacts, occupations, and activities of a rural community. A tour is conducted from the festival site out into the community and features another mill—one of the last old-fashioned horse-driven sorghum mills in the Bluegrass.

The beauty and charm of the old mills, which were often nestled in a setting of rock and trees, are attested by the few surviving examples and the photographs or sketches of the many that have been razed or allowed to fall into ruin. Their loss represents an aesthetic impoverishment of the historic Bluegrass landscape.

EARLY INNS AND TAVERNS

Closely associated with the mills of the early Bluegrass were inns and taverns; both were centers of social interaction and communication, and the mills supplied the distilleries with mill-ground corn, which was promptly transformed into whiskey—an obligatory beverage for every successful inn and tavern.

The very earliest inns and taverns were built primarily of logs. The first Bourbon County tavern was a log structure kept by Thomas West and known appropriately as West's Tavern. In later years, when it was weatherboarded and coated with a red wash, it was called West's Red

One of the last horse-powered sorghum mills in the Bluegrass, in Boyle County (Photo courtesy of Forkland Community Heritage Committee)

Tavern. Another famous weatherboarded log tavern was Love Tavern in Frankfort, built about 1786. Used first as a residence, it was the only structure in town sufficiently large to accommodate the 1792 General Assembly; in old photographs it looks like a typical log-framed house of the day, and it stood until 1870. In rural areas, taverns continued being built with logs at least into the 1820s. One of Franklin County's most popular country inns was William Owen's Tavern, a two-story poplar structure built in 1820 as a family home, but in 1821 converted into a tavern.

Such conversions of structures from private residences to inns or taverns, or vice versa, were common in the early Bluegrass. The Old Crow Inn of Boyle County, one of the oldest stone structures in Central Kentucky, has been an inn and restaurant for much of its history but it was originally built in 1794 as a private residence, probably by Thomas Barbee, the first postmaster in Kentucky. This Greek Revival building—seven-bay asymmetrical, two-stories—in the tradition of Bluegrass hospitality, welcomed travelers as private guests long before it ever became a public enterprise. This same conversion pattern—private to public use—was followed by such historic Bluegrass inns and taverns as Johnston's Inn (Bourbon County), Colby Tavern (Clark County), and Offutt-Cole Tavern (Woodford County), all of which are still standing (and will be discussed later). Indeed, numerous old Bluegrass inns and taverns stand structurally intact to this day. Testifying to their sturdy construction is the legend (reminiscent of the John Hunt Morgan story related earlier) about a popular inn at Harrodsburg, the Allin House. Supposedly a man rode his white horse in the tavern door, through the main lobby, and up to the bar, where he ordered his drink, consumed it, an then nonchalantly rode back out again.

The typical tavern or inn provided stables, a bar, food, a taproom for socializing, and "accommodations"—sleeping quarters of a sort. At that time in Bluegrass history, alcohol was actually safer to drink than the water, but evidently innkeepers were as adverse to extending credit then as now. Over the bar of one such taproom was hung the sign:

> My liquor's good, my measure's just.
> But, honest sirs, I will not trust.

Most inns and taverns also served food, although choice and quality varied widely. The usual offering was a continuously cooking stew—also found almost universally in rural homes at the time—into which water and fresh meat and vegetables were periodically added. A large room was frequently available for dances and other types of folk entertainment, and the weary travelers could have a place to sleep—although, it was said, in some taverns "the beds had a private life of their own;" thus many men preferred to sleep in the relatively clean hay of the stable. For such hospitality and creature comforts the traveler paid what was called tavern rates, usually set by the county court; in Franklin County, writes Carl E. Kramer, "A single traveler on horseback could obtain a night's lodging, eat three meals, and stable and feed his horse for the princely sum of $1.25. Liquor was extra, with prices ranging from 12 ½ cents for a half-pint of whiskey to $2.00 a quart for Madeira and other imported wines."

Inns as Social Centers   The early inns and taverns were much more than just stopping places for travelers; indeed, their social and political significance to the community far outweighed their importance to wayfarers. The tavern was a respectable resort for males at all leisure hours; it was a combination social club, informal courthouse, political forum, and saloon. Often the only newspaper in the community was found there; the small sheet saw hard usage, passed from hand to hand. Some could hardly read it, and others only pretended; over the bar of one taproom was posted the notice: "Gentlemen learning to spell are requested to use last week's newsletter."

Militia drills and sales of cattle and horses were frequently held near inns and taverns. Assemblages of all kinds met there, and officials did much of their work in the taproom, taking depositions, issuing licenses, holding elections. In the towns and villages the custom of sitting out in front of the hostelry developed; rows of chairs or benches were provided—even part of the street might be preempted by community loungers who made the tavern or inn their headquarters and passed time in talk and games while they awaited the arrival or departure of the stage, their big event of the day. In fact, early inns and taverns constituted an acceptable common ground where all segments of Bluegrass society could meet together for business and share in entertainment and conviviality. As Kentucky historian and geologist Willard Rouse Jillson observed:

Here, in an elemental society, where hunters in deerskin coats and breeches and coonskin caps met, mingled, and bartered . . . with cultured gentlemen from the eastern tidewater towns and plantations dressed in broadcloth and silk tops, tavern jollity afforded the principal amusement of life. . . . With an ample supply of good food and drink, including a deal of handmade corn whiskey, the patrons passed the long cold winter nights in a pleasant roundabout of story, jest, and rollicking song.

Early taverns were not frequented solely by males, however; they were used for performances of all sorts: fortune tellers and ventriloquists; exhibitions of waxworks, dwarfs, assorted freaks, and musical clocks; political speechmaking; musical concerts, balls, and dances; lottery drawings—a favorite means for schools and churches to raise money—and so on. Society belles and beaux from all parts of Kentucky and surrounding states came to the Bourbon House in Paris for sixty-five years to enjoy the dances held during the county fair. The most famous and popular tavern in Paris, however, and center for much of the early social life of the Bluegrass was Duncan Tavern. Two stories tall, with high basement and attic, and containing twenty rooms, Duncan Tavern is an imposing five-bay, double-pile stone Georgian structure, built at a time—around 1788—when most of the surrounding buildings were constructed of logs. The tavern's structure and interior woodwork were made of the finest Kentucky hardwoods; girders, beams, and joists were of oak or ash; huge sleepers have retained their original bark after 200 years and are still sound; laths are of hand-split hickory, floors are ash. After 150 years of continuous operation, the old building, threatened with destruction, was restored by the Kentucky Society of the Daughters of the American Revolution, who furnished it with authentic period pieces and maintain it today as a historic public shrine.

While Paris was the very early social and cultural nucleus of the northeastern Bluegrass, Danville, in Boyle County, was the early cultural capital of the southwestern Bluegrass. Danville was also the first political center for the entire Commonwealth and site of the ten constitutional conventions held from 1784 to 1792, which led to Kentucky statehood. Several taverns were established there, one of which was Grayson Tavern, built possibly as early as 1786, and soon thereafter called the most prestigious meeting place in the West; consequently, it was a popular spot for politicians debating the issues of Kentucky statehood. This L-shaped, two-story frame structure was eventually converted to a private residence and is preserved today as part of the restored Constitution Square complex.

A second historic tavern in the area, which also catered to noted lawyers, famous politicians, and wealthy planters, was Chiles or Morgan Row Tavern in Harrodsburg. The tavern was the scene of gala balls and political celebrations, serving good food to local citizens and the traveling public alike. Reflecting the popularity of the tavern is the story of its busy innkeeper, who had no time even to count his profits and would sweep the day's receipts into his hat. Constructed in the early 1800s, Morgan Row is Kentucky's oldest completely standing example of the row house. Built of solid brick, locally burned and mortared with river sand, limestone, and "pike dust" (pulverized clay), Morgan Row is a four-unit structure, two and three stories high, with a partial basement of solid hand-hewn stone. The center unit, the oldest and largest section, which probably housed the original tavern, contains some rather unusual architectural features, including a rare stone fireplace with stone shelf and hearth intact, plus two carved wooden arches, which served as a pass-through into the dining room. In the north unit, the last added to the row, is the first built-in sideboard known in the Bluegrass. Today the exterior of the row house conforms precisely to its original design, and much of the interior has been either restored or at least renovated.

Lexington quickly established itself as the hub for all social, cultural, and economic activities, and hence it was in Lexington that the most famous of Bluegrass taverns, Postlethwait's, prospered. Compared to Duncan and Grayson taverns, Postlethwait's was a latecomer, opened in 1797 by Captain John Postlethwait, a Revolutionary War officer, but it was built on the site of Lexington's very first tavern, opened sometime around 1784–1786 by Captain James Bray, whose sign promised "Entertainment for Man and Beast." ("Entertainment" at that time meant "hospitable reception.") Much of Postlethwait's success can be attributed to the personality of its owner, as noted on a historical plaque that once marked the tavern site:

In addition to being "mine host extraordinary," a fantastical figure in the matter of dress, a suave speaker in demand at social and political functions, banker, business man and onetime city treasurer, Captain Postlethwait was a man with a singular ability for making and holding friends in all walks of life.

Postlethwait was host to, among others, Andrew Jackson, James Monroe, Aaron Burr, and the Marquis de Lafayette. His tavern was not only a warm and welcoming stopover for travelers but also the district post office, the center where passing couriers dropped off news of distant places, and the scene of heated discussions about politics, education, current events, and, of most importance, horse racing and the development of Bluegrass horses and other purebred livestock.

Surviving several fires and the vicissitudes of history, Postlethwait's, under the name Phoenix Hotel, remained a flourishing establishment for nearly 200 years until, in 1981, the old hotel was finally and irrevocably razed.

Rural Inns   Not all prosperous early Bluegrass inns were located in towns and villages; many were strategically placed on established stagecoach routes between settlements, particularly on roads radiating out from Lexington. Three such establishments, sharing various common characteristics, were Johnston's Inn, Offutt-Cole Tavern, and Colby Tavern. The oldest of the three, Johnston's, appears on John Filson's 1784 map of Kentucky, situated five miles west of Paris on the original road from Lexington to Maysville; this was one of the earliest roads in the Bluegrass, also mentioned by Filson as "Smith's waggon-road," and the first in the Commonwealth to be macadamized. Johnston's was a favorite stopping place for travelers, and as many as fifty Conestoga wagons sat at times in its wagonyard. Equally well located was the Offutt-Cole Tavern, the first tavern on the first stagecoach line running on Frankfort Pike from Lexington to Frankfort. In antebellum days, the tavern was host to many political rallies for Scott, Woodford, and Fayette counties, and the Clays, and many others were frequent visitors.

Perhaps the most important rural tavern in the Bluegrass was Colby Tavern, which also prospered primarily because of its location on a major stagecoach route, Colby Pike. During the early 1800s, this was the favorite route for businessmen and lawyers such as Henry Clay who, traveling from Lexington to Winchester, could ride to Colby Station, spend the night at the tavern, and then ride on to Winchester alert and ready for business the next morning. The tavern also benefited from horseback riders and stagecoach travelers, including families accompanied by their servants journeying from the Deep South to Olympian Springs in Bath County, who paused there for rest and refreshment. Its beds were clean and comfortable, and its cooking renowned. J. Winston Coleman, Jr. wrote:

Prices...were 25c for breakfast; dinner 37 ½ cents and supper 50 cents. Lodging was figured at 12 ½ cents; "cyder and beer" brought 6 ¼ cents per quart.... "Cherry Bounce of Whiskey" was a favorite drink...which brought 12 ½ cents per half pint. For the more aristocratic traveler, a "toddy of foreign materials" commanded 37 cents per drink.

All three taverns were constructed in two or three stages, apparently growing as their families or businesses increased, and are essentially I-house forms, or modifications thereof. A one-story brick side wing containing a keeping room and bar was added to Johnston's Inn before 1800, and in the early 1800s the old log main structure was replaced by the present red brick I-house main block with a unique Greek Revival double-recessed entrance. Offutt's, built for a private residence prior to 1790 (some say as early as 1780), began as a one-and-one-half story log house, later covered with solid cherry weatherboarding; about ten years later, the house was leased to Horatio Offutt who built a brick, modified I-house addition directly abutting the original structure, for use as a tavern and, in 1804, as a stagecoach inn. The tavern was operated from 1812 to 1839 by Richard Cole, whose son James was father of Zerelda Cole James, mother of the notorious Jesse and Frank. An interesting feature of the old inn is a partition between two of the upstairs rooms, which is operated by a system of weights and pulleys in the ceiling and can be raised to create a ballroom. Construction of Colby Tavern was begun in 1820 by Colby Taylor, evidently for the primary purpose of serving as an inn and stagecoach stop; eventually, an *identical* ell was added to the tavern. The earlier section was probably used for eating and sleeping (it can be identified by features such as shorter doors), and the later one contained the customary second-floor ballroom. Each wing of the tavern was essentially a domestic central-passage I-house with double doors and asymmetrical bays. As was the practice with many Bluegrass homes, the bricks for the tavern were hand pressed on the property, and some still bear the fingerprints or initials of their makers.

The business fortunes of all three taverns faded when the roads on which they were located lost their status as principal routes between Lexington and outlying towns. Eventually all three became private residences. Johnston's was purchased in 1832 by a member of the Clay family, renamed Rosedale, and remained in the family until 1956. Again renamed, this time Auberge, Johnston has been celebrated by its present owners who composed a song about its long history: "You're standing still upon the hill and may you ever be." Offutt-Cole experienced a series of transformations. For a while it was operated as Black Horse Tavern, then, from 1848 to 1880, as a tollgate house, then private residence until 1979, when it was deeded to the Woodford County Historical Society, restored, and designated by the Commonwealth as a historical site. Colby Tavern reverted to a family residence around the time of the Civil War, and for almost a century served as a tenant house, which use, rather ironically, preserved its original structure, although the older wing was partially torn down and remodeled. Finally, after several years of

abandonment and neglect, during which time cows wandered in and out
its missing doors, and rain and snow fell through its broken window-
panes, the old tavern was purchased in 1988 by a young Clark County
couple, who are remodeling and restoring it to its antebellum glory.

Though most of the early hostelries, like Johnston, Offutt-Cole, and
Colby Taverns, have ceased to function as businesses (the famous Talbott
Inn at Bardstown in the Outer Bluegrass is the exception), the tradition
of inns and taverns in the Bluegrass continues to flourish. Serving
traditional Bluegrass fare, much of it from old folk recipes, and entertaining guests with traditional Bluegrass hospitality, modern establishments such as Harrodsburg's Beaumont Inn and Shakertown in Mercer
County continue to welcome the Central Kentucky traveler.

CHURCHES

The very earliest Bluegrass pioneers were so preoccupied with surviving
that they had little time or energy to worry about the condition of their
souls. Nevertheless, churches—or meeting houses as they were called—
were among some of the frontier's earliest structures. The first church in
Kentucky was erected in December 1781, at Craig's Station by Lewis
Craig's "traveling church," a Baptist congregation which had fled what
they considered religious persecution by the Episcopal Church of Virginia. They had journeyed as a group to Kentucky in search of freedom of
conscience and a piece of good land. Almost overnight, new churches
came into existence, not only Baptist but also Presbyterian, Methodist,
and Catholic. Indeed, scholars have noted that—with the exception of
the Mormon expansion west into Utah—no other region in this country
was settled with the accompanying religious fervor demonstrated by early
Kentuckians.

Typically, the first meeting houses were of round-log construction,
but built a bit larger and with more precise workmanship than were
cabins; indeed, some of the earliest meeting houses *were* cabins. The first
Methodist Conference west of the Alleghenies was held in 1790 at
Masterson's Station, the home of Brother Masterson, a plain log structure built near a large spring. For two or three days there was virtually
round-the-clock preaching, and many souls repented and others were
converted. The old building was razed in the early 1900s, and today only
a photograph and a historic marker testify to its existence. Unfortunately,
most other early log churches in the Bluegrass have shared the misfor-
tunes of Masterson's Station. Today only one is left intact—the Cane
Ridge Meeting House in Bourbon County.

Cane Ridge Meeting House   Cane Ridge—the location, not the church—was named by Daniel Boone, sometime in the 1770s, after the dense, gigantic canebrake covering a fifteen-mile ridge. Close to the crest of this ridge a Presbyterian meeting house was built in 1791 by settlers primarily from North Carolina, directed there by Boone and led by the Rev. Robert W. Finley. Approximately 50 feet long and 30 feet wide with 15-foot ceilings—possibly the largest one-room log structure in the United States—Cane Ridge was constructed of hand-hewn blue ash cut from the surrounding virgin forest. Because few ash trees grew near the intended site, but in small clusters in scattered areas, some huge logs had to be transported to the Ridge. According to legend, the cane was so thick and so tall that men were forced to climb tall trees in order to direct the men dragging the logs which way to turn. Although the early pioneers probably did not realize it, their choice of blue ash was fortunate, for the wood is resistent to nearly all insects, especially the termite, and this contributed to the longevity of the building.

Set on a stone foundation, the meeting house was built so that its ends faced east and west, with doors at each end and the main entrance from the west. A long aisle extended from door to door. The two-story building was fairly tall for a log structure, most of which are notoriously short. Alcoves or offsets, approximately 2 feet deep and 8 feet long, were built into the north and south walls, and the pulpit was located in the north alcove; Rhodes Thompson, a historian of Cane Ridge, describes the pulpit as "boxed up, with entrance at the side reached by several steps, and its elevation was so considerable that the speaker literally looked down upon the audience." The roof was made of hand-sawn sheating and covered by wooden shakes that were held in place by wooden pins, or treenails. Not one nail, not one piece of metal, was used in the original building (although a few have been added since, for reinforcement).

Inside the meeting house a large U-shaped gallery was built around two end walls and one long wall of the structure. A remarkable piece of frontier folk engineering, the gallery, or balcony, was built for those slaves of the landowners who attended the services. Although considered as members of the congregation in full standing, blacks were segregated upstairs, a seating arrangement that positioned them, perhaps ironically, above the heads of their masters. A note in the margin of the clerk's roster in the early 1800s noted that the congregation consisted of more that 225 adult members, one-third white males, one-third white females, and one-third "persons of color." There were no inside stairs to this gallery; instead, slaves climbed up and down by an outside ladder that leaned against the west-end wall and entered the balcony via an opening above the entrance door. The gallery, remarkable for its large size, was

Cane Ridge Meeting
House, Bourbon County
(Photo courtesy of Cane
Ridge Preservation
Project)

cantilevered at the center; that is, it projected out over its center supports below. Resting solely on eighteen posts, it was free-standing and not attached to the walls at any point—a truly astonishing structural achievement of engineering, requiring wedging and fitting and balancing.

This three-sided gallery no doubt reflected the influence of the English parish church, as did other interior aspects of Cane Ridge: the positioning of the high pulpit on a long wall, and the seating arrangement—one section facing the pulpit and one section on either side facing toward the center. As most Cane Ridge settlers were only a generation removed from Britain, such adherence to traditional interior arrangements is not surprising.

In 1829 it was decided to "modernize" the old church to make it more comfortable. Since most of the black members had left to attend churches of their own—known for their liberal attitudes toward slavery, many in the Cane Ridge congregation had probably freed their slaves—the gallery was removed and a ceiling put in under the great beams. The lower interior walls were plastered; a plank floor was laid; seats with back supports were installed; glass windows replaced the wooden shutters; and the outside was weatherboarded—making Cane Ridge look like hundreds of other little white country churches sitting on a hill. Further changes came in 1882, when the original pulpit was torn out and a small, free-standing one was placed before the east entrance, which was closed.

Seating was also replaced and rearranged into two sections facing the east-end pulpit. Apparently the congregation was attempting to conform more closely to the nave-plan, gable-end orientation of other churches in the area. A second plank floor was laid—this one remains in the meeting house today—and a large potbellied stove (the only source of heat Cane Ridge ever had) was set in the middle of the church, its flue and chimney going out the center of the roof.

By 1921 the congregation had become so small that it disbanded, and the property was deeded to a board of trustees; in 1932, after accumulating considerable support and money, the decision was made to return the church as nearly as possible to its original structure. This process, resembling somewhat the slow-motion rewinding of a video cassette, involved tearing off weatherboarding, removing the glass windows and rehanging solid wooden shutters, removing the stove and its flue and chimney, scraping plaster off the walls, rebuilding the pulpit in the north alcove, reopening the east entrance, placing the seats back in the round, tearing down the ceiling, and—perhaps the most amazing feat of all—reassembling the original gallery. For 103 years the various pieces of this gallery had been part of a barn on a nearby farm belonging to a church family. Used for stall dividers, part of a hayloft, etc., the wood had survived through four or five generations of this family who, in 1932, very happily gave it all back to the church. When skilled restoration craftsmen reassembled the gallery in the meeting house, it fit back in precisely like the day it was taken out; only three pieces were missing and had to be reconstructed. Today the gallery is frequently used—the curator says it is probably more secure than the main floor—and is a source of admiration and fascination for engineering and architectural students and the visiting public alike.

Cane Ridge Meeting House is presently enshrined, so to speak, within a stone superstructure, dedicated in 1957, which protects the old log church from the weather. The stone utilized for this superstructure, unique to Cane Ridge and found only within a six-mile radius, is a tan or golden colored surface limestone. In the church cemetery huge blocks of this same limestone, some weighing in excess of 4,400 pounds, form "ledgers" covering individual graves. Ledgers are named for the inscriptions on their top surfaces and are not uncommon in English parish churchyards; however, they are rare in the United States. Although they look like vaults or sepulchers they are not hollow but rather single, solid blocks of limestone. The Cane Ridge cemetery contains at least twenty of these ledger stones, dating from 1801, and a few can be found in other Bluegrass cemeteries, including some at North Middletown and at least one in Winchester. One can only marvel at the ingenuity and skill required to cut and maneuver these huge blocks of stone.

When all other early log churches in the Bluegrass were either torn down and replaced by brick or stone structures or abandoned and allowed to fall into ruin, why does Cane Ridge, after nearly 200 years, continue to exist? The answer, of course, is that the old meeting house was the site of two historical religious phenomena—the Cane Ridge Revival of 1801 and the birth of the Christian Church (Disciples of Christ) in 1804, events which combined to make it probably *the most famous church on the western frontier!*

A prominent event in what historians have called the Great Revival, the Cane Ridge Revival in August of 1801 has been described by Tom Clark as "possibly the greatest emotional upheaval on the early American frontier." An estimated 20,000–30,000 people attended, traveling by wagon, cart, carriage, horse, and foot from all over Kentucky and surrounding states, at that time the largest gathering in frontier history. They remained at Cane Ridge for seven days and six nights, camping on the church grounds and listening to preaching by twenty-five to thirty Presbyterian, Methodist, and Baptist ministers, which continued all day and into much of the night. In his autobiography, James B. Finley, who came to the revival a skeptic, but nonetheless experienced its emotional power and later became a Methodist minister, describes a scene he calls "awful beyond description:"

A vast crowd . . . collected together. The noise was like the roar of Niagara. The vast sea of human beings seemed to be agitated as if by a storm. I counted seven ministers, all preaching at one time, some on stumps, others in wagons, and one . . . standing on a tree which had, in falling, lodged against another.

Many in the crowd became hysterical during impassioned exhortations, sobbing and shrieking or flinging themselves to the ground in ecstatic seizures. Some sang fervently while others barked like dogs (called "treeing the devil"); others danced wildly or jerked their heads and bodies with incessant spasmodic contortions. One observor quipped, "There were those who came to scoff but stayed to jerk;" many claimed to "have seen the light." The revival finally came to a close for purely logistical reasons—food for people and animals had been exhausted. So they went home, and stories of the event were carried with them. The Cane Ridge experience had established camp-meeting revivalism as an American tradition.

The minister at Cane Ridge during the revival was Barton W. Stone, Robert Finley having left in 1796 for rather dubious reasons—he was evidently charged with drunkenness, or at least with over-imbibing. In 1803, two years after the revival, Stone (like Finley, from North Carolina, though born in Maryland), along with five of his companion preachers, was severely criticized by the Presbyterian elders for the liberal views and the demonstrations associated with the revival movement, and they were officially expelled from the Presbyterian Church. The following year—1804—Cane Ridge became the first congregation of the Stone movement, whose members referred to themselves as simply Christians. Spreading rapidly, the "Christian movement" joined with a similar movement led by two Presbyterian ministers from Pennsylvania, Thomas Campbell and his son Alexander, and together these two movements formed the Christian Church, Disciples of Christ, which now numbers over one million members. It was during the centennial anniversary of that union that the old Cane Ridge Meeting House, as the parent church to the new denomination, was restored to its primitive appearance. Today Barton Stone's legacy to the old meeting house is documented in a folk museum on the church grounds, which houses items relating to Stone, Cane Ridge, and the beginnings of the Christian Church, and other artifacts. Three miles from the meeting house is a small, one-room log cabin, where Stone lived and raised his family during his tenure at Cane Ridge. Weatherboarded outside and plastered within, the little structure now serves as a bedroom wing to a large two-story farmhouse which has been attached to it, perhaps serving as a fitting symbol of the old log meeting house from which evolved a modern church.

Old Stone Meeting House   With the exception of Cane Ridge, the early log churches in the Bluegrass were replaced as soon as possible with stone or brick, and it is primarily these structures, particularly stone, that now stand as examples of traditional church architecture. An excellent example of the progression from log to stone is the Old Stone Meeting House (Providence Baptist Church) in Clark County, the oldest constituted Baptist Church in Kentucky—some say the oldest continuous congregation west of the Alleghenies. Old Stone was founded in 1785 by one of the "traveling churches" from Virginia, and it is claimed that Daniel Boone and his family attended services in the 1790s. The first meeting house was of log construction, with, legend says, "100 holes for fighting the Indians," but before 1793 the congregation had erected a one-room stone structure, 40 by 50 feet, from limestone blocks quarried about a quarter of a mile away. Like most other early churches in the Bluegrass (but not Cane Ridge), Old Stone was built on a floor plan similar to that of modern churches: central nave, gables at the entrance end and the pulpit/altar end. The long facades have three bays, each with a jack arch (flat arch) still discernible in the stone work. In a traditional region such as the rural Bluegrass, church architecture is viewed much as congregations view their religious beliefs—as irrefutably correct—and consequently neither changes much over time. However, in the late 1880s the windows of Old Stone were changed to the lancet shape to conform to the then-prevailing view that Gothic architecture was more appropriate for church buildings. At one time Old Stone was an important center of population: in the early nineteenth century, court notices—informing defendants of offenses of which they had been accused—were affixed to the church door immediately after divine services.

After nearly seventy-five years, however, the congregation wanted a larger and more elaborate house of worship, and in 1870 Old Stone was deeded to the "colored" Baptists, who continue to worship there to this today. Not surprisingly, the old church has had many a tale attached to it over the years. A favorite is the story of the inebriated fox hunter. The church's locale is excellent fox-hunting country, and one rainy evening an old country squire, known for his love of both hunting and Kentucky bourbon, took temporary refuge in Old Stone during a revival meeting to warm up and dry out. Slipping in quietly, he sat in the back of the balcony, over the door (in early days, the slave gallery) and listened while the black preacher expounded on his text "The Judgment Day." The old squire then dozed off, and awakened just as the preacher was warming up to his climax, vigorously warning his congregation of the "Wrath to Come" on the "Last Day when the angel Gabriel would sound his trumpet." At that, the old Squire, still fortified with alcoholic stimulant, put the fox horn to his lips and let out a tremendous blast. The ensuing pandemonium can well be imagined. The preacher—so the tale goes—seeing that he was cut off from both windows and doors, dived under the pulpit, exclaiming loudly, "Hallelujah! Hell fire! Damn a church with only one door."

Today, secluded in a valley near the end of a one-lane gravel road and surrounded by giant trees and an old graveyard filled with briars and pokeberries rambling over blackened and broken tombstones, and an old stone fence separating the churchyard from rolling, wooded hills, the Old Stone Meeting House continues to stand as a living testimony to some of the Bluegrass' oldest traditions.*

Other Stone Churches   Nearly as old as Old Stone and similar in form and structure is Walnut Hill Presbyterian Church in Fayette County. It is the oldest standing Presbyterian church building in the Commonwealth, erected in 1801 on land donated by General Levi Todd, grandfather of Mary Todd Lincoln. Preceded by a small 1785 log building, the present 40 by 50 feet stone church looks much as it did 190

---

*While Old Stone has been a black church since 1870, the Pleasant Green Missionary Baptist Church in Lexington has the distinction of being the oldest black church in the Bluegrass. It has been a black congregation *continuously* since 1790, and located on the same spot since 1822. The church was famous for its mass baptisms, which drew hundreds to witness the immersions in a Lexington pond.

1890s black mass baptism in Lexington; preacher is Sanford Howard (Photo courtesy of Kentucky Historical Society)

years ago except for the Gothic arches and stained-glass windows and the removal of the slave galleries accomplished in an 1880s remodeling. Two other early stone Presbyterian churches—Pisgah in Woodford County and Ebenezer in Jessamine—share the architectural characteristics of Walnut Hill, but especially Pisgah has undergone similar Gothic modifications.

A few early stone church structures in the Bluegrass have been converted to other uses. Cooper's Run Baptist Church in Bourbon County, built 1803, has served both as a hemp factory and later as a Runnymeade Farm livestock barn for almost 175 years and remains in an excellent state of preservation. Unlike the other stone church structures discussed, however, Cooper's Run was apparently not built according to the nave plan; its entrance was originally in the center of one side, but this has now been walled up and doors installed at either end. Also, as Langsam and Johnson note, the floor planks on the second story

still reveal a pattern indicating that like the somewhat earlier log Cane Ridge Meetinghouse...the original balcony was U-shaped, leaving only a relatively small proportion of open space above the sanctuary in the center of one side.

There is also evidence of at least one corner stairway to this exceptionally high and deep loft-balcony.

In addition to these early stone churches and of course the Cane Ridge Meeting House, the Bluegrass contains one other notable example of early religious folk architecture, the Old Mud Meeting House near Harrodsburg in Mercer County. The first Dutch Reformed Church west of the Alleghenies, erected in 1800, Old Mud's claim to fame rests on its peculiar structure. Set on a fieldstone foundation, its distinct framing was constructed of sturdy oaken timbers, and the walls were filled with mud mixed with straw and sticks, thus the name "Old Mud." As in the case of Cane Ridge, "improvements" were initiated over the years, such as covering the exterior with siding and plastering the interior walls. In 1849, according to records, extensive repairs were undertaken: windows were lowered; shutters hung; new doors cut; the exterior painted; and a suitable pulpit was built. (The old, evidently unsuitable pulpit was a lofty wine-cup affair with a spiral staircase.) Such changes, of course, completely destroyed the individuality of Old Mud; after falling into disuse and being abandoned, the old church, fortunately, was deeded in 1928 to the Mercer County Historical Society, which has restored the building as closely as possible to its 1800s appearance.

New Sects and Denominations   Kentuckians have always been enthusiastic about religion and its possible heavenly rewards, a fact richly attested to by the numerous old, and not so old, church buildings located around the Bluegrass. The constantly increasing number of new churches is in part the result of another Kentucky trait, a disposition toward religious disputations and resultant schisms, noted by Clark McMeekin:

When the requisites for getting there [Heaven] become a matter of disagreement in a church, the usual solution was for one group to break away and start another branch, same denomination. As far as we can determine, Kentucky's record along this line is unrivaled.

This has led to the use of some peculiar "houses" of worship—school cafeterias, banks, business buildings, and converted private residences. On occasion, it has also been partially responsible for another religious folk architectural form, the so-called store-front church.

Usually, but not solely, associated with Pentecostal or Evangelical movements, store-front churches in the Bluegrass are generally a phenomenon of the smaller, outlying towns and are often located on main streets (though they come and go, Lexington presently has at least two, both in shopping strips). Traditionally mission churches—"a soul-saving

Store-front church in Winchester with religious objects in the windows (Photo by Jerry Schureman)

station" as one young pastor put it—they consist of small, newly formed congregations who, because of limited finances, rent business places or stores in which to meet and worship. Such congregations frequently move from one location to another, often because of lease problems and/or rent increases, but also in search of more space because membership often increases rather dramatically.

The outside of the store-front church looks like an ordinary downtown store building except for some type of church sign, usually displayed behind the windows or painted on them, though sometimes hanging on the outside of the building. Folk-art religious scenes or quotes from the Scriptures or moralistic statements are also sometimes painted on the windows using various materials such as soap, Bon Ami, crayons, or spray paint; sometimes curtains cover the windows. The *inside* of the store-front church, however, resembles, as closely as original architecture and the affluence of its members allow, the interior of a traditional church. Folding chairs, or even pews are often arranged with a center aisle, and face a pulpit and altar area, possibly raised, and located across one wall. Also in this area may be a piano, perhaps with a curtain around its back, a place for the choir, and even displays of flowers or some sort of greenery. These trappings, with the addition of painted walls and perhaps carpeting, create the impression, particularly when facing the altar/pulpit area, of being inside a traditional church, especially if the room is large and the store-front windows not visible.

Nevertheless, store-front churches are intended to be temporary church abodes; their members, primarily poor and/or working-class whites, usually wish eventually to build or buy a traditional church structure, no doubt recognizing that a certain social stigma attaches to their church solely because of its location. Until "the Lord leads them in that direction," however, most members would agree with the comments of one convert concerning people who "feel sort of lowered" to have to walk into a store-front church: "If they feel too good to come into a store-front building, they might not make it into heaven, either."

Although Kentucky is considered a Bible Belt State with strong Fundamentalist and Evangelical traditions, various scholars have noted its ambivalence towards "sin." Eslie Asbury observes that Kentucky's "famous products, whiskey, horses, politics and women, are all romantic and 'sinful.'" Often, of course, the Kentuckians who pore over the racing form and/or frequent the neighborhood tavern on Saturday are not the same Kentuckians who crowd into Fundamentalist churches on Sunday; yet many see no reason that one activity should preclude participation in the other. This apparent incongruity is perhaps difficult for outsiders to understand, but a little incongruity is not unknown in individual Kentuckians, who see nothing odd in devotion to both piety and pleasure.

Other Bluegrass social traditions are in some ways also similar to those of other Kentucky regions. In other ways, however, Bluegrass customs are as distinctive as the geography of the Region itself.

Bluegrass Folk Customs and Other Traditional Activities

CHAPTER 8

Folk Traditions of the Bluegrass Horse World

When the younger sons of Virginia's landed gentry immigrated to the Bluegrass, they brought with them an inherited love of horses and a long tradition of horse breeding and racing. Virginia plantations had for years imported the finest Thoroughbreds from England, where that superior strain had been developed by wealthy breeders for sport, and for use by the English cavalry, by combining the legendary endurance and swiftness of the Darley Arabian, the Godolphin Arabian, and the Byerly Turk, all famous breeds from the Middle East. An ancient legend, sometimes related by Bluegrass horse people, attests to the selection process Arabs used to choose the most outstanding of these superb animals. A number of horses were hobbled in the desert for a long time without water and then were cut loose near an oasis. As they raced toward the water, the Arabs blew their horns, a signal to the horses to come to them; those that responded to the call, turning away from the oasis, were the only ones chosen as worthy to sire and bear the future generations.

Not only Thoroughbreds but the Standardbred horse also is descended from these three bloodlines; however, for Standardbred stallions, the Darley Arabian is the only unbroken line of the three, and it also provides the most sires for Thoroughbreds. Although best known for its Thoroughbreds, the Bluegrass is also an important breeding and training region for Standardbreds, both trotters and pacers. Approximately one half of the major harness-race winners are Kentucky foals. A third Bluegrass breed, the Saddlebred, is native to the Region, having been originally developed by early pioneers, who needed a hardy, intelligent, and sure-footed riding horse.

HORSES IN THE EARLY BLUEGRASS

Fine horses have always been the pride of the Bluegrass gentry, and horse people take great pains to perfect the hereditary lineage of their animals. Legend has it that Daniel Boone maintained that "every man needs a wife, a gun—and a good horse." Note that only the horse needed to be "good." An old Bluegrass proverb stipulates, "A good horse never stumbles and a good wife never grumbles." To assure that the finest horses would be available, Boone himself introduced a bill "for improving the breed of horses" at the first legislative assembly held in Kentucky. Good horses were so highly valued that men were tempted to steal them, and horse thieves were punished severely if caught. One early horse thief in Frankfort, for example, was sentenced to two years, part of it to be served in solitary confinement on a "low and coarse diet." He probably considered himself lucky; prior to 1800, such a crime could call for the death sentence, and indeed, on April 2, 1799, one Augustine Adams was hanged in Frankfort's public square for stealing a horse. As recently as 1977 a thief cut two wire fences and stole a Thoroughbred mare from Claiborne Farm. The theft was the talk of the Bluegrass; the farm offered a reward, and the media so exploited the situation that the thief became frightened and made no attempt to sell the mare or to demand a ransom. She was found several months later in Tompkinsville, near the Tennessee line, and returned to Claiborne; the thief served a five year prison term for the crime.

Deceptive Practices   A popular early unethical, if not illegal, flimflam—now obviated by computerized central record-keeping—was the deceptive recitation of a horse's fabricated lineage. A favorite Clark County tale, here retold by Lawrence Thompson, relates how an amateur horseman from Cincinnati tried to sell a "Thoroughbred" to the mayor of Winchester—a knowledgeable horseman with a sense of humor.

[The Cincinnati man] offered to show the pedigree, and it looked like the royal blood of horsedom: "Bay horse, Bluegrass, foaled in 1877, sire Black Samson, dam Young Phyllis; Black Samson by Breastplate, dam Lady Waxey; Young Phyllis by Blue Jeans, dam Mattie J.; Mattie J. by Cyclone Wilkes, dam Miss Tormentor; Miss Tormentor by Tuscarora II, dam Ada V.; Breastplate by Frank, dam Jellico; Jellico by Bucephalus, dam Princess; Bucephalus by Sir William, dam Euphalia." [The mayor] listened attentively and then commented gravely. . . . "There's nothing the matter with the name of your horse. . . . Bluegrass is a very good name . . . ; but Black Samson is, or was, when living, a jack. Young Phyllis was a shorthorn cow; Breastplate was a shorthorn bull; Lady Waxey was a famous saddle mare; Cyclone Wilkes is a trotting stallion, owned in Bourbon County; Miss Tormentor was a Jersey cow; Tuscarora II is a gray mule down on Four Mile Creek; *Ada V.* is a steamboat on the Kentucky River; Frank is a yellow dog in Simpson's livery stable; Jellico is an old mare mule in one of Brown's coal carts; Bucephalus is the gelding they drive to the Winchester hose reel; Princess is a Berkshire sow; Sir William is Rodney Haggard's goat; and Euphalia is one of Dr. Wash Miller's Southdown ewes."

Court Day in Lexington, November 1897 (Photo courtesy of University of Kentucky Libraries)

For most early Bluegrass horsemen, more important than its pedigree were a horse's racing abilities and appearance, and both could be doctored. One of the favorite haunts of those who practiced such chicanery was the occasional and itinerant meeting place known as the "swapping ring." This was often held during Court Day, the first Monday in the month, where nearly anything could be bought, traded, bartered, or swapped.

A tradition transplanted from Virginia, Court Day was an occasion for politicking, conducting business, socializing, sport wagering, and drinking. It was also the favorite time for farmers to sell or swap animals, especially horses and mules. So many horses and mules were traded at Frankfort's Court Day that the town's Main Street was nicknamed Jockey Alley; and Lexington's Court Day was nicknamed Mule Day.*

*Eventually, town dwellers became disenchanted with Court Day; and the noise, congestion, filth and tangential activities such as politicking and arguing, gambling, whoring, fighting, swearing, and drunkenness, that invariably accompany such licentious folk gatherings, prompted town fathers to close them down forever. Lexington's Court Day, for example, was officially declared a "public nuisance" and abolished in 1921.

Mule traders often kept a "mule book," in which they listed the markings and other characteristics of any mule they acquired; carried with them, the mule book helped locate a mule that was a near twin to the one they owned, so they could have a matched pair. Such mule and horse trading was to the poor man what horse meets were to the rich—his sport, his chance to match wits with his fellows, his way of displaying expertise and perhaps getting the best of a bargain.

However, would-be buyers had to be well versed in the ingenious deceptions practiced by some "hoss traders." A racehorse with a defective windpipe was hardest to unload; unscrupulous traders would stuff various objects up the horse's nostrils to disguise the condition. An unruly horse could be calmed by stuffing his nostrils with cotton laced with ether or other anesthetic. Sluggish steeds were often enlivened with a burr under the saddle, or crumpled leaves or wads of paper could be put in their ears to make them prance and shake their heads like a spirited racer; some even gave tired old horses drugs to enliven them. Other drugs—such as arsenic coated on its tongue—could make a malnourished horse appear fleshed out. Although the folk practice of determining the age of a horse by examining its teeth has some merit, especially up to age six, older horses' ages are more difficult to ascertain, and some traders used chemicals to color and reshape aged teeth; or, if a horse were a "cribber"—one that chews on its crib (manger) or anything else in sight—its teeth were often wedged to make them sore, to prevent its chewing.

Today, of course, the Jockey Club's records preclude fabrication of pedigree, and horse sales in the Bluegrass are devoid of such chicanery and gross mistreatment of the horses. Most such shenanigans were practiced by itinerant traders, not by Bluegrass gentry, whose handshake or gentleman's word was traditionally as good as another man's airtight contract. Such means of concluding business is practiced by a few gentry even today. However, in today's sales, especially of yearlings, some traditional practices continue to be used to showcase these prized animals as attractively as possible.

The Highest Pride of a Kentuckian   According to tradition, the first *authentic* Thoroughbred, a filly, was brought to Lexington in 1779. Just ten years later, Fayette County alone contained 9,607 horses. The *Kentucky Gazette* carried the first advertisement of a stallion in 1788, and in 1797, Blaze, the first Thoroughbred stallion to stand at stud in Kentucky, was brought to Scott County. Breeding increased so that in 1805 the *Gazette* found it necessary to begin a special annual supplement to provide information about available stallions. Apparently breeding was a lucrative business, for, in order to protect public sensibilities, as notes Lawrence Thompson, legislation had to be enacted to "restrain over-zealous horsemen from 'standing' their stallions in . . . public places." To protect fine broodmares, legislators also allowed their owners to geld mature stallions "caught running at large." Despite such legal restrictions, dockets of early courts were inundated with litigation concerning horses and their owners.

Early nineteenth century travelers to the Bluegrass noted: "A handsome horse is the highest pride of a Kentuckian." "For some time past the inhabitants of Kentucky have engaged in breeding horses. . . . Almost all . . . employ great care in breeding and improving the breeds. . . . If a traveler arrives, his horse is valued as soon as they see him." A later traveler commented upon the "horseyness" of the Bluegrass: "One drops into horse talk immediately on alighting from the train at Lexington, and does not emerge from it again till he takes his departure. It is the one subject always in order."

In testimony to the fact that the Bluegrass has produced superior horses, many horse and turf connoisseurs would probably cite the 1850-born colt Lexington as perhaps the greatest of all the early racers. At the end of his racing career he was retired to stud at Woodburn Farm in Woodford County, where he became an equally famous sire. Eventually, Lexington became blind and was given the respectful epithet "the blind hero of Woodburn." John Hervey, an equine historian known for his conservative evaluations, called Lexington "the most illustrious, the most historically significant, and in his influence as a progenitor, the most potent and far-reaching of American Thoroughbreds." Although Lexington died at the age of twenty-five, his skeleton continues to stand erect, encased in glass at the Smithsonian Institution.

A modern testimony to the pride and love modern Bluegrass residents have for their horses is a bumper sticker seen all over the Region: "Have You Hugged Your Horse Today?" Although it is an obvious parody, many Kentuckians do "hug" their horses, both figuratively and literally.

Since early settlement days, then, horses have been central to a traditional Bluegrass way of life. Today that way of life involves primarily the wealthy and privileged gentry, but it also affects a great many others, such as various professionals, business people, farm employees, and other working-class people. There are three basic categories of horse farms today: (1) full-scale operations where all facets of horse raising are carried out, including training; (2) commercial farms where training is often not undertaken; and (3) the newest type farm, the stallion-only or stud farm, where breeding is the principal activity. Most of these farms are gentleman farms. In 1980 Karl Raitz noted the considerable importance of today's gentleman farms and horse activities in the Bluegrass, saying that the "value of horses sold in Fayette County in 1969, for example, exceeded the total value of all farm products sold in three quarters of the counties of Kentucky." As Bluegrass horse scholar Edward L. Bowen observes:

Clearly we are no longer speaking of a pursuit having much economic similarity to the hobby of gentleman farmers of 200 years ago. . . . As figures have reached into six, seven, and even eight figures, the Kentucky horseman has become a businessman as well as a man of the land. . . . [and] thousands of Kentuckians are employed in ancillary roles. . . . In tradition, sentiment, and fiscal figures, the horse world *is* much of Kentucky.

Raitz further notes that the "gentleman farmer is also a sportsman. He has played a leading role in establishing sports associated with horses—the race, the trot, and the hunt." Of the many social activities, customs, and other traditions that have been created by horse people, racing was one of the first.

RACING

Even in the early settlement era, racing, for many Bluegrass residents, was the most popular recreation; and early primitive race courses or tracks were quickly established and races were held, sometimes even despite the possibility of imminent Indian attack. For instance, as early as 1788 the following notice appeared in Lexington's paper, *The Kentucky Gazette:*

> Notice is hereby given that several gentlemen propose a meeting
> at the
> CRAB ORCHARD on the 4th of JULY
> in perfect readiness to move early the next morning
> through the wilderness.
> As it is very dangerous on account of the Indians it is
> hoped each person will go well armed.

Even today, over good roads, Crab Orchard is about fifty miles from Lexington, so the difficult trip and the Indian threat were considerable prices to pay for a day of folk revelry and racing.

Street Racing   To indulge their passion for racing without traveling such distances, many early Bluegrass residents simply raced their horses up and down the main streets of towns. Racing took place on Lexington's Main Street, and also at "Humble's Path" in Harrodsburg, and on the streets of Georgetown, Paris, Frankfort, Versailles, Winchester, Danville, and other Inner Bluegrass towns. Many such early "racetracks"

Horse show day, Paris
1880s (Photo courtesy of
Kentucky Historical
Society)

resembled obstacle courses, since stumps often protruded from the dirt. During one such street race in 1795, in Nicholas County (then still part of Bourbon County), an arrogant Virginian appeared with a fine Thoroughbred and boasted he could outrun any Bluegrass horse around. Such a taunt was too much for Kentucky pride to swallow. Lawrence Thompson relates what happened:

The local gentry bet their worldly goods—mostly animal skins—that a ragged and barefoot lad from their community could ride two horses at once and beat the Virginian. Barely two hundred yards from the starting line one of the two horses had to leap a stump. The youthful stunt rider's equilibrium was upset but he was not thrown; and, in spite of this handicap, the two...horses soon overtook the Virginian and finished a full length ahead of him. In the midst of the general rejoicing over Kentucky's victory, the modest lad sneaked away.

That "modest lad" would later gain the laudatory nickname of "Old Stonehammer," and was none other than Thomas Metcalfe (discussed earlier), who as an adult became a stonemason and later governor and U. S. senator. No doubt Metcalfe's popularity was due in part to that legend. In fact, it was a tradition in the early Bluegrass that a man could not only gain respect but could also decisively win an ongoing argument by beating his opponent in a horse race.

Street racing was such a popular activity that a path for racing was designated in Lexington as early as 1780, and in 1789 the first public course, called Race Field, was laid out, bounded by Main, Georgetown, Third, and Jefferson Streets. Such races quickly became traditional; in Lexington, by 1791, a three-day racing meet was held every October. Such street races were subject to varying rules. For instance, in one type of race, each rider had to ride *someone else's* horse, and the *last* horse across the finish line won; consequently, each rider was compelled to race his mount to the utmost, in the hopes that his own horse would be last and thus win.

One of the local gentry in Jessamine County once sponsored a street race, stating the rules would allow "anything with four legs and hair on" to be entered. He had bought an expensive Thoroughbred racer in Virginia and wanted to show up the local talent; he set the purse at $50. It so happened that a farm boy had trained a bull to ride to saddle, and on the day of the race, he appeared with his bull and demanded that it be entered, according to the rules. Although the owner of the Thoroughbred objected, he lived up to his word and allowed the bull to be entered. At the start of the race, the farm boy immediately dug his spurs into the bull and blew a tin horn he was carrying, which caused the poor beast to emit a "dreadful bellow" and surge ahead, with the oxhide the boy had draped over him flapping furiously in the wind. All this so startled the horses that they bolted and ran off in every direction except the right one, and the bull easily crossed the finish line alone. Of course, everyone but the boy objected and demanded another heat, one in which the boy could not use the horn and had to remove the oxhide; the second heat also provided a $50 purse. Again the boy dug his spurs into the bull, this time so fiercely that the bull bellowed even more loudly, and the skittish horses bolted once again; and thus the boy and his bull won the second heat as well. With his $100 prize, it is said that the lad purchased blacksmithing equipment and, after working for many years, died in the 1860s at age eighty-five. Instead of money, sometimes the prize was the losing horse, or equine equipment, or—no small prize—a wagonload of tobacco.

Soon, however, the unpleasantness accompanying such folk revelries— dust and excrement created by the horses (and the crowds), the gambling and drinking, the noise, rowdiness, and even brawls—caused the town fathers to frown upon these licentious and boisterous proceedings, and in 1793 Lexington passed an ordinance banning street racing. The town did condescend, however, to allow horse owners and admirers to continue to use the "lower end" of an area called the "Commons" (Water Street), where stud horses could still be shown.

The Jockey Club   Not to be thwarted, disgruntled racing enthusiasts, in 1797, gathered at one of their favorite watering holes, Postlethwait's Tavern, and organized the Jockey Club, the first such esoterically specialized group in Kentucky. The Club's first act was to lay plans for a race course, which was built later that same year on ground now occupied by the serene and beautiful Lexington Cemetery. A circular grass track one mile in length, it was named Williams Race Track, and races were held there for the next twelve years. It is perhaps somehow fitting that many Bluegrass famous now lie in the very soil upon which their forebears raced their great Thoroughbreds, thus adding a literal meaning to the old Bluegrass saying, "All men are equal on and under the Turf." In thanks for the part Postlethwait's played in the formation of the Club and the Track, and for the convenience of wagerers, the first bets were for a time placed with the tavern.

The Kentucky Association   The next step in the establishment of racing as paramount in Kentucky was the formation of the Kentucky Association, on July 23, 1826, "to improve the breed of horses by encouraging the sports of the turf." One of the founders was Henry Clay, who—with four friends—bought a famous racehorse named Buzzard for $5,500 (perhaps the first syndicated Bluegrass stallion); the animal's pedigree filled a full newspaper column. Buzzard stood at stud at Ashland, Clay's estate, where in 1831 Clay built a private racetrack and started a breeding program. However, Clay, like nearly every early Bluegrass gentleman farmer, also raised other purebred stock. He is credited with having imported, in 1832, the first Catalonian jackass into Kentucky (Spanish jacks were the largest and finest available and produced excellent mules); and it is also believed that he imported the first Hereford cattle directly from England, and possibly even Merino sheep.

During much of the antebellum era, breeding of purebred livestock of all sorts was nearly as important in the Bluegrass as horse breeding. So proud were owners of their purebred livestock that many paid artists to paint their portraits—$60 for a horse, $40 for a bull, and $30 for a cow. At first the paintings were hung in the barns and stables, but soon they were promoted to the office, then to the home, where many were displayed on walls alongside family members' portraits. Such displays are a widespread tradition in the Region. Nevertheless, horses were most Bluegrass Kentuckians' true passion, reflected in the huge crowds attending the races.

From 1828 to 1834 the Kentucky Association purchased sixty-five acres of land, at what is now 5th and Race Streets in Lexington, and constructed a one-mile dirt track, grandstand, stables, and other buildings. The Kentucky Association track, which was used for racing for over 100 years, soon came to be better known throughout the racing world by its folk name "Chittlin' Switch." "Switch" refers to the railroad switch, where cars carrying horses were shunted onto the siding at the track. A "chittlin'" ("chitterling" in the dictionary) is made from the small intestines of the pig—a delicacy once especially relished among Kentucky's black population but also popular with white trainers, jockeys, and even owners. Chittlin' Switch was the site of county fairs and livestock shows as well as races. (The judges' stand was actually part of the cow pens.) One sportswriter charged that the track was "constructed strictly as an affront to whatever muse presides over architecture," and indeed it was poorly structured and ill maintained. This apparently did not bother the patrons—except in 1889 when a storm caused the roof to leak so much that water dripped into the patrons' whiskey glasses. Chittlin' Switch was the only track in the country to continue racing practically without interruption throughout the Civil War. Races were held regularly until 1933 when the Kentucky Association was dissolved; the track, the oldest in the United States, was razed in 1935.

Keeneland   That same year, an open meeting was held, convened by prominent local Bluegrass gentleman farmers. It drew over 200 horse people and turf enthusiasts. Leaders of the group formed the Keeneland Association, and went on to establish what would become perhaps the most traditional racetrack in the country: Keeneland, built on land that had been granted to the Keene family by Patrick Henry, five miles west of Lexington. Actually, construction of the track was begun several years earlier by John Oliver "Jack Keene" on a part of his old family estate on Versailles Pike. Intending it as a private track, Keene built a part of it each year—for eight or ten years—until his money ran out, after which the Keeneland Association purchased the property and completed the track, one of the fastest in America. From the start Keeneland has been a nonprofit operation and donates much of its earnings to charity, to education, and to research.

With over 25,000 in attendance and $535,497 wagered, Keeneland held its first race in October 1936, and it inaugurated both the Breeder's Stakes and the Ashland Stakes (named for Henry Clay's home). For a number of years the far end of Keeneland's grandstand constituted a segregated section for black patrons, an arrangement remembered well by one Bluegrass lady who as a young girl regularly attended the races. Her family's black cook, also an avid racing fan, was uncommonly adept at picking winners, so the girl would frequently seek out the cook in the black section to ask for tips. Always mindful of tradition—for instance, the track refuses even today to use an electrified public address system to call races—Keeneland in 1937 continued the Blue Grass Stakes, which had been held at the Kentucky Association Track (Chittlin' Switch) and which had been—and still is—an important preparatory race for the Kentucky Derby.* The iron gate posts at the entrance to Keeneland were salvaged from the track's predecessor, and the original "KA" emblem on the posts is now assumed as the Keeneland Association emblem. Even in modern times Keeneland has endeavored to maintain as many of the racing traditions of the past as possible, to keep racing a gentleman's sport, or, as the track is fond of saying, to keep "racing as it was meant to be." As one racing fan commented, Keeneland is "based on the idea that racing is a rather expensive amusement and not an avenue to sudden and undeserved riches."

The folklore of Thoroughbred racing is vast and varied, and would, no doubt, fill several volumes if fully documented, but a select sampling of such traditions can be recounted. Stories about famous horses are legion, including several illustrating the great "heart"—a folk term meaning stamina, and a never-say-die spirit—of Bluegrass horses.

LEGENDS OF THE TURF

One of the earliest of such stories concerns the famous Dare Devil, who was entered in an 1805 race at the crude track in Lexington. This track was so poorly laid out that in one spot a board fence was erected to warn jockeys of an approaching sharp turn. Booked in races at Frankfort the previous day, Dare Devil was ridden back to Lexington in the mud just in time to enter the field. However, he was not acquainted with the track, and when he came to the wooden fence, he simply jumped it as would an experienced hunter; the jockey then turned him around and made him jump it again, and Dare Devil still won the race by several lengths. A similar story, no doubt apocryphal, is often related about a Bluegrass mare in foal, racing at an out-of-state track where sentiment was against her in favor of local entries. The mare, being well ahead in the field at the backstretch, stopped to drop her foal; she then recovered and finished first, and her foal, the story continues, came in second.

A similar oft-related story—this one authentic—has become a legend among turf raconteurs. It concerns the unbeaten colt Graustark of historic Darby Dan Farm. Here is sports editor Billy Reed's eloquent version of the 1966 event:

*The famous Kentucky Derby—called the most exciting two minutes in sports—is held at equally famous Churchill Downs. The week-long pre-Derby festivities and the extravaganza at the track on Derby day—the first Saturday in May—are traditions of wide renown. However, because Churchill Downs is in Louisville, outside the Inner Bluegrass Region, neither it nor the Derby are discussed here as *Bluegrass* traditions. Many Bluegrass people do attend the Derby, but many others celebrate it at home.

He supposedly had the longest stride since Man O' War and the finest chance for a Triple Crown . . . since Citation in 1948. His final tuneup was . . . [Keeneland's] Blue Grass Stakes only nine days before the Run for the Roses in Louisville.

On an afternoon that was cold, wet and rainy, Graustark and jockey Braulio Baeza stepped onto a sloppy track that was about the same texture as the rich Kentucky burgoo sold by Keeneland's concession stands. He was such a prohibitive favorite that only two, Abe's Hope and Rehabilitate, had been entered . . . [as] token opposition, the smallest Blue Grass field since 1942.

As soon as the horses broke from the gate, the mighty Graustark began to draw powerfully away. On the backstretch, it looked as if his winning margin would easily surpass the six lengths that then was the stakes record. But then the unthinkable happened. Suddenly Graustark began to slow down. As he came into the turn for home, Abe's Hope came to him and they fought neck and neck, mud flying with every stride, down the stretch to the wire. The photo-finish . . . revealed that, in the last stride, Abe's Hope had a nose in front.

Only later was it learned that Graustark had run the last half-mile or so on a broken foot. Imagine that. Everytime his foot hit the slop, the pain had to be excruciating. Yet he still fought to the end, straining to win. That was his last race—but a young writer's introduction to why generations of Kentuckians have grown misty-eyed at the sight of a great thoroughbred. Even now, when asked to define the elusive element that makes this game special, a fellow's thoughts turn to Graustark . . . laboring through the mud at Keeneland on his broken foot. This is class. This is courage. This is racing.

Colonel Chinn   Almost as numerous as famous horse stories are tales about human heroes of the Bluegrass turf, such as the late Colonel Phil Chinn, who not only loved to raise and race horses but to buy and sell them as well. Reportedly, Chinn would go to any lengths to sell a horse, and he especially liked to sell to rich "Yankees;" his motto, he was quoted as saying, was "Let the Yankee Beware." He used to stay up all night entertaining potential buyers, and by morning, Chinn said, "You could sell them anything. They couldn't even *see* the horses." Colonel Chinn was basically an honest man, and yet the story most frequently related about him tends to cast a shadow on his reputation. The story concerns the allegation of his dubious sale, in 1901, of an "unraced two-year-old of royal lineage that couldn't outrun a fat man." The story recounts that Chinn had tried everything to make the colt into a racer, to no avail; so his only recourse was to find a gullible buyer, preferably a Yankee. At a restaurant Chinn supposedly met one of the wealthy New Yorkers who frequently visit the Bluegrass, eager to buy a potential stakes winner at a bargain price from some down-on-his-luck breeder; this one was looking for a two-year-old who could do three furlongs in thirty-five seconds, and he was willing to pay $50,000 for him. The

Colonel had an idea. His alleged conspiracy, according to the legend, is outlined by horsemen Jack Lohman and Arnold Kirkpatrick:

He told the wealthy New Yorker that he had just the horse for him and to be at his barn the next morning so he could show him off in a work at Keeneland. Promptly at six the Colonel's fish arrived ready for the hook. The colt, whose looks complemented his royal pedigree, pranced and showed off as he rounded the barn. . . . he bowed his neck and looked for all the world like a stakes horse. Col. Chinn had instructed the rider to make the colt look like a champion. And that he did. With two quick pops of the whip, he broke the colt off at the three-eighths and the colt worked a very rapid :34 3/5! After a hot breakfast in the track kitchen, the deal was made!

There were some comments by horsemen that the track must have been extremely fast that morning, because more than one two-year-old went three furlongs in 34 and faster! But the next day times were back to normal.

No one had even noticed that, at midnight . . . Col. Chinn and his groom had gone out to Keeneland [sic] and dug up the three-eighths pole and moved it a hundred feet closer to the finish line! [He moved it back, of course, that night after the sale.]

Buyer beware.

Though he was a shrewd horse trader, Chinn achieved great respect in the horse world, as had his father before him; in fact, Kentucky's first racing statute was called the Chinn Act, after "Black Jack," Phil's father. Of the young Chinn, one horseman says, "Bluegrass farmers should erect a monument to Colonel Chinn. By creating a market for yearlings, he took more tobacco farmers from behind the plow than the International tractor." Consequently, many Bluegrass horsemen did not believe the Colonel could stoop to such unscrupulous shenanigans as outlined in the above legend. Therefore, just five days after the alleged event (embellished versions of the story were already widely circulated), horsemen formed a committee of inquiry, as outlined by horse scholar Kent Hollingsworth:

It is about time to put to rest—again—this canard about the colonel. During more than half a century . . . Chinn bought and sold more horses than any man who ever turned a blade of bluegrass. He dealt . . . in horses . . . in five figures during an era when a stakes-class horse could be purchased for $2,000. He traded with . . . people in many countries, and . . . the financial arrangements usually were intricate. . . . *Caveat emptor* in horse trading was more widely understood and buyer and seller grappled for the best hold. "In truth," Col. Chinn said shortly before his death in 1962, "I did not always reveal my full knowledge of the animal [to be sold]. . . ." Chinn did not, however, cause the three-eighths pole at . . . [Chittlin' Switch] to be moved 44 feet and three inches closer to the finish line on Oct. 24, 1901, according to the findings of an investigating committee made up of the most prominent horsemen in Kentucky.

The committee discovered that the real culprit was one Dan O'Brien, an Irish trainer who, acting as agent, sold the colt and pocketed (allegedly) a handsome profit for the ruse. In his testimony, however, O'Brien implicated Chinn as an accessory—a charge which Chinn described as "an absolute lie, and is as base a lie as could come out of the foulest mouth that lives." Evidently, O'Brien, relying upon Chinn's reputation and contacts, told the Colonel he had a good colt for sale for $10,000, and worked the colt for Chinn (after having previously moved the pole in question, unbeknown to Chinn). Duly impressed by the colt's performance, Chinn told his father who, as a favor, called a buyer in New York to tell him a fast Bluegrass colt was for sale, but in fact the New Yorker never bought the colt.

Trickster Tales   This widely circulated legend reveals several truths about folklore. After nearly ninety years, although long since disproved, the story is still being told, attesting to the tenacity of tradition, even in the face of conflicting evidence. As in much oral folklore, the "facts" vary with the teller and the version. However, folklorists realize that with such tales it is often neither the veracity of the teller nor the historical accuracy of the information that accounts for the tale's longevity. Instead, its social and psychological *function* is often the principal motivating factor in the story's popularity. This particular kind of story is called a trickster tale. In such tales, the local culture hero (here Colonel Chinn) always plays pranks or tricks on, or otherwise outwits, those from an outside culture—particularly those outsiders who consider themselves superior to the locals. Frequently pompous, arrogant, overbearing, and condescending in their demeanor, such outsiders are often perceived as attempting to "take" what they consider to be the "ignorant" or "backward" locals; in a trickster tale, however, it is always the outsider who is disgracefully "taken." The main reason this tale exists, therefore, is not to slander Colonel Chinn or to recount historical "facts," but to bolster local self-esteem. The tale's popularity stems from the fact that Chinn, as a Bluegrass folk hero, outwits an outsider who, in the opinion of those telling and hearing the tale, probably would have cheated Chinn given the opportunity. That Chinn cheats him first is incidental. Chinn is the "good old boy" local folk hero and representative of all locals who hear and tell the story; and it is his shrewdness in outsmarting the New York city slicker that both tellers and hearers relish and vicariously share, and this accounts for the popularity of the story. The tale's implied message is: We Bluegrass people are not the backward hicks New Yorkers and Yankees think we are; in fact, we usually outsmart all of you when the chips are down.

Such trickster tales, on all sorts of topics, abound in the Bluegrass, and throughout Kentucky. Probably they flourish, in part at least, because Kentuckians have frequently been victims of negative stereotypes. Some of the gentry find the "mint julep on the veranda" stereotype humorous, and some find it offensive, but it is widespread and popular and has led to innumerable folk anecdotes, such as this one regularly told among South Carolina horse people:

A wealthy Kentucky breeder was entertaining a member of the British nobility, also a horseman, at his farm. It was a bland spring afternoon, and instead of taking his visitor from stall to stall, or field to field, the Kentuckian ordered the grooms to lead the broodmares and yearlings past the front porch, where they could be inspected from the comfort of a chair. If you've ever been in Kentucky, you know what happened next. A man in white coat appeared, bearing two juleps, with straws and mint sticking out of them.

"You know, sir," said the host, as he settled back to sip, "the greatest pleasures in life are thoroughbred horses and good whiskey."

"A very sound thought," said the visitor, "though I imagine that in England the preference would be for a high tea and a good fast cricket match."

Out on the lawn a groom holding a broodmare turned wondering to another.

"Do you suppose," he said slowly, "that neither of them gentlemens has heard of women and watermelon?"

Such folk anecdotes, like trickster tales, simultaneously reveal how ridiculous stereotypes are, and therefore help to dispel them. In actuality, life on a modern horse farm demands, as one horseman says, "thirty-five hours a day, eight days a week;" all Englishmen do not revere cricket; and all blacks do not like watermelon. As for financial rewards, one of the best storytellers in the horse business had a favorite joke about its economic difficulties: "It's easy to make a small fortune raising Thoroughbreds. . . . Just start with a large fortune."

TRICKS OF THE TRADE

Just as many shenanigans were used to sell horses, over the years numerous traditional strategies have been employed to gain a racing advantage. Official rules, controls, and regulations are now so thorough and sophisticated, however, that most such methods and devices can no longer be used. In earlier times, according to those who have spent their lives in turf pursuits, using *any* trick or device to gain an advantage was "just accepted." Many trainers used batteries to give horses a slight charge just before the race, thinking it would increase the animal's speed. Drugs were commonly used, and even today, on occasion, attempts to drug a horse are made, but most fail, thanks to a variety of detection tests, such as those given after a race in the "spit box," the area where test specimens are drawn from horses.

A widespread custom for many trainers is to "daylight" exceptional horses—that is, to get up long before daylight to work the horse before anyone else, including the clocker, arrives at the track, in hopes of keeping the horse's distance times a secret. The old practice of substituting a better horse—one that closely resembled the horse entered in a race—is now precluded by modern foolproof identification procedures, principally the Jockey Club's requirement that all Thoroughbreds receive a permanent tattoo on the inside upper lip. In addition, many tracks photograph the vestigal toe—a growth on every horse's lower inside leg, called a chestnut or night eye, which serves as a kind of fingerprint. Prior to these modern means of identification, substitutes were used so often that the practice gave rise to terms such as "horse of another color," "dark horse," and "ringer"—all still heard today, although not usually in their original sense. Modern photography has also precluded many jockey tricks, such as crowding another rider into the rail or even hitting one another with whips.

Horse Mascots   One trick, aimed at gaining an advantage prior to the race, gave rise to the folk expression "to get your goat." Thoroughbreds hate to be alone, and over the years it was discovered that, for some inexplicable reason, they particularly like to have goats around, even in their stalls. Thus many owners shipped their Thoroughbreds' goats to the track to keep the high-strung horses pacified. It became apparent that one way to excite your opponent's horse and put him off his form was to steal his mascot—thus "to get your goat" meant, and still means, to upset someone so that he is vulnerable. Other favorite mascots for Thoroughbreds are ponies, cats and dogs, and even game or fighting cocks and chickens.

A poignant example of this buddy system occurred when Peanuts, the pony mascot for a horse named Exterminator, died unexpectedly. The Thoroughbred refused to eat for two days, so, to convince him that Peanuts would not be there any longer, the pony's remains were put in the stall with him overnight; it was only after Exterminator lay with his head across his dead friend's body all night that he finally accepted that Peanuts was gone. Exterminator started to eat, soon received another pony mascot, and lived to a ripe old age.

According to another old racing custom, whenever a trainer fails to have a horse in the money for an entire meet, it is traditional that the track management present him with a duck. The custom supposedly began at a track with an infield lake that had ducks on it; the track gave one of the ducks to an out-of-the-money trainer so he wouldn't "starve."

Originally meant to be a joke, it became a tradition, and is sometimes still followed, for luck.

Courting Lady Luck   In addition to these customs and tricks of the trade, a great number of superstitions and taboos have been employed through the years to curry favor with Lady Luck. Many of those connected with a horse in a race—owners, trainers, jockeys, and grooms alike—refuse to have their photographs taken prior to the race. Some even refrain from talking with other people except their racing team. Others keep their fingers crossed until the race is over. Some believe particular actions will either elicit good luck or avert bad luck. To kill a cricket in a horse stall, especially in the stallion barn, will bring bad luck, so grooms gently shoo them out instead. Brooms used at one track should not be taken to the next track, and the handles of the old brooms should be broken when you leave. Some people either eat, or refrain from eating, certain foods on race day.

Many horse people, especially jockeys, fear the number 13. At the 1932 Derby, the jockey assigned to ride Colonel Bradley's Burgoo King (see Chapter 16) discovered that the horse not only carried the number 13 but had also drawn the thirteenth starting position—double jeopardy. The jockey talked the jockey of Forward Pass into switching mounts for the famed race. Burgoo King won; Forward Pass finished nineteenth. (This would seem to indicate that the superstition is not valid; however, only three horses at the thirteenth pole position have ever won the Derby.)

As a precaution against getting thrown, superstitious jockeys often toss their new silks on the dirty ground—so as not to tempt fate with an immaculate outfit. Many jockeys, owners, and trainers take it amiss if their horse is the Derby favorite—they say it would jeopardize his chances of winning.

Good luck charms and techniques abound, of course. Sometimes a bettor will put a silver coin in his shoe before going to the track. An untold number of systems will help pick a winner—some as bizarre as using color schemes of silks or colors of the horses, or complicated numerical tabulations to determine if the horse and the bettor have sympathetic equations. Some schemes have even been computerized. Yet, perhaps the best scheme is that followed by what turf fans sometimes call "stoopers"—ticket scavengers who, stooping over to sift through the piles of discarded tickets on the floor, hope to find a winning ticket some careless or ignorant bettor has discarded; the stoopers often fare rather well.

Popular with nonhorse people the world over is the ancient belief in the efficacy of the horseshoe, always to be hung with the open end up "so the luck will not run out." Ask most Bluegrass horsemen about the horseshoe's powers of good luck, however, and the pragmatic reply will probably be: "The only 'lucky' horseshoes are those on the horse that wins the race"—a common Bluegrass expression. A popular local Bluegrass trickster tale, related here by Lawrence Thompson, concerns Man O' War's black groom, Will Harbut, who supposedly sold hundreds of the great stallion's "authentic" horseshoes to gullible tourists.

During Man O' War's declining years his inseparable companion was a colorful Negro, Will Harbutt [sic]. Will was something of a financial genius as well as a skilled horse trainer. He would spot a particularly fanatical admirer of Big Red [the legendary Thoroughbred's nickname] and would sidle up to him, murmuring, "Look here what I is got, Boss."

"Great Scott, man, that looks like one of his racing plates [shoes]! What do you want for it?"

Will would look down at the ground and shift his feet and reply: "I don't know, boss. I is jest a poor ol' nigger that never had much money. . . ."

Almost invariably the tourist would whip out his wallet and say, "Here take these two tens and let me have that shoe. That ought to be a fair price."

Today there are enough of Man O' War's racing plates hanging on the walls of turf fans to build a new grandstand at Keeneland. But Will never sold the real article.

BIG RED

One "real article"—a shoe Man O' War actually did wear in his last race—is displayed, along with shoes of other greats, at Keeneland; ironically, however, Big Red never raced on a Bluegrass track. Will Harbut loved Man O' War and called him the "mostest hoss in the world," his ultimate epithet, and claimed that being Big Red's groom was the most important job in the world, one he preferred even to being President. Big Red was equally fond of his constant companion; a charming picture of Will hugging Big Red appeared on the cover of a 1941 issue of *Saturday Evening Post*. It is not surprising that Will and the great horse died just weeks apart, in 1947. Will always kept a ledger for visitors to sign when they came to see Man O' War, and at his death there were sixty-three ledgers, with 1,323,000 names of people from all over the world. The famous champion was often treated more like a human than a horse, and was even given birthday parties with cakes, flowers, and guests. His twenty-first birthday party (in 1938) was even broadcast on the radio for all his many fans to enjoy, one of whom was Kentucky's governor, "Happy" Chandler, who commented that at long last Man O' War was old enough to vote so things were bound to get better. For many

Man O' War at his twenty-first birthday party, held by his groom, Will Harbut (Photo courtesy of The Blood-Horse archives)

of his fans, Big Red and his groom Will typified the Bluegrass. For the Bluegrass horse world, they were idols to be emulated. Big Red lives on in his progeny—what horsemen call his "get"—and Will's son became a groom in his father's image.

Man O' War also lives today in Bluegrass legend because of his highly elaborate funeral. When an expensive stallion dies, it is the custom to bury only his head, his heart, and his testicles—those parts considered most symbolically representative of his fame. However, Big Red was so beloved the owners could not bring themselves to dissect him; instead, they accorded him an open-casket funeral. He was the first horse to be embalmed, requiring twenty-three bottles of fluid (a human body needs only two), and he was the first horse to lie in state—for two days, so mourners, numbering in the thousands, could pay their respects. Left open so the remains could be viewed, his custom-built, solid-oak casket measured 6 feet tall, 10 wide, 3 ½ deep, and was lined with the yellow and black racing colors of Faraway Farm, where the great stallion was buried. It required thirteen farm hands, using a homemade sling, to lower the body into the casket; a derrick then moved the gigantic casket to the viewing site and lowered it into the grave. The base of the gravestone was of New Hampshire granite on which was placed a bronze life-size statue by French sculptor Herbert Haseltine. Flanked by sixteen pin oaks and thirty pyramidal hornbeams, one hornbeam for each year of Big Red's life, the grave was surrounded by a 10-foot moat and a circular

Bedford-stone wall. Wearing the farm's racing colors, the local American Legion post—called the Man O' War Post—played taps, and at least six notable dignitaries delivered eulogies. Though many more had come to see him lying in state, over 2,000 also attended the funeral service, and many filed by and patted Big Red as they had when he was alive. Many mourners, judging from photos of the funeral, were black—present, perhaps, to show their respect for the gentle, talented Will Harbut as much as for the famous horse. Page Cooper and Roger Treat summarize the feelings the great horse aroused in many: "Man O' War was dead, but the fact that his body lay under a granite slab in a Kentucky pasture made little difference. He already had become a legend, a part of the folk history of great Americans."

Today, Man O' War's gravesite has been moved and occupies the place of honor at the Kentucky Horse Park. No other horse has ever been accorded such obsequies, or been remembered so fervently for so long.

THE MEN WHO WORK THE HORSES

One of the oldest traditions of the gentry—dating back to the settlement era, when slavery provided free labor—was to have black grooms and trainers for prized horses. Once racing was established, blacks became jockeys as well. Aristides, the winner of the first Kentucky Derby in 1875, was ridden by a black jockey named Oliver Lewis, and of the fifteen jockeys in that inaugural Derby, fourteen were black. Over the years, eleven Derby winners have had black jockeys, the last being James Winkfield, who won in both 1901 and 1902. Seven of these early Derby-winning black jockeys were from Lexington.

Some blacks were also trainers; in fact Kingman, the horse on which famous black jockey Isaac Murphy won the Derby in 1891, also had a black trainer, Dudley Allen, a former slave who fought in the Civil War and after the conflict "made a lot of money training horses." One black trainer, Ed Brown, whose nickname was "Brown-Dick," was considered by some of his peers as "the greatest trainer of all time, white or black"; he was born a slave and was bought by "Lord" Alexander, one of the more noteworthy gentry-horsemen. Apparently, once freed, Brown-Dick owned horses himself, among them Ben-Brush, one of the greatest sires in this country. "All of the hosses that's high class has Ben-Brush's blood in 'em—Sea Biscuit for instance," claimed one of Brown's peers, who also said Brown "trained the first hoss to run a mile and a quarter in 2:07," a "record that stood for about twenty-five years." Clearly, as others have noted, black trainers and jockeys played a significant role in the early Bluegrass horse culture. Yet, more blacks were employed as grooms than in any other job, as even a cursory examination of the horse tradition will reveal. For instance, most grooms shown leading a horse in *Country Estates of the Blue Grass*, published in 1902, are black.

Good Hands   Black grooms were joined at the track by some of the innumerable Irish immigrants to the Region, the greatest number of whom came during and after the Potato Famine in the 1840s and 1850s; few became jockeys, but at the track many became "hot-walkers"—stable hands who, to cool a horse down slowly after a race or workout, walk the animal and intermittently hose him down with water. Although some believe that it was an "innate love for animals" that led many Irish to work with horses in America, local Bluegrass horse people offer two other explanations why both blacks and Irish excel in handling horses: both have "silver tongues" with soothing, musical, reassuring voices, and both have "good hands." In fact, according to two general managers of prestigious Bluegrass horse farms, having good hands is almost *the* prime requisite for *any* horseman; moreover, they claim that someone who does not have good hands can, in a few minutes, ruin months of work with a high-strung Thoroughbred. Thoroughbreds often possess a nervous disposition and are full of fear and apprehension of anything strange or new. Evidently, the success of both blacks and Irish as early grooms was due, at least in part, to their gentle, caring, soft-spoken, and reassuring control over their temperamental charges.

Today neither blacks nor Irish are involved in Bluegrass horse activities to any appreciable extent. Blacks first left the farms during and after the Civil War, and poor whites, some of them no doubt Irish, took over many black positions in the Bluegrass. Ranks of both black and Irish horsemen were further depleted during the two World Wars; when they returned, most former horsemen sought other work, often using skills they learned in the military. According to modern Bluegrass horsemen, the few black horse people who remained tended to drift away from the horse business during the Civil Rights era. Today, few of them seek jobs as horsemen.

Horse farm jobs that were in former times held by blacks and Irish and later by white males are today on occasion filled by women, some of whom have assumed important roles. Calumet Farm, for example, has a woman vet and a woman in charge of the breeding shed—roles that are traditionally filled by men and crucial to the success of the farm.

Most modern blacks, like most whites, are too tall and heavy to be jockeys, so more and more jockeys are of Hispanic descent or from the rural Deep South, where common people have been less well-nourished and thus have grown up with small, lightweight frames. A number of jockeys come from the Louisiana bayous, a region which has a long-standing tradition of "country" horse racing, where youngsters begin racing at age eight or nine and become experienced jockeys at the numerous rural tracks.

No doubt because both were on the lower ends of the socioeconomic scale and often lived in close proximity, there evidently was some occasional miscegenation between blacks and Irish. In the Bluegrass the most famous product of such union was Isaac Burns Murphy, a "black" jockey with an Irish name, who proved that selective breeding evidently works with jockeys as well as Thoroughbreds. His expert handling of them, on the ground or in the saddle, was renowned, an ability some might credit to his inherited black/Irish folk traits of gentleness, a smooth tongue, and love of animals. Breaking many records in his time, Murphy raced from 1875 to 1895, winning 628, or 44.5 percent, of his races, including three Kentucky Derbies, four American Derbies in Chicago, and five Latonia Derbies. Murphy rode with long stirrups, as was the fashion in his day, and rarely used a whip on his mounts. A man of unimpeachable honesty, Murphy had a national reputation as a gentleman. During one race, his horse fell over another that was down, and Murphy, though injured himself, pulled the other jockey off the track to safety. Murphy's talent and reputation earned him the ultimate honor in the Bluegrass: a grave near the remains of Man O' War at the entrance to the Kentucky Horse Park. He is truly a Bluegrass folk hero.

STANDARDBRED AND SADDLEBRED

Not to be outdone by Thoroughbred racing, Standardbred and Saddlebred enthusiasts, in 1875, under the auspices of the Kentucky Agricultural & Mechanical Association, built a race course and elaborate grandstand as part of a new Lexington fairgrounds complex, where fairs, shows, carnivals, circuses, and all sorts of other folk festivals and events have been held continuously ever since. This has been, for instance, the site of two traditional fairs in the Region: the Bluegrass Fair (still held) and the Colored Fair (no longer held). The Junior League Horse Show, begun in 1937 and now the largest outdoor horse show in the country, has also been held at this fairgrounds.

As it is in many Bluegrass activities, tradition is respected and perpetuated in the numerous horse shows in the Region, which are held at least annually in nearly all Bluegrass towns, often in conjunction with the traditional county fair. In part because the Saddlebred horse was developed in the Region, the term "horse show" has a different meaning in the Bluegrass from similar affairs in other parts of the country; it usually refers to the exhibiting and judging of Saddlebred horses for their spectacular beauty of form and gaits and their easy-riding qualities. As racing tended to dominate Lexington fairgrounds activities, in 1892 fairgrounds control was transferred to the Kentucky Trotting Horse Breeders Association, and in 1942 it was put under control of the Kentucky Trots Breeders Association and came to be called by its folk name, the Red Mile. In 1893, what has come to be the oldest traditional harness stakes race in America, the Kentucky Futurity, was established here. Today, the principal racing events are the fall and spring trotting meets, and the Red Mile, with its packed-clay track, enjoys a reputation in racing circles as the most traditional and fastest such course in the country.

Of the many record-breaking trotters, Nancy Hanks, of the Gay Nineties era—today buried on the Madden farm, Hamburg Place—was one of the Region's most admired. An amusing story is often told about her, as recorded by Bradley Smith:

Old-timers among the trotting fraternity tell the story of how a group of lady sightseers came to Lexington to see the historic sights and to visit the antebellum houses.... [Hearing that] Nancy Hanks was buried nearby...they inquired... [and] were given directions to proceed four miles east of town on the Winchester Pike. The ladies arrived at Hamburg Place and laid their wreath upon the grave of the...trotting mare, *Nancy Hanks*. Upon returning, one of the ladies remarked, "Those crazy Kentuckians paid an unusual honor to Mr. Lincoln's mother. They put a circle of monuments shaped like a horseshoe around it and a lovely statue of a horse over her grave!"

By the time they discovered their embarrassing mistake many versions of the story were already being circulated.

Many of the same traditions representative of Thoroughbred racing, especially in the form of superstitions, tricks of the trade, and methods for gaining an advantage, are also present at the trots, though with some differences. One common method to gain an advantage is to "stiff" in a race; a driver deliberately holds his horse back, either to increase the odds in later races or to get the horse placed in a lower class, where it has a better chance of winning; this is usually done with either chronically ill or poorly performing horses. The formal restrictions are upheld and maintained by most drivers, but some people do give trotters medications. Some are "jugged"—injected in the jugular vein—with vitamins, and even though state law requires that the procedure be performed by a vet, some small stables do it themselves to save money.

There is a class division, and sometimes friction, between Standardbred and Thoroughbred horse people; as a Thoroughbred horsewoman said, "They go their way and we go ours." Some Thoroughbred people label Standardbreds with the derogatory epithet "jugheads"—a reference to jugging, which Thoroughbred people dislike. Purses tend not to be large at trotting tracks, and expenses of buying, raising, and maintaining a good trotter or pacer are high. When feed and grain costs increase incrementally but purses remain constant, owners will often turn to traditional shortcuts to win.

As in Thoroughbred racing, most trots people feel they are "almost like a separate community," and they value honesty and integrity above all characteristics, along with horse "savvy" and a winner, and the money and prestige that accompany it.

HORSE WORLD FASHIONS AND CUSTOMS

Racing and horse activities in the Bluegrass quickly became "fashionable," especially for the ladies, as they increasingly used the gatherings as opportunities to display their newest fashions, garner the latest gossip, and set the newest trend. Joe Jordan describes the wife of a Gay Nineties playboy:

Lexington old-timers still grope for words ... to describe the loveliness of the flashing dark-eyed girl, who ... actually sat in a box at the Lexington Trots and smoked a cigarette—the first time a scandalous thing had ever been done in public in the conservative old center of culture [Lexington]. Women were shocked—and men quit watching the races.

When one considers that in 1900 an actress was committed to the psychiatric ward at Bellevue for smoking cigarettes, it is no wonder that the staid old Athens of the West was aghast at this new female effrontery. In more modern times, another nearly scandalous event occurred at the Lexington Trots when a horse named Fuzzy-Wuzzy, the entry of a prominent horsewoman, had to be withdrawn from the race. The crowd roared when the loudspeaker blared the announcement: "Mrs. [So-and-so] scratched her Fuzzy-Wuzzy." Also, it was at Chittlin' Switch, as tradition has it, that a woman hung her silk purse at the finish line to be collected by the winner, thus giving rise to the term "purse" for the winner's reward. For years no fashionable woman would attend the Derby without the obligatory new spring hat and white gloves, and many women still feel they would not be properly attired for the "Run For the Roses" without them.

Coaching in the Bluegrass   Possession of a fancy carriage quickly became de rigueur for antebellum Bluegrass gentry, as noted by Squire Coleman:

Every farmer or planter had his elegant carriage and his one-horse buggy for himself, while the younger members of his family were well supplied with horses and ponies "to use when their inclination leads them to gallop uncontrolled from one neighbor's house to the other." Some of the well-to-do folks "around Lexington had coaches and carriages that cost one thousand dollars." Of the costly equipages, the two-horse victoria and barouche were status symbols of the rich, driven by an aged Negro coachman in livery who felt to the fullest degree the importance of his white folks family.

Many an early gentleman farmer who owned a good trotter or pacer drove it himself in the trials. One of the first wealthy absentee-owners was August Belmont I, first president of the Jockey Club, whose successful Nursery Stud (established 1885) was (long after Belmont's death) the birthplace of Man O' War. Hester Wilson remembers the arrival of the absentee-owner Harkness family to its Walnut Hall estate in the early twentieth century, heralded by a bugle announcing the approach of the tallyho long before it came into sight:

Four well-matched horses prance[d] by, driven by a coachman in the regalia of a Buckingham guard—tall silk hat, red coat with shining brass buttons, white trousers, and polished boots. The footman swung from the rear step, and it was he who blew the bugle ever so often, so that the silvery tones wafted far across the countryside and were heard several miles away.

Outings and Impromptu Races   During the early 1900s, groups of carriage riders would meet at Fayette Park in Lexington and then drive out to the country together for an afternoon's outing, a recreation also enjoyed in other Bluegrass towns. Courting was carried out in the buggy, much as the car is used today, and some of the favorite lover's lanes were the Region's covered bridges, where "sparking" was sheltered from view. This gave covered bridges the name "kissing bridges." Other similarities between buggies and cars are numerous. After church on Sunday, members of the congregation would challenge one another to a race, often up and down in front of the church. If one buggy passed another on the way home, it was often considered an affront and a challenge to race—often all the way home. A Jessamine County resident tells a story about her mother, who was driving a buggy home from church and passed a buggy driven by a man, which made him angry; so she hurled the traditional challenge at him, "Come on let's go," and they raced the entire eight miles to town. Even stagecoaches raced one another over early Bluegrass roads, the drivers egged on by their passengers, who reportedly would not tolerate another coach passing them. To this day, many Bluegrass drivers do not like to be passed on the highway—a dangerous pattern—and visitors often comment how frequently local drivers accelerate when someone attempts to pass (such auto driving patterns are often regionally peculiar manifestations of unconsciously learned normative behavior). These early spontaneous races were also precursors to the modern custom of "dragging," "playing chicken" and so on, in which Bluegrass youth challenge each other in sophisticated steel "buggies" all over country lanes. Many of these cars and pickups are what I call "high-riders," as they are raised off the ground with custom undercarriages and gigantic wheels, some so high as to require a ladder to get in and out. The making, racing, and displaying of these customized modern "carriages" is a widespread folk activity in the Region.

Another early precursory practice was the custom of driving one's favorite horse and buggy up and down the streets and around selected areas of town. In Bourbon County one lady remembers that a local sweet shop was the favorite place for buggy riders to congregate. Today, it is called cruising, and is, of course, done in cars, especially ones with sophisticated sound systems and other electronics. As in earlier times, the favorite locations to cruise are still eating places, especially fast-food restaurants, and, a close second, a shopping-center parking lot, especially at night after the stores close.

However, in Kentucky, horse racing is still the premier sport. The main purpose of horse races, in addition to the sheer joy of either riding them or watching them run, is to prove that one's horse is better bred, better raised, and better trained than others, which in turn implies that the owner is a superior horseman. The purse at a big race is often considerable, and yet prestige, pride, and reputation constitute rewards that are, for most modern Bluegrass gentry, equally important. Consequently, in the always uncertain business of breeding Thoroughbreds, Standardbreds, and Saddlebreds, many tried-and-true methods, procedures, and activities have become traditional. The degree of belief in such methods, and the likelihood of their continuation, is often in direct proportion to the degree of success attained when they are used. Acceptance and use of such traditional methods is also often directly related to two other factors: the lack of scientific applications available for necessary recurring, cyclical horse farm operations; and the degree of uncertainty and presence of risk—consequently the necessity of having "luck" and tradition on your side.

Traditional Horse Farm Procedures

According to English tradition, the birthday for all Thoroughbreds is set at January 1. Racing in England ended in the fall and did not resume until spring, so the idle period between meets was chosen to advance the ages of the horses. In 1833 the American Jockey Club decided to follow the English example. Thus, no matter when a foal is actually born—even during the last few days of December, as is sometimes the case—on New Year's Day, it becomes one year old.* Many people see this traditional date as the source of a number of problems, particularly with regard to the sale of yearlings.

THE BREEDING CYCLE

A mare's normal gestation period is 342 days and her natural heat cycles—lasting from eighteen to twenty-one days—usually occur from about April until August. If she conceives, she will drop her foal in the spring and summer months when weather is agreeable. This means that late foals, which will officially become one year old on January 1, are nonetheless often not sufficiently developed to bring a good price at the preferred yearling sales the following July. Moreover, many horse people harbor the folk belief that "the earlier the foal the better the foal," although this has never been scientifically substantiated. In any event, many farms endeavor in various ways—some scientific, some folk—to get the mare in heat and bred in time to foal as early as possible.

Formerly, the traditional breeding season extended from about February 15 to June 15 and was attuned to nature, that being the time of year when most mares come into heat, the stallion's sperm becomes more active, and the weather is conducive to breeding for a spring foal. Left to breed in accord with natural rhythms, however, a mare's foaling date gets

---

*Apparently the only exception to this tradition was Man O' War, whose groom, Will Harbut, claimed was "the onlyest horse to have a birthday"—March 29.

a little later each year, thus making it increasingly difficult to get her in foal; this is one reason horses have the lowest reproduction rate of nearly all domestic animals. In fact, Jockey Club records reveal that only a little more than 50 percent of mares bred the previous year have foals registered, indicating that a great number of farms do not get their mares in foal. The economics of a modern horse farm require that 75–80 percent of the mares should foal each year if the farm is to survive. Bluegrass horsemen say that most good farms in the Region average about 85 percent; the two principal farms used in this research, Claiborne and Darby Dan, maintain an in-foal rate of 92 percent and 91 percent respectively. In an attempt to emulate such success, many farms have extended the breeding season, some beginning as early as January 15, and others—believing a late foal is better than no foal at all—breed as late as July 15. In this instance, folk belief—that early foals are superior—coincides with economic necessity; that is, successful modern horse farms must endeavor, one way or another, to get as many mares as possible in foal each year, and the earlier the better.

Every spring mares from around the world are shipped to the Bluegrass to be bred to famous sires.* Thus a stallion has to service a high number of mares—often two, or even three, every day—so every effort is made to get a mare in foal as soon as possible. Many are bred on the first heat after delivering the current year's foal, called the foal heat or the nine-day heat period. Therefore, counting the 342-day gestation period, it is possible—but not often probable—to get a mare in foal again 351 days from her last breeding. Even if she is in heat, however, it is often pure luck for the mare to conceive with the first "cover"—a term derived from the fact that the stallion "covers" the mare's back with his body during breeding. With so many mares being "booked"—the term for a breeding date—to just a few stallions, and as many popular stallions have full "books" all season, the importance of obtaining conception during the first cover is understandable. The breeding schedule, especially with much-touted stallions, often becomes a hectic juggling act for the secretaries, farm manager, and stallion manager. Often five or more mares, scheduled to be serviced by the same stallion, are in heat and ready to ovulate at the same time. Although a mare may be in heat from eighteen to twenty-one days, the most advantageous time to breed her is twenty-four hours prior to ovulation, which makes the booking job even more exacting. Artificial insemination obviates some of the uncertainty but is used only with Standardbreds and Saddlebreds, not Thoroughbreds. In endeavors to have some managerial control over the Thoroughbred's

---

*One horseman repeated a prevalent superstition: "Never ship 'em with salt in the van—that's bad luck."

natural reproductive rhythms, many horse farms use a combination of folk and scientific methods.

Teasing the Mares   To ascertain when and at what stage a mare is in heat, horsemen have for generations used a procedure called teasing the mares, or simply teasing. This involves exposing the mare to a "teaser"—a male horse, usually of inferior grade, whose nearness can arouse sexual excitement in a "ready" female—and assessing her reactions to his presence. Teasing, however, is not as simple as it might appear. In fact, most Bluegrass horsemen consider the teasing program to be the most crucial activity of a successful breeding operation, one to be conducted only by dedicated, experienced employees who are familiar with both the mares and the teaser. Most farm managers appoint their best people to do the teasing and keep them in that job year in and year out.

A teaser can be any male horse that is not unruly; most farms use stallions, but a gelding that has been shot full of male hormones will sometimes work as well. Many farms prefer either very large or very small stallions as teasers, since they have more difficulty actually entering a normal-size mare—something no teaser is ever allowed to do. Thus, a number of farms even use Shetland pony stallions, and at least one farm uses a sterile stallion—said, in folk parlance, to "shoot blanks"—just in case. Since the teaser will visit—often every day during breeding season—numerous mares, the vast majority of whom will be anestrous (not in heat) and therefore prone to kick, bite, and otherwise assault him, no expensive Thoroughbred stallion is ever used as a teaser; he could easily be injured in his duties of courting and titillating the temperamental mares. To put up with the frustrations and the often violent rejections, a teaser must be calm, easy to handle, and even sophisticated in performing his courting duties. One of the teasers I watched stood out as easily the best; the head teasing man said of him, "He knows *exactly* what he's doing."

The teasing procedure is carried out daily during the breeding season. It is almost always an early-morning routine, and is performed in one of two ways: out-of-doors using a teasing "bar" or "chute," which is merely a reinforced section of fence outside the broodmare barns, usually padded with rubber or other material to protect the horses; or inside the barn, the teaser taken from stall to stall.

In the outdoor method, the teaser is put on a lead and taken to every barn on the farm where there are mares to be teased; to get from barn to barn the teaser usually trots alongside the teasing men's vehicle while the man on the passenger side holds his lead out the window. The mares are brought out from the barn one at a time and led over to the teasing bar, behind which, on the inside of the paddock, stands the teaser, still held on his lead by the head teasing man. The helper backs the mare up to the teasing bar, and the teaser puts his head over the fence and endeavors to nibble, smell, and brush his head against the mare's rump, at which overture the mare will respond one way or the other depending upon her state of readiness to be bred. If not in heat, she will most often nicker loudly, sometimes laying her ears back—a signal to watch out— and frequently kick backward at the stallion even though he is on the other side of the fence (hence the padded, reinforced bar). If she is in heat, she will, in the teasing men's parlance, "stand quiet at the bar (or chute)" and respond more or less favorably to the teaser's advances, depending on how "hot" she is; if she is just coming in heat, she may still protest, but only mildly; but if she is "hotter than a firecracker" —possibly very near ovulation—she will "show" to the teaser and "break down," meaning her vulva will dilate and contract and she may even expel urine—both positive signs that she needs to be palpated by the vet that very morning and, depending upon his findings, booked for breeding that day, schedule permitting. If she is in full heat and "stands quiet," some over-zealous teasers actually try to climb the fence to get to her (here again the padding saves the horses from injury).

In the inside method, the teaser is taken from stall to stall to court the mares; the stall door is opened and the teaser is allowed to stick his head and neck into the stall. Because new foals are in the stalls with their mothers—as discussed above, attempts are made to rebreed the mares even during their foal heat—some farms do not like this inside method, fearing injury to new foals. Many anestrous mares kick the sides of their stalls—which are not padded—and even rear up in their fierce efforts to thwart the teaser's advances. Yet, most mares are quite expert at directing their protests toward the teaser, and their foals are in very little danger. Also, in the outside method of teasing, the foal has to be left alone in the stall while its dam is taken outside to the teasing bar, and the foal usually whinnies and raises a fuss, which may excite its mother as well as the other foals and even the other mares, thus making an accurate reading of the mare's reaction to the teaser more difficult. Both traditional methods of teasing have their pros and cons, and both continue to be used by successful Bluegrass horse farms.

Although most mares—in heat or not—exhibit broadly similar responses to the teaser's advances, each mare nevertheless has her own peculiar quirks. Some, even though not ready to ovulate, will "stand quiet" and apparently accept the teaser's advances; more temperamental mares, though ready to ovulate, will protest the stallion's overtures. Also, some teasers and some mares apparently just like each other and will exhibit that affection. A number of stallions, for example, seem to prefer

An over-zealous teaser trying to get to a mare in heat that is "standing quiet at the bar" (Photo by author)

lighter colored mares, especially gray mares—an equine version of "blondes have more fun"—which also suggests that the old song, "The old gray mare ain't what she used to be" may have as yet uncomprehended profundity imbedded in its verses. Consequently, the teasing men must know each individual mare well enough to be able to "read" her reactions to the stallion's dalliances during teasing without jumping to incorrect conclusions, for although it is a proven folk method, teasing is not an exact science.

In addition, a good teaser is indispensable, and some small Bluegrass farms breed and train non-Thoroughbred stallions to supply top teasers. Most farms keep a number of teasers on hand to ensure that this crucial aspect of the breeding process will not be delayed by the unforseen illness or injury of any one teaser. To "reward" a teaser and to keep him from becoming *too* frustrated, he is allowed on occasion to breed a nurse mare—a non-Thoroughbred mare that acts as surrogate mother for an orphaned foal or one whose dam is dry, ill, or otherwise incapable of nursing (some Thoroughbred mares will reject their own foals—sometimes violently).

The teaser may also be used in two other ways: to "jump" and to stimulate "maidens" (females that have never been bred) or mares that for some reason are difficult to breed. To perform these "mounting tasks," a teaser truly expert at his job is required—such as the one mentioned above who is so sophisticated that during normal teasing he hardly ever gets an erection. A teaser is allowed to "jump" a mare as though actual breeding is to take place in order to familiarize her with having a stallion on her back and to accentuate her heat in preparation for—and usually just prior to—actual breeding to her booked stallion. When jumping is done, the teaser often wears a shield—an apronlike device sold at tack shops—to prevent him from entering the female; some teasing men call this shield the teaser's britches, and will say "now ol' [horse's name] has got to get his britches on" when the teaser is scheduled to jump a maiden. A number of teasing men, however, prefer not to use britches; instead they prevent the teaser from entering the female simply by holding back his penis with their hands. Instead of the jumping procedure, some farms prefer to put a female—especially an unruly one—in a stall adjoining the teaser's, where a small hinged window has been cut in the common wall so that, when opened, the teaser is able to stick his head through it to excite her, usually without any physical contact at all.

After the daily teasing rounds, the vet examines the mares, especially those in heat, those close to ovulation, and those already bred. If a mare is in heat and a booking date is available, he often injects her with a drug to induce ovulation and arranges for her booking with the stallion. Data obtained from the teasing operation and the vet's findings, along with data about bookings, the breeding date of the mare, the state of foal development, etc., are crucial. One Bluegrass farm manager has devised an ingenious color-coded chart on which he can track the breeding state and progress of every mare on the farm at a glance, and he updates it daily. He keeps the chart on a stand next to his desk and says, "That's all of it right there—all the important breeding information on every mare—so we know what's been done and what we got to do."

In their efforts to breed for early foals and to induce heat in mares earlier than the natural spring cycle, some farms have adopted the practice of placing electric lights in the barns to fool the mares into believing spring has already arrived; the lights work with the stallions as well, apparently activating the sperm. One very successful farm, for instance, starts leaving the lights on in the barns in December when they bring the mares in at 4 p.m.; at first the "daylight" is artificially extended by three hours, and then increased by one hour per month until April, by which time many mares, and stallions alike, have been deceived by the lights into believing it is time for their breeding season. The lights work so well that some farms can begin teasing as early as January 20–February 1. When the mare is ready to ovulate—as determined by the teasing process and the vet's inspection—she is taken to the breeding shed and prepared for her stallion. In earlier times, breeding was often done outdoors or, more often, in the farm's tobacco barn, which doubled as a breeding shed.

The Breeding Shed   Because either of the breeding pair—but more likely the mare—may become unruly, today's breeding shed is often padded to protect both the animals and their handlers. In fact, grooms stress that of all procedures on a horse farm, those in the breeding shed are the most dangerous; for example, I witnessed an unruly mare kick a groom square in the stomach, but fortunately he did not sustain a severe injury. The mare is usually controlled with a homemade device called a twitch—a stout stick, from 2 to 5 feet long and about 2 inches thick, of hard wood, usually hickory or oak, with a short piece of leather or rope looped through a hole drilled in the stoutest tip. The rope is placed around the mare's sensitive nose and upper lip, and the stick is twisted until the rope is snugged tight, giving the handler a leveraged hold on the animal. A particularly obstreperous mare is further controlled by a second, or even a third, twitch secured around her ear(s). Sometimes her legs are also hobbled. Thus she is prevented from rearing and/or wheeling or—it is hoped—kicking, should she resist being covered by the stallion. Still, some mares, in sheer panic or contrariness, have been known to break away, often tossing their grooms against the wall or to the floor, and then having to be chased, calmed, and returned to the shed. Once she is secured, the mare's genitals are washed with a mild solution as she stands with her head toward the wall. By this stage a portion of her tail nearest her rump has been wrapped and tied so that her entire tail can be easily pulled aside for unobstructed access for the stallion; if caught at penetration, the mare's tail hairs could actually cut his penis, a serious injury to the expensive stallion, perhaps resulting in delays or even cancellations of bookings, and therefore loss of lucrative stud fees.

When the mare is ready, the head stallion groom leads the stallion in and up to her, at which time both he and the mare begin to prance, snort, nicker, etc. Once the stallion begins to get an erection, the head groom quickly leads him to a nearby area of the shed where, wearing rubber gloves, he fully extends the stallion's penis and washes it with a mild solution. The gloves are worn to protect the stallion's penis from fingernail scratches as well as for hygienic reasons. Each stallion has his own bucket with his name on it, used only to wash his penis, and the buckets are never switched. After washing, the groom leads the stallion back to the mare, who is being held by two or three other grooms. (Both mare and stallion are firmly held at all times during the entire process.) With encouragement from his groom and by nipping and sniffing at the mare, the stallion soon has a full erection and begins to mount, at which time the groom actually guides the stallion's penis into the mare—sometimes called grooming the stallion, and the groom himself is sometimes called the pilot. Upon penetration, especially with a maiden or a small mare, a stallion roll—of foam rubber, covered with plastic so it can be washed and kept sterile—is placed between the stallion and the mare to avoid complete penetration and possible injury to the mare. (The roll resembles a giant roll of paper towels, or a large rolling pin, since it has handles on the ends.) Sometimes, the stallion groom—or especially the vet, if one is present—as soon as the stallion withdraws, will catch some of the semen in his hand, which is protected by a shoulder-length plastic glove, and push it into the mare's vagina as far as possible. This step is called the human service. After breeding, the stallion is washed once again and led back to his stall; then the mare is released and led out.

In the breeding shed, highly sexed stallions sometimes become overly excited and must be pacified, usually with soothing words from their grooms, or some are timid and must be vocally reassured. Folk stories about "timid studs" are relished. One stallion, the story goes, was so shy that in his efforts to escape he once backed out of the breeding shed into a water trough. Nasrullah, an early (1949) high-priced syndicated stallion, was not timid but vicious, particularly toward people he disliked; stories are told how he often attacked his vet and how he refused to mount a mare in the breeding shed if his owner were present—as though he spitefully resented the role of managed, syndicated, money-making stud. Reportedly the owner had once used a broom to subdue him, and Nasrullah never forgot it. Another popular story tells how a well-known horseman, before Nasrullah's amazing record as a sire was established, once refused to buy the unruly animal for a mere $15,000. Though violent, and even grudgeful, Nasrullah nonetheless covered many mares and sired famous champions. If an over-sexed—called rank—stallion, is truly impossible to handle, he may be gelded.

Obviously the above procedures are incompatible with a romantic view of raising horses, but Thoroughbred farms are run as a business, and these procedures have been developed over the years through both tradition and science to minimize injury, disease, and infection, and to maximize the natural breeding process. Some of the best farms boast that conception occurs after an average of only two covers, whereas in olden days numerous covers were usually required, which tended to "wear out" or even seriously injure the mares; moreover, if a mare remained barren she was often either destroyed or turned into a farm animal and worked to death, something that seldom occurs today. Modern scientific procedures discover and correct many reproductive problems, and sterile precautions enable farms in the Region to stamp out equine venereal infections. The breeding shed is kept as antiseptic as possible, and many have special floors that can be scoured or even completely replaced at regular intervals.

During the actual breeding, the grooms and others present often comment on the process with the frankness of many male groups when the subject is sex: "What's the matter with him—can't he get it up this morning?" "Why he's plumb tuckered out from yesterday's mares." "He don't want to get on her—give him a little help there [So-and-so]." "Watch her now—she sure don't like this even if he is a million dollar job!" "That's a cover"—"he's finished, look at his tail twitch!" "She's bred now, for sure"—and so on.

Such traditional joking notwithstanding, grooms assigned to the breeding shed are expert at their jobs, as are most horse-farm people. One horseman, who had brought his maiden from a different farm to be bred, commented, "It's always a pleasure to watch these people do their jobs; they're so good at it, and they always take a lot of pleasure in it." A groom from another farm, who had delivered an especially temperamental mare to be bred—one that required a great deal of handling, including five men, hobbles, and three twitches—commented, "Man, I thought you was gonna put the whole tack shop on her, but you got her bred all right; you always do." Not only is there a great deal of respect for fellow horsemen's expertise, but nearly all horsemen seem to love their work, often exclaiming they would not exchange it for any other way of life.

Breeding Traditions   Although they control the breeding process, most Thoroughbred farms still want to keep it as traditional and natural as possible, and this is one reason they have not resorted to artificial insemination. Another is fear of change. Many horse people believe to some extent that luck can be a significant factor in success or failure, and consequently, when certain practices have proved successful over time, breeders are not prone to change; hence traditions often arise and are perpetuated. The owner of one large and successful farm— though he could well afford to do so, many times over—nonetheless for years refused to replace his old stallion barn and breeding shed. Some of the best Thoroughbreds of modern times had been sired in that old breeding shed by stallions stabled in that old barn, and he was reluctant to alter the pattern—possibly defying the "fates" and changing his luck.

In breeding race horses, the time-honored wisdom is "Breed the best to the best and hope for the best." However, endless theories and systems—called nicks—have been created for analyzing potential breeding results. Although most are folk systems, a significant few are scientifically generated efforts to trace genealogical patterns or to understand better and evaluate the physical attributes of highly pedigreed horses. Many of the latter use computer-based data banks, which can produce, in a matter of minutes, analytical readouts of genealogical data, racing or sales results, etc., that once required weeks to obtain. Other computerized systems analyze such factors as proper size and "balance" of conformation, or a racehorse's stride. One such system, created by an MIT professor, also provides insights into the reasons and potential for lameness in horses. However, many of the systems are reminiscent of gamblers' ingenious and convoluted strategies to beat the roulette wheel or make a million at the track. Because no mating system has proved infallible, and many are obviously pseudoscientific, many racing writers and horsemen look upon breeding as something of a "genetic lottery." Most of these folk systems are based upon analyses of selected, acclaimed stallions that have consistently transmitted a particular, highly desirable trait to a number of their get. Although the dam is at least as important as the stallion in producing winners—some top horse people say even more so—most nicks use the stallion's record simply because he sires from forty to fifty foals annually, whereas a mare, no matter her quality, will produce, at best, one per year; thus the stallion simply provides more foals—data—for the system.

The decision of which mare is to be bred to which stallion is, however, not just a matter of desirability; it requires money and, sometimes, acquaintance with the owners of the stallion and, if boarded, the owners of the farm where the stallion stands at stud. Most stallion owners—plural because prestigious stallions standing at stud today are syndicated, usually with forty shares—obviously prefer their animal to service only the best mares; a stallion with a "high-quality book" means that the majority of the forty to fifty mares he will service have enviable records for producing winning foals. For this reason—despite the traditional rule-of-thumb that sets fees at about one fourth of the mare's value—stud fees are high, frequently in the range of $15,000–$250,000 (an unverified rumor had one stud fee set at $750,000). Stud fees have been high in the Bluegrass since very early days; in 1865, for example, Lexington's, at $500, was the highest in the country, and Man O' War was the first to command a $5,000 stud fee, astronomical at that time. Accompanying such high prices is often a great deal of bargaining, finagling, and sub rosa dealing. Often, personal connections or acquaintance between the parties will result in a more attractive financial arrangement, assuming both the mare and the stallion are acceptable to the other party. In addition, some Bluegrass gentry who have been lifelong friends— even though they may be fierce competitors on the track—will breed to nearly any match the other desires, and usually under a financial arrangement unavailable to outsiders. Furthermore, most shares of syndicated stallions are sold to members of the breeding fraternity or other close acquaintances, and usually each shareholder is entitled to breed one mare per year to the stallion for as long as it stands at stud, often on a "guaranteed live foal" basis. Hence, members of the esoteric breeding community are in enviable positions, not available to just anyone. Such intimate folk networks—called "good old boy" networks, especially among those on a lower socioeconomic stratum—have existed for years in the Bluegrass and function in nearly all social activities as well as in breeding arrangements.

Consequently, who you are and whom you know is often crucial in dealing successfully with many Bluegrass gentry. In this way they have elaborated a general Kentucky trait—to ask upon first meeting where a person is from and, if he is from a known area, who his relatives are. At the informal level such inquiries amount to on-the-spot genealogy; the inquirer endeavors to trace the stranger's pedigree, to ascertain what the two might have, or whom they might know, in common. This pattern is often observed, for example, when older people ask a younger person, "Now whose girl [boy] are you, anyway?" The youngster then names her/his parents and the oldster, if he only vaguely knows them, will ask, "Now was your momma a [last name] before she married?" If he has it right, he then might say, "and your granddaddy was [first and last names]—*why I know you!*" The older person may never have seen the youngster before, but once such genealogical identity is established, the youngster is accepted. Moreover, specific cultural traits, ideas, expectations, and obligations will be forever associated with the youngster because of her/his genealogy and the perception of her/his ancestors' position in the community. Thus, genealogy and culture are intricately entwined in everyday social relationships and constitute a significant part of many Bluegrass residents' perception of themselves and the Region. This folk pattern functions on all levels, even the economic, as in breeding arrangements for expensive horses.

Soon after she has conceived, the mare, especially if she is an older producer, will have her vulva partially sewn together by the vet to prevent "wind sucking," a mare's habit of drawing air into her vagina in everyday physical activities, which could also suck in foreign matter and cause infection. Windsucking occurs especially in older mares whose vulvas often have lost their muscular tone. Selective breeding to accentuate racing characteristics has also given the Thoroughbred a rump that slants abnormally forward, often causing uterine infections in the mare, another reason for the practice of suturing her vulva; the sutures are not removed until the mare is about to foal.

WEANING THE FOALS

Before the mare can deliver the foal she is carrying, her current foal must be weaned. After being bred in the spring, often shortly following the birth of her foal from last-year's breeding, the pregnant mare spends the summer being observed by the vet and farm employees, taking vitamins, and leisurely cavorting with her offspring in the farm's beautiful grazing parks—providing splendid scenic Bluegrass memories and photo opportunities for tourists. When the weather cools in the fall, usually the first part of October, weaning begins. Most farms wean the same time every year; it is a tradition on Claiborne Farm, for instance, that weaning is always done on one day, the first Tuesday in October. By that time most spring foals have been nursing over six months and already nibble at feed.

Not only are fall's cooler temperatures more pleasant for weaning, an inherently stressful process for both foals and dams, but fall has also been chosen because of ancient folkloric belief in conducting husbandry procedures according to the signs of the zodiac. For years *The Blood-Horse* magazine, avidly read by nearly all horse people, has published a calendar with the current month's "signs." To quote the magazine, "The sign is a zodiacal tracking, by which some horsemen traditionally have determined the best time for weaning and certain other husbandry decisions." Horsemen say that during the first part of October the "signs" are usually "down" or "on their way down"—that is, according to the zodiac, planetary influences that rule the lower parts of the body—the legs and feet—are usually dominant during the first part of October. Under no circumstances should the "signs" that rule the head, neck, digestive system, or udder be dominant, as that would adversely affect weaning. To help dry the mare's udder without encountering problems, ideally the signs should be "below the knee" (as they also should be when a male is gelded). Because weaning is a crucial process—during which the future temperament and demeanor of a Thoroughbred can be decidedly influenced—most horsemen will use astrological signs, and anything else, to enhance the chances for a positive weaning experience. Although some horsemen scoff at such traditional procedures, probably the majority nonetheless follow them. At one time *The Blood-Horse* ceased publishing its monthly zodiacal calendar, but readers created such an uproar that the editors decided to continue it. One horseman candidly expressed his pragmatic folk belief, also held by many others:

How much truth is there to such things? I'll never find out by not doing them, because you've gone through so much effort and worry and expense to get that foal out and on the ground that I'll never risk it to find out.... So many strange things can happen that you just wonder... there must be something to these things.... So over the years the things that have worked you stick to; and things that haven't ... you drop.

Weaning Procedures   There are two basic weaning procedures, both traditional methods: pasture weaning and stall weaning. Pasture weaning, the most prevalent method, can be done in two ways, abruptly or at slow intervals. The abrupt method, used traditionally by Claiborne Farm, involves separating all foals from their dams, grouping them by age and sex, and moving them to another, distant, pasture in one day's time. If possible, foals that have been together since birth are kept together so that the buddy system will ameliorate the frightening experience. Usually the older foals have already been somewhat naturally weaned by their mothers so they are less skittish, but all to some extent call to their mothers with whinnies and resist the grooms' efforts to separate them. Such a mass exercise requires a great number of workers; at Claiborne, for instance, eighty-some hands, each having a specific role in the preplanned coordinated weaning, take part; Claiborne's manager indicates the importance of the exercise by joking that if a hand is absent on weaning day, "he better be either in the funeral home or the hospital." In the afternoon the foals are rounded up from their new pastures and taken to their new barns; to catch them requires about twenty-five men per ten foals in a pasture—a sight that is often comical and to some even fun—"if you can call it fun to chase the little rascals all over the pasture," says an experienced hand. Apparently because they all experience the same thing at the same time, weanlings soon begin to accept their new lot in life as inevitable. Though a hectic day for weanlings, mares, and horsemen alike, the traumatic weaning procedure is accomplished in one day, and adherents of this approach claim that it is preferable to stretching out the process over a period of time.

Interval pasture weaning, also begun in the fall, involves removing two mares at a time from the pasture, leaving their foals with the rest of the mares—usually anywhere from eight to ten—and their foals; some farms do this at feeding time when the mares and foals are often preoccupied with eating and less likely to notice that the mares have been taken away. This is continued over a period of days until all the mares have been removed to other pastures. Adherents of this system maintain that it is less traumatic for the separated foals, which still have the company of all the other foals and mares left in their pasture; however, the dams that are removed, of course, still suffer a sudden stressful separation from their foals.

Stall weaning is traumatic for both mares and foals, and is consequently not as widely used as pasture weaning. Usually two foals are put in a stall together and their dams removed. Some believe that the initial stall confinement is too unnatural and frightening for the foals and that they are more prone to become sick or injure themselves in the stalls than if they were in the pasture. Also, as in most situations when two foals are weaned together, the two foals will eventually have to be weaned from each other, creating an additional, though less difficult, step.

Whichever traditional method is used, after being separated, the foals and mares alike are strategically grouped. Weanlings are divided by age, and even though equine puberty does not usually occur until about fifteen months, they are also separated by sex, just in case; moreover, fillies together are usually not as rambunctious as the spirited young colts, who in their playful antics could cause injury in mixed groups. A great deal of care is given to the well-being and correct behavior of the weanlings. They continue to be "turned out" in the pasture each morning, as they had been with their mothers, only now as a group of youngsters. One highly successful farm manager uses the daily "turning out" to examine both the foals and their dams; he stands at the gate and closely scrutinizes each horse as it passes, alert for any illness or abnormality; in this way he says, "I see every one of the horses on this farm at least twice every day."

Most horsemen insist that young horses are highly imitative—weanling see, weanling do—so the turning-out process is formally structured, punctual, and synchronized. Each weanling has its own halter, fitted shortly after birth and constantly worn, one of the most important pieces of training equipment. While still in its stall, each weanling has a short lead fastened to its halter, and then, when all are ready, each is led simultaneously from its stall by a groom and all walked to the pasture together, almost procession-like—just as when the mares were present, only then the mare was led by the groom's left hand and the foal by the right. The same pattern is followed when they are brought back in the afternoon. Each youngster is put on its lead in the field, and when all are ready, they are marched back to the barn as an orderly group. Many farms use an older, often barren mare to draw reluctant weanlings to the gate, but soon they learn to come on their own as part of the group. The idea is to establish and maintain patterns. A number of weanlings, accustomed to the behavior patterns of their dams, will readily respond and do what is expected, and these actually teach the others by example the proper behavior expected of a well-brought-up horse. Foals are like schoolchildren and treated as such; they are influenced by the company they keep, and they must be taught. As one horseman puts it, "That first day after weaning is the first day of their new life, and we want to make sure we teach them the right way to behave; they'll learn enough bad habits on their own."

FOALING

Mares are grouped according to their anticipated foaling dates and assigned to appropriate broodmare barns and pastures. It is interesting that mares may in their lifetimes on any one farm eventually be moved to a number of pastures and barns, whereas a stallion is invariably assigned to one stall and one paddock, both of which often bear his name. Mares grouped for early foaling are brought into the foaling barn usually in December, where they come under the knowing eye of the foaling crew. Members of the foaling crew must be experienced and knowledgeable, calm, quiet, reassuring, patient, reliable, and willing and able to be easily awakened at all hours of the night. Life or death of the foal and/or mare may depend upon any or all of these characteristics.

Although all farms have vets on call, and some even have vets in residence, the foaling crew may be the only ones present if the mare delivers unexpectedly; in fact, it is standard procedure on some farms for the foaling crew to handle all normal deliveries, calling the vet only in times of emergency. Much of the foaling crew's competence has been supplemented, of course, by the vet's scientific knowledge and procedures, but they owe perhaps just as much of their expertise to years of on-the-job training and experience in the traditional methods that have worked for generations.*

When the mare is close to delivery, the foal will drop and extend her abdomen, and she may begin "waxing." Waxing refers to the appearance of a wax-like substance on the mare's teats, and is taken as a sign she is about to foal; however, while many mares wax just hours before foaling, some mares wax for days and others not at all. Some mares "heat up" prior to foaling, meaning they actually sweat, or at least their temperatures rise; however, heating up can also mean the foal is simply changing position, but not ready for birth. If a foal is not properly positioned, the mare will panic and actually push her insides out in an effort to deliver

---

*Members of the foaling crew are fond of telling stories about "stupid" or pompous vets, especially ones fresh out of college who think they know it all and often commit blunders after ignoring the advice of the foaling crew member(s). Most wise vets heed the foaling crew's advice and even ask for their astute observations, such as the signs to watch for in the pregnant mare. Just as folk knowledge holds that one can predict the sex of human babies by the way the fetus is carried, so horsemen claim to predict the sex of the foal by the appearance of the mare.

and relieve herself of the pain; in such cases the foaling man's knowledgeable assistance to the vet is vital. Since no scientifically accurate method exists of predicting delivery times, horsemen traditionally look to "the signs." If a mare has not foaled when expected, many an experienced foaling man will look at the almanac and say, "Well, there's a change of moon next week; she'll foal then."

Just as tales about unruly or timid stallions are relished, stories about foaling experiences are popular and often become traditional, especially ones about unusual events, such as this mean mare tale:

This woman had this mare and she hadn't had a live foal out of her, 'cause she killed them all, the mare did. Just went after them when she got done foaling and savaged them. She asked me, "Could you foal this mare for me?" And I said, "I'll foal her for you." And I went and watched that mare, and as soon as she broke water I tied her up to the wall and stood right there with a twitch and I told her, "You bitch, you hurt that foal and I'll knock the hell out of you!" And I stood right there with that twitch and her tied to the wall until that foal was up and nursing. And once it finally nursed, she was okay and she took it and raised it. But that was the only foal that woman got out of the mare 'cause she killed them all 'cept that one. And that woman named that foal after me 'cause I saved its life. I wasn't going to let her kill *that* foal!

Many mares prefer to be alone during actual delivery, and some will even hold back the process if they are being observed; so the foaling crew must be as unobtrusive as possible when the delivery is imminent. The mare will usually become restless and "walk her stall," paw the ground, and so on—signs that the foal is about to appear. Once the mare lies down, her labor is usually very brief; and the actual birth, if normal, requires only a few minutes. The foal arrives head and front feet first, and the dam stands almost immediately after the foal is completely delivered—a protective instinct. Perhaps because its mother is standing and/or it is hungry, the foal usually stands and nurses within the first thirty minutes after birth. If any aspect of this process is not normal, the vet and foaling crew must discover and correct the problem(s).

Not only does the foaling groom usually assist the vet in the delivery, he/she can also be invaluable in caring for the foal during its crucial first three days of life. Foaling time is fraught with uncertainty; consequently, a number of traditional beliefs, taboos, and rituals attend it. Perhaps the most prevalent taboo warns against the use of rye straw bedding in the foaling barn because, as horsemen say, "It'll make a mare 'slip' her foal." To "slip" means to abort the foal, so most horsemen adamantly refuse to have rye straw in the foaling barns, but will use it for yearling and stallion stalls. Though not often observed today, another traditional practice is to hang a string of onions in the stall in the belief that "any viruses around will go *in* the onions." To court good luck, mascots of all kinds abound in all horse barns, and one prominent Bluegrass horseman firmly believes that bluebirds, especially around the foaling barns, bring good luck.

FOLK VETERINARY MEDICINE

Before the advent of modern veterinary practices, folk medicines and practices abounded. Still seen on occasion is Raleigh Salve, once used for nearly any ailment. One horseman remembers an old vet who had been in the cavalry and favored Raleigh Salve and a lot of other folk remedies because he had used them on Army horses. Representative of most horsemen's attitude today is this comment of a prominent farm manager: "Medicine is the most modern aspect of the farm operation."

Before modern vets and scientific equine medicine were readily available, the farrier was often the person consulted for folk cures. Frequently he recommended hoof poultices—of cow manure, crushed onions, peat moss, linseed oil, and assorted other ingredients. So popular were such mixtures that commercial versions were sold across the counter: O.K. Hoof Remedy, Harrold's Hoof Ointment, and Strap Veterinary & Hoof Ointment—the last touted as also able to "cure a horse from head to toe, being good for collar galls, car bruises, sore tendons, and contracted heels." Some, such as Continental Ointment, were supposedly also good for chapped hands and other human skin problems. Through the years, human and equine folk medicine have shared many common ingredients to create remedies for all sorts of ailments—an old pattern that has reappeared in the modern Bluegrass, as outlined in a recent (1989) Lexington *Herald-Leader* article:

The latest in hair care comes straight from the horse's mane. . . . [Lexingtonians] are dipping their hair in Mane 'N Tail, a conditioner marketed for horses . . . to make manes and tails thicker, longer and silkier. . . . [It's] 20 years old . . . but only recently has its popularity soared among humans. . . . "Ninety-nine percent of the people buying it are women" [said a Pinkston's Turf Goods clerk]. . . . [He described one woman] who used the stuff on her horses first. . . . [She] wanted a short cut to grow out. She put on Mane 'N Tail every night for two weeks, slept on it and rinsed it out the next day. . . . "It works on the horses' tails," she said. "Why wouldn't it work on our heads?" [which is a typical example of "folk logic"]

Breeders Supply & Equipment Co., a Lexington wholesaler, has more than quadrupled its supply of the conditioner to meet demand. . . . "I'm not certain how in the world it got started. . . . I sincerely have my doubts about it" [said an executive of the wholesaler]....[A Lexington businessman] was reluctant to try...[it] at first. But...[he] used it for three months...and [says] his receding hairline is less noticeable.... "Everybody loves it. These women are coming in and buying it like it's going out of style" [said another wholesaler].

Horse hair conditioner is not the only horse product in vogue....Some people use horse liniments to soothe sore muscles and...women frequently buy hoof moisturizer and use it on their nails....One woman...walked into the store, opened a jar of hoof moisturizer...dabbed it on her fingernails and then put the jar back on the shelf and left the store....[The clerk said] "We ought to open a whole line of crossover...equine Homo sapien products."

THE FARRIER

Today very few farms have a resident farrier. In antebellum times one or more of the slaves was designated the farrier; and even after the Civil War a former slave—often a resident of a nearby black hamlet—often worked as a farrier. Gradually farriery was assumed by the whites who began to replace black horsemen on most farms, and as it became less and less the custom for hands to live on the estate, the traditional work of the farrier was performed at the blacksmith shop. However, when the once-ubiquitous smithy—often as common as today's gas station—started to become obsolete in the 1930s, many blacksmiths specialized as farriers and began to make regular "house calls" to the farms, as is done today.* Most modern farriers have a truck of some sort fully equipped with all necessary tools and materials; a few even carry a miniature forge and work entirely out of the mobile rig. A recent movement among some Bluegrass farriers has been to establish complete blacksmith shops, although they in no way resemble the many early Bluegrass smithies, which not only shod horses, but did nearly *all* iron and metal work for the Region; moreover, early smiths performed all general tool, implement, and equipment repairs and provided the ironwork for wagons, farm sleds, and buggies.

Early blacksmiths were considered to be notoriously dirty, a belief reflected in an anecdote about one such smith who refused to bathe or shave. He was visited once each year by the local men who, after making him strip, scrubbed both him and his clothes with lye soap and shaved him. Blacksmith shops were often favorite meeting places for horsemen and other males, where storytelling, gossip, and swapping flourished. Swapping was sometimes so involved that reportedly one man unintentionally

*It is interesting that the work patterns of the country medical doctor and the farrier have completely reversed.

ended up with the hound he had originally swapped. Farmers also frequented the smithy for help with problems on the farm, for advice was freely shared. A modern substitute for this function of the blacksmith shop is a farm managers' club, which meets once every month for fellowship and exchange of information; often a vet or other scientific equine specialist is an invited speaker. Like his blacksmith predecessor, today's mobile farrier is often a storyteller and serves as a conduit for all sorts of information about the life of the horseman. However, unlike the early blacksmith, who had an assistant called a striker, most Bluegrass farriers today, except for an occasional apprentice or partnership arrangement, work alone.

Today's typical Bluegrass farrier has several farms under contract and visits them on a regular schedule, usually every thirty days, to perform routine trimming and any other special tasks required. A good farrier can trim and clean the hooves of about forty to fifty horses during a long summer day, and he can shoe twelve to fifteen yearlings a day, or six to eight mature horses. Like the vet, and *anyone* on the farm, he is also on call for emergencies. While the shift from resident to independent craftsman was a major change in lifestyle, other aspects of farriery have remained much the same—tools, methods, and procedures. Indeed, even though quasi–formal schooling in the traditional craft is available—the headquarters of the American Farriers Association is now located at the Kentucky Horse Park near Lexington—some farriers still use a modified version of the old apprentice system, during which novices learn the traditional craft in the traditional manner—imitative, hands-on, learn-by-doing. A good example of the difference involves trimming the "frog," the soft cartilagelike center of the horse's hoof. Formal training usually advises against trimming the frog, since it can easily be cut too deeply and bleed, become infected, and lead to serious problems, even lameness. However, one top farrier of thirty years experience contends, "If you don't trim the frog it actually leads to more problems; it's a matter of how you do it; you got to be careful, and your knife can't slip." He trims it in a diamond shape, explaining, "You got to know your horse; some will bleed easier than others, so you got to be careful with them." In no way can a formal school teach a farrier such intimate, specialized folk knowledge; so, in spite of sophisticated modern techniques and new equipment, much of what the farrier does is still learned and performed in traditional folkloric mode.

Perhaps the most significant modern change in the farrier's equipment has been the introduction of lighter and more malleable aluminum plates (shoes) for race horses. Too, some horses require custom shoes to correct congenital defects in conformation (like corrective human footwear) or aberrant patterns in stride, and this is where the farrier's

traditional skills and experience are most needed. In fact, some maintain
that a person is not a true farrier unless he can make his own shoes from
"blanks;" however, farriers still use "keg" shoes—a term from earlier
times when "ready-to-wear" shoes were sold in kegs—today available
from many places, even Japan.

Select Yearling Sales

Shortly after the foaling, teasing, and breeding season has once again
gotten underway, the yearlings—last year's crop of foals—begin rapidly
developing the conformation characteristics of the Thoroughbred. It is
then that decisions and preparations for the select—or preferred—summer
sales must begin.

Yearlings—actual ages can range from seven to nineteen months—
selected for the sales are those considered to have the best potential to
command high prices, and some farms choose and start preparing them
for the July sales as early as March or April. Of course, many farms keep
some yearlings to train themselves, and decisions about which to keep
and which to sell are among the most difficult the farm managers and
owners face. The hectic process of preparing the yearlings selected for
sale is described by one successful farm manager:

You've got about 100 days . . . I call it a "football field" . . . we go about one yard a
day, and sale day is the goal line . . . and when we get down to a few yards it gets a
little rougher as you don't want any blemishes or injuries on that yearling
then. . . . The last ten days we walk him an hour a day . . . [and] sale day he shows
he's got what it takes . . . that he's been raised right.

Color and Markings   In selecting yearlings for the preferred
sales, most horsemen are acutely aware of the wide range of prejudices,
superstitions, and folk beliefs harbored by most potential buyers; most
concern a horse's color, markings, size, conformation, and general appearance. Many horsemen shy away from a roan; supposedly, its mottled
"indefinite" coloring signifies an indefinite ability as well, and many
maintain that roans are lazy. (This belief is so widespread that fewer bets
are made on roans than on any other color of horse.) Consequently, roan
yearlings are rarely chosen for the select sales. Other factors being equal,
most horsemen prefer bays, either light or dark (sometimes a dark bay is
called brown), and chestnuts; bays are believed to be easily handled and
even-tempered, and chestnuts are thought to be high-spirited but man-
ageable. Consequently, yearlings with these colorings are often chosen for
the select sales. Black or gray Thoroughbreds are few in number, but

they are often popular with racetrack crowds; however, along with roans, many horsemen consider both blacks and grays to be "abnormal." Moreover, black horses are thought to be potentially malicious, and gray ones gentle and proud (thus gray mares are more readily accepted than gray stallions).

In addition to coloring, a Thoroughbred's markings are believed to indicate its potential. A Thoroughbred with more than one white stocking—especially one with four—is fated to be a loser on the turf and as a sire. Yet Lexington, one of the greatest of racers and sires, had four white feet, as did Gallant Fox, the only Triple-Crown winner to sire another—Omaha. Both Whirlaway, Calumet Farm's 1941 Derby champion, and Secretariat, Claiborne Farm's 1973 Triple-Crown winner (who, as another much beloved horse, was given Man O' War's endearing folk name "Big Red"), had three white feet; and Swaps, with two white stockings, was one of the most celebrated of modern Thoroughbreds. However, none of this alters the folk belief that white stockings are a bad sign. Conversely, if a Thoroughbred has only one white stocking, many believe that characteristic *increases* his chances of becoming a champion. Coincidence—positive or negative—is taken as certain corroboration of the superstition's predictive power, and any number of winners with one white foot—such as Count Fleet and Equipoise—are cited to validate belief in the superstition, so widespread that it has been set to an oft-repeated folk rhyme:

> One white stocking, run him for your life,
> Two white stockings, give him to your wife,
> Three white stockings, give him to some man,
> Four white stockings, sell him if you can.

Today, markings of all sorts—head and body as well as legs—are photographed and described in detail for Jockey Club records, and a team of auction-house officials—all horse experts—inspects each nominated yearling and selects only the best, supposedly limiting their appraisals to pedigree, health, temperament, and conformation characteristics. However, even such experts are not always immune to folk beliefs.

Conformation   Folk beliefs about a horse's appearance and conformation are legion. A Thoroughbred should not be "pig-eyed," because horsemen believe that indicates stubbornness, nor should it be "pop-eyed." Rather, its eyes—often believed to indicate its spirit, temperament, and heart—must be alert and bright, and perhaps a bit curious, but not mean or angry. The head should be neither too large nor too small, and more "dish-faced" than "Roman-nosed"—the former hinting at Arabic ancestry and the latter a draft-horse trait. No Thoroughbred that is "muley-eared" or "lop-eared" will bring a high price; rather, the ears should point toward the front at a 45-degree angle, indicating alertness, intelligence, and spirit. Its mouth should align properly, enabling the animal to chew easily; a "parrot mouth" (overbite) or "monkey mouth" (underbite) can cause digestive problems. The Thoroughbred should not be "sway-back," "slab-sided" (which might mean respiratory problems), or too long in the back, which makes running more tiring.

A long neck is often an asset to racing ability, as are firmly developed muscles on a "well-sprung" chest, but it is the legs, feet, and hooves that are most crucial and are therefore scrutinized most closely. As the saying goes, "No foot (or leg), no horse." Feet must be neither "pigeon-toed" nor "duck-footed"—either could hinder racing ability. Legs should be neither "back at the knee" nor "over at the knee," called "knee-sprung," which could create too much leg strain; nor should legs be "knock-kneed," "bow-legged," or "sickle-hocked."

These are only a few of the major terms and associated beliefs known by most horse people. Yet, all such beliefs notwithstanding, "A beautifully conformed yearling with the best pedigree can be a dud," says one horseman. Conversely, a misshapen horse that looks as though it were put together with rejected spare parts can on occasion put the handsomest animals to shame. As Bluegrass horse people say, "On the track, pretty is as pretty does." A case in point is John Henry.

Born in Bourbon County of ignoble, unimpressive parentage, John Henry was so "knee-sprung" that vets considered him likely to "come apart at the seams" if ever raced. Consequently, he was sold at Keeneland's winter sale (where horsemen dispose of unlikely yearlings early rather than go to the expense of preparing them for the select sales) for a mere $1,100. Although he was "smallish"—some said a runt*—as a young stallion John Henry was oversexed and unruly, nearly impossible to train, so his new owner gelded him and sold him at the winter sale for $2,200, but he was returned because of his terrible knees. He was then sold two more times before his last owner, a New York businessman, decided to race him. The unsightly, "back at the knees" John Henry became the first horse to win totals of $3, $4, $5, and $6 million; and, until surpassed by Alysheba's earnings, John Henry held the world's record in purse winnings (over $6.5 million); and he still holds the record for a gelding. "Unsightly," "knee-sprung," and "smallish" though he is,

---

*However, one does not say such things at the sales. An unwritten code of ethics among horse people, and even buyers—especially at the sales—dictates that, no matter how misshapen or otherwise undesirable in appearance it is, one should never "bad mouth" another man's horse.

today John Henry is stabled at the Kentucky Horse Park in its Hall of Champions as living testimony to the unpredictability of "genetic engineering," conformation clues, temperament tips, and all of the rest of the systems, nicks, folk beliefs and practices, and sophisticated scientific methods used to predict quality in Thoroughbreds.

Preparing for the Sales   Once a yearling has been chosen for the select sales, it is turned over to a groom, who heaps constant meticulous attention upon it for hours every day until it is sold. Most farms keep yearlings in the barn all day, turning them out only at night, thus protecting their coats from the sun, which can cause fading. During the day they are often force-fed a special diet—which usually includes vitamins and tonics to increase their appetites—designed to develop their musculature and fill them out as much as possible. Poultices are regularly applied to soften hooves, cool legs, and improve circulation; every speck of foreign matter is removed from the hooves and feet, and a dressing, often homemade with a pine tar and oil base (sometimes linseed or fish oil), is applied to the hooves to keep them soft and shiny. In general, they are cleaned, curried, brushed, clipped and otherwise rendered immaculate for sale day. If the farm is able to afford expensive exercise equipment, the animal's young muscles are toned up on treadmills and customized "swimming pools." Grooms also teach the yearlings how to stand to enhance the sought-after true Thoroughbred appearance—calm but alert with eyes bright, ears forward, legs slightly apart, all of which show off the animal's head, legs, and body muscles to best advantage. Just days before the sale, the yearlings' manes and tails are "pulled" to make them even and often treated with tonics for appearance, and their facial hair is clipped. Pampering and primping continues, and even intensifies, up to sale day; in fact, grooms continue polishing the yearlings until just seconds before they enter the sales arena. Usually the last "prep" is to oil and polish the animal's hooves and wipe its body with a lustrous hair polish. Racing columnist Joe Palmer comments about such preparations:

It is the business of every seller to put his product on the market as attractively as possible, just as if he were a jeweler or a grocer or a politician. And it is the business of the buyer to see through every subterfuge . . . to distinguish between decoration and quality. If a man can be induced to go another thousand because a yearling has been rubbed sleek and had his mane and tail done up with . . . ribbons, that's just good showmanship or bad judgment, depending on which side you're on.

Some sellers employ rather subtle subterfuges when yearlings are being scrutinized by potential buyers. Before the auction, when buyers visit yearlings in their stalls and paddocks, the groom holding and leading the yearling being inspected may position himself so as to block the buyer's view of any known blemishes or undesirable characteristics. Another strategy used at the auction itself is simply to assign the smallest groom to the job of handler so his small stature will make the yearlings loom even larger.

The Auction   A number of traditions are also evident in the actual sales process. One racing fan characterizes the sale as an "Easter egg hunt," and another analogy compares it to an "auction of unraced custom-built racing cars." The sales arena is usually packed with millionaires, or their agents, some with virtually bottomless pockets, all eager to own the next Triple Crown winner and/or a share of lucrative stud fees.★

The highly sophisticated and expensive sales arena is no place for the novice or the gullible, as attested by stories about sales shenanigans. One novice enlisted the aid of a knowledgeable horseman to help him buy a yearling; during the sale, he left for another of several drinks to bolster his courage, instructing the horseman, if the desired yearling came up before his return, to "buy him . . . never mind how much." When he returned, he learned, much to his chagrin, that he had just paid $25,000 for the yearling, a very high price at that time. Rumor had it that the "knowledgeable horseman" was actually the owner of the yearling and had intentionally run up the bid. Yearlings of dubious quality are sometimes sold by "pinhookers," men who buy weanlings or yearlings and prepare them for either the yearling or two-year-old sales. Pinhookers often consider eye appeal more important than actual potential, so, although a number of pinhookers are competent horsemen, some earn a living by creating mere window dressing.

The sales pavilion has been likened to a Greek amphitheater, a prize ring, a circus, and a theater-in-the-round—all settings that glorify performance—and rightly so—for the sales are conducted with pomp and ritual. Interaction crackles between the auctioneer, the bidders, and the assistants who roam the crowd expertly culling out those likely to bid higher, deftly encouraging them to do so. This cajolery is accompanied

---

★More and more today Japanese and other wealthy foreigners—especially Arabs, a number of whom even own prime Bluegrass horse facilities—are influential buyers in Bluegrass horse sales. In fact, a weekly TV business news program reported that due to the 1990 Iraqi invasion of Kuwait and the subsequent Desert Storm, Keeneland's summer sale suffered because Arabs were noticeably absent. Considering the Thoroughbred's Arabic genesis and present day yearling sales to Middle Eastern Sheiks, the Thoroughbred-Arab connection seems to have come full circle.

Typical scene, Keeneland
yearling auction (Photo
courtesy of Keeneland
Association)

by the auctioneer's staccato and rapid-fire traditional chant, as described by folklorist Wm. Hugh Jansen:

The auctioneer's undulating chant soars over the buzz of socializing. . . . It plays back and forward sliding over about four adjacent notes in the scale, punctuated by gavel raps upon the board under the chanter's elbow. The pistol-sharp reports sometimes send the jittery yearling rearing and pitching . . . perhaps with the conscious realization by the auctioneer that . . . show of spirit is not to the seller's disadvantage. . . . The syllables rush over each other so rapidly as to be only occasionally understood—even . . . inititates do not always understand. The chant is almost a drone, lulling, soporific, but pleasant and musical as it comes over a totally-unnecessary microphone. . . . Never taking his eyes off the auctioneer, an expert whispers, "He knows what they ought to bring, and he tries not to stop until then. Of course if he gets a couple of suckers, he doesn't. . . ." Time and again, the auctioneer abandons his singing chant for a sentence or two in shouted oratorical harangue. Sometimes it seems to be merely to break the spell spun by the chant.... Too, it gives variety. Sometimes the purpose is to make a point or to calm a momentary unruliness....

Some of that "shouted oratorical harangue" has become traditional among auctioneers, who use it to stir up the crowd, such as: "I hope the hell she runs faster than you're bidding," or "Hey, let's everybody wake up here. We got more horse than that." "Now you hillbillies keep quiet and listen to what's going on." "Aw, I swear, you can get chicken faster than anyone I ever saw," and so on. (These same techniques and some of the same phrases—altered only enough to accommodate the different context—are, of course, used by other auctioneers, particularly those who auction land, furniture, and other personal goods at the many popular auctions in the Region.) The king of horse auctioneers was George Swinebroad, who has become a Bluegrass legend. Swinebroad and his announcer comprised a team that, in the 1940s, could, with a combination of bullying and joking with bidders and by taking advantage of their egos and insecurities, "empty every wallet in the pavilion faster than a band of pickpockets." Their aggressive auctioneering style is credited with changing what was once a buyer's market, selling only three or four yearlings an hour, to a seller's market that moved as many as eighteen yearlings through the auction every hour.

Such auctioneering is, of course, deeply rooted in American folk traditions; in fact, horse scholars Tom Biracree and Wendy Insinger trace the horse auctioneer's chant to two nineteenth-century Bluegrass brothers who combined the folk style of their preacher-father's temperance sermons with the "country wit and singsong chant" of local tobacco and farm auctioneers to produce the hybrid of horse auctioneering perfected by Swinebroad. Folklorist Jansen noted the evangelical overtones in Bluegrass yearling auctions:

[A] listener is conscious that it is not merely a repetition of numbers, but of jumbled, compressed phrases, repeated in a fashion almost exactly like the "speaking in tongues" of the old-fashioned preaching...impossible to reproduce...on paper.

RACERS-IN-THE-MAKING

Naming   Once acquired, the yearling must be officially named by its new owner, provided it was not named previously, and few are if destined for the sales. Today, names must be approved by the Jockey Club, and must be more or less original which, considering that nearly 50,000 new foals are born each year, can be a vexing problem. Well over a half-million names are already used and therefore ineligible, as are any

Thoroughbred names from the past seventeen years, any famous horse's name—such as Man O' War—any name with political or advertising connotations, any obscene name in any language, and names of living people without permission. If numbers are used, they must be spelled out, and no name can be longer than eighteen characters. The yearling's name application must be filed with the Jockey Club by November 1 of its yearling year; if previously named, it can be changed for a fee of $100, but considering the difficulty in finding an acceptable name, this is seldom done. The most traditional procedure is to choose a name that derives from the yearling's sire and/or dam.

Efforts to choose a name within the above guidelines have yielded many humorous and oft-repeated stories. One owner's application—each application lists three possible names—was returned three times marked "Not Available." Since all nine suggested names were not available, the yearling's owner sent in as his tenth choice the name "Not Available," and it was approved. Another anecdote concerns the founder of the famous Elmendorf Farm; in 1877, after his wife returned from a shopping trip to New York, where she had spent lavishly on her wardrobe, he named a promising two-year-old Spendthrift after her. (Of course, the horse became famous, and its name was later assumed as the name of another famous Bluegrass farm.) Not to be outdone, the next year his wife named Spendthrift's new brother Miser after her husband.

Serendipitous names are legion, as are names of places (Omaha and Stalingrad) and people (Ugly Mary and Mrs. Cornwallis, and Secretariat was named after the farm's secretary), foreign names (Toujours Prêt—"always ready," and Dinard—a French town), names from songs, dances, or other current fads (Disco Dance and Green Alligator), sports names (Goal Keeper and Forward Pass), and names derived strictly from fancy or owners' idiosyncrasies. Mrs. Hancock, owner of Claiborne farm, prefers the shortest names possible, ideally consisting of only one five-letter word and one syllable. Colonel E. R. Bradley, owner of Idle Hour Farm, supposedly because both his name and that of his first famous Thoroughbred began with the letter *B*, gave *all* of his horses names that began with the letter *B*. Many became famous and one, Black Toney, sired so many of the others that today his statue stands at Darby Dan Farm, a remnant of Bradley's old Idle Hour Farm. Darby Dan has its own traditional method of naming its horses. Each fall a group of fifty or more people is invited to the farm on a Sunday afternoon after church. All the yearlings it has decided to keep are paraded before the group and the yearlings' genealogies are provided. Whoever submits an acceptable name wins a prize—a silver mint julep cup.

The horse Nancy Hanks was named for Lincoln's mother, but a macabre folktale is often erroneously cited as the source of the famous trotter's name. A young girl named Nancy, crossed in love, hanged herself in the family attic, using hanks of yarn. Sentimental verse commemorated this sad tale, in the course of which her homemade rope got confused with the family's surname (long since forgotten), and the girl went down in local history as Nancy Hanks. It is this Nancy "Hanks" who is sometimes mistakenly said to be the source of the trotter's name.

Breaking   After receiving its folk name, a yearling must be broken and trained by its new owner (or its home farm if it was not sold) in preparation for becoming a racer. Traditional skills and procedures are religiously followed in this process, although a number of horsemen contend that the term "breaking" is a misnomer, for one never wants to impair or "break" a yearling's spirit or "heart." Some farms prefer to send their yearlings to specialists in these important stages of developing turf winners. Perhaps because the temperamental Thoroughbreds seem to respond favorably to soothing human voices, many such training facilities are located in the South, where the prevailing dulcet drawl may be a factor in mollifying these high-strung animals as they learn to become responsive and spirited—yet controllable—racing machines. On those Bluegrass farms that do their own breaking and training, it is only during such activities that Thoroughbreds are actually ridden—a sight few visitors will ever see. On most Bluegrass horse farms, horses are for breeding and racing, not for pleasure riding, a fact kept uppermost in mind during breaking. Consequently, most breaking and training is conducted in sequestered areas of the farm.

Having been handled from birth, says one trainer, "Most yearlings are not man shy, so the breaking/training process is just a matter of teaching them new forms of familiar human contact." The first phase, called bucking out, is done in the stall and lasts three days, if the yearling "hasn't got much buck in him." After all loose objects are removed from the stall, a saddle pad is laid across the yearling's back and a surcingle is put around him and slightly tightened. Control is maintained with a halter using the Chiffney bit, which is a brass ring, the top half of which rests in the yearling's mouth on the gums, teeth, and tongue; this bit, which lacks the harshness of a regular bit, is used to accustom yearlings to the presence of metal in the mouth. Previously, the yearling's "wolf teeth"—small back teeth that would have interfered with the bit and caused a sore mouth—were pulled in preparation for the bit. Care is always taken not to use the bit excessively, which might create a "hard-mouthed" horse—a condition reducing his value as a racer.

If he responds to the blanket and surcingle without fear or fight, he is then "turned around a few times in the stall," the surcingle is further tightened, and he is turned again. This process is repeated until the surcingle is about as tight as a saddle strap would be. Then, while a groom holds the halter, the exercise person—preferably of small, light-weight frame—slowly, gently, and lightly lies across the yearling—a practice called belly-busting—and this is continued until the yearling is no longer frightened by the new experience.

"If all this is OK," says the trainer, "then you go ahead and straddle him the first day, and maybe even 'figure-eight' him some." That is, the exercise person sits astride his back, and the groom leads him around the stall. This is done for two days.

The third day a bridle is added—an item most horsemen are quick to call "the most important piece of equipment you'll ever put on a horse." At this crucial stage, it is extremely important that handlers have "good hands." On the fourth day, a saddle without stirrups is put on him and he is "figure-eighted" some more. This slow process is continued for several days, after which the yearling is moved from the yearling barn to the training barn.

Training   Farms allow as long as six weeks for breaking, and anywhere from two to six months, or even more, for training. This long slow process is sometimes called hacking (from the "hackamore"—a homemade, loose, soft rope bridle used for generations for breaking and training) and is common today, whereas in the past training was often more hurried and rigorous.

The first day at the training barn the yearlings are turned out so they can familiarize themselves with a new pasture and surroundings. Up to this stage they have been kept in groups of eight to ten, but at the training barn they are further separated, often two to a group, and these new associations frequently continue at the track and throughout their racing careers. Early the next morning—about 6 a.m., before being turned out—the new arrivals are taken for a walk, often just up and down the shed row; the next day, they are walked over the training track and grounds to let them become comfortable, and "If everybody's OK, we might even jog a bit on the track."

The new racers-in-the-making are often led to the track by a lead pony (non-Thoroughbred), which remains stabled at the track and is therefore familiar with the surroundings, a traditional procedure that works wonders in calming the newly arrived, often skittish, yearlings. Moreover, the training track is usually located in a quiet and serene part of the farm, an environment conducive to peaceful and pleasurable daily routines, for both trainer and horse. Many horsemen contend that the breaking and training period is "the best part of the year on the farm," as it allows them to observe the development of the horses they have worked with from conception, and which are on their way to proving that all that work will be rewarded at the track.

In the following weeks they will be walked, jogged, and galloped and then, reversing both directions and procedures, galloped, jogged, and walked, until they are able to "breeze"—perform a smooth and easy but brisk workout on the track, usually for one-half mile (a gallop is often over two miles). The new strain on their legs is relieved with usually homemade poultices, the ingredients of which are selected to improve circulation and cool muscles.

The young Thoroughbreds will race for a while, the length of time dependent upon their degree of success or failure, or the concerns of their owners. Then, for one reason or another, they will retire from racing; fillies become broodmares, and winning colts become—it is hoped—virile stallions. An illustrious horse with an impressive track record is usually syndicated—sold to a group of investors who share in the profits from his stud fees, earned at some prestigious Bluegrass farm, where he is either boarded or owned. If the mare becomes barren, or if the stallion loses his virility, and they have become famous champions, they are then usually simply turned out, to live the rest of their lives in the peaceful Bluegrass "grazing parks." An unpleasant reality is that some not-so-famous or obscure horses are sold for pet food, and some have been sent to France, where horsemeat is used as human food.

Horse Cemeteries

When a much beloved horse dies, it is usually buried in—if there is one—the farm's horse cemetery. Many Bluegrass horse farms do have such cemeteries—a revered tradition—where stones and monuments are erected over the graves. Such memorials vary in splendor in proportion to the achievements and renown of those they memorialize. Just recently the famed Secretariat was buried on Claiborne Farm; like Man O' War, he was buried intact in a huge oak coffin, though his burial was nothing like the funeral accorded Man O' War. A 1982 list compiled by the Keeneland Association Library documents the graves of over 150 famous Bluegrass horses. "Why do we have the cemeteries? I think it's out of the respect and love we have for those classic racehorses," says C. V. "Sonny" Whitney, Bluegrass gentleman farmer of wide reputation. "We put in the graveyard what you might say were the leading, most successful horses, the very top that were produced on this farm." This Bluegrass custom began in 1875 when A. J. Alexander memorialized the grave of Lexington with a marble shaft, the first recorded horse monument in the country. In 1887 and 1893, Alexander's gesture was imitated

Calumet Farm's horse cemetery (Photo by Jerry Schureman)

by his neighbor Frank Harper, who erected ornate marble gravestones for his great racers and sires Ten Broeck and Longfellow. Perhaps the most elaborate horse cemetery is on the illustrious Calumet Farm, home of the greatest number of Derby winners, where just recently Alydar was buried. Over forty other horses lie buried on its beautiful grounds, planted with flowers and trees, and in the center stands a marble monument to Calumet's eight Derby-winning immortals: Citation, Forward Pass, Hill Gail, Iron Liege, Pensive, Ponder, Tim Tam, Whirlaway.

Calumet's horse cemetery was designed by the farm manager, who made "a rough draft on a piece of shelf paper," and at breakfast one morning the farm's owners, the Markeys, promptly approved it. A brass replica of the Derby trophy on top of the central monument was originally crowned with a tiny figurine of a horse and jockey, which, sadly, was stolen, probably by souvenir filchers. If nothing else, such thievery—not unheard of in other Bluegrass horse cemeteries—attests to the widespread reverence accorded the area's famous horses.

A final catalyst to the tradition of postmortem tributes to Bluegrass horses was provided in 1897 by James R. Keene, who, although considered a rather cold-hearted man, nevertheless buried his famous Domino under the laudatory epitaph: "Here lies the fleetest runner the American turf has ever known, and one of the gamest and most generous of horses." Not to be outdone by Keene's gesture, other horsemen in the Region created horse cemeteries for their own famous steeds, a tradition that continues today. As a newspaper article noted, Epona, the Greek goddess of horsemen "would surely be pleased with many of the tributes that the caretakers of Thoroughbreds have built to immortalize their charges."

Controversial Memorial   Though most Bluegrass horse memorials generate a degree of reverence from sightseers, one is the subject of a continuing humorous—and some say scandalous—legend. It is the statue, erected on Lexington's courthouse lawn, of the Region's most famous Confederate, General John Hunt Morgan, astride his equally famous mare Black Bess—the same horse he rode through his house to escape Federal pursuers. The following is Burton Milward's version of the Morgan/Black Bess legend:

The statue had been created by the noted sculptor, Pompero Coppini, and cast in bronze; the granite base had been carved and erected, and all had been installed under closely guarded wraps by the day of the unveiling, October 18, 1911.

A tremendous crowd assembled: The veterans of Morgan's own command and of other Civil War regiments, Confederate and Union; the United Daughters of the Confederacy in their finest gowns; the distinguished speakers, public officials and guests, and a horde of on-lookers.

The fateful moment came. The cords that held the drapes were pulled . . . Morgan was revealed astride . . . Good God! . . . a stallion.

A gasp of horror arose from thousands of throats. Morgan, as EVERYBODY knew, had ridden through the war on a mare, his favorite Black Bess.

The Daughters almost fainted en masse as cries of "Shame, Shame" reverberated from the walls of downtown buildings. Coppini would have been lynched if he could have been found.

Indeed, another version of the legend, told by William H. Townsend, says that Coppini escaped the angry mob gathering at Lexington's Union Station—his intended escape route from the Bluegrass—only by having the police escort him to Winchester to catch his train.

What the outraged crowd did not know was that this mount represented a compromise between Coppini's original model and the monument committee's preference for Black Bess. Coppini believed that the horse should be a stallion, because a mare was "too fragile and small for an equestrian statue of heroic proportions"; since Morgan had ridden a male horse (actually a gelding) during the war—a "big horse"—longer than he had Black Bess, Coppini's original model had depicted Morgan on a stallion, but one of huge size and—to the monument committee—grotesque proportions. The committee was aghast, proclaimed the model a hammer-headed nag unfit to carry a Bluegrass hero, and rejected it outright. So vehemently did one Lexingtonian criticize the beleaguered sculptor that Coppini challenged him to a duel—evidently he knew *that* Bluegrass tradition—but Judge James H. Mulligan interceded. The upshot was a compromise: the committee would accept a stallion as long as it was one of proper Bluegrass Thoroughbred size and conformation. However, public consternation was not appeased. People wanted Morgan riding his own favorite little mare.

The statue's "masculine equipment" for many years was the target of the annual ritualistic pranks of graduating high school seniors who would, in the dark of night, paint the scrotum a bright red. Though a folk prank, such painting had a serious function—it kept in the folk conscious and called to public attention the fact that it was a grotesque and blatant effrontery to depict Morgan's beloved Bess with male genitalia. To make matters worse, efforts of workers to remove the "paint jobs" only served to polish the statue's genitalia to a high gleaming sheen; all of this, furthermore, not only called more attention to the statue—no doubt not of the sort Coppini intended—but also created an entirely new reason for the continuation of the legend, now in modern "dress," so to speak.

Of course, the original legend is just that—a legend. According to Milward, "there ascended from the vast crowd a prolonged and enthusiastic cheer, not groans and curses," when the statue was unveiled. Yet the "historic" account is not the one most people know; rather it is the folk version that lives on the lips of untold thousands and generations of Bluegrass residents. Their hero Morgan should be riding his Bess—that is the prevailing folk wisdom related again and again in the legend, and the views of all the elite culture artists, historians, and committees in the world will never change it.

Folk culture is central not only to horse legends but in various forms permeates most Bluegrass horse activities—whether breeding, raising, training, buying and selling, racing, or memorializing them. Yet despite all the new scientific as well as traditional methods employed, the ultimate result is often seen as a matter of "luck"—another component of folk culture; in fact, many horse people would say that, in the final analysis, raising and racing horses is a gamble.

The Gaming Spirit

Travelers to the early environs of the Bluegrass frequently commented on what one Scottish visitor described as "the strange affinity for gambling and horse racing" among Kentucky gentlemen. In 1837, William P. Fessenden, who visited Lexington with Daniel Webster, wrote:

The Kentuckians . . . value themselves greatly in their breed of horses, and enter into the spirit of such an occasion, and it is not disagreeable to see such men as Clay, Crittenden, Robinson and others of that stamp apparently as much excited, talking as loudly, betting as freely, drinking as deeply and swearing as excessively as the jockeys themselves.

Apparently caught up in the excitement of such an event, Fessenden reported that he himself had bet, and lost, eight "hailstorms" (brandy juleps) on a horse. From time immemorial interpersonal, informal gambling and social drinking have been traditional, much relished activities, and only in modern human history have such activities been viewed as either illegal or sinful—illegal because, if they are done without official controls, the government cannot tax them, and sinful because they can lead to excesses, such as drunkenness, or neglect of family and obligations.

AT THE TRACK

Excess in anything is perhaps undesirable, but for many Bluegrass residents occasional drinking and gambling have been two of the threads making up the traditional fabric of life—not only acceptable, but traditionally expected of a gentleman. One of the more successful of Bluegrass legendary gamblers was Bourbon County native Riley Grannan, who ran up, and lost—with equal equanimity—at least half a dozen fortunes. According to one of the many stories about his colorful career, Grannan, temporarily broke, was preparing to send a suit to the cleaners when he discovered in a pocket a forgotten fifty-dollar bill. He went straight to the racetrack and in one afternoon parlayed the fifty into twenty thousand dollars. An equally colorful gambler was the previously mentioned Colonel Chinn, a man of immense personal charm and honor, as well as the sharpest horse salesman in the Bluegrass; nonetheless, from time to time, the Colonel found himself short of cash. On one such occasion, according to a story retold by Bradley Smith, he wired his good friend, W. T. Anderson, another big-time wagerer, saying: "COULD USE $25,000. PLEASE REPLY." Anderson answered: "ANYONE WHO CAN USE $25,000 CAN USE $50,000. MONEY ORDER HEREWITH."

Whether Colonel Chinn wagered this $50,000 profitably is not known, for even the most knowledgeable of horsemen could not be assured of uninterrupted success at the track, as attested by the experiences of Colonel E. R. Bradley during the 1921 Kentucky Derby. Bradley planned to win that race with a stallion called Black Servant. Not doubting the speed and stamina of his horse, the Colonel bet heavily on him, even entering in the race another fast horse, Behave Yourself, as pacemaker for his favorite. Bradley's strategy failed, for Behave Yourself, apparently not living up to his name, refused to be controlled by his jockey, caught up with Black Servant in the stretch, and passed him at the finish. Although visibly disappointed, the Colonel gallantly remarked, "Some washer-woman probably had her two dollars on Behave Yourself, and her winnings will mean more to her than my losses will to me."

The unpredictability of race horses, and the fallibility of so-called experts in selecting winners, is the subject of numerous stories, one of the more humorous of which—related by Bradley Smith—concerns two gentlemen who, considering themselves discerning judges of horseflesh, attended the races at Keeneland. They were perturbed to find—their vaunted expertise notwithstanding—that they were losing heavily on every race, whereas two elderly ladies standing nearby were cashing in tickets right and left. Finally, one of the gentlemen stepped over to the ladies, congratulated them on their good luck, and inquired about their system for selecting winners. "Oh," replied the elder of the two, "we have lots of systems. Today we're betting on the horses with the longest tails."

Gambling in the Bluegrass was not limited to the gentry, of course. Another colorful Bluegrass personality was Price McGrath. Although of humble origins, he became an inveterate old gambler and, after winning $105,000 in a single night in New York, came back to Kentucky to found McGrathiana farm, where he lived like a Bluegrass squire. He continued to gamble and to lighten the pockets of the Bluegrass "sporting brotherhood" right up to his death in 1881. McGrath was also the owner of Aristides, winner of the first Kentucky Derby in 1875. The following year, McGrath was challenged to race Aristides against the famous Ten Broeck of Woodford County at Lexington's Chittlin' Switch. All Woodford County turned out, ready to bet heavily on Ten Broeck. Lawrence Thompson retells the ensuing legendary events:

McGrath stood in the track taking all . . . bets that the Woodford County boys would place. . . . [It is claimed he] bet between $12,000 and $20,000, and he made no record of his wagers. A friend advised McGrath to jot down some of the names of the bettors, warning that every man at the track would claim a bet with McGrath if Ten Broeck won. "Don't you worry, sonny," the veteran gambler calmly replied, "the red hoss will keep the books. . . ." All turfdom knows how "the red hoss" [Aristides] [finished] . . . a full forty yards ahead of Ten Broeck.

Legend further has it that all Woodford County went bankrupt and that the day after the race the line to the local "home finance company's doors in Versailles stretched around the block."

BILLIARDS AND CARDS

Kentuckians' wagering and games of chance were not, of course, limited to horse racing. Despite the protests of local reformists, facilities for card games, billiards, and other opportunities to lay wagers were available at every inn and tavern. In early days, as it still is today, billiards was an exceptionally popular game, and one version was even called "Kentucky." (Although later, to the glory of the Bluegrass chivalry, the game was renamed "Jennie Lind" because of billiard players' admiration for the "Swedish Nightingale.")* One famous Bluegrass tavern, Morgan Row in Harrodsburg, boasted a gambling room that never closed. Virtually windowless, with white plaster walls on which winnings and losses were scrawled, the gambling room was open only to known patrons who were carefully scrutinized through a slit in the door before being admitted. When gambling houses from other areas of the country needed sharp dealers, it was said they could be recruited at Morgan Row. During the Civil War, a running poker game was supposedly interrupted by the Battle of Perryville being fought only ten miles away; the gamblers, wishing to observe the spectacle, left the tavern, but they first took the precaution of laying a drunk across the table to prevent anyone from tampering with the chips.

Poker, Kentucky style, was developed to a fine art. The stakes in some games were so extravagantly high that fortunes could be made or lost in a single evening. One of the most incorrigible addicts of the poker

---

*It is interesting to note the change over the years in the class of people frequenting pool rooms. In former times the billiard parlor was a gathering place for gentlemen of both upper and middle class. Today, most Bluegrass pool rooms—which are so numerous as to deserve a separate study—are usually a favorite haunt of working-class males and even those on the lowest rung of the socioeconomic ladder.

table was the redoubtable Henry Clay, who was an inveterate gambler. Clay and his good friend John Bradford, editor of the *Kentucky Gazette*, once ended a game of cards with Bradford the loser by some $40,000. When Bradford asked how the account should be settled, Clay suggested that Bradford's note for $500 would be satisfactory. Shortly thereafter, Clay and Bradford played again, but this time Clay was the loser, by about $60,000, whereupon he returned the $500 note to the editor, and both men were satisfied. Unfortunately, however, most gambling debts were not settled so amicably, and poker games often ended in brawls, duels, and bloodshed.

OTHER ''SPORTING'' EVENTS

Nineteenth-century Kentuckians would bet on almost anything or turn almost any situation into an opportunity for a game of chance. Pioneer Kentuckians most frequently bet on their marksmanship. However, on the frontier, and continuing for years after, wagering was also popular during bearbaiting, cockfights, and similar "sporting" events, including the frequent "no holds barred" fist fights and wrestling matches popular among working-class Kentuckians, especially on Court Day. Forming a makeshift ring around the combatants—who clubbed, gouged, bit, scratched, kicked and, in the words of a visiting New Englander, engaged in other canine modes of fighting—the spectators would bet on their favorites until one man either shouted "enough" or lapsed into unconsciousness, and a winner was declared. Such unrestricted brawls were so common that a section of one Bluegrass town—Winchester—was nicknamed Battle Row.

Stagecoach drivers invented a popular game called Penny-on-the-Bottle, which they played in idle moments. The idea was to snap the whip so precisely that a penny—positioned on the lip of a whiskey bottle—would be knocked off without upsetting the bottle; if one driver upset the bottle, he had to stand drinks for the rest.

Quite different from these free-for-all bets were the private lotteries for worthy causes such as schools, public roads, and canals, which were successfully held by special permission of the Kentucky Assembly until 1890 when they were finally declared illegal by the revised state constitution—only to be renewed by the Commonwealth itself when in recent years it established a state lottery.

No doubt public sentiment against gambling and horse racing increased in direct proportion to the growth of Fundamentalist religious fervor. For some Bluegrass churches, however, an unequivocal condemnation of these "works of the devil" proved to be untenable. The

Christian Church at Midway (Woodford County) was built and maintained primarily through monies provided by J. W. (Uncle Jim) Parrish (1862–1940), a wealthy parishioner and successful breeder of race horses. Once, when the church needed a pipe organ, Uncle Jim suggested the decision be postponed for a week, because his Rolled Stocking was running in a stakes race at Latonia next Saturday, and if the horse won, the congregation could afford the organ. Rolled Stocking won—no doubt with the undivided backing of the congregation—and the organ was installed. A few years later the church again was searching for funds, this time to repair the outside of the building and to redecorate within. Parrish was shipping a horse to Chicago. "If he wins," he said, "get started on the painting." Again, the horse won, and the church was painted. Returning to Midway after a month's absence, Parrish attended services on the following Sunday, and was highly pleased with the refurbishing. In fact, as he looked about him, he begin to grin. The inside of the church had—apparently inadvertently—been done up in Uncle Jim's racing colors—terra cotta and straw.

Handbooks   Despite some religious opposition, then, racing and gambling in the Bluegrass continued to be profitable folk pastimes, both for the wealthy and the general populace. During the first part of the twentieth century, reaching their peak in popularity during the 1930s, so-called handbooks flourished in the Bluegrass, particularly Lexington. Most of these betting establishments were housed on second floors above legitimate businesses in downtown Lexington, particularly bars and theatres; however, what is now known as the historic Mary Todd Lincoln house, which stands close to the center of downtown Lexington, was at one time a handbook establishment. One could place a bet on almost anything through a handbook but the emphasis was, of course, on horse racing. Although they were illegal, they were apparently tolerated by the police, because they operated quite openly. Each handbook catered to its own patrons and provided, as did early Kentucky taverns, common gathering places for males of all socioeconomic levels, including many of the employees of the surrounding Bluegrass horse farms. The walls of handbook establishments were usually covered with charts showing the races being run at various locations all over the United States, and seats or chairs were provided so wagerers could await race results in comfort. To avoid competition with Keeneland, a gentleman's agreement declared that all the handbooks would be closed during the Keeneland racing season.

Some handbook operations were quite large. The handbook business in Lexington was so profitable that one operator gained a national reputation as a "big money lay-off man"—that is, one who accepted bets from other bookies, to spread the risk. Others were small enterprises operating out of the back of grocery stores and the like, so small that some would accept a 25-cent bet. Many handbook operators were considered respectable members of the community, donated to churches and charities, helped their patrons with financial problems and employment, and were scrupulously honest. One such operator, nicknamed Deacon, had as a customer an elderly black gentleman named Sam who, though blind, loved to shoot craps. They would play for hours over the phone, Deacon throwing the dice, telling Sam what point he made, then Sam directing Deacon what to do next. As the story goes, Deacon always paid Sam the exact amount he had won.

An amiable relationship between handbook operators and their patrons continued until World War II, when large numbers of soldiers were stationed in the Bluegrass, and the Federal government, deeming it necessary to protect the morality of its troops, joined with the more righteous among Lexington's populace and had the handbook establishments (as well as the brothels) closed down.

As often happens when a conflict occurs between elite and folk culture, the folk culture merely changes its form of expression. In this case, the tacitly approved, publicly accepted handbook establishments, which provided outlets for the folk propensity for gambling, were eliminated by the legal and institutional powers of elite culture; however, that power could not eliminate the reason for those establishments—the folk impulse prevalent among many to gamble. Gambling moved from the highly visible handbooks to the sub rosa activities of the bookie. One informant recalls that, during his college years, he entered a certain music store in a downtown Bluegrass city and saw ten phones sitting on a large desk with little slips of paper strewn about them. Not until years later did he realize that the owner sold few pianos but made many "books." Even today in the Bluegrass, a number of bookmakers are located in otherwise legal stores, in both the black and white communities. One well-known white store and two busy commercial locations in black neighborhoods were pointed out to me just recently as also being "bookie joints." The immediate environs of one of the black bookie joints is also the scene of public drinking—a liquor store is not far away—and, weather permitting, all sorts of other gambling, such as craps and cards, take place on the hoods of cars or on the ground. As often happens in such an atmosphere, arguments and fights frequently break out, so much so that the area has won itself the unenviable name "Bucket of Blood."

Thus if one knows the right places to go and the right people to see and has the acceptable references, bets can be placed at nearly any time for nearly any kind of activity. In general, most illegal betting activities are folk culture. (This does not mean, however, that all folk culture is illegal, only that most illegal activities are folk.) Perhaps recognizing the proclivity to gamble among a good many of its populace, as well as adhering to the folk proverb, "If you can't beat 'em, join 'em," the Commonwealth has increasingly assumed computerized oversight of race-track betting, and, most recently, has also initiated a state lottery; both profit the Commonwealth financially.

As in years past, members of all segments of contemporary Bluegrass society participate in the tradition of wagering on beautiful horses, whether by way of the legal system sanctioned by the Commonwealth, or the illegal, folk system of bookies. Some no doubt utilize both systems. Many horse farm employees avidly follow the bloodlines and careers of the Thoroughbreds with which they have worked and back them with their money. Even farriers, who are usually independent contractors moving from farm to farm, may display an amazing knowledge about their clients' horses; one young farrier, after looking at the brass name-plate on the halter of a mare, rattled off from memory her string of racing accomplishments and winnings. Such knowledge is frequently used to choose horses before placing bets.

Among working-class Kentuckians, wagering is probably most popu-lar before the Kentucky Derby. Each May employees of nearly every public or private business, factory, office, and institution—even elementary and secondary schools—spontaneously participate in betting pools for the Derby, then gather in private homes, bars, and other watering places to watch and celebrate the traditional, romantic Run for the Roses. A minister's widow, who had been opposed to racing and betting all her life, was nonetheless, at the age of seventy-five, attending her first race. After waving in her first winner and watching his numbers put up, she said cheerfully: "You know, I don't see anything bad about this." As the old Kentucky saying puts it: "There is little wrong with anyone around a racetrack that a winner won't cure."

Another well-known Bluegrass horse activity—often used, erroneously, to typify the gentry—and one inspiring a wide range of activities throughout the calendar year—many of which constitute perhaps the most ancient folk traditions and customs seen in the Bluegrass—is the gentleman's venerable sport of fox hunting.

CHAPTER 11

"Riding to Hound"

Fox hunting, which provides opportunity for both sport and social interaction, is considered by many to be one of the Region's strongest links with Mother England.

HUNT CLUBS

Located outside Lexington, on the Fayette–Clark County line, is the oldest nationally recognized hunt club in the area (established in 1880) and the third oldest in the nation—the Iroquois Hunt, named after the first American horse to win the English Derby. The Iroquois Hunt has been appropriately headquartered, since 1928, at the historic, ivy-covered Grimes Mill. A Joint Master of the Hounds—whose father served in that same office for forty-three years—explained: "There's a whole lot of tradition and color in [fox hunting] . . . a whole lot of manners, politeness and protocol . . . from the dress, to the language, to the way we conduct the sport."

In keeping with this adherence to tradition, the Iroquois opens its annual hunting season with a ceremony originating centuries ago in Belgium but observed by only a handful of American hunt clubs, the Blessing of the Hounds. This ceremony, held the first Saturday in November, has traditionally been conducted by an Episcopal bishop or priest, often from nearby St. Hubert's Episcopal Church. Standing upon an old millstone, holding a hunting staff in one hand and a prayer book in the other, the cleric says a prayer and delivers a sermon. Then, the scarlet-coated hunters are blessed, each one kneeling before the priest to receive an individual benison for safety and a good hunt as well as a medal on which has been engraved the club logo and an image of a kneeling Saint Hubert, patron saint of the hunt. Horses and hounds are then blessed, and, finally, in more recent years, the fox is blessed: "That he may run the good race and 'go to ground' "—that is, escape. Viewing the Blessing of the Hounds as part of the Church's ongoing blessings for all matters of life and work relating to its members, one officiating priest from St. Hubert's explained: "The blessing is in the long tradition of . . . the Church of England, of which we are a branch. . . . Everything

Blessing of the Hounds
at the Iroquois Hunt, in
front of the historic
Grimes Mill, November
1990 (Photo by author)

that people did was very much a part of the church, and in this church, horses are important."

Horses and Hounds   Because the Bluegrass is horse country, many of the horses used for fox hunting are specially trained pedigreed breeds; indeed, probably a higher number of pedigreed mounts are found in the Iroquois than in any other hunt club in the nation. Some Iroquois members believe, however, that Thoroughbreds, because they tend to be nervous and high strung, are not as adaptable to hunting as are other breeds, such as the Appaloosa, or as crossbreeds. The latter can be almost anything, but among the more popular combinations is the cross between a Thoroughbred and a Quarter Horse. Like Thoroughbred people, fox hunters also harbor traditional prejudices about a horse's coloring and conformation. A man in the market for a hunter is warned, in a different version of the "white feet" quatrain:

> One white foot, buy the horse;
> Two white feet, try him;
> Three white feet, doubt him;
> Four white feet, do without him.

Sometimes the advice is more blunt: "Four white feet and a long white nose, knock him in the head and feed him to the crows."

Whatever the breed, the hunter must be properly trained, a service provided by Iroquois huntsman, Patrick Murphy, and his daughter, who manages the club stables. Preparatory to a hunt, the lower and underneath portions of the horse's body are closely clipped to minimize the accumulation of mud and debris. Although clipping itself is a longstanding tradition, individual riders vary in their opinions of quantity and design of such clipping, and the result is that some horses are clipped in unique patterns. If a horse has a reputation as a kicker, a bright red warning ribbon is tied near the root of its tail.

Sharing the limelight with the horse are the hounds. The responsibility for breeding, training, caring, and controlling the Iroquois hounds during the hunt also belongs to the huntsman. Murphy inherited his position at the Iroquois from his father, who had hunted in Ireland before emigrating to Kentucky in 1948. Fox hunting is rife with elaborate traditions, and thus Murphy's methods, procedures, and knowledge in general were absorbed from his father and generations of men "riding to hound" before him. Murphy breeds and trains approximately twenty pups a year, maintaining a pack of thirty couples, or sixty dogs, though only twenty couples are hunted at any one time. His hounds are primarily crossbred, a cross between the American fox hound, developed and bred first in Virginia and Kentucky, and the English fox hound, a combination he considers best for Bluegrass terrain. (In 1905 a hunting match pitted a pack of American hounds against a pack of English hounds; the colonials won.) A bit larger than American hounds, the English hounds have difficulty finding a way through the wire fences surrounding much of the Bluegrass farmland and, in addition, Murphy believes, they "don't have the best noses in the world." However, he tries "to keep about a quarter English in them for discipline. They're a little easier to handle." The quality of Kentucky hounds is widely admitted, and it is interesting that early breeders attributed, with geologic and geographic determinism, the excellence of Kentucky foxhounds to the underlying Bluegrass limestone, as noted by Roger D. Williams:

Kentucky has always been noted for its beautiful women, fine horses, and good whiskey. As horses and hounds always go together, it is not, therefore, surprising that the records both of the bench and hound field trials show conclusively that the very best foxhounds . . . come from Kentucky. . . . The horses and hounds of Kentucky are superior to those of all other states . . . [because] the water contains a larger percentage of phosphate of lime than any other section, and the effect of this upon stamina, size, and bone is well known.

The relative value placed upon one's hounds is humorously revealed in an 1886 place-name legend about Cream Ridge in Jessamine County.

One J. Fuller Brash was walking along the ridge when he met Bruner R. Close, stingiest man anywhere. J. Fuller suddenly blurted out that he wished to borrow $1 from Mr. Close to feed his family and another $17 to buy licenses for his hounds. Mr. Close instantly creamed him with a warped tobacco stick he was using as a walking cane. Creamed Ridge in time was shortened to its present name.

Murphy's excellent hounds are "pack broke"—that is, he has trained them to run in a pack, which he controls via his voice and his horn. He directs the pack to an area where he knows a fox lives, and with any luck the hounds pick up the scent, and the chase is on. Two "whippers-in" —club members who are superior horsemen—ride with the pack to help keep the hounds together. A hound "carrying the mail"—that is, at the front of the pack—has to be "a pretty good hound," Murphy asserts. Foxes, he notes, run approximately the same routes they did forty years ago (evidently foxes have traditions too). Eventually the fox "goes to ground," meaning he scampers into a hole. A couple of hounds will then "bay the hole," and the hunt is ended. Murphy then blows his horn and leads the pack away to find another fox. The fox is not harmed. Murphy maintains that the objective of "riding to hound" is not to kill or catch the fox but to have the pleasure of riding across country and watching the hounds do their work. This is in contrast to English practice, where the fox is dug out of its hole and killed. "They must have more foxes over there," Murphy commented wryly.

The Fox   Indeed, many fox hunters hold Reynard in high esteem and tell many tales—some of them *tall*—of his cunning and skills. In one story, a fox steals a wooden decoy duck and uses it to lure wild ducks. In another, the fox, after outpacing the panting hounds, sits on a hill to watch the hounds run around searching for him. Concerning the fox's tail a whole body of legend exists. A fox annoyed by fleas waded into deepening water until they were all congregated on the brush of his tail and then shook it, consigning the fleas to a watery grave. Some hunters say a fox will avoid cornfields and other plowed ground to prevent the weighty accumulation of mud on his tail, or will take a swim to clean the mud from it. Held in considerably less esteem than the fox is the coyote, a newcomer to Kentucky in the last five or six years. Murphy says the hounds will attempt to run a coyote the same way they do a fox, but the whippers-in attempt to spot any coyote (or deer) in the area and signal so the hounds can be turned. Hunters want the dogs to chase the fox—as tradition dictates—not a coyote or other animal, but the dogs, of course, do not know that.

Following the hounds and fox as closely as possible throughout the hunt are the hunters on horseback. Behind them are nonjumping riders, the "hilltopping group," club members who ride along the ridges to watch and follow the run from a distance. This group allows the inexperienced or unsure rider—or the very young or old—to participate in the sport. Active hunters range in age from the early teens to the mideighties. According to one Iroquois member, living in hunt country is a "way of life," and riding to hound together creates a bond "like an extension of your family."

Socializing   The kinship fostered by participation in the hunt is reinforced by various social activities, such as hunt breakfasts, dinners, and parties. In the early spring, the club hosts a day of steeplechase racing, open to the public, but it is in the early fall that its most exciting event is held, the Iroquois Hunt Club Barbeque and Trials. Held in behalf of the farmers over whose land the hunt rides, the day includes breakfast for members and landowners, steeplechase trials which determine what members ride what class of hunt, the presentation of the Iroquois hounds by the Masters, the huntsman, and the whips, and a barbeque. Although primarily a treat and tribute to the landowners, without whose permission and cooperation the hunt could not be conducted ("the fox knows no property lines"), the events (except the breakfast) are open to the public for a small admission fee. Members are dressed in traditional attire: either spotless white or tan breeches, knee-high black boots, black velvet hunting bowlers, and scarlet coats with black collars and blue piping. The scarlet coats are traditionally called pinks, not for their color but after the Englishman, by the name of Pink, who first made them.

Although it is the oldest, the Iroquois is not the only hunt club in the Bluegrass. The Woodford Hounds, located in Versailles, was established in 1981. The tradition of fox hunting in Woodford County, however, considerably antedates the establishment of the club; indeed, one of the greatest fox hounds of all time, Big Stride, was bred and hunted there. Legend claims that in the 1920s the blind congressman from Ohio, Roy Gillan, traveled all the way to Versailles just to feel Big Stride's muscles. A marble shaft marking the famous dog's grave bears the inscription: "A wonderful hound, the greatest of all times. (Records live, opinions die.)" The members of the Woodford Hounds apparently are as enthusiastic hunters as are those of the Iroquois; in the 1988–1989 season their hounds (crossbred and American) went out sixty-nine times, as compared to sixty for the Iroquois. A third organized hunt club, the Long Run Hounds, is located in the Outer Bluegrass, near Louisville.

The zeal of the Kentucky fox hunter is the subject of many a folk story; a favorite, retold here by Lawrence Thompson, concerns James Campbell of Mercer County, who was the grandfather of Carry Nation and the owner of Sounder, one of the most celebrated fox hounds of its day.

Campbell . . . was not baptized until middle age, and when he finally decided to submit to immersion, he held up the actual proceedings for several hours. Just as he was ready to go under, he heard Sounder barking in the forest . . . and he felt compelled to interrupt the rite long enough to find out what was exciting the hound.

NIGHT HUNTING

The joys of fox hunting in the Bluegrass are not limited, of course, to members of organized hunt clubs; Thompson has called fox hunting "a great leveller," enjoyed alike by "one-gallus tenant farmers" and "scarlet-coated heirs to the great Bluegrass fortunes." The former are particularly fond of "night hunting." In a fashion similar to "'coon hunting," night fox hunters gather with their hounds on a hilltop, light a fire, perhaps drink a bit, and turn their dogs loose to hunt. Each man can recognize the voices of his own hounds, and the hunters may sit around the fire all night, enjoying the thrill of the chase by just listening to their baying dogs. Attesting to the glories of night hunting—and the importance placed upon a prized fox hound—is this statement by Kentucky Court of Appeals Judge Eugene Siler, during a court case over the death of a hound from a fall into an open well while running a fox:

In the great fraternity of fox hunters, a man's hound is a pearl of considerable price. A common man may freely enjoy without tax or ticket the open air symphony of the melodious harmony of a pack of hounds on a cool, clear night and therein finds that life is good if not somewhat glorious. He often recognizes the distinct voice of his own dog and takes pardonable pride in the leadership of that dog running out there ahead of all the rest. . . . The hound that runs the bushy tail with enthusiasm is just a little lower in the fox hunter's affection than his children. And although habitual fox hunters toil but little and spin but spasmodically, yet Solomon in his palmiest days never had more of a wealth of real happiness than one of these fox hunters, a wealth to which the hounds make a nightly contribution. Sometimes a man goes fox hunting just for the music, sometimes he goes for surcease from unhappy home life, sometimes he goes in pure pride over the "best dog in the country."

Other hunting and "sporting" folk traditions, primarily of the common folk, are widespread in Kentucky and the Bluegrass.

12

Guns, Rods and Reels, and Baited Fields

From the earliest settlement, weapons were, of harsh necessity, the most important items in a household, but they—and their expert use—were also romanticized and quickly acquired symbolic significance. Today, weapons, and the sporting traditions surrounding them, are still often romanticized.

HUNTING

On the frontier the preservation of life depended upon the skills and tenacity of the hunter. No ability was more lauded; a great hunter was the ideal man. Not only did hunting provide meat, hides, and fur for pioneer families, but fur and peltry also served as money to exchange for salt, iron, rifles, and other necessities. Currency was estimated in bucks, or deer hides, which were in demand for working men's aprons; the skin of a buck was valued at one dollar; that of a doe, half a dollar.

Some settlers hunted every day, and of those who declined to hunt on the Sabbath were many who refrained not for religious reasons, but only because of a superstition that whoever hunted on Sundays was certain to have bad luck the rest of the week. Squirrels were so plentiful in the early Bluegrass that they were considered a menace, and thousands were slaughtered. In 1793 a law was enacted that required every white male over sixteen to kill a certain number of crows and squirrels each year. From pioneer times, every boy was given a rifle at the age of twelve or so, and thereafter he regularly hunted squirrels, turkeys, and raccoons.

Displays of Marksmanship Expertise in marksmanship was so highly valued that shooting competitions were a favorite pastime, wherein every man could display his skills. Audubon, the noted ornithologist, who lived in Kentucky from 1808 to 1819, marveled at the marksmanship displayed in such shooting matches as "driving the nail," "snuffing the candle," and "barking a squirrel," and he described them in an 1831 essay. From about 40 yards, each rifleman in turn shot at a nail partially imbedded in a tree, the object being to hit the nail square on its head and drive it in. If he missed entirely, the shooter was considered "an indifferent marksman," and even bending the nail was unacceptable. Those who managed to drive in the nail then competed to determine the consistently best shot. To polish one's skills at night hunting, a candle was placed 50 yards away in the dark; the object was to snuff out the candle at least three shots out of seven, an accomplishment that brought hurrahs from bystanders. Supposedly, such skill enabled a shooter to hit the eye of his quarry at night, since the light from a torch would reflect from an animal's eye. Perhaps the most demanding of shooting abilities, barking the squirrel, was performed for Audubon by Daniel Boone himself, who along with George Rogers Clark excelled at this display of marksmanship. The object was to hit the bark of the tree so close to the squirrel that the concussion and flying bark either stunned or killed the animal without even grazing its skin. According to Audubon, squirrels were so plentiful that Boone stood in one spot for hours barking squirrels and "procured as many squirrels as we wished"—almost a brag.

Flyting   Displays of such marksmanship were often accompanied by braggadocio. Kentuckians would boast, for example, that they could only eat squirrels shot through the left eye, else they might get indigestion. Such boasts were but an extension of the even more widespread tall-tale and flyting tradition associated particularly with early Kentuckians. These extreme boasts were so commonly recited that they were often set to rhyme or song or formulaic chant. One Southern Congressman visiting Kentucky was told by a local that he could "jump higher, squat lower, dive deeper, stay under longer, and come up dryer... whip his weight in wildcats, and let a zebra kick him every fifteen minutes." Such colorful declarations were soon exploited and satirized in novels, stories, and vaudeville where they quickly were accepted as accurate, stereotypical characteristics of Kentuckians, as in an 1830s James Paulding drama, whose main character spouted:

Mister, I can whip my weight in wildcats—my name is [Colonel] Nimrod Wildfire—half horse, half alligator, and a touch of airthquake; that's got the prettiest sister, the fastest horse, and ugliest dog in the district, and can outrun, out jump, throw down, drag out, and whip any man in Kaintuck.

In the same era, the main character of a popular novel bellowed:

Straunger, my name's [Captain] Ralph Stackpole [meaning a captain of horse-thieves], and I'm a ring-tailed squealer...I'm a gentleman, and my name's *Fight!* Foot and hand, tooth and nail, claw and mud-scraper, knife, gun, and tomahawk, or any other way you choose to take me....Cock-a-doodle-doo!

These boasting, flyting, and hyperbolic tale telling traditions were epitomized by frontier riverboatmen, who excelled in their performance, chief among them being the king of the keelboatmen and the "great grand-daddy of . . . practical jokesters in Kentucky," the immortal Mike Fink. Mike bandied about declaring, "I'm a ringtailed squealer, I love wimmin, and I'm chock full of fight." Yet Mike was most renowned for his marksmanship, and won the laudatory nickname "Bang All" for his shooting skills, demonstrated at many local matches; he was frequently barred from competing because no one could match him. He once shot the tails off three pigs to teach a farmer a lesson; but his most daring feat involved shooting a hole in a cup of whiskey as it rested on an accomplice's head. According to one version of his death (there were at least ten), this act also cost him his life. Supposedly, Mike and his accomplice had argued over a squaw, so at the next occasion to shoot the cup, Mike lowered his sights and shot his rival dead between the eyes; the man's friend allegedly revenged him by killing Mike.

The Long Rifle   The incredible marksmanship of early Bluegrass residents was in part attributed to the remarkable accuracy of the so-called Kentucky long rifle,* a superb example of folk craftsmanship. Kentuckian's sharpshooting, *and* braggadocio, was nowhere more convincingly demonstrated and historically documented than during the 1815 battle of New Orleans. Kentuckians with their "squirrel rifles" —along with frontier volunteers from other parts of the South—poured such a deadly fire on the hapless British troops that they lost 2,000 men to the Americans' seventy-one. In appreciation, the song "The Hunters of Kentucky" was dedicated to them and sung nationwide in vaudeville performances.

> There stood John Bull in martial pomp,
>   But here stood old Kentucky!
> O Kentucky, the hunters of Kentucky,
>   The hunters of Kentucky! . . .
>
> And if daring foe annoys,
>   Whate'er his strength and forces,
> We'll show him that Kentucky boys
>   Are "alligator horses."
> O Kentucky, the hunters of Kentucky,
>   The hunters of Kentucky!

---

*The long rifle, also known locally as a squirrel gun, actually originated in Pennsylvania— probably made by some anonymous German-Swiss immigrant gunsmith—and is more correctly called, therefore, the Pennsylvania long rifle. Yet, it was in the hands of Kentucky frontiersmen that it became famous.

A long rifle was usually crafted by hand to the individual owner's size, dimensions, preferences, and intended use. The small, lightweight stock was custom-carved, usually from apple, walnut, or maple wood, especially tiger-striped or curly maple. While the intended owner demonstrated his shooting style, numerous measurements were taken, and the stock was fitted to him as accurately and precisely as though it were a glove. It was truly a customized weapon, and Bluegrass folk craftsmen excelled in its creation. The world's best long-rifle craftsman was reputed to be Benjamin Mills of Harrodsburg.

Owners were so enamored of their long rifles that many were given names, as were powder horns which, like the rifles, were usually inscribed and carved with personal names, markings, and even intricate and beautiful embellishments of folk art. Today, both are considered museum-quality treasures. Modern craftsmen in the Bluegrass do create excellent reproductions, however, and a number of black-powder clubs exist which endeavor to preserve an accurate picture of frontier-hunter life. In addition to making the reproductions, they hold shooting matches and even bivouacs in the country, in as near to frontier fashion as modernity permits: buckskin and linsey-woolsey clothing, coonskin caps, lean-to shelters, etc. Among these modern frontier aficionados the traditional long rifle has been elevated to a position of near-worship. The most recent tribute to Kentuckians' hunting prowess and marksmanship and to their traditional long rifle occurred in August, 1990, when the image of the rifle with a powder horn draped over it was chosen as the official logo for the U.S.S. *Kentucky*. (The *Kentucky*, the Navy's newest nuclear submarine, is appropriately lauded as the "Thoroughbred of the fleet.") Thus it was a perfect matching of the oldest and the newest, and most accurate and deadly, of American weapons, and a continuation of the tradition of Kentuckians being, as noted by an Englishman, "the best warriors in the United States." Such efforts of glorification and emulation as the black powder clubs and the sub logo—romantic, and in the case of the sub, elite culture, efforts though they may be—are nonetheless direct descendants of early folk traditions.

MANLINESS

The wanton slaughter, the violence, and the love of firearms among many early Kentuckians—and even among some modern ones—may be an inheritance from early explorers, who of necessity were adventurous and lawless. Although the caricature of the early settler depicted him as a barbarously comical character, the alligator-horse was in fact a sinister figure, embodying both animal cunning and brute force. Such a stereotype was to a degree rooted in fact. Arthur K. Moore has described Kentucky frontiersmen as symbols "of murderous and lustful anarchy ... aggressive," with "self-assurance bordering on arrogance, belligerent independence, and inordinate pride of person, family, possessions, and homeland." Although many were socially inferior and poverty-stricken, says Moore, Bluegrass frontiersmen were proud and resourceful, determined "to alter the humble role assigned to them by their betters in the East." In doing so, many "asserted ... their natural prerogatives to level out class distinctions, tinker with political machinery, worship orgiastically, and set aside the Mosiac Decalogue at pleasure."

Partially mitigating such violent tendencies among the first generation of settlers was the presence of a considerable number of people who valued their European cultural heritage and strove to establish its traditions in the Bluegrass—hence Lexington's appellation as "The Athens of the West," the founding of Transylvania as the first institution of higher learning west of the Alleghenies, and the early establishment of a primary and secondary public school system. Notwithstanding these influences, for the larger populace they were ineffectual, and the common man's folk worldview of "manly" ideals prevailed. As T. P. Abernethy wrote, "The challenge of the wilderness was so largely to physical prowess [that] brawn came to be the most respected of all endowments and education in time came to be looked upon not only as unnecessary, but as something effete, not quite becoming to men of virility."

Central to this concept of manliness was, of course, hunting, and it followed that esteem increased in direct proportion to demonstrated evidence of skills in tracking and marksmanship. Moreover, a hunter's life came to be increasingly rationalized and even glorified. The preacher James B. Finley, who had grown up on the Kentucky frontier, wrote:

A hunter's life is one of constant excitement. He is always on the look-out, and filled with constant expectation. His narratives always possess a thrilling interest, and are listened to with the greatest attention. His wants are but few, and he is not disturbed with cankering care about the future. His employment does not lead him to covetousness, and he is always characterized by a generous hospitality [a highly valued Bluegrass trait]. His hut or cabin is always a sure asylum for the hungry and destitute.

Thus, such romanticized portrayal of hunting held that it was "manly" to pursue and kill wild animals. Hunting became a challenge by which a man could establish and demonstrate his worth. So pervasive and accepted was this propensity to equate "manhood" with hunting that even highly educated gentry fell under its spell—as many others do to this day.

The Cousins Clay: Henry and Cassius   Even the highly educated and urbane Henry Clay, on one noteworthy occasion, was compelled to prove his proficiency with the long rifle. The legend is retold here by William C. Davis:

In 1803, when Henry Clay was stumping Fayette County for a seat in the legislature, he suddenly found himself challenged by a yeoman in the audience to display his prowess with the long rifle. No man who could not shoot fair and straight deserved to sit in the state house. Manfully, "Harry of the West" [one of Clay's nicknames] shouldered the piece, discharged the fatal ball, and peered through the smoke to learn his fate. His aim was true, and he won the backwoodsman's vote and the cheer of the crowd. Only years later did he confess that "I had never before fired a rifle, and have not since."

Henry *was* adept, however, at employing the much revered long rifle in a metaphorical sense when his political career was in jeopardy. Robb Sagendorph records a legend about Henry. Because of Henry's vote on a controversial issue, an old influential friend—in his younger days an avid hunter—sadly informed Clay he could no longer support him for re-election. Henry replied, "If you had a very good rifle, and one day it failed to fire, would you break it to pieces . . . or would you pick the flint and try it again?" The old hunter answered with tears in his eyes, "No, Harry, I would pick the flint and try her again; and I'll try you again; give us your hand." Clay was re-elected.

Although they were cousins and both became Bluegrass legends in their own time, Henry and Cassius Clay could not have been more temperamentally different, as revealed in their nicknames. Henry, a diplomatic man of words, was given the epithet the Great Compromiser, while his cousin, a man of action, yielded to no one and was called the Lion of White Hall. Henry did fight duels, but only reluctantly and somewhat ineffectually, whereas Cassius extolled the folk associations and equations of manliness with weapons proficiency and excelled in their use. One of the innumerable Cassius legends, related by Gerald Carson, describes the venerable old firebrand's death, rifle at his side.

Clay was a dead shot, could sever a string at ten paces three times out of five. In his first duel both Clay and his adversary fired three times, missed, and shook hands. Afterwards a friend asked Clay how he could have missed when he had this marvelous ability to cut a string with a bullet.

"The darned string had no pistol in its hand," he explained.

When Clay was ninety-three . . . and legally adjudged to be out of his mind, the old man lay dying on a hot day while a large fly buzzed noisily on the bedroom ceiling. Deeply annoyed, the old fighter propped himself up in bed, took aim with his rifle, blasted a hole where the fly had been, and died.

Another legend, tangential to this one about Cassius' death, curiously concerns the statue over his cousin Henry's grave, a central focus of the Lexington cemetery since Henry's death in 1852, here retold by Squire Coleman:

[Cassius] lived a lonely life in the big mansion, and when he was nearly 93, he died of a kidney ailment on . . . July 23, 1903, he was the oldest living graduate of Yale University. At the time of his passing a severe electrical storm swept over central Kentucky, and a bolt of lightning knocked the head off the lofty statue of Henry Clay in the Lexington Cemetery.

Some considered the storm and its decapitation of Henry's statute a fitting climax to Cassius' turbulent life and a symbolic comment on which philosophy was more appropriate for a Bluegrass gentleman farmer aristocrat—Henry's compromising and "effete" position being toppled by Cassius' "manly" "thunder and lightning."*

Bearbaiting and Ganderpulling   This often violent attitude toward daily life gave rise to a number of distinctly rowdy forms of sport: bearbaiting, cockfighting, and ganderpulling—all thought by some, then and now, to be inherently cruel and inhumane.

Although Lawrence Thompson maintains that ganderpulling ranked "second only to horse racing as the most beloved sport of the rampaging frontier," as far as can be determined it has not survived. The "sport" was so popular at one time that a section of one town in the Outer Bluegrass was called Gandertown, as it was the ganderpulling gathering center for the Region. This "sport" involved suspending a gander by its feet from a revolving wheel atop a tall pole; the unfortunate bird's neck was then heavily greased, and contestants would thunder by the pole on horseback and attempt to jerk off the gander's head; the first to succeed won the contest.

Like ganderpulling, bearbaiting has been relegated to the past, though in early years it was a popular activity. The most common procedure was to unleash dogs on the chained, hapless bear, money being wagered on the canine most likely to engage the bear most fiercely and emerge unscathed. The 1814 Paris paper, for example, carried a notice of a bearbaiting at a private home where a three-year-old was to fight five dogs every half-hour "according to the regulations to be made known at the time of entering." For refreshment at this event, one-half of a she-bear was barbecued, said to be "as good a dinner furnished as the

---

*Cassius Clay, the former boxing champion, was named after the legendary Bluegrass abolitionist, and has also become a legend—and, like his namesake, in a very ostentatious manner.

country can provide." Ironically, although it was itself a bloody display of violent cruelty, the bearbaiting permitted no "quarrelsome person . . . to remain a guest as peace and harmony. . . [was] promoted and expected." When bears were unavailable, it was not unusual to stage a dogfight, supposedly to keep the dogs ready for real quarry. Such quasi–hunting activities no doubt whetted both hunters' and dogs' ferocity and also served to polish the dogs' skills and initiate any untried dogs into the dangers and techniques of the hunt. However, the match also served as a showcase for the symbolic and psychological vicarious aggrandizement of a hunter's prowess and superiority over the, sometimes threatening, animal world.

Cockfighting   Neither bearbaiting nor ganderpulling was a gentleman's activity, but cockfighting, from the earliest times, involved both the gentry and the common man. (Today, it is a sport of working-classes, and cocks are called the "poor man's race horse.") David Hawke writes:

Cockfighting . . . flourished everywhere in early America. An Anglican minister . . . [recorded] without remorse the fights he attended in New York. . . . Bets ran high at every fight, and often tempers, too, when any hint of a fixed match surfaced; a beak coated with garlic to repulse an opponent, a shot of brandy to enhance a cock's self-confidence were tricks used by owners. The cocks were trained to kill and equipped with honed steel spurs to speed their work.

Tom Clark has called cockfighting in the Bluegrass the "illicit consort of horse breeding and racing," and until the 1950s many horse farms had cockpits on their premises, usually in the center aisle of a tobacco barn. Cockfighting was almost as honored a sport as horse racing. Though today cockfighting, which is often a family activity, continues to be popular in the Bluegrass, betting on a cockfight is illegal. Therefore, it is usually staged surreptitiously, sometimes still in the center aisle of a tobacco barn. Today, a number of gentleman farms still keep gamecocks on the premises, usually in the horse barns to serve as mascots, since horses seem to appreciate their presence. Moreover, as raising gamecocks has never been illegal, today they are raised, as they were in the past, in any number of places, even in towns. Recently, in the backyard of a house in a poor Lexington neighborhood, gamecocks were discovered being raised to sell to the many cockfighters in the Region. Lifelong residents of Irishtown also remember gamecocks being raised in their neighborhood. The legal status of cockfighting was recently debated in the Kentucky Legislature, some legislators wishing to outlaw the sport altogether, others preferring simply to tax the proceeds like any other business. Attesting to cockfighting's current popularity, supporters and

Cockfighters proudly displaying a trophy and champion cocks, with homemade pens in background (Photo by author)

dissenters across the Commonwealth argued the issue, as in this newspaper dialogue, where the sport was said in fact to be

ordained by nature. . . . You can't, and don't have to force these beautiful and proud birds to fight. Fighting is their breeding and heritage. To fight is all they live for. . . . Cockfighters value their roosters as if they were thoroughbreds; and well they should, considering the money they bring in. The best money-making arenas are well known to all owners . . . from the local county and surrounding counties to Lexington. . . . Prizes for a win can approach $3,000 . . . a day or more. . . . Cockfighters hold tenaciously to their sport. . . . It is no more cruel than slaughter houses or chickens that are kept up day and night in mass assembly egg-laying factories. . . . It is probably no more cruel than horse racing, considering that the horse is used for the sole purpose of making money. . . .

All debaters, pro or con, seem to agree that cockfighting will continue, no matter its legal status, and like other tenacious and long-standing traditions, the sport has evolved an equally complex and esoteric folk idiom, as noted by Lawrence Thompson:

Kentucky chicken fighters have developed their own peculiar glossary. Yearling cocks are "stags," and . . . are kept on "walks" (natural habitat) when not fighting [hence the folk term "cock of the walk," said of a man who pompously flaunts his status]. However, during the off-season the chicken is painstakingly trained by being "flirted" (tossed to develop wing muscles) and "fluttered" (held by the thighs). In the pit the chickens may fight in "hacks" (single fights) or in "mains" (fifteen to twenty-one fowls pitted against one another). Chickens may be "game," "close hitters," "bloody heelers," "ready fighters" with "good mouths," or "quick to come to the point." But woe unto a "dunghill" chicken, one who will not fight, for his fate is more shameful than that of the cowardly bull. However, whereas many an unwilling *toro* has provided a toothsome beefsteak, game chicken is rarely a delicacy. Owners "dry them out" by giving them only as much water as is necessary for health and rub the skin with oil of peppermint just before fights.

Peak fighting age for cocks is three years; by four they are worn out. To revive a "brained" cock (one with a head injury), the owner strokes its neck and head repeatedly, but this treatment often fails to work and the bird dies.

Today cockfighting is but one of the outdoor folk sports participated in by many Bluegrass working–class males, a surprising number of whom still follow a traditional outdoor way of life.

MODERN HUNTING AND OTHER OUTDOOR TRADITIONS

Typical of a considerable number of older Bluegrass males is seventy-eight-year-old Lexingtonian Clay Smith; as outlined by Art Lander, Jr., Smith has "lived close to the land" most of his life, digging ginseng and raising tobacco in the summer and trapping mink and muskrat and hunting rabbits and quail in the fall. However, as a boy, squirrels were his first quarry, hunted with a .22 rifle he earned as a prize for selling $12 worth of mail-order garden seeds. His hunting dog Bounce always accompanied him and "was a legend. If there's a dog heaven, he's there," says the old hunter. The dog demanded that his master be a perfect marksman. "If I'd miss a squirrel, that dog would go crazy, running around . . . barking. I'd tell Bounce, just hold still boy, I'll get that squirrel on the next shot."

Whenever he could, Smith would head to the creek with a cane pole and some nightcrawlers to catch a mess of redeye or small mouth bass . . . . Through the years Smith also hunted raccoons with Walker dogs, but he never cared much for deer hunting. . . . Smith said he had gate keys to farms all over Fayette County. "All the farmers trusted me to fish and hunt on their property," he said. [In the Depression, Smith, as a teenager, picked produce on farms to sell on Lexington's streets—a folk occupation also engaged in by residents of Irishtown.] The day . . . Broker's Tip won the 1933 Kentucky Derby, Smith brought a load of fresh produce to Idle Hour Stock Farm [owned by Broker's Tip owner Colonel

Sheriff Burns of Mercer County proudly displaying his knife collection (Photo by author)

E.R. Bradley, who was in a good mood and glad to see Smith]. "He knew he had a good chance to win the Derby. . . . He told the cook to feed me breakfast and give me some of his best whiskey."

Such subsistence hunting/fishing/trapping/part-time farming lifestyle is another manifestation of the make-do mode of living and a common experience in earlier times, and it is interesting to note that the gentry—as in the Bradley/Smith connection here—often played a significant role in such patterns of subsistence living by providing part-time farm work, permitting fishing and hunting, and even by purchasing the fruits of the common man's labors. During hard times, many men of necessity took up the rifle and the fishing pole to provide for themselves and their families, but others did so simply because they cherished that traditional way of life.

One sees evidence of the hunting/fishing/sportsman tradition everywhere in the Bluegrass. Nearly every small-town barber shop has an array of "outdoorsman" and "gun" magazines, their pages dog-eared and often worn through; the same magazines are also found in physician's offices, automobile dealerships and garages and gas stations, and anywhere men gather. Nearly every town has its sportsmans' clubs, and most have target ranges. Not only do gun and sportsman stores enjoy a thriving business, but hardware, discount, and department stores are incomplete without sizable gun/fishing/outdoorsman sections. Many dealers and devotees travel hundreds of miles to attend periodic Bluegrass gun and knife shows, held either by local clubs or by commercial interests, where nearly any sort of firearm or cutting edge imaginable can be bought, sold, or traded. Bluegrass males of all socioeconomic classes trade and collect knives, and one can see this activity at nearly any informal male gathering. The National Knife Collector's Association is headquartered in Tennessee, but officials say that Kentuckians have always comprised a huge proportion of their membership.

The logo of the NRA (National Rifle Association) is seen everywhere on caps and jackets and especially on bumper stickers, usually on a pickup truck—often with oversize wheels—along with an occasional NRA political statement against gun control. The pickup may have dogs on board and almost invariably a gun rack across the inside rear window, often holding one or more guns or, more rarely, a hunting-quality bow or a fishing rod, or even a baseball bat or other club—an obvious association with potential violence as well as with sporting activities. Pickup gun racks belonging to stockmen or sheepmen sometimes display canes (the national sheepdog trials have historically been held in the Bluegrass). Many pickup drivers, especially those under forty, sport a beard or mustache, wear longish hair, usually smoke and/or chew, play rock or country music, wear work pants of denim, corduroy, or khaki, either a work shirt or a T-shirt (often sporting another logo) or in winter a plaid shirt, and work shoes or tennis shoes or boots (often cowboy). The older male will likely be clean-shaven and have short hair and may prefer a car to a pickup. *Most* often seen on young or old—even on grade-school boys—is the ubiquitous baseball cap, usually with yet another logo, often of a farm supply or contracting or automobile or truck company, or simply a favorite "down home" or "good ol' boy" slogan. The baseball cap is *the* one most commonly worn contemporary badge of identification, belonging, and manhood, especially for adult rural or working-class men. These common characteristics of manliness are emulated by so many rural men that they make up a readily discernible folk pattern, not only in the Bluegrass, but across Kentucky.

This traditional heritage of guns and hunting and fishing has led on occasion to some embarrassing and illegal situations. For instance, just a few years ago a group of lawyers, elected officials, and other respected people of one Bluegrass town were caught red-handed hunting doves illegally in a baited field. Likewise, frogs are regularly gigged illegally, and deer and other game such as turtles are shot by some men whenever they see them.

Turtles, however, are more commonly taken by traditional methods.

Lexie Slusher of Clark County shows how to catch a turtle (Photo by author)

In the fall and early winter, before it is too cold, turtle hunters wade in ponds and creeks and dig turtles out of the muddy banks, where they have burrowed to hibernate. Although some men actually dig them out with their hands—a dangerous pastime called noodling, presumably descriptive of their shredded flesh if grabbed by a snapper—most hunters prefer other methods. A number of men use an ingenious device to hook turtles lodged in the mud. The long steel rod from the side of old-fashioned bedsprings is bent on one end at a 90-degree angle to form a handle and at a 45-degree angle on the other end to form a hook. The turtle hunter stands in the pond or creek and inserts the hook end into the muddy bank and feels for snapping turtles, and when he locates one, he hooks it and pulls it out, holding tightly to the handle. The men say the sound made by the metal hook on the snapper's shell is unmistakable. During the warmer months turtles are taken with baited hooks, as in fishing. Most hunters use a hook and line, tied to a stake on the bank. The hook is baited with some tempting morsel—Lexie Slusher of Clark County, an expert at this, uses dove gizzards—and the line is tossed out and left for as long as a day. Others jug-fish for turtles by simply attaching a baited hook and line to plastic jugs and placing the jugs around a pond. The success rate of these methods often runs to 50 percent. Turtle meat is relished and even considered a delicacy, but one must know both how to clean and prepare turtles to bring out their best flavor. As Simon Bronner has noted, turtle hunting, as well as the consumption of their meat, constitutes one of the oldest hunting/culinary traditions known—one that has remained largely unaltered by the influences of commercialism.

Fishing folktales are nearly as plentiful as fishermen. A favorite anecdote, as it was related to me, concerns a farmer who loved to "dynamite" fish—toss a lighted stick into a lake and scoop up dead or stunned fish that float to the surface.

A game warden heard of his illegal pastime and paid him a visit disguised as a fisherman wanting to try the farmer's pond. After fishing a bit without success, he asked if the farmer ever heard of dynamiting fish. Not fooled, the farmer said he had heard of it but never had done it; so the warden asked if he had any dynamite so they could try it. The farmer took the warden out in the boat and lit a stick of dynamite, but gave it to the warden, who immediately panicked and threw it overboard. When the fish rose to the top, the farmer said, "Well look at that, you sure do know how to get fish the easy way."

Obviously, this is another trickster tale, and provides both narrator and audience vicarious delight in outwitting an adversary bent on halting a traditional method of taking fish.

All of the above examples notwithstanding, most fishing and hunting in Kentucky is conducted within the bounds of legality. Nearly one third of the population purchase legal permits, and in fact the state legislature recently enacted a hunter-harassment law to protect legal hunters from animal-rights activists who sometimes hound them in the field. However, the law has never been tested.

The pervasive emphasis upon guns, hunting, and shooting has on occasion led to assaults against people. Killings do occur, often as the result of a personal disagreement, where the readily available knife or gun is put to use to defend one's honor or one's position or to "settle the argument once and for all;" as in fistfights and such, these most often occur among those on the lower rungs of Bluegrass socioeconomic strata. However, as recently as 1990, one of the parties to an altercation between two Lexington lawyers chose a traditional Bluegrass method to settle the dispute; he shot the other attorney.

The early gentry were by no means immune to violence either, but among gentlemen killing one's enemy had to be done according to a carefully regulated, well understood "code of honor," thus assuring that the act be performed with elegance and civility.

13

The Code Duello

From the earliest days of Bluegrass settlement, homicide was a relatively common occurrence. Kentucky historian Robert M. Ireland describes early nineteenth century attitudes:

Life . . . was both hard and turbulent, and often short for many men who tried to get themselves established in that fast growing section of young America. Reckless gambling, hard drinking and fighting to the death with pistol and knife were the order of the day. Men fought for their rights and for their lives.

While gambling and drinking were certainly common precursors to violent encounters, they were not, in and of themselves, lethal activities. Rather, the practice of carrying concealed weapons, such as small derringers, sharp-pointed dirks or even larger knives like the bowie, and cane swords, together with the adherence to the "code of honor" which led to formal and de facto dueling—all traditions within the mainstream of Southern culture—provided the means for murder.

As early as the 1830s a Scottish visitor to Kentucky reported seeing well-dressed men carrying dirks; he noted that they not only picked their teeth with these "murderous blades" but also had the disconcerting habit of opening and closing their knives, or whetting them on their boots, during conversations. About the same time, an English visitor to Lexington was shocked to find so cultured a center with so many dirks for sale. Evidently, the habit of carrying such weapons, and using them, became more prevalent after the Civil War. In 1871, a prominent Kentucky judge, William Pryor, attributed "nearly every case of murder or manslaughter . . . to the pernicious practice of carrying concealed weapons," and the Louisville *Courier-Journal* declared the habit "so universal that when a gentleman orders a pair of pantaloons, the tailor inserts a pistol pocket, without any instructions to that effect, almost as inevitably as he inserts side-pockets." A verse of the famous poem "In Kentucky" (see Chapter 2, p. 22) also proclaims, in only half-jest:

> Hip pockets are the thickest,
> Pistol hands the slickest,
> The cylinder turns quickest
> > In Kentucky.

Laws to prohibit the carrying of such concealed weapons were beset with loopholes and exceptions and, according to an 1889 Fayette County judge, were seldom enforced and, when enforced, seldom resulted in a conviction. The right of men to carry concealed weapons was defended by many with the same argument used today by proponents of the private possession of firearms—that is, it was a God-given liberty, protected by the Second Amendment. Supporting the practice was the acceptance by many Kentuckians of the so-called code of honor. So universal was dueling in early days that the 1799 General Assembly passed an act to check the spread of honor killings. Fines and prison terms were imposed, and duelists were disqualified from holding public office for seven years—a particularly harsh penalty for politically-minded Kentuckians. Evidently this law was ineffectual in persuading Kentuckians to reject the code of honor. In 1854 Matt Ward redressed the humiliation of his younger brother by killing the schoolmaster who had publicly labeled the boy a liar and whipped him and then refused to explain or apologize for his actions. During the trial, in which Ward's defense rested upon the jurors' acceptance of the code of honor, Ward's attorney instructed the jurors "that a person had a 'legal right' to arm himself from the soles of his feet to his head." Ward was acquitted.

DEFENDING ONE'S HONOR

A polished, ritualized form of dueling, the code of honor in the Bluegrass was a tradition that originated in Europe and Britain and arrived in Kentucky by way of Virginia. According to the code, if a gentleman felt his honor besmirched, he had to demand instant satisfaction, for a gentleman could not accept an insult or even a slight. Honor concerned one's own reputation, of course, but also that of one's family, one's friends, one's political allies, and above all, one's women. A difference of opinion in politics, or some other issue, no matter how trivial, could cause one man to call out another. However, the most frequent cause of "affairs of honor" was offensive personal remarks—political vituperation or name calling.

This period in Bluegrass history was one of intense and vitriolic abuse, written and oral, and this in turn provoked physical violence. A man was expected to "resent" an affront, and if he failed to challenge the offender and obtain revenge—which often meant the death of one or the other—he was regarded as a coward and a public disgrace. His friends might desert him, his family be reviled. Likewise, if a man refused to accept a challenge, he was considered undeserving of life, and handbills might be circulated or posted in conspicuous places, calling him a liar, coward, poltroon, vile wretch, slanderer. One such "flaming handbill" was tacked up all over Paris in the summer of 1848:

To The World!!

Austin B. Wickham,

Having resorted to low, cowardly and dishonorable means, for the purpose of injuring my character and standing, and having refused honorable satisfaction, which I have demanded; I avail myself of this opportunity of publishing him to the world as a reclaimless liar, an infamous scoundrel, a black hearted villian, an arrant coward, a worthless vagabond and an imported miscreant, a base poltroon and a dishonor to his country.

William B. Victor

It is small wonder that few men failed to challenge an insult or to accept the gage. The code duello was observed in the Bluegrass for a little more than seventy-five years—from 1790 to several years after the Civil War—and became such a prominent feature of Kentucky culture that even today every person taking an oath of public office, from the governor on down to a notary public, must swear that he has never fought a duel, carried a challenge, or acted as a second.

In its most formal sense, the code consisted of a series of challenges, responses, negotiations, and so on, and was adhered to primarily by the upper classes. Dueling occurred only between gentlemen of equal social standing, and a conflict with a man of inferior station was conducted not with a rapier or pistol but with a cane. In the eighteenth century, the use of the traditional rapier in duels was gradually replaced by the dueling pistol.* Such a change probably encouraged dueling, for pistols demanded far less skill and training than sword play. A fine set of dueling pistols, writes Squire Coleman, became a gentleman's source of pride:

With the older and aristocratic families that emigrated from the eastern states came their fine sets of duelling pistols, fitted in elaborate mahogany cases, complete with powder measure, bullet molds, and ramrods. These were treasured heirlooms and guarded with great family pride.

Occasionally men dueled with shotguns or rifles, and as noted earlier, Cassius M. Clay—a maverick in dueling as in most things—preferred the bowie knife, which he wielded with consummate skill. Clay's legendary prowess with a blade was due in part at least to his special custom-made knife, described by Willian Townsend as "the wickedest looking knife" any Kentuckian "had ever seen or heard of." Clay wore it strapped under

*However, in 1798 the *Gazette* announced the opening of a new fencing school for "the young gentlemen of Lexington."

his left arm, handle down, held in place by a spring at the hilt. It had a seven-inch, razor-sharp, curved, double-edged blade. Clay had but to grasp the handle with his right hand and thrust the blade into the navel of his advancing foe.

Famous Duels   One of the first important Kentucky engagements under the code duello was the 1801 meeting between Dr. James Chambers and Judge John Rowan. While playing cards and drinking, the two men, both of whom considered themselves classical scholars, got into a heated argument over which was the better master of the dead languages. Rowan called Chambers a liar, and a fistfight broke out during which the inebriated Rowan pounded a nearby stone chimney instead of Chambers' nose, breaking one of his thumbs. A duel ensued. The meeting took place on a foggy morning in February. The two men took their places back to back, marched ten paces, turned and fired. On the second round Chambers was wounded, and he died the next day; Rowan was arrested but freed after a preliminary hearing. He later became a member of Congress and a U.S. Senator, and the rencounter, as it was called in Kentucky, never hurt his career. (A New York journalist once quipped that a rencounter was a barroom brawl between colonels.)

So powerful a grip did the code of honor have upon a gentleman's conduct that even so sober and respected a citizen as Henry Clay, the Great Compromiser, participated in duels. The first of these was in 1809, when Clay was thirty-two, and his opponent was Humphrey Marshall (formerly a U.S. Senator from Kentucky in the 4th Congress). Political opponents and sharply divided over the Jeffersonian embargo, the two men actually came to ungentlemanly blows in the Kentucky House after Clay had made a harsh speech against Marshall, who then jumped up and called Clay a liar. A duel ensued, and Clay received a slight hip wound. Although in later years Clay condemned the practice of dueling, he yielded to the customs of the time and never rejected the code completely. In 1826, while Secretary of State under President John Quincy Adams, Clay was the victim of a series of verbal assaults by the eccentric John Randolph, U. S. Senator from Virginia; in exasperation, Clay challenged the senator to a duel. That meeting, described by Senator Thomas Hart Benton as one of the last "high-toned" duels he ever witnessed, was fought in Virginia; Randolph, as the challenged, had the choice of weapons and place, and he desired, if he fell, to "die on the soil of the Old Dominion." The two men met, exchanged fire (neither was hit), and—honor satisfied—parted courteously.

Not all duels were so dignified, or conducted so elegantly. Attorney John Waring, as Lawrence Thompson writes, was considered the most dangerous man in the State. He was evidently not quite sane; he wasted time in petty vengeances as well as lethal ones—tacking doggerel, comic-valentine verse upon the gateposts of men he disliked, for example. [Waring had] several notches on his gun and . . . talked of filling his saddlebags with human ears [of his dueling victims].

Hated and feared, Waring was eventually killed in Versailles—shot from ambush.

Not all Bluegrass gentlemen, of course, assented to affairs of honor but, wishing to avoid being the subject of flaming handbills, chose to substitute shrewdness for bravado. A challenged Lexingtonian, for example, chose for weapons "muskets loaded with grapeshot and two balls . . . at five paces." His challenger, convinced his opponent was either insane or suicidal, quickly forgot the quarrel. A similar duel in Clark County was thwarted when the challenged party chose rifles at 90 yards. Abraham Lincoln—born in Kentucky though an Illinoisan at the time—was once challenged to a duel; asked his preference of weapons, he replied, "How about cow-dung at five paces?" In the Bluegrass, however, such gentlemen were clearly a minority.

DEATH OF THE CODE

The demise of dueling as a gentleman's pastime was eventually brought about by a combination of the temperance movement, public sentiment, and the law. (Ironically, the law alone, as long as public opinion supported dueling, effected little change.) Many applauded its wane, arguing that dueling allowed an excellent marksman to be aggressive and insulting with impunity—he could always win the resulting challenge. Others, however, contended that the traditional custom actually saved lives.

The code, first of all, enforced a cooling-off period. Challenger and challenged were separated and all negotiations were conducted through seconds, who attempted to arrange a peaceful accommodation between the two combatants. These negotiations could last for days—long enough for rage to dissipate and discretion to take over. If the duel actually took place, a lonely site was chosen to prevent injuring bystanders with stray bullets; a referee stood by to insure fair play; and a physician was present to attend to wounds. Often the parties deliberately misfired—as probably happened in the Clay-Randolph affair—so that no blood was shed. Thus a good case could be made that dueling served as a safety valve for heat-of-the-moment overreaction.

Moreover, proponents of dueling claimed that with its demise came an increase in brawling and street fights, labeled by historians as de facto duels, as noted by Robert M. Ireland:

The guarantees of fair play found in the duel did not exist in the street fight, and often one party surprised and killed the other without much, if any, warning and without an opportunity to draw a weapon. Just as often, parties might begin on fairly even terms, but one would ultimately gain a clear advantage and even shoot or stab the other in the back. Laws against dueling, according to its defenders, only aided the coward who could escape the code duello's insistence upon a fair fight and capitalize upon the street fight's anarchy by in effect ambushing his opponent.

However, it has not been proved that former duelists were those who engaged in brawls. More likely, street fighting was the poor man's way of settling a quarrel, whereas his betters now took their squabbles to court. This was not always true, however.

One of the more famous of these nineteenth century Bluegrass de facto duels occurred in 1889 between two prominent Lexington lawyers, Colonel Armistead M. Swope and Judge William Cassius Goodloe. Bitter rivals for leadership in the Republican Party, the two were long-standing antagonists, who had exchanged so many virulent insults that friends had to arrange a formal truce, and the enemies retracted their offending statements in writing. This rapprochement was short-lived, however. Swope confided to a friend that his affairs with Goodloe had reached the point where something had to be done, else he would be imputed a coward, something no Bluegrass gentleman could tolerate. Goodloe, for his part, was the favorite nephew of the fiery old abolitionist Cassius Clay. According to one account, "Uncle Cass" gave his nephew a knife from his own large assortment with the following directive: "Now you take this knife, William Cassius. If Armistead Swope insults you again and you don't kill him, you're no Clay. I never want to see you again."

The inevitable altercation occurred at the Lexington post office. Swope, a large man with a splendid physique, drew a .38 revolver, and Goodloe, small in stature, used his uncle's long knife. Swope fired two shots, hitting Goodloe in the abdomen, and Goodloe plunged his knife into Swope at least thirteen times. Swope died immediately and Goodloe a couple of days later. Though saddened by his nephew's death, Cassius Clay was nonetheless proud that Goodloe had behaved like a true Clay; with tears rolling down his cheeks, he said to a friend, "I couldn't have done better myself."

Traces Remain   The elevation of Cassius Marcellus Clay to something akin to folk hero reflects the admiration and approval Bluegrass Kentuckians pay to the code of honor by which he lived his turbulent life. There even lingers a certain wistful regret that a man can no longer conduct his affairs in an honorable fashion but must, under the threat of severe legal retribution, submit to the inevitable insults of others.

Thus, although dueling in the Bluegrass is a custom of the past, the tradition of personal honor may still on occasion be violently upheld. Blatant effronteries are still avoided in Bluegrass society; one does not, for example, stare or look disdainfully at another, nor laugh or poke fun, nor accuse or challenge another's right to do something. In driving one does not critically honk a horn at someone—even if that person is violating a driving law—nor pull out too closely in front of another vehicle. Such actions are interpreted as infringements upon individual rights, or as implying an assumption of superiority, and are sometimes answered with violence. Recently, a male pickup driver stopped in traffic behind a woman's car that had just previously pulled out in front of him, got out, walked to the "offending" car, and tore out the driver's side window, which was partially rolled down; he then returned to his pickup and drove away, leaving the frightened woman perplexed and helpless.

Today the modern legal structure and its penalties have tempered most violent reactions to such real or imagined affronts. The tendency now is for the aggrieved party simply to disassociate himself from the insulter, to cease speaking to him, to have nothing more to do with him. Some people have been known to leave restaurants if an enemy is present, not wanting to give the impression they are eating together. Such denial of an insulter's existence may last for years, or a lifetime. Today, Bluegrass violence is usually associated with lower socioeconomic classes and most often occurs when sworn enemies or other combatants are in their cups.

CHAPTER 14

Bourbon: Kentucky's "Hosesome Beverage"

An early citizen of the Bluegrass once wrote to the *Gazette* that through-out the Union it was said that "horse-jockeying and tippling is [our] chief employment." Regrettably, the Bluegrass must share with other regions of the country its enjoyment of "horse-jockeying." In no way, however, does the Commonwealth concede parity to any state when it comes to the distilling of bourbon. As many an old Kentucky Colonel might have said (in the words of Harry Harrison Kroll), "I'll have you know, suh, that bourbon is a Kentucky produce, the name duly patented in the U.S. Patent Office. Call liquor made in any other state bourbon—except maybe for some small brewings down in the heathen state of Tennessee, where a provincial by the name of Jack Daniel operates—and I'll challenge you to a duel on the field of honor, and the hell with the law!"

Indeed, bourbon has been officially declared a unique national prod-uct by the U.S. Congress. When in 1990 the Navy's twelfth Trident nuclear submarine was christened the U.S.S. *Kentucky*, the bottle broken over its prow contained not the traditional champagne but bourbon—a special blend of eight brands of Kentucky bourbon.

Earlier commemorative uses of the "hosesome beverage" have been noted. When the massive limestone towers supporting High Bridge, which spanned the Kentucky River at the Jessamine-Mercer County line, were built in the 1850s, a bottle of premium bourbon was supposedly sealed in each tower by the masons to commemorate the occasion. The bridge was demolished in 1929; however, no one would ever admit to finding the whiskey. Bourbon was even used as decoration for Christmas trees in churches. One churchman recalls: "Nobody thought anything about it. The colored lights made the bottles pretty."

THE FIRST BOURBON MAKER

Beyond the sure knowledge that bourbon belongs to Kentucky, and specifically to Bluegrass Kentucky, the state's historians have not been able to progress, for, like most folk inventions, the exact location and date or even the maker of the first Kentucky bourbon have been as elusive as the delicate aroma of bourbon itself. As to the original creator, several names have been proffered, the most intriguing of which is Virginian Elijah Craig, fiery Baptist preacher and brother of the more famous Lewis Craig, leader of the "traveling church," and builder of Kentucky's first meeting house in 1781. Elijah, after serving several jail sentences in Culpeper and Orange counties, Virginia, for expressing his dissenting religious opinions, removed himself to Kentucky in 1786, carrying with him, according to bourbon historian Harry Harrison Kroll, "French millstones, a wooden still, and a gentleman's taste for . . . whiskey." He settled in Georgetown (Scott County) and, when he wasn't preaching and engaging in religious controversy, developed a recipe for distilling whiskey from corn and rye—with perhaps a little wheat added—malted barley, and yeast from wild crab apples.

Two other candidates for the "birthing of bourbon" were Pennsylvanians Jacob Spears and John Hamilton, both of whom moved to Bourbon County in the 1780s and began distilling, Hamilton on his farm and Spears in conjunction with a milling enterprise. Spears floated his barrels of whiskey by flatboat down to New Orleans, where he became known for his superior distillate. The Frenchmen called it bourbon, because of its source.*

Other contenders for creator of bourbon included John Ritchie, Wattie Boone, Evan Williams, Henry Hudson Wathen, Jacob Beam, Daniel Stewart, and Elijah Pepper. Wathen, Beam, and Pepper were all patriarchs of bourbon-making families. Pepper settled at Old Pepper Spring near Lexington sometime around 1776 and built a log-cabin distillery about 1800; the Pepper family continued distilling for over a century, selling their product under the trademark "Old 1776—Born with the Republic." Boone was, of course, a near relative of Daniel; he and Ritchie both settled in the Outer Bluegrass (Nelson County) in 1776 and began making whiskey around 1780. Thomas Lincoln, Abe's father, is thought to have worked in the Boone distillery for a time, and young Abraham was supposed to have carried his father's dinner to him in a split-oak basket and assisted him in his work (although Abraham was only seven when the family left Kentucky). According to a story related by Kroll, Uncle Wattie predicted that, "[Abe] is bound to make a great man, no matter what trade he follows. If he goes into the whiskey business, he'll be the best distiller in the land."

*Gerald Carson defines bourbon as, "A whiskey distilled at 160 proof or lower from a fermented mash with corn not less than fifty-one percent of the grain used. All bourbon must be stored in charred new oak cooperage."

Today, after the passing of more than two centuries, it is impossible to determine the precise origins of bourbon. In truth, there were innumerable folk distillers in pioneer Kentucky; an estimated 500 stills were in operation in 1792 and 2,000 by 1812. Writing in his memoirs, Ebenezer Stedman, a midnineteenth century Bluegrass papermaker, estimated (perhaps somewhat on the high side) that "Nine tenths of the farmers had a small Still house on Each Farm, and did not make more than two Barrels of Whiskey per week." This whiskey was not only used "amongst the family" but was also sold or traded for items the family did not produce, as whiskey frequently substituted for money in frontier commerce. (When Thomas Lincoln sold his Kentucky farm in 1817, he received as the greater part of the sales price ten barrels of whiskey.) Most early Kentuckians were honest, plain folk who were already accustomed to living in the wilderness, and when they came to the Bluegrass, they raised their cabins, cultivated corn patches, and set up the furnaces and pot stills. They thought no more of making whiskey than they did of performing other everyday subsistence tasks. Prominent among their numbers were the Scotch-Irish—folk distillers perhaps since the sixth century—who poured into the Bluegrass, bringing with them their whiskey making traditions and the firm belief that whiskey, not bread, was the staff of life.

General Aid to Well-Being   Indeed, *rye* whiskey—for rye was the available grain—had been a "medicinal drink" in the eastern colonies for years, a role which the frontier corn whiskey quickly assumed. Whiskey was used as a preventative, a cure, and a general aid to well-being; it was particularly good for snakebite, fallen arches, chills and fever, and "women's complaints," including prolapse of the uterus. One drink enabled a man to run faster, to jump higher, and to shoot better—or to think he did. Whiskey rations were often provided to working hands and slaves in the belief that it yielded up more work than increasing wages. The frontier churches had not yet taken a stand on temperance, and almost everybody took a sip, including preachers and Christians. Even children were given a bit, and there were numerous apocryphal stories about how many gallons of whiskey were required to raise a family without a cow. Whiskey was considered a staple commodity, as essential as meat and flour. One popular tale tells of a Kentuckian carrying a sack of corn to a gristmill, whose neighbor, upon seeing him, comments: "Look at that feller going yonder to grind a turn a corn. Bet right now he ain't got a pint of liquor in his house." Summing up the role played by whiskey on the Kentucky frontier, Stedman, the aforementioned Bluegrass papermaker wrote:

In the Early days of Kentucky one Small drink woold Stimulate the Whole Sistom. One Could feel it in their feets, hands, and in Evry part. There was a warm Glow of Feeling, a Stimulus of Strength, of Beaurency [buoyancy] of feeling, a Something of Reaction of Joy in place of Sorrow. It Brot out Kind feelings of the Heart, Made men sociable. And in them days Evry Boddy invited Evry Boddy That came to their house to partake of this hosesome Beverage.

Producing generous quantities of this "hosesome" beverage became in the early decades of the 1800s a lucrative side business for approximately one out of every five Bluegrass farmers. Although most historians do not mention it, the Grimes Mill complex originally included a distillery, and the area evidently bustled with farmers converting their grain to alcohol. By constructing both distillery and mill, a farmer could convert his excess grains (and perhaps a share of his neighbor's) to liquor, which, when compared to the raw ingredients, would not spoil, was more easily transported, and brought more attractive prices. (A pack pony could carry only four bushels of raw grain to market but twenty-four bushels after it was distilled into whiskey.) Moreover, the spent stillage or still slops—the used-up mash after the run—was rich in protein and made peerless food for the farmer's hogs and cows. Similar dealcoholized distillers' grains are still used today in the Bluegrass to supplement the diets of livestock, and a university study is presently investigating the possibility of feeding "whiskey leavings" to fish-farm catfish. Reportedly, the experiment is progressing well; the fish appear to like the aroma of the mash-supplemented pellets and therefore eat more.

PERFECTING THE "RECIPE"

The first Kentucky whiskey was probably distilled from rye, as it had been in the East, but the Bluegrass grew corn, wonderful corn, and one day some distiller—or distillers—probably threw some corn in to supplement the rye and the basic formula for Kentucky bourbon—corn for strength and body, rye for mellow flavor—was born.

The second, probably also fortuitous, discovery by Bluegrass distillers was that aging their brew in charred white oak barrels enormously improved its quality, changing white corn whiskey into amber bourbon. The use of new charred barrels is a distinctive feature of Kentucky bourbon, distinguishing it from other whiskeys of the world. Canadians use charred barrels but not new ones, and the Scots employ old Sherry casks. The origin of this charring in Kentucky—although Scots and Irish distillers have reportedly aged their product in charred wood for a thousand years—has given rise to various legends. In one account, an early distiller, who stored his liquor in barrels previously containing saltfish, scorched the insides to destroy the fish smell and subsequently discovered that the scorched barrels improved both flavor and color. In a second tale, a frugal old Scots cooper accidentally charred a batch of white oak staves, and rather than discard them, he worked them up into barrels with the scorched surface inside and sold them to a distiller. Months later, when the distiller tasted his product, he found the whiskey not only had a mellower, tastier "sippage" but also had a nice russet color. A third tale contends that a Bourbon County farmer hid a barrel of ordinary Pennsylvania whiskey under the dirt floor of his barn, which was later struck by lightning and burned to the ground. Upon excavation, the charred barrel was discovered to have lent a smoother flavor and a ruddy color to the distillate.

It has also been conjectured that the beneficial effect upon whiskey of aging in wood was caused by a forced wait—first for the spring rise of the rivers and then the long, slow journey down the Ohio and the Mississippi to New Orleans. Supposedly, the gentle rocking of the boat also helped convert the original "bald face" whiskey to "old whiskey."★ However, as Gerald Carson notes, "So far as aging is concerned . . . until the Civil War period, the Kentucky distiller disposed at once of his white whiskey, usually to the whiskey trade in Cincinnati or Louisville. The aging, if any, was carried out by the purchaser."

The Distiller's Craft   Each distiller developed his own formula, techniques, and discoveries, based upon his experiences in the trade, and about which he was less than garrulous. The excellence of his run depended upon his abilities, his intuition, and chance; wide variations in the quality of the product were thus inevitable. Nevertheless, the newly distilled whiskey, whatever its strength, quality, or purity, was bartered to peddlers touring the Bluegrass with pack animals in exchange for Eastern trade goods.

Such "generic" whiskey, colorless, with a pungent odor and a biting taste, was sold in the East as "Kentucky whiskey." At home in the Bluegrass, it was commonly called domestic whiskey, or table or family whiskey. The term "family whiskey" indicated a product of higher quality—whose distiller had gotten "the pig tracks out of it." A second or third-class product was ordinary red-eye. This latter product, also called "shine" or "rot gut," was often served in establishments of questionable reputation such as the taverns in Frankfort's slum neighbor-

★"Bald face" refers to bald face hornets—just as "hot" to handle as the whiskey. The journey perhaps explains why the French so prized Jacob Spears' distillate.

hood, the Craw. Ripe bourbon was frequently referred to as sour mash or fire copper whiskey.

Just when the term "bourbon" was first used for Kentucky corn-and-rye whiskey is impossible to say—perhaps as early as the 1830s. The earliest printed mention of bourbon occurred in the mid-1840s; scattered examples were found in the 1850s and several in the 1860s. After the Civil War, the term became common. At its best, Kentucky's famous bourbon possesses a unique and delightful depth of flavor with a lingering aroma known to appreciative Kentuckians as the "farewell."

In traditional image, bourbon is as closely linked to Kentucky as its famous Colonels. (A mint julep, properly speaking, must be made of bourbon.) A famous couplet, composed in 1825 by Chief Justice John Marshall proclaimed:

In the Blue Grass region, a paradox was born,
The corn was full of kernels, and the Colonels full of corn.

Describing a particular phial of this famed liquor, distilled in 1845, Kentucky sage, editor, and social philosopher, "Marse Henry" Watterson wrote:

It was re-barreled in 1860 by James Ford.

It never paid no taxes.

It was hid in the bushes ... in spite of its disloyal practices and Ku Klux associations, it is soft and mild, and can say as Champ Ferguson [Confederate guerrilla] said when he cut Billy Still's ears off, "Why, I wouldn't hurt a fly."

Like many Bluegrass estates, many antebellum whiskey-making families fell victim to the ravages of the Civil War, and the business firms that replaced them were more often than not controlled by bankers, merchants, lawyers, and so on. Fortunately, these newcomers maintained a sincere respect for the bourbon-making tradition, and many founded new generations of bourbon aristocracy. Observing the Old World custom of a "family calling," distillers passed their old formulas and methods on to their sons, and the sons to the grandsons, and so on. Frequently, one bourbon-making family intermarried with another, and thus helped create a bourbon elite. The antebellum gristmill operator who made whiskey as a sideline had become a Kentucky gentleman with traditions to respect and preserve. Even under the direction of these new scions of bourbon, however, distilling remained essentially a folk craft.

The Master Distiller   The term "master distiller" was applied to the man responsible for the actual operation of the still, the man who controlled the process of condensing alcohol from grain. He was responsible for both quantity and quality—how good the product tasted, how well it sold, and how its reputation fared over the years. Sometimes the owner of the still was his own master distiller; sometimes he hired another man to do the "stilling." In either case, the occupation was not a textbook profession, but a folk art. One of the best master distillers of the era, for example, could neither read nor write, but he knew bourbon. Gerald Carson says of him:

He didn't know an ester from an aldehyde. He had, however, an uncanny sense of just when to draw the [still] beer off. He knew grain, and could produce his own yeast. He kept to his standards by taste and smell and could confidently ask a buyer to rub a few drops between his hands, gently inhale and catch the redolence of apples, a sound test for a sound bourbon.

The judgment of some of the old taste-testers bordered upon the miraculous. They have been known to name the county, the exact valley, the creek bottom, in which an aromatic bourbon was made. What they knew came not out of books but out of bottles.

Such informal learning process is one of the hallmarks—if not *the* hallmark—of folk culture.

Even in a modern Bluegrass distillery, the source of the master distiller's knowledge is primarily folk, passed down by tradition and gleaned slowly over long years of experience. In spite of many scientific innovations—today, computer-controlled procedures—the crux of distilling remains primarily a folk art, and the quality of the product continues to be tested in the folk manner—by the human taste buds, not by chemical analysis. The secret to distilling good whiskey was pinpointed by John Muir, a banker to the bourbon distillers:

One of the most wonderful drinks of whiskey I ever had was made by this old Negro who could neither read nor write. But his pies and pickles and preserves were right. You can make fine whiskey on the kitchen stove in a pot still. You can make fine whiskey in a modern plant that cost a million dollars to build. On the other hand you can make a terrible whiskey on the kitchen stove in a pot still and some of the modern distilleries manage to do pretty bad, too. It's the touch.

BOURBON AND BLUEGRASS TRADITIONS

Itself the offspring of a rich folk heritage, bourbon has, in turn, significantly affected other Bluegrass traditions. As observed by Lawrence Thompson: "The whole atmosphere of the Kentucky tradition is permeated with the aroma of fine whiskey. . . ." In the early days of the Region, liquor was sold not by the drink but by the jug or flask, thus necessitating enormous consumption to finish the supply at hand. A British traveler once described Kentuckians as being able to "swig whiskey from goat flasks for half a minute without ejecting their quids of tobacco." During the popular Court Day, merchants sold whiskey by the "tickler," a slender bottle holding a half-pint—just enough to tickle, and by day's end, according to James Lane Allen, "wellnigh a whole town would be tickled."★

A widespread folk saying holds that the traditional Kentucky breakfast is "a fifth of Bourbon, a sirloin steak, and a hound dog." The dog relieved the diner of the necessity of consuming the steak. It has been said that only Kentuckians appreciate the true value of bourbon. The story is told that, during Prohibition, a Danville native was at a New York speakeasy with a client when a waiter offered them a bottle of prewar bourbon. When informed the price was $30.00—a staggering sum in the 1920s—the New Yorker protested, "That's robbery! Don't buy it." "I insist," replied the Kentuckian. "This is the *first time I ever have paid what good bourbon is really worth.*"

Many other tales about Kentuckians and their bourbon have proliferated, one of the better known concerning two senators and their legendary powers of taste. The setting and details vary from version to version, but the story features two Kentuckians sampling a barrel of whiskey. One insists he tastes leather in the whiskey; the other replies, "It's not leather you taste, it's *iron.*" Determined to settle the argument, they eventually consume the whiskey, demolish the cask, and find a tiny carpet tack in a small leather washer.

"What a dreary world," wrote Bernard Mayo, in his choice description of Kentucky as the Goshen of the Western World, "if a free-born son of Old Kentuc couldn't take his gum-tickler (about a gill of spirits) of a morning or his phlegm-cutter (a double dose) before breakfast; his anti-fogmatic (a similar dram) before dinner; and a few gall-breakers (about a half pint) during the day."

BOURBON AND POLITICS

Perhaps no aspect of Bluegrass tradition has been so interlaced with the heady fumes of bourbon whiskey as have the twin arts (at least in Kentucky) of politics and oratory.

Henry Clay himself was particularly fond of Old Crow, one of the earliest of Kentucky bourbons, distilled in Frankfort and formulated in the 1830s by James Crow, a Scots immigrant, who is credited with

★Allen observed that the Court Day pleasures of drinking and fighting "went marvellously well together. The drinking led up to the fighting, and the fighting led up to the drinking; and this amiable co-operation might be prolonged at will."

introducing the sour-mash process. It is said that after Clay had taken two drinks of Old Crow, he and Jim Crow were comrades; after half a jug they were brothers for life. When Clay went to Washington, he carried a keg with him. Fortified and inspired by Old Crow, so the legend goes, Clay's eloquence awed the noble senators who, after getting a whiff of him, demanded "What the goddam hell you been drinking, Henry?" Old Crow's reputation was made.

Power of Speech   Clay's gifts of persuasion were firmly within the evolution of Bluegrass political tradition: eminence in oratory and the art of picturesque invective coupled with the consumption of Kentucky bourbon. Some have contended that it is actually the lime in the water—from the underlying strata of blue limestone in the Region—that endows bourbon—and the oratory—with a special velvety flavor. Be that as it may, Kentucky political history is certainly replete with stories of victories achieved by way of a silver tongue and bourbon whiskey. In the 1915 governor's race the candidates—Republican Edwin P. Morrow and Democrat Augustus Owsley Stanley—were both great speakers. Personal friends and lovers of good bourbon, they sat down together, each with his bottle, to prepare for a joint debate. Said Morrow to Stanley (as Kroll tells it), "I'm going to beat hell out of you in this race, and right now I'm going to drink you under the table!" "Like hell you are!" Stanley replied, and they started drinking. By some sleight of hand, Morrow managed to empty much of his bottle into Stanley's. When they finally sat down for the debate, Morrow "politely" allowed Stanley to sit by the stove. Kroll tells what happened next:

Morrow spoke first. He had the audience pretty much with him, for he was just enough in his cups to put up a whale of an oration. Then Stanley got up . . . reeling a little and looking sort of pale around the gills . . . . The heat of the stove and all that liquor—his and most of Morrow's—were too much for him and he turned white in the face and vomited right there before all those folks. That cooked his goose then and there, for if there is anything a Kentucky audience can't abide it's a man who can't tote his liquor like a gentleman. Stanley mopped his mouth, got a deep breath, and turned loose that big voice of his. "Gentlemen, it always did make me puke to hear a damned Republican, especially that fellow Morrow, and you'll just have to forgive me."

The audience "broke into a great clapping," and Stanley proceeded with one of the best speeches of his political career. A few weeks later he won the election by 470 votes.

According to legend, the public career of another Bluegrass politician was reportedly saved by a ten-gallon cask of Old Crow. In 1875 Joseph C. S. Blackburn of Versailles was in a hot political race for representative with Ed Marshall, and although Marshall was a brilliant campaigner, Blackburn had one advantage: he owned the very last cask of Jim Crow's whiskey known to exist. Crow had died in 1856, and although W. A. Gaines & Company kept his name alive and distilled bourbon according to his method, the distillation of the original Old Crow died with its creator. Bourbon historian Gerald Carson retells the story:

With his political career at stake, Blackburn decanted the precious fluid into small cruets. He would take a stubborn Marshall supporter aside and tell him all about Crow and his wonderful whiskey and then, as an old account puts it, he "poured the liquor into his soul."

"As you drink that, sir," Blackburn would say, "I want you to remember that you are helping to destroy the most precious heirloom of my family. It is the last bit of genuine Crow whiskey in the world. Observe, sir, that you do not need to gulp down a tumbler of water after swallowing the liquor to keep it from burning your gullet. On the contrary, you know instinctively that to drink water with it would be a crime. All I ask of you is to remember that you are getting something in this liquor that all the money of an Indian prince cannot buy. Drink it, sir, and give your soul up to the Lord. Then if you can vote for Ed Marshall I cannot complain, because it will be the Lord's act!"

Blackburn beat Marshall in a walk.

Blackburn was not the only one to extol the virtues of Jim Crow's distillate. The lofty praise to Old Crow, here outlined by Kroll, would do justice to the purple rhetoric of many a Bluegrass politician, as well as to earlier flyting traditions:

Down in Nashville, Tennessee, Andrew Jackson got a snort and became a convert. William Henry Harrison drank of it and went into ecstasies. It was shipped across the high seas and crowned heads were made dizzy by it . . . .

Horse racers wagered Crow's whiskey instead of money. A quart of it would be incentive enough to make men swim rivers, wade through boggy swamps, and fight varmints. It would also make men stand on their heads. . . . It drove skeletons from feasts, and made throats that swallowed it sing songs of joy. Sweeter was it than wild honey, and its smell was more perfumed than are the lilies that grow in the valley of Hebron. Its fame traveled over mountains so tall that small boys could stand on the tops and tickle the feet of angels; across the plateaus where the willow and honeysuckle grew side by side, over billowy fields of grain, through meadows and marshes, down through the cotton fields of Georgia and Mississippi, the pine forest of Alabama, and laid its merit and its fame at the feet of the barons of the south.

Wooing the Voters: Outdoor Barbecues and Debates

Although expensive Old Crow was not usually devoted to such a use, bourbon was (and is) an indispensable ingredient of the great political barbecues held to launch campaigns and stage political debates. All-day events held in warm weather, such barbecues were occasions for indulging in oratory, arguing, eating, drinking, and fighting (not necessarily in that order of importance). Set out to quench participants' inevitable thirst was a hogshead of whiskey toddy, and according to a description by Thomas Allen, a guest at one such nineteenth-century Fourth of July picnic, it was paid devoted attention all through the day until evening the liquor had been drunk down so far that "only a long-legged and long-armed man could reach it with his cup." Hundreds of men, too full to get up, lay about on the grass, and a number of fistfights broke out. A constable indiscreetly attempted to intervene in one, whereupon the combatants stopped swinging at each other and turned on him. As Allen left the picnic, "Sim Drake lost his balance trying to dip up another cup of toddy," and fell into the hogshead.

After the debates and the picnics came the elections, and in the antebellum Bluegrass it was the custom for each candidate on election day to provide a free barrel of whiskey, with his name lettered on its side, for supporters. Tin cups were hung around the outside of the barrel and a bouquet of mint and a few pounds of sugar were thrown into it, creating a crude, potent version of mint julep. Not surprisingly, the presence of such refreshment near a polling place often caused fights, especially since, in some elections, the polls remained open for three days. James I. Robertson, Jr. describes a typical three-day election:

By nightfall of the first day, drunkenness and a craving for excitement were the usual forms of behavior. By the second day, nervous temperaments opened the way to numerous fights. The third day was basically a survival of the fittest between the opposing candidates, with sometimes as many as four barrels of whiskey being tapped at one polling site. Occasionally a candidate would holler out for "all true sons of Ol' Kentuck to come to the trough and liquor!"

Sharply critical of the prevailing folk method of electioneering, William Littell, legal scholar and political satirist, in an 1814 article, "Too Much Spirit," burlesqued the campaign debts of a perennially unsuccessful candidate for political office: "For introducing myself as a candidate, 100 half pints of whiskey." "Treating those who had voted for me last year, 200 half pints." "For the purpose of shewing that I was attached to diets and drinks of domestic growth and manufacture, and was disposed to encourage them," 100 half pints. "Expenses of the election days," $90. Notwithstanding such stinging denunciations, whiskey's integral role in Bluegrass politicking was little changed during the nineteenth century. Prohibitionists attempted to mitigate drinking at the polls—in Clark County they provided free ice cream to voters—but vast quantities of free liquor continued to provide election days with scenes of drunken brawls, maimings, or even killings.

DRY LAWS

By the early 1900s, the Commonwealth had developed something akin to schizophrenia concerning its bourbon. On the one hand, the Bluegrass continued to be famous for its fine whiskeys, with $160 million of capital invested in distilleries in 1908. On the other hand, the state was 97 percent dry, a local-option law having made the home of bourbon virtually a desert long before the Eighteenth Amendment.* Adding injury to insult, hatchet-wielding Carry Nation, the inveterate foe of the saloon, was born in Garrard County.†

When national Prohibition became official on January 16, 1920, the effect upon the bourbon distilleries, essentially family affairs, was devastating. Some attempted to remain in business by operating under federal permits to distill medicinal spirits; others endeavored to produce industrial alcohol from grain sorghum or to manufacture vinegar by further fermenting the alcohol. None of these substitute businesses was very successful. Distilling was all most of these people knew. Overnight they were dispossessed of property, livelihood, a traditional way of life.

An anecdote is told of a disgruntled doughboy who, returning to the Bluegrass after World War I—"the war to make the world safe for democracy"—discovered that whiskey was no longer a legal beverage. Staring at the slogan "Born with the Republic," displayed on the wall of the old Pepper Distillery, he suggested it be updated: "Born with the Republic—Died with Democracy."

Determined to avoid this fate, a lady distiller by the name of Mrs. O'Brian, who had inherited the family business of Waterfill & Frazier, dismantled her distillery, loaded it onto freight cars, and carried the entire business south into Mexico. She was a friend of Jeremiah Beam, son of Jim Beam, who sent a man down to help her get started. Her new product, it was said, sorely missed the Kentucky limestone water, so

*Today, of Kentucky's 120 counties seventy-six are dry, thirty wet, and fourteen "moist" (partially dry/wet); and in the Inner Bluegrass, five are wet, three dry, and one moist. Because of the historical abuse of alcohol during elections, law requires, as in other states, that on election day sales of any alcoholic beverages be suspended until after the polls close.

†Carrie's grandfather, James Campbell, who lived in Mercer County, was devoted to his morning toddy. While the family was at breakfast he would ceremoniously stir butter, brandy, sugar, and hot water into a tall glass. He then gave each child a spoonful and quaffed the rest.

Oscar Pepper Distillery employees, 1883 (Photo courtesy of Kentucky Historical Society)

Mrs. O'Brian ordered tank cars filled with pure Bluegrass water hauled down to Mexico. Thereafter, her distillate, except for a slight taint from the tanks, lived up to the original mixture, and was shipped back into the States and sold illicitly. After Repeal, the lady again crated up her distillery and returned to Kentucky.

Making Shine   All of the illegal whiskey during Prohibition did not come from south—or north—of the border. Within the United States, making "shine" or "bathtub gin" became a national pastime. In the popular imagination, the Kentucky moonshiner epitomized this activity; the stereotype pictured him hidden away in some "holler," where the "Revenooers" (the ATF men) could not locate him, cooking up a batch of rotgut corn whiskey.

In the Bluegrass, illicit distilling of whiskey was not, of course, a child solely of Prohibition. Instead, it developed side by side with the legal distilling industry, encouraged by increasing Federal taxation. The large capital investments necessitated by continuing refinements in the distillation process also placed small distillers in a difficult position, and some chose to avoid the problem by ceasing to operate legally. In the Bluegrass Region, bootlegging—the purchase of alcohol in "wet" counties (those allowing liquor sales) and transporting and selling it in "dry" counties (those prohibiting liquor sales)—is more prevalent than making shine. Nevertheless, one can still find, in the sequestered fringes of the Bluegrass, a few stills producing "woods whiskey." Samples of it have, from time to time, accompanied student research projects directed by this writer. This wildcat corn is not bourbon, and its quality has apparently changed little since frontier days when a gulp of raw white lightning was like the kick of a mule. An old folktale recounts the meeting of a Kentucky woodsman, carrying a jug of whiskey and a rifle, with a Yankee surveyor; Bradley Smith retells it:

The woodsman pushed the jug into the stranger's hands and then stepped back and aimed his gun at the frightened surveyor. "Take a drink," he commanded. The northerner gulped down a few swallows of the fiery liquid. The Kentuckian took back the jug and handed his gun to the stranger. "Now," he insisted, "you make me take a drink!"

Another version, set more than 150 years later, is retold by Lawrence Thompson. The main characters are a "staid burgher of Winchester" and a hillman; the liquor, however, remains the same, as attested by the hillman; "Now hold that there gun squar' on me. . . . It's the only way I can get the damned stuff down myself!"

REPEAL

Ironically, when Repeal did come in April of 1933 the first legally produced whiskey was evidently little improvement over moonshine. According to a contemporary master distiller with five generations of experience behind him, the reason for this poor quality was primarily economic: many distillers could not afford to wait while their whiskey aged properly. The resulting product, bottled and sold after only two years of aging, was appropriately called "headache whiskey." Kentucky journalist and humorist Irvin S. Cobb describes the stuff:

It smells like gangrene starting in a mildewed silo; it tastes like the wrath to come, and when you absorb a deep swig of it, you have the sensations of having swallowed a lighted kerosene lamp. A sudden violent jolt of it has been known to stop the victim's watch, snap both his suspenders, and crack his glass eye right across—all in the same motion.

Nevertheless, many of the old bourbon families scrambled to get back into the business; some did not succeed, and almost all of them were forced to go north to obtain capital. With Yankee money came outside power and influence, and distilling was changed from a family affair to big business. This is another example of elite culture (official, governmental) intervention into folk culture affairs, bringing devastating results. The geographical center of the bourbon industry also completed a shift—away from the Inner Bluegrass counties (begun even before Prohibition) to the Outer Bluegrass area around Bardstown and Louisville. In 1872, a touring reporter for the New York *World* wrote that "for more than a mile before you reach one of these immense Bourbon County distilleries" one could smell the pigs penned on the property and fed the stillage. In 1990 not one distillery is located in the county that, according to folk tradition, gave birth to bourbon.

In Lexington the Lexington Brewery, one of the largest structures on Main Street when it was erected in 1898, closed with Prohibition and was demolished in 1941. Likewise, the old Pepper distillery, one of Kentucky's earliest and largest, is defunct; and the Old Taylor and Old Crow Distilleries on Glenns Creek, in Franklin and Woodford Counties respectively, are no longer productive. The only Inner Bluegrass county continuing to produce bourbon is Franklin, where Ancient Age is distilled, although there are still three distilleries located in Lawrenceburg (Anderson County) on the very fringe of the Inner Bluegrass, three or four miles beyond the Woodford County line. Except for three distilleries located in Daviess County in western Kentucky, the remaining plants cluster in the Outer Bluegrass Region surrounding Louisville and especially Bardstown, which has affectionately been dubbed Bourbonville USA. More whiskey is produced per square mile in Bardstown than anywhere else in the world; and it is home of the fascinating Oscar Goetz Museum of Whiskey History, which houses a wealth of distilling artifacts.

Between roughly 1840 and 1870 bourbon distillers began to build factories in Nelson County, to take advantage of the many limestone springs in the area. Master Distiller Booker Noe, whose family has made whiskey in the area for over 200 years, also attributes the lure of the locale to the presence of hardwood trees for manufacturing barrels, proximity to the Ohio River, which provided transportation, and climate, especially humidity levels and fluctuating temperatures conducive to aging bourbon. An additional factor may have been the substantial Catholic population of the county as well as considerable numbers of people of German descent—both traditions more tolerant of alcoholic beverages than the historically Fundamentalist Protestantism of the Inner Bluegrass. (At least since the days of the Great Revival, evangelistic churches have carried on a relentless battle against Demon Rum.) For example, during a summer drought in Nelson County sometime before Prohibition, Jim Beam, whose distillery was nearby, piped water from his water supply to Nazareth, the Catholic school and convent; in gratitude, the nuns had the girls at the school pray for Jim Beam every night.

The Bourbon Industry Today

Tradition has always played an integral role in the bourbon business. In the early 1960s, Carson observed that "even today, in the era of large corporations operated by professional administrators, an executive of a distilling company will mention that his great-grandpappy had a still at the forks of the creek. . . ."

A premier example of such a family distilling tradition is the Beam family, whose numerous sons have been presiding over Kentucky mash tubs for seven generations. The progenitor of the Kentucky family was Jacob Beam, of German stock, who first tried to distill whiskey around Cumberland Gap but discovered that coal country produced terrible whiskey; he moved on to the vicinity of Bardstown in the Outer Bluegrass and constructed a still there around 1788. One of Jacob's grandsons, David, fathered four boys and four girls, ensuring a plentiful supply of Beams for the growing distilling industry. One of those sons was Jim Beam, who inherited the business from his father in 1892 and ran it until Prohibition; his major whiskey was named Old Tub, after the early process, which involved hand-stirring the mash in large tubs. During Prohibition Beam sold the distillery, preferring to sever connections with the family tradition to serving time in prison, and he and his son, Jeremiah, tried their hands at other businesses, but without much success. When repeal came in 1933, Jim Beam, then approximately seventy years old, immediately applied for a distilling license and began working on his yeast, which is one of the crucial ingredients of good bourbon. (Indeed a Civil War story tells of a Bluegrass family whose yeast jug was about to be smashed by a blue-coated sergeant; the entire household attacked him en masse to save their jug of yeast.)

The Crucial Ingredient   Yeast is traditionally made by first creating a medium or "slurry" of barley malts and hops, combined with limestone water—Bluegrass limestone water supposedly teams up perfectly with yeast. This mixture is then cooked and, with the addition of a little sulfur to hold the bacteria down, set out in the air to "let the yeast come to it." The strain of yeast that Jim Beam created in 1933 by this folk method is the same strain used today to produce Jim Beam whiskey. Whereas some distillers use "laboratory" yeast—that is, yeast developed in laboratory test tubes and kept pure by artificial methods—Beam's yeast is "wild" or "spontaneous" or "jug yeast." Called simply stock, it is stored in a copper jug, and when the supply runs low, a new slurry in a new jug is inoculated with the old stock, a process which has maintained this strain for almost sixty years. So prized and guarded a secret is this yeast that some years ago, when the master distiller of Heaven Hill, also a Beam, requested a sample of it from his brother, the master distiller at Jim Beam Distillery, he was refused.

Today the master distiller responsible for care and maintenance and use of this yeast is Booker Noe (quoted above), the grandson of Jim Beam and nephew of Jeremiah. Brought by his grandfather to visit the distillery when only a little boy, Noe began working there part-time at approximately twelve years of age, and became master distiller in the late 1960s. In the meantime, the actual ownership of the distillery had passed from Beam hands, bought by American Brands in 1968; nevertheless, according to Noe, the corporation has not tried to alter the traditional whiskey-making process. The original formula, or "recipe," for Jim Beam bourbon, handed down from Jacob Beam, typewritten and bearing the signatures of both Jim and Jeremiah Beam, was given to Noe by Jeremiah and is secured in his private lockbox, a document he plans to give eventually to his own son, a seventh-generation Beam distiller.

A new super-premium high-proof bourbon honors Booker Noe and is named after him. Aged in the heart of the warehouse for eight years, Booker Noe bourbon is 121.4 proof* and is bottled straight from the barrel. It is, Noe assures us, the "natural stuff"—undiluted, uncut, unfiltered—and worth more than $100 a bottle in Japan. Ironically, it is essentially "barrel" or "jug" whiskey—the kind that, years ago, before Prohibition, was sold straight from the barrel to customers arriving with their own jugs, the cheapest way to buy it. No doubt the original barrel whiskey was not aged for eight long years, and certainly it was not packaged so attractively—or cost as much—as that sold to the Japanese.

Heaven Hill distillery also markets extensively to the Japanese by promoting its ties to tradition. It proudly publicizes its association with the Beam dynasty of master distillers, a branch of which has provided it with master distillers for several generations. Even the site of Heaven Hill itself has promotable "ancestors," for it was here that the Heavenhill family began distilling whiskey in the 1780s and the recipe for Heaven Hill whiskey was first developed. In fact, the son of that early distiller, William Heavenhill, who also distilled whiskey at this site, was the first white child born in the Kentucky wilderness; legend says he was born in a damp hole where a large spring gushed out—limestone water, of course—while his father and neighbors fought off Indians.

---

*"Proof" is the folk term for alcoholic strength. Originally it was "gunpowder proof," so-called because early distillers determined the potency of their products by igniting a mixture of half gunpowder and half bourbon. If the powder would not burn at all, the alcohol content was too low. If it blazed up brightly, it was too high. If the mixture burned slowly and evenly, especially with a blue flame, it was labeled "100 percent perfect" or "proved."

Another significant site in the annals of bourbon-making history is the Maker's Mark Distillery (formerly the Star Hill Distillery), the only distillery to be placed on the National Register of Historic Places. An old country distillery purchased in 1953 and lovingly restored by T. William (Bill) Samuels, Maker's Mark is presently under the care of Bill Samuels, Jr., a seventh generation distiller. The first Kentucky Samuels settled here in 1780 on a sixty-acre tract granted by Virginia governor Patrick Henry and promptly launched what is a Kentucky distilling dynasty. Today, as Bruce Allar laments, "the Samuels are the last of a breed, the only one of the original Scotch-Irish clans still in the bourbon business." Samuels produces only one label—Maker's Mark—advertised as "the softest spoken of the bourbons" and produced in very limited quantities (thirty-eight barrels a day compared with an industry average of 600). Much of the distilling process is accomplished by hand, and some procedures—such as the rotation from floor to floor of barrels of whiskey while they age, a practice now abandoned by larger distilleries—are still customary at Maker's Mark. The grains continue to ferment in nineteenth century vats, and the youngest Samuels continues to taste and evaluate his whiskey as did his father, who described his taste-testing technique as follows: "I sit and *smell*. Taste . . . and smell buds are the same. Sometimes we sip, but barely, and we never drink. That would ruin the sense of smell . . . even when we sip we don't swallow, for a few swallows would anesthetize the buds and you would miss that elusive bouquet which is the hallmark of quality." Described by one connoisseur as pure Kentucky champagne, Maker's Mark may bear eloquent testimony to the efficacy of distilling folkways.

Mint Julep   There are at least two traditional ways in which bourbon is habitually consumed in the Bluegrass. The first is called "bourbon and branch water," a combination of whiskey and water, preferably spring, poured over ice cubes. This is a favorite of many Bluegrass gentlemen, including Booker Noe himself and the writer of this book. The second traditional form in which bourbon whiskey is enjoyed—and which has become the unofficial Kentucky Derby drink— is the much celebrated mint julep.

Cold and frosty to the touch, the mint julep is a delicate concoction traditionally composed of mint, sugar, bourbon, and water. A genuine Kentucky Derby mint julep must be served in a frosted silver julep cup—originally coin silver, about 4 inches tall and 3 inches in diameter— and all ingredients must be native to Kentucky: the water must be cold and fresh from a limestone spring; the bourbon, at least eight-year-old Kentucky straight; and the mint, picked after the most recent dawn, when the dew is still fresh on its leaves. A mint julep is not, however, merely the product of a formula; it is a folk ceremony, a heritage of the Old South. Symbolizing the traditions of hospitality and domestic joy, it is a rite that must not be entrusted to a novice or a "Damn Yankee." According to an old saying, the grave of a true Southerner can always be identified by the mint, springing from the innumerable mint juleps consumed over his lifetime, which grows on the plot.

As to which Southern state gave birth to this delectable drink, Virginia, Maryland, Georgia, and even Louisiana have all vied for the honor. Bluegrass Kentuckians, however, agree with Larry Thompson—a scholar and a native of North Carolina, who therefore should be objective in his deliberations—who wrote: "There is but one bonafide mint julep, and it is as indigenous to the Bluegrass as gin and bitters is to the diet of a London charwoman."

Also subject to sharp disagreement is whether the mint should be crushed or merely bruised. The editorial offices of the Louisville *Courier-Journal* and the Richmond *Time-Dispatch* once debated this point eruditely. What distresses Kentuckians even more, however, is the use of "alien" —that is, nonbourbon—liquors in julep making. New Yorkers, it is reported, gulp down "juleps hideously concocted with creme de menthe and maraschino cherries" and Marylanders sometimes pour in rye whiskey— an act which led Kentucky humorist, Colonel Irvin S. Cobb, to write: "Any guy who'd put rye in a mint julep and crush the leaves, would put scorpions in a baby's bed."

Notwithstanding all this wrangling and poetics, some scholars have contended that the popularity of the julep is more a creation of folk fancy than of fact. The Kentucky mint julep has always been the drink of special occasions, and few juleps are drunk in Kentucky today except at Derby time. However, the folk mystique of the Bluegrass has been much enriched by the mint julep, and the quintessential recipe for julep making provided by Lexington lawyer-journalist J. Soule Smith (who was called the Falcon, and whose eloquent prose must certainly have been at least partially mint julep inspired) is a classic of Bluegrass folk oratory:

Then comes the zenith of man's pleasure. Then comes the julep—the mint julep. Who has not tasted one has lived in vain. The honey of Hymettus brought no such solace to the soul; the nectar of the Gods is tame beside it. It is the very dream of drinks, the vision of sweet quaffings. The Bourbon and the mint are lovers. . . . The mint dips its infant leaf into the same stream that makes the Bourbon what it is. . . . Gracious and kind it is, living only for the sake of others. The crushing of it only makes its sweetness more apparent. Like a woman's heart, it gives its sweetest aroma when bruised. Among the first to greet the spring, it comes. . . . It is virgin then. But soon it must be married to Old Bourbon. His great heart, his warmth of temperament, and that affinity which no one understands, demands the wedding. . . . Take from the cold spring some water, pure as angels are; mix with it sugar till it seems like oil. Then take a glass and crush your mint within it with a spoon—crush it around the borders of the glass and leave no place untouched. Then throw the mint away—it is a sacrifice. Fill with cracked ice the glass; pour in the quantity of Bourbon which you want. It trickles slowly through the ice. Let it have time to cool, then pour your sugared water over it. No spoon is needed, no stirring is allowed—just let it stand for a moment. Then around the brim place sprigs of mint, so that the one who drinks may find a taste and odor at one draught.

When it is made, sip it slowly. August suns are shining, the breath of the south wind is upon you. It is fragrant, cold and sweet—it is seductive. No maiden's kiss is tenderer or more refreshing; no maiden's touch could be more passionate. Sip it and dream—you cannot dream amiss. Sip it and dream, it is a dream itself. No other land can give so sweet a solace of your cares; no other liquor soothes you so in melancholy days. Sip it and say there is no solace for the soul, no tonic for the body like Old Bourbon whiskey.

Also, many devotees would ask, "What's a julep without a cigar?"

15

Burley Tobacco: From Hand to Mouth

Since pioneer days tobacco has been an important cash crop in the Bluegrass, and—as it was in Virginia—a medium of exchange and a substitute for money. A Clark Countian, writing in a newspaper in the early 1920s, lamented:

It was so many pounds of tobacco for a day's work, or for a horse or cow, and finally when taxes were levied it was so many pounds of tobacco. Tobacco was sent back over the mountains to Virginia on pack horses as a currency...with which to purchase various articles needed by settlers.

When courts were established...all [their] fees and services...were paid with tobacco, thus it will be seen that an article unsuitable for either food or raiment, used only to gratify an unnatural but acquired taste for a filthy practice, took position above every other article of production.

CHEWING TOBACCO

Pioneer Kentuckians were indeed enthusiastic adherents of the "filthy practice," boasting of their prowess with tobacco and whiskey alike: "I'm the *ginewine* article...I can outrun, outjump, outswim, chaw more tobacco and spit less, and drink more whiskey and keep soberer than any other man in these localities!" "Eatin' terbacky"—an appropriate term, since about as much juice was swallowed as spit—was a common diversion, and one that newcomers and visitors considered particularly nauseating. One such visitor commented, "There was not a man who appears to have a single earthly object in view except spitting...." Others estimated that the average chewer spit at least once every minute, expectorating a half pint of juice per hour. Worse yet, spittoons and cuspidors were largely unknown on the frontier, and even when present were no competition to floor and walls. Illustrating this is a many-versioned tale about a tobacco chewing visitor to a well-kept Bluegrass home. The lady of the house quietly directs a servant boy to move the cuspidor so that the visitor will spit in it and not on her clean floors. The visitor, however, keeps spitting in different places, forcing the boy to scoot the cuspidor frantically around the room in an attempt to catch the spray of ambeer. Finally the visitor bellows: "Madam, if that little rascal doesn't stop moving that thing around, I'm going to spit right in it!"

Such profuse chewing and spitting was a serious problem for overnight guests at crowded frontier inns and taverns. Since pegs on which to hang clothes were seldom found in taverns, guests were faced with a choice: either sleep in their clothes or pile them on the floor, where they risked being spattered with ambeer (tobacco juice spittle). Legend claims Jessamine County's town of Spears was named for one such spitter of ambeer. Bob Fain retells the place-name legend:

One of the first settlers was Tobacco Ned Cuspidor [itself an obvious folk name]. Mrs. Cuspidor was herself famous, for her looks. People delighted in asking Ned how he told his wife from his goat. He would shift his chew, spit ambeer—"Sput!" and drawl, "Why's her ears." Meaning that she had the larger ears. Heard, and not written, his reply came out, "Sput'sears." In time, Spears.

Today, homemade spittoons are commonplace, usually any container with an opening wide enough for the spitters to hit; some even make portable ambeer catchers from pop bottles or cans and carry them along wherever they go—an improvement over indiscriminate use of the floor.

Early Kentuckians' predilection for "chewing" over "smoking" tobacco was both philosophical and practical. Their preference for chewing was partly a frontier rejection of the culture of the Eastern seaboard, where smoking and snuffing prevailed. Many pioneers considered smoking—not to mention taking snuff—to be effete and degenerate. The early Kentuckian reveled in his own way of doing things, and that included chewing his tobacco and not smoking it. He also believed chewing was more practical.

Twist and Plug   "Twist" chewing tobacco was cheap and readily available; it was convenient to use—one did not have to stop work to fill and light a pipe, one's hands were free to continue working, and a chewer's spittoon was the whole outdoors. Settlers learned from the Indians how to twist leaves tightly into a kind of braided rope, which could be folded up and carried in the pocket. From this twist one could bite off a "chaw" at will. To make the chaw more palatable, frontiersmen fabricated "sweet plug." This was made by wadding the chaw into a hole in a stump or log and liberally lacing it with some kind of sweetening, preferably alcoholic, and leaving it to ferment. It emerged as a tightly compressed cake of tobacco called a plug.

Long "twists"—the products of a widespread Kentucky traditional folk craft—can still be found hanging in Bluegrass country stores, and "smokeless tobacco" remains popular among numerous rural and small-town Bluegrass Kentuckians.* In addition, snuff, formerly snuffed up the nose (hence the name), is now "dipped" and held between the cheek and gums, and has become a popular substitute for chewing tobacco. The shape of the small round can in which snuff is packaged can be seen rolled up in the sleeve of a T-shirt or outlined in a tight blue-jeans back pocket.

WHITE BURLEY

By 1840 Kentucky ranked second only to Virginia in production of tobacco. This was a dark-leaf variety, cured with fire of either hickory wood or charcoal and sometimes called Little Frederic and Big Frederic tobacco. The amount of tobacco cultivated in the Bluegrass counties, however, was minuscule compared to that of some western Kentucky counties. Until after the Civil War the major cash crop in the Bluegrass was hemp, and a certain amount of hemp continues to be grown—nowadays in the form of marijuana, an illegal folk enterprise. In 1864, however, Kentucky White Burley was discovered—not in the Bluegrass, to the chagrin of Kentuckians, but in Brown County, Ohio. The new plant, named for its greenish white or pale green coloring early in the growing season, was particularly adaptable to the Central Kentucky limestone soil, and it thrived in the Bluegrass. By the 1890s, White Burley had replaced hemp as the major Bluegrass money crop, and today Kentucky produces the second largest tobacco crop in the country, surpassed only by North Carolina, and Lexington is reputed to be the world's largest Burley market.

In the contemporary Bluegrass, Burley is grown mainly on small and medium-sized farms. Many tobacco patches are cared for by rural families whose main income is provided by a nonfarming occupation; the father (and perhaps mother) works for a nearby manufacturing or service

---

*The Bluegrass—indeed all of Kentucky—has a high incidence of oral cancer, a fact recognized by both in-state and out-of-state medical people. For example, at the University of Kentucky Medical Center, a newly arrived ear, nose, and throat specialist from the upper Midwest explained he had come to Lexington because he was interested in oral cancer, much of it caused by tobacco. However, because tobacco is so central to the state economy, political pressures are brought to bear when it is maligned or its use prohibited, even in the interest of health. When the director of the Fayette County Health Department attempted to institute a "no smoking" policy on Health Department premises, he was deluged with protests from other state agencies; likewise, when the Fayette County Board of Education proposed to ban use of tobacco on school property, protests were heard all over the Commonwealth.

industry in the day and tends the tobacco evenings and on weekends. Such arrangements are almost always family affairs with children and both parents participating in the work, especially in its most time-consuming aspects, such as setting, cutting, and stripping. Few horse farms raise their own tobacco, rather a tenant cares for the crop full-time, or the farm leases its allotment acreage to a nearby farmer who then raises the crop on his own land. This allotment arrangement is a traditional practice in Kentucky; indeed there are many more tobacco allotments in Kentucky than farms. Agricultural areas that have been converted to urban or suburban use—the Bluegrass Airport, for example—retain active tobacco allotments, which are usually leased to enterprising farmers.

A Hand Operation   The entire process of growing White Burley tobacco involves traditional methods. Some steps, it is true, have been modified or even eliminated by technological advancements. Pesticides have virtually eliminated such pests as the hornworm—the huge green tobacco caterpillar that farmers once caught by hand and crushed between thumb and forefinger. "Suckers," secondary leaves that appear after the plant head or blossom has been "topped," which once had to be hand-cut, are now chemically retarded. Cultivating by horse and hoe has been largely replaced by herbicides and tractor and plow. Mechanized transplanters have facilitated the setting of young plants, and the use of a baler (to compress the stripped leaves into huge bales) has reduced stripping time; however, both procedures still require much time-consuming hand work and expertise. Family-oriented, part-time operations sometimes find it economically impossible to utilize scientific farming techniques and equipment. Moreover, relatively few labor-reducing technologies have been introduced into the farming of Burley tobacco. Consequently, the planting, cultivation, and especially the harvesting of Burley is labor intensive, even on the larger farms. As one elderly tobacco farmer put it, "There's nothing you can do about tobacco that isn't hard."

Less than 2 percent of the cropland in Kentucky is planted in tobacco, but raising that crop consumes approximately 25 percent of the productive farm labor. Scarcity of labor is a continuing problem; indeed, during the harvest season of 1990, a local television station featured a news piece lamenting the lack of skilled labor to cut the tobacco. Most people not familiar with tobacco farming do not realize how much hand labor is required to harvest the leaf.

Raising the Leaf   The production of Burley follows a precise yearly calendar. Each step in this production has been conducted within the same yearly time period, and in the same order, since Burley was

Pulling tobacco plants from seedbed for transplanting, a family activity (Photo by author)

first cultivated. Not only does each step reflect folk knowledge, but it is often described in folk terms. In the first months of the year, the seedbed or "tobacco bed" is selected and prepared. The bed is shaded with a "tobacco cloth"—sometimes called a plant cloth or tobacco canvas or tobacco cotton—which is suspended just above the sprouting plants on stakes, or sometimes on soft-drink bottles turned upside down and stuck into the ground. Once the seedlings are well started, usually six to ten weeks after sowing, the best looking ones are pulled and transplanted—usually an entire-family task—to the patches where they will complete their growth. They are set out in rows 3 to 5 feet apart, one plant every 12 to 16 inches. Traditionally, this is done by hand, but a hand-operated transplanter or a tractor-drawn transplanter—with family members riding on it, setting plants—is available, and either can speed up the process somewhat. By the end of July or early August, when the plant is about to flower, it must be "topped"—that is, the entire patch must be walked, row by row, and the budding blooms broken or cut off each plant. White Burley is "topped high," leaving most of the leaves (as many as twenty) on the stalk. Topping firms up the leaves and improves their development.

During the last half of August and early September, the plants are cut (that is, harvested) with a "tobacco knife," a kind of thin, lightweight hatchet (which, if handmade, is a folk-culture tool). Cut stalks are "spiked" on "tobacco sticks," which are removed from the field after a few days to the tobacco barn—traditionally a male task—where they are hung on the tiers to cure. White Burley is air-cured—that is, unlike the dark tobacco of Western Kentucky (fire-cured) and the lemon-colored leaf of the Carolinas (flue-cured), it is hung in a ventilated barn and allowed to mellow naturally. Tobacco barns (as discussed in Chapter 6) are specially made to allow for a maximum of air circulation to avoid "house burn"—damage caused by a fungus that develops when there is too much moisture—and "pole rot."

In October or November, after the leaf is "in case"—ready to strip—the sticks laden with cured tobacco are removed from the tiers in the barn and carried to the "stripping shed." To strip the leaves, the worker lays a stalk on a "stripping bench (or table)" and pulls off the leaves by hand; the leaf is then sorted into grades according to color, texture, size, and physical condition. There were originally six grades, beginning at the bottom of the stalk: "dog-trash" or "spoge," "trash," "lug," "brightleaf," "redleaf," and "tips." Today, most farmers strip off in two or three grades: "trash" meaning those leaves closest to the ground, "lug" the middle leaves, and "red" the top leaves. A time-consuming, bone-chilling process, stripping is often done on an assembly-line basis, with each member of the farmer's family stripping a particular grade.

After stripping, each grade is tied into "hands" of ten to twenty leaves; or if the farmer has access to a baler, leaves are laid in a box and pressed and tied. The discarded tobacco stalks are a rich source of fertilizer, and farmers spread them on their fields so that winter rains can leach the nutrients into the soil. Even in Bluegrass towns, one can occasionally see lawns, especially those recently seeded, crisscrossed with tobacco stalks as a folk alternative to commercial lawn services (pop culture). As a last step, the graded tobacco is usually taken to an area tobacco market—not only Lexington but most Bluegrass towns of any size have one—and sold at auction. Auctioning begins the last half of November and lasts through the first half of January, and since the result of an auction—how high a price one's leaf brings—is recompense for an entire year of arduous labor, auction time is anxiety time. An unknown farmer's wife is frequently quoted: "The tobacco market has spoiled Christmas around here for years." For those Bluegrass farmers, especially tenant farmers—many of whom live on the edge of poverty—a poor crop with an accompanying low price at the auction is devastating. To an observer, the lined, sunburned face of a farmer whose crop has failed to bring a good price becomes a haunting, heart-rending memory.

Tobacco Auctions   Tobacco auctioneering itself is a traditional artistic communicative medium. To be fully appreciated, the auctioneer's rapid singsong must be heard—perhaps "experienced" would be the

A typical tobacco auction
(Photo courtesy of
University of Kentucky
Libraries)

better word—in the context of an actual tobacco auction; print can in no
way do justice to this special kind of traditional folk speech. In the words
of one old-time auctioneer, "crying a sale" (or "calling a sale") requires
a tongue that is "loose at both ends and in the middle." As is the case
with many folk arts, auctioneering is now taught by elite culture institutions in six-week courses. Such classes, however, may instruct the novice
in the theoretical fundamentals, but perfecting the auctioneering art
remains a folk process—younger auctioneers listening and learning from
older practitioners at the sales. An experienced Jessamine County auctioneer, who occasionally teaches at auction schools, maintains that
although formal classes help, they cannot make an auctioneer. He himself
learned by watching the tobacco market and from experience. Moreover,
he believes a man must be honest, possess a good voice, love people
(selfish people make poor auctioneers), and have auctioneering in the
blood. "You can't make a hamburger out of a egg," he says, "You've got
to have a certain amount of it in you."

The sale itself is held in a huge tobacco warehouse (the largest said to
be in Lexington), where farmers' "baskets" and "hogsheads" and piles
and bales of tobacco have been graded, labeled, and arranged in long
rows. A basket is a shallow circular or rectangular container, usually
woven of wood, on which "loose" tobacco is stacked, enabling it to be
moved around the warehouse more easily. A hogshead is a huge container, often wood, for compressed leaves; eighteenth century hogsheads held
only about 600 pounds, but today they average twice that. Most tobacco
auctioned in the Bluegrass is "loose leaf"—not baled or compressed in

hogsheads—hence the terms "loose-leaf auction," "loose floor," "loose-leaf warehouse," and so on.

The auctioneer and a group of tobacco company buyers walk down a row—often at a rather brisk clip—preceded by the warehouse representative, who has familiarized himself with the tobacco and knows the farmer's reputation for growing quality, or inferior, leaf. (Some desperate or dishonest farmers have been known to place heavy objects in the middle of their pile of tobacco, or keep their crop moist on purpose, thus artificially increasing its weight). The auctioneer and warehouseman communicate back and forth about each crop to be sold, and the auctioneer begins his rapid-fire chant and responds to buyers' bids, always endeavoring to get them to increase it. All during this process, everyone involved usually feels, lifts, crushes, smells, and in other ways examines and discusses the tobacco at bid. When it is obvious that no one will increase the bid, or when he realizes that the last bid was more than fair, the auctioneer sings out "Sold [name of tobacco company winning the bid]," and the group proceeds to the next pile. All the while, the farmers, and often their families as well, stand on the sidelines with expressions of hope, anxiety, or despair—but seldom glee—on their faces. Sometimes they approach the warehouseman, endeavoring to get him to ask the auctioneer to do his best to get a higher price; if the farmer has a good reputation/relationship with the warehouseman, this strategy can possibly get him a few more cents per pound for his crop. So, as in economic arrangements for stud fees among horse breeders (discussed in Chapter 9), a "good ol' boy" system sometimes influences the price a farmer gets for his crop.

Tobacco in Folk Belief

Not surprisingly, as it is so important to the Bluegrass, tobacco is the focus of sundry folk beliefs and superstitions. In folk medicine, a tobacco leaf will cure a carbuncle; tobacco juice will cure warts; tobacco smoke will cure a baby's colic; in early days, tiny bags of crushed tobacco worn around the neck warded off evil and illness; and keeping tobacco juice in the mouth prevents dental caries. (This last item would no doubt come as a great surprise to the U.S. Public Health Service.)

Carrying tobacco seeds (or buckeyes) is believed to bring good luck. Yet, smoking can be unlucky; one Lexington home-brew maker claimed that his concoction would explode if he smoked during its preparation. Likewise, a two-pack-a-day Scott County horse trainer supposedly desisted from smoking whenever one of his horses was running; he was convinced that, if he lighted up, his horse was certain to run a poor race. Refusing a "chaw" if offered one is bad luck; and if given a knife to cut the plug, one must return the knife, handle first and with the blade in the same position as when received—either open or closed—or it is bad luck, and will sever the friendship. Many Kentucky males consider it a sign of manliness to use tobacco; and one often hears the assertion, "Why I wouldn't trust a man who didn't smoke or take a drink either one." The superior quality of Bluegrass tobacco has, on occasion, been noted even by horses. A Thoroughbred named Beaucaire was popular among tourists because he would mooch tobacco in any form—cigarettes, cigars, twists, even snuff—by sticking out his tongue whenever a visitor came near. Whether or not he used a spittoon is not recorded, but he apparently thrived on the weed. Just as race horses evidently relished a treat of bourbon after (sometimes even before) a race, such ingestion perhaps is logical—in essence, Bluegrass pride (horses) enjoying Bluegrass pride (bourbon and tobacco).

A 1990 study revealed that the per capita percentage of Kentuckians who still smoke is higher than that of any other state. To defend their habit, and as a response to the effort to ban tobacco, more and more Kentuckians today display a bumper sticker on their cars: "I Smoke, and I Vote." Indeed, criticism of tobacco can start a fight—almost as quickly as criticism of Kentucky ham or other native food.

"Grease Spots in the Air," Lamb Fries, and Other Bluegrass Epicurean Delights

Culinary variety was not one of the advantages of being an early settler in the Bluegrass. An assortment of nuts and wild greens and fruits were available in season, but until crops could be planted and harvested, pioneers subsisted primarily on wild game: bear, deer, turkey, and squirrel. So many turkeys—flocks numbering in the hundreds were not at all unusual—were killed and consumed that turkey pot pie became a common dish, so common that one settler reputedly declared he "never wanted to eat any more as long as he lived." Too, turkey breasts and venison often served as "bread" when flour and meal were in short supply. Of more serious consequences to the pioneers than mere surfeit of meat was the folk belief that an all-protein diet prevented conception. A legend maintains that the wives of settlers in 1780 began to "breed pretty fast" only after their corn crop was harvested in 1781.

The role that corn eventually played in frontier life cannot be overstated. Corn did not require plowed soil to grow; it could be planted anywhere convenient, even among stumps in newly cleared fields. Every part of the plant was used: stalks and leaves for fodder; shucks to stuff pillows and mattresses and for scrubbing floors; cobs for toys and pipes and to use as fuel, along with dried corn silk, which also was used to smoke in hard times; kernels to eat in various preparations—fresh when first picked, or as parched corn later, or ground as meal for a variety of breads that could be made more easily and more quickly than wheat breads; and, of course, corn could be turned into whiskey. In many respects, corn was the salvation of the early settlers, and its use is still central to many Bluegrass culinary traditions. Parched corn, for instance, is still a tradition in the Bluegrass and stems from Native American cuisine; in fact, a recent study of Kentuckians who have traditionally used parched corn revealed that a significant percentage of them also have some Indian ancestry.

In addition to corn, Bluegrass settlers planted cabbage, squash, pumpkins, sweet potatoes, beans, turnips, cucumbers, peas, and lettuce. Some of these plants—corn, beans, squash, and pumpkin—had been wild plants domesticated by Indian tribes and were probably borrowed from them by early settlers. White potatoes were not popular until the nineteenth century when the English and Scots, whose foodways formed the foundation of Kentucky culinary traditions, accepted the Irish alternative to sweet potatoes. Tomatoes, thought to be poison, were not eaten until even later. Though they took much longer to mature, fruit trees, including apple, cherry, plum, peach, and pear, were also planted. In addition to providing desserts and inserting some much needed vitamins and variety into the pioneer diet, many of these fruits, plus wild berries, grapes, and even vegetables and wild greens were used to make wine. Interestingly, this tradition of wine making continues to flourish in today's Bluegrass. Both apples and peaches were favored for converting into brandy, and apples were used to make "apple jack," a fermented cider, while raisins fermented in fruit juice created "raisin jack." From apples also came vinegar, used both for pickling and for flavoring greens, pies, and other foods. Hogs were raised for meat and lard, and pork, eaten either fresh or preserved, became the Region's favorite meat. Cattle likewise provided meat (beef was usually eaten fresh), and cows produced rich dairy products. Finally, chickens were raised, for both meat and eggs.

SUMPTUOUS MEALS

Utilizing these basic foodstuffs, Bluegrass settlers created as lavish a repast as their circumstances would support. Perhaps because of their experience with scarcity—not only as settlers on the American frontier but also as heirs of Old World hunger and deprivation—early Kentuckians loved their food in sumptuous quantities. At communal gatherings, such as house or barn raisings, corn shuckings, log rollings and so on—often called workins'—the preparation and eating of food played a central role; and in the individual household, food, no matter the quantity or quality, was generously shared with guests. Food and drink—usually alcoholic—was (and still is) the primary focus of Bluegrass hospitality. In 1813, Colonel William Whitley hosted this breakfast on his acreage near Crab Orchard; Burton Milward elaborates upon Tom Clark's description:

"There was chicken, soup with rice, baked Ohio River salmon, bacon, cabbage, beans, barbecued lamb, roast duck, applesauce, roast turkey, cranberry sauce, roast beef, broiled squirrel, leg of bear, baked opossum, sweet potatoes, roasting ears, hominy, boiled potatoes, baked sweet potatoes, stewed tomatoes, hot cakes, corn dodgers," and a large assortment of desserts and beverages, including, of course, old Kentucky bourbon.

Though plentiful, Kentucky cooking has never been pretentious; however, a convivial gathering and appealing table have always been important. These twin folk traditions—lots of food and drink and gracious hospitality—have flourished in the kitchens of Bluegrass homes from horse-farm mansions to tar-paper shacks.

The traditional cuisine emerging from these kitchens has manifested a decidedly Southern flavor: fried chicken or catfish; green beans cooked with enough pork grease to wink back at you; fried okra; soup beans or greens cooked with ham or salt pork; sweet potatoes, including sweet potato pie; black-eyed peas; and corn in all its variations—cornbread, hush puppies, hominy, grits, mush, spoonbread, corn pudding, fritters, hoecake, "roasten ears," fried corn, cornbread dressing, and so on. Such a cuisinary kinship is not surprising, since the Region has historically been identified with Southern culture. Nonetheless, Bluegrass culinary traditions are in some ways unique.

LAMB FRIES

One of these unique traditions is the eating of "lamb fries," a euphemism for the testicles of a lamb. Perhaps the popularity of this dish in the Region is a modern example of the Bluegrass pioneer tradition that maintained that all available resources (including all parts of slaughtered animals) should be used. People unfamiliar with the tradition of lamb fries have sometimes erroneously equated them with "Kentucky or mountain oysters;" actually, mountain oysters are invariably hog gonads, and lamb fries are always lamb testicles. Prepared country-style—removed of all skin and "strings," soaked in salt water for an hour or so, then halved or sliced lengthwise, breaded with corn meal and a little flour, fried once over lightly in lard (today, vegetable shortening), and then served with cream gravy—lamb fries have been considered a Bluegrass delicacy for almost 200 years. Conversely, neither beef nor hog testicles are usually as well liked, much less considered a delicacy; many people object that both are "too tough," and that hog gonads are "awfully strong tasting."

Not only was the area a big producer of lambs at one time, but sheep raised in the eastern mountains were also transported to Lexington for slaughter, thus providing an abundant supply of lamb testicles for consumption. Curiously, lamb itself never became a Bluegrass specialty,

The S & N Market in Lexington, a fourth-generation family neighborhood store, regularly features Lamb Fries and Chittlins' (Photo by Jerry Schureman)

although leg of lamb and other such cuts were of course eaten by the more prosperous. Today, although most lamb testicles are not produced in the Region, the tradition of eating lamb fries has persisted, using meat grown elsewhere; and some area stores regularly feature them.

The very traditionality of the dish has negated, for residents of the Bluegrass, the embarrassment normally associated with consuming animal testicles, a nonchalance not shared by most out-of-staters. A lady from Virginia, visiting the Bluegrass for a racing event, tasted her first lamb fries at a party. She enjoyed the delicacy and wished, upon her return home, to buy some; but she was always too embarrassed to explain to her butcher exactly what she wanted. Not so afflicted, Bluegrass residents not only prepare and eat lamb fries in the privacy of their homes, but several area restaurants regularly include them on their menus and, to the puzzlement of out-of-staters, advertise "LAMB FRIES" on their outdoor signs. No doubt in an effort to capitalize on the tradition, Hall's on the River—a popular Bluegrass restaurant that works hard to portray itself as a "down home" eatery—has included "turkey fries" on its menu alongside lamb fries. Lamb fries have been served at Hall's for generations, and are a specialty of the restaurant's black cook, Miss Jean Bell, who has prepared them there for over twenty-five years. Waitresses at Hall's must put up with many inane witticisms from male customers about turkey fries: "How many dozen do you gotta have to make a mouthful?" "Do you get a magnifying glass to eat 'em with?" To make matters worse, the waitress is equally embarrassed and perplexed for an explanation when tourists who are truly ignorant about both dishes ask, "What in the world are lamb and turkey fries?"

There is an odd divergence between the sexes on the subject of lamb fries. Though some women do have an aversion to discussing the origin of the dish, they rarely dislike eating it. Many women consider lamb fries to be one of the more delicious of Bluegrass traditional culinary delights; in other words, women view them differently *as a dish*. Conversely, many men, who are quick to point out and joke about the dish's sexual connotations, are not nearly as enthusiastic about eating them; many do not even like to talk about eating them, except in a sexual-joking way. Evidently, they feel that testicles of any kind are "too close to home" to eat with a hearty appetite. Those who do eat them usually do so quietly at home, as a dish prepared by their wives. Thus, while both sexes relish lamb fries as a delicacy, Bluegrass women are usually quicker to extol their culinary merits. "Oh, why they're *good* eatin', they're a delicacy. . . . I wish I had some right now," says a lady who has enjoyed lamb fries in her extended family for four generations. When asked if it was the men who usually wanted lamb fries and bought them, prepared them, and then enjoyed them more, she replied, with a mildly condescending look, "Oh no, it's *always* the women." That is a view corroborated by Miss Jean Bell and other of Hall's employees and by other local people who relish them. In fact, Hall's female kitchen manager asserts, "It's the women who really like 'em the most. Now some men like 'em, but not many fix 'em. I think it's too close to home for some of them. And you know, women might like to fix them especially when they're mad at their husbands and thinking about that every time they slice one up. I know I do that sometimes."

PORK DISHES

As attested by Colonel Whitley's breakfast, Kentuckians have always been great meat eaters. The favorite and most commonly eaten meat of the Bluegrass is not lamb fries, however, but pork. Pork was consumed in such quantities, in all its myriad forms, that in 1846 at least 8,000 hogs were slaughtered in Mercer County alone. As noted earlier, one of Lexington's early racetracks was called Chittlin' Switch—indeed, some people called the town itself Chittlin' Town—and with good reason. These small intestines of hogs, deep-fried a crisp and crunchy brown, were once served, it is said, at Johnnie Furlong's hole-in-the-wall restau-

Miss Jean Bell, cook at Hall's on the River for over twenty-five years, preparing her traditional Lamb Fries dish (Photo by Jerry Schureman)

rant in the heart of Lexington. As Bradley Smith describes it, "The hog entrails were cooked in a large lard can and the cleanliness of the 'kitchen' was such that one patron suggested that if Johnnie's cook could be induced to take a bath the health department would raise the sanitation rating from a 'D' to a 'C' card."

No portion of the hog was wasted; every part was used except its squeal—a farmer's joke, later utilized by Chicago meat packers. Pigs' feet and tails were eaten by poor whites and especially blacks. Even the head—bones and all—was boiled and mashed and congealed to make souse, or headcheese. Among the more familiar pork products popular in the Bluegrass are bacon and sausage, pork sausage being so prized that a collector of heirloom Kentucky recipes insisted that "no book on Kentucky food would be complete without a recipe for pork sausage." Nevertheless, it is eclipsed in fame and regard by the incomparable Kentucky country ham.

Kentucky Ham   As one Bluegrass chauvinist proclaims, "Much of the flavor of the old days still resides in the old ham, the Kentucky ham, sir, not that tasteless dried up rind called the Virginia ham." Attempting to account for the unique quality of this Kentucky folk delicacy, cookbook author Marion Flexner declares:

There is something about the flavor of a Kentucky cured ham that cannot be found in any other. It is richer, more nut-like and delicate than those of Virginia, Indiana, or any other state. Perhaps this flavor is due to the way the meat is cured. Perhaps the Kentucky hickory smoke is more fragrant than in other States, or perhaps the secret lies in the cooking. At any rate, hickory-smoked old country ham is perhaps Kentucky's most distinctive entry for the Culinary Hall of Fame.

In fact, Tom Clark goes so far as to claim, "It is nip and tuck between Kentucky bourbon and Kentucky ham" as to which is more famous. Kentuckians, he contends, "disdain to discuss the subject [of ham] with anybody else" and offer their sympathy to Virginians "because of their lack of discrimination in aged hog meat." Illustrating in what high regard the Kentucky ham is held is a tale of how the family of Judge Samuel Todd of Bellepoint (now part of Frankfort) entertained General William Henry Harrison; nothing was too good for the famed Indian fighter, so the Todds served him an elegant dinner, the central delicacy of which was a molasses-cured ham that had been buried in wood ashes for nine years. In fact, as Kentucky epicureans insist, even the term "Kentucky ham" is synonymous with hospitality. As Alvin Harlow notes, Kentucky's most famous region takes it even a bit further: "In the Bluegrass, it was either an insult to a dinner guest or a confession that you were tottering on the verge of poverty if you failed to serve a slice of ham with your fried chicken."

Kentucky ham can either be salt-cured or sugar-cured—heated arguments have been launched over which procedure produces a better-flavored ham—and multitudinous folk recipes exist for both preparations. A humorous old belief contends that your true connoisseur of hog meat always picks the left ham for curing, because a hog scratches himself with his right foot, which is thought to toughen the meat. A diet of spent mash from a whiskey still is also supposed to improve the taste of the meat. Customarily aged from six months to three years—Kentuckians cannot seem to agree upon one precise aging period—Kentucky hams typically exhibit mold spots on the outside, which must be scrubbed off with a stiff brush before cooking.

The hams may be slow baked, simmered, steamed, or boiled and "wrapped"—partially cooked by boiling, then covered or wrapped with cloth etc., and allowed to cool overnight to complete the cooking process; this latter preparation is preferred by many, especially with salt-cured hams which, even Kentuckians admit, may be quite salty. One traditional recipe recommends, for example, that, preparatory to cooking, the ham be placed in a pan under continuously running water and left there for thirty hours! After it is cooked, country ham is cut the "Kentucky way"—that is, tissue-paper thin. The meat is a dark reddish-brown, flecked with white. These white fleckings, which are in fact "medals of merit" used to identify the genuine article, have inspired a series of anecdotes wherein strangers, usually Yankees, believe the ham to be spoiled and either refuse to eat it or throw it away. Kentucky country ham is also delicious when fried, in which case it is cut a little thicker and fried in a hot skillet. In this way, another wonderful Kentucky specialty—red-eye gravy—can be prepared to accompany the meat.

The gravy gets its name from the small round bone, often reddish in color, in the center of a slice of ham. Heated arguments have taken place over how best to prepare—or "raise"—the gravy. Some contend that a spoonful of coffee must be added for "color;" others insist on plain tap water. Allan Trout, a red-eye gravy gourmand, proclaims:

The most nourishing liquid in this world is the gravy that fried ham gives up.... There is abundant life in ham gravy. It will put hair on the hairless chest of a man, or bloom into the pale cheeks of a woman. Breast-fed babies whose mothers eat ham gravy are destined to develop sturdy bodies and sound minds. Biscuits sopped in ham gravy will satisfy the gnawing appetite of a growing boy quicker than any combination of the patented foods . . . praised by radio announcers.

Trout facetiously pointed out the futility of the sacrilegious suggestion that Kentucky's ham gravy be bottled and sold:

But ham and gravy is a lopsided combination. The gravy always gives out before the ham. Nine times out of ten, the platter will be half full of ham when the last drop of gravy has been soaked up by the bread on some eager diner's plate. I have seen a bowl of gravy emptied on the first round, but with enough ham left for the second table.

That, sir, is why we cannot bottle ham gravy to sell to gravy lovers. A surplus of ham gravy cannot be attained.

Admittedly, Bluegrass Kentuckians like their gravy, not only red-eye gravy, but also cream gravy, prepared with either cream or milk. Cream gravy almost invariably accompanies certain meat dishes, such as lamb fries, fried chicken and fried chicken livers, country fried steak, and perhaps most common, fried sausage; and where there is gravy in Kentucky, there must also be biscuits upon which to pour it.

BREAD STUFFS

Ubiquitous throughout the Bluegrass, biscuits are made in a variety of sizes, shapes, and textures and from differing recipes, depending upon who is preparing them, and why. Biscuits are a breakfast staple—combined with gravy, sausage or ham, butter, preserves, molasses, or jelly, and sometimes eggs, fried potatoes, and fried apples. Concerning biscuits for breakfast, one respected Bluegrass cook recalls her mother saying, "It is a very lazy woman who has toast. You can't serve toast hot—biscuits you can cover up." Such a hearty breakfast is, of course, a carryover from Kentucky's rural past, when most people were engaged in the physically taxing occupation of farming. Today such breakfasts are still eaten by many farm people—the cafeteria at Keeneland serves a similar breakfast to horse people—and school cafeterias in the area regularly serve a variant of this meal (usually minus the gravy) for both breakfast and lunch. A traditional affair for over half a century, the Governor's Derby Breakfast, served each year at the Capitol to approximately 12,000 people, features similar fare: country ham and sausage, biscuits, eggs, cheese grits, and fried apples. Various fast–food restaurants in the Region also cater to this traditional culinary custom by hawking a variety of biscuit/egg/sausage/ham/bacon/gravy combinations.

Beaten Biscuits   Probably the most famous of Bluegrass biscuits are beaten biscuits, so-called because the dough must be vigorously beaten with a rolling pin or a flatiron or kneaded on a beaten biscuit roller. Kentucky culinary authority Charles Patteson says beaten "doesn't mean whipped together for lightness with an egg beater or whisk; it means placed on a flat surface and pounded with a blunt instrument ... [even] a tire iron will do. . . . Granny used to beat 'em with a musket." This is done for a protracted period of time, twenty to thirty minutes, until, in the words of a black cook noted for her delicious biscuits, it is "silky satin and talks back to you"—that is, the dough becomes smooth and satiny, and the blisters forming in it go "plop–plop." Some suggest that all this beating also serves to vent the cook's weekly accumulation of pent-up frustrations. Amazingly long lived even without refrigeration, beaten biscuits can be stored for several months in an airtight container. In the past they were often considered a Sunday biscuit.

Today, minute slivers of old Kentucky country ham ("minute" because it is so overpoweringly salty) are served between hot, buttered beaten biscuits as delicacies at social affairs. As Woodford County black cook "Miss Susie" Jackson says, "If you have a party around here [the Bluegrass] and don't have beaten biscuit and Kentucky ham, why you ain't had no party at all. They *means* 'hospitality.'" She should know, for she has prepared beaten biscuits for most of her adult life, and now at age eighty-eight she is asked to provide them for a wide variety of occasions, not the least of which was a New York banquet honoring Kentucky's first lady governor, Martha Layne Collins. Working alone in her small kitchen, Miss Susie made seventy-five dozen of her renowned biscuits for that meal. For years, she regularly sent ten dozen every Friday to a Florida customer. When asked why her beaten biscuits are so popular, she quickly says that people claim they are easier than other beaten biscuits to slice into two halves, something that has to be done in order to use them for party hors d'oeurves. Miss Susie says, "You see, I got a secret ingredient and a secret process and they make my beaten biscuit all good and crunchy but not crumbly—you know, most other people's break and crumble when you try to cut 'em, but mine don't. And whenever I see a recipe for beaten biscuit, I read it and say, 'Ah, they don't have my secret ingredient.'" She told me that secret ingredient but asked me not to say, and "Anyway," she said, "they wouldn't know how much to put in."

Miss Susie has perfected not only her biscuit recipe but her process for making them as well. Beaten biscuits were at one time so popular that special machines were manufactured with marble tops and rollers to knead the dough. Miss Susie has two of these. The rollers of one must be turned by hand; but the other—called DeMuth Improved Beaten Biscuit Machine, made by Gem Sales Co., Lexington, Kentucky—was taken apart by her cousin and motorized with parts from an old washing machine and other discarded appliances. Miss Susie likes to use it because beating the dough by hand, or even turning the rollers, is extremely strenuous and fatiguing work; moreover, at a certain stage of kneading with the machine, she does something special to the dough (she said not to tell)—the second of her secret approaches to creating what many consider the best beaten biscuits in the Bluegrass.

Although they were probably originally a creation of those on the

Miss Susie Jackson making her world famous beaten biscuits on her homemade, motorized biscuit beater (Photo by Jerry Schureman)

lower socioeconomic end of the Bluegrass table, beaten biscuits have become traditional fare for all classes of society in the Region, and are especially relished by horse world people. An "after the races" light meal at Glencrest Farm, for example, included "Buttered Beaten Biscuits with Sliced Ham." Around Derby time, beaten biscuits are also served with Derby Spread, a blending of butter, bourbon, and Roquefort cheese.

In more recent years, small biscuits have become popular; cocktails at the Elmendorf Farm, for instance, features as a finger food "Kentucky Country Ham on Tiny Biscuits." Similar combinations of ham or sausage and small biscuits—although not usually "beaten," rather soda biscuits or baking powder or even yeast—are also popular at festive activities among the less affluent, as are also sausage balls, which consist of a mixture of bulk sausage, biscuit mix, and shredded sharp cheese formed into small balls and baked.

Biscuits in the Bluegrass are not, of course, limited to breakfasts and party foods; they often accompany other meals, and are also served as snacks—hot or cold—combined with potato and green onion; or smeared with butter and honey or sorghum or jelly, or crumbled at night into milk or buttermilk. At these times, however, biscuits must share the table with another bread, which antedates even the biscuit in Bluegrass cuisine—cornbread.

Cornbread   If pressed to choose the one food that has, more than any other, shaped Bluegrass culinary tradition, one would have to point to corn. Edible at almost any stage of growth, and adaptable to an impressive array of dishes, corn not only provided early settlers directly with sundry food dishes but also fattened their hogs, thus helping to create the famed rural twosome, hog and hominy. Corn was also easy to grow in the limestone soil, proving the old Bluegrass saying: "If you drive a nail into the ground at night, it will come up a spike in the morning." In contrast, wheat did not at first grow well in the uncultivated soils of the Bluegrass, and even when it did become a common crop, the grain was so valuable that often it was sold rather than consumed. Thus, cornmeal in the form of hoecakes or corn dodgers became the staff of life for most early settlers.

In general, most Kentucky cornbreads were traditionally prepared on a griddle—a method of cooking traditional with the Scots, and which may have been adopted in the Bluegrass because of the innumerable Scotch-Irish immigrants. Bake ovens were few and far between on the frontier—though a few cornbreads like spoon bread were baked in heavy Dutch ovens directly over the coals of a hearth fire. Ingredients were few: meal, eggs, soda, water or milk. Corn lacks gluten, so buttermilk was preferred to sweet milk if soda was unavailable—it helped "raise" the bread. Also, without artificial refrigeration, sweet milk was quick to curdle in summer. It has been said that buttermilk is as common to traditional Kentucky cooking as Thoroughbreds are to the Bluegrass. Sugar was seldom an ingredient; it was one of the few staples early settlers had to buy and would have been too dear for use in cornbread. Instead, to satisfy a sweet tooth, honey or maple syrup and, later on, sorghum molasses was smeared on a piece of cornbread. This traditional way of preparing and eating cornbread is still followed in the Bluegrass, despite the ready availability today of sugar, soda, fresh milk, ovens, and refrigerators.

Hoecakes are among the most basic of cornbreads, requiring only meal and water, a bit of salt and pork grease, and a hot griddle. In pioneer days these were also baked on a rock or board slanted toward the fire, so that heat emanating from within the fireplace baked the bread—a baking method utilized in Scotland and Ireland with oat cakes. The results were called johnny, or journey, cake, because hoecake was often carried by travelers. Another simple cornbread, which has been especially popular with black cooks, is hot water cornbread; cornmeal is combined with boiling water before being fried. A special treat at hog butchering time is cracklin' bread, made by adding cracklin's (crisp bits left over from lard making) to the basic cornbread batter, and then either frying or baking it. Corn dodgers are small, hard, practically indestructible cornbread pocket food, which people could carry around to snack on. More elegant are thin-batter corn cakes fried on a hot griddle so that they have lacy edges. At the apex of the cornbreads is, of course, spoon bread, the richest of all Bluegrass cornbreads, requiring extra eggs, milk and butter, and sometimes the addition of grits as well as cornmeal. All of these cornbreads, and many more, are important components of traditional Bluegrass meals, particularly dinner (the noon meal) and supper (the evening meal), as well as of a delicious bedtime snack called crumble-in—cornbread combined with milk or buttermilk in a glass, eaten with a spoon.

VEGETABLE DISHES

Cornbread complements many traditional Bluegrass dishes, foremost among them soup beans, usually pinto but sometimes white. Numerous small Mom–and–Pop restaurants, which cater to a working-class clientele, serve fried cornbread and pinto beans as standard fare.

Slow-Cooking and Frying As prepared at these Mom–and–Pop restaurants, beans are cooked with ham or pork jowl. Indeed, ham or bacon grease or hog jowl is an indispensable ingredient of many traditional Bluegrass vegetable dishes, which are complemented by cornbread almost as deliciously as are soup beans. These dishes include fresh green beans—with or without new potatoes or squash on top—cabbage, and greens. Usually such dishes are put on the stove and allowed to simmer for several hours, perhaps all day. (The liquid left over after cooking greens in this manner is called "pot likker.") This style of cooking, especially of greens, is traditional among black cooks, but since black women cooked not only for their own families, but for many white families as well, greens cooked all day with pork also became a widespread favorite among whites in the Bluegrass. A custom during the first half of this century was "toting the basket." A black cook would take all the leftovers from the white family's meals home to her own family, and it was tacitly understood that she would cook ample biscuits, potatoes, vegetables, and dessert to feed both families. Consequently, black cooking traditions have exerted considerable influence upon middle and upper income Bluegrass family food customs.

At the same time, poor whites observed many of the same cooking and eating customs as did blacks. Both groups ate meats such as pig's feet or headcheese or pork jowl—all considered undesirable by more affluent whites. Likewise, both had extensive folk knowledge of "wild greens," different kinds of which are often mixed together and cooked in one pot. One poor white, a lifelong resident of Lexington's Irishtown, casually named approximately a dozen different types of wild greens that even today he picks and slow-cooks with bacon grease or hog jowl.

A second traditional method for cooking vegetables is frying. Depending upon the vegetable, it may or may not be first rolled in a cornmeal mixture, and then fried in bacon or ham grease. Potatoes, green tomatoes, corn, hominy, okra, and occasionally even cabbage and "poke" (greens) are fried. Potatoes are also served mashed, particularly when accompanying meats, such as fried chicken or ham, with which gravy is traditionally prepared. Ripe tomatoes are stewed or baked with bread, or combined with macaroni, for unpretentious dishes. Corn-on-the-cob is a summer favorite, of course, but a more elaborate corn dish, also traditional in the Bluegrass, is corn pudding, a delicious creation of cut corn, milk or cream, eggs, and butter. Cut corn is also sometimes combined with lima or butter beans or even green beans to form a kind of succotash, although, in general, traditional Bluegrass cooking does not favor mixtures of different foods, such as casseroles. Several vegetables are creamed, however, such as corn, peas, and a combination of new potatoes and peas.

A few vegetables are eaten raw; in general, however, not many traditional Bluegrass green salad dishes contain totally raw vegetables; instead, they are wilted or steamed in bacon or ham grease. However, raw sliced tomatoes are popular—a favorite traditional snack is tomato on biscuit—and raw cabbage in the form of coleslaw, with a mayonnaise dressing (in years past it was often a "boiled" dressing made from eggs, butter, vinegar, cream, etc.) is eaten as are green onions and lettuce. Concerning the last item, a very special variety of lettuce, called by its folk name "Bibb lettuce" or sometimes "Kentucky Limestone Bibb," is native to the Bluegrass.

Bibb Lettuce Kentucky Limestone Bibb, described in superlative terms by Central Kentucky writers, is purported to be the "finest lettuce in the world," the "Orchid of the Salad World." Jack Clowes says:

People who have never encountered Kentucky Bibb lettuce have a joy to live for. It's a beautiful plant with crisp, deep-green leaves that cluster like rose petals only not as dense. Its texture and its flavor are utterly delightful. . . . You don't have to have cultivated taste buds to enjoy Bibb.

Bibb lettuce was first developed and grown by Judge John ("Jack") B. Bibb, a native Virginian who settled in Frankfort in 1845. Judge Bibb never patented or protected or even named his lettuce; he only grew it, providing friends and neighbors with seeds, and evidently ate it, for he lived to the ripe old age of ninety-five. The lettuce was not grown commercially until the early 1920s, when the owner of a Louisville greenhouse, William Genenwein, rather circuitously obtained a pinch of the seed for his business. As the story goes, Genenwein's friend, the horse trainer for a wealthy Jefferson County industrialist, upon whose estate the lettuce was grown, enticed the estate gardener with a bottle of prime whiskey and received in return some seed, which he then passed on to Genenwein. Genenwein refused to sell any of the seed, and the lettuce remained a profitable family monopoly as long as it was grown in his greenhouses. After about seven years, however, Genenwein decided to increase production by growing an additional crop outdoors, and the inevitable happened: someone crept onto the property and carried off some Bibb seedlings. Genenwein's monopoly was ended.

Kentucky Bibb is best complemented by homemade salad dressing. One recipe suggests to forget the olive oil and substitute your own warm bacon grease; another, a favorite recipe for seven generations of the Scott family of Frankfort, calls for "real maple syrup," "real olive oil," "malt vinegar" and spices.

The elegance of Bibb lettuce is matched by only one other vegetable that flourishes in the Bluegrass soil—asparagus. Both Bibb lettuce and asparagus are considered Derby specialties, since both are in season in May, but they also appear frequently on traditional Bluegrass menus. Some menus devised by the racing elite combine Bluegrass delicacies so that the meal becomes a virtual mirror of the Region's traditional cuisine.

One such Derby menu was Spendthrift Farm's Post Derby Breakfast: Turkey Hash with Corn Cakes; Country Ham; Lamb Fries with Cream Gravy; Creamed Sweetbreads; Fresh Asparagus; Grits; Corn Pudding; Creamed Eggs; Corn Muffins; and Beaten Biscuits. Derby Eve Dinner at the C. V. Whitney Farm features almost as many traditional Bluegrass dishes: Mint Juleps; Thin Slices of Old Kentucky Ham in Buttered Beaten Biscuits; Chicken Finger Pies; Fresh Wild Greens; Corn Puffs; and Bibb Lettuce Salad. Likewise the Post Derby Lunch at Forest Retreat Farm serves guests Kentucky Cured Country Ham; Turkey and Dressing; Green Beans; Corn Pudding; and Biscuits. Finally, the Bluegrass Farm hosts a "country" supper: Southern Fried Chicken; Country Ham; Black-eyed Peas; Green Beans; Sliced Fresh Tomatoes with Onions; and Cornbread.

FISH FRIES AND WILD GAME FEASTS

Another traditional Bluegrass supper, enjoyed by people from all strata of Bluegrass society, is the fish fry. Kentucky fish fries, it is claimed, have been popular since the days of Daniel Boone when he and two compan-

ions discovered large schools of fish in the shallow waters below the falls
on Lulbegrud Creek. Removing their coats and attaching them to a staff
so as to make a crude seine, the three men netted as many as they wanted
and launched the first fish fry in Kentucky history. Fish fries today are
customarily accompanied by baked beans (cooked with jowl bacon and
sorghum molasses for a distinctive Kentucky flavor), hush puppies, and
coleslaw, and sometimes fried potatoes, fried onion rings, fried banana
peppers, and beer cheese. (Beer cheese is an old Kentucky favorite, made
hot and spicy, which at one time decked every saloon bar, and today is
another specialty of Hall's on the River.) Such a menu is also served at
the Fayette County Crescent Farm, a comparatively new horse farm,
with modern buildings and training facilities but a traditional cuisine.

Among Bluegrass Kentuckians of more modest means, the fish fry
takes the form of a group party: the host provides the fish (often caught
by him), and guests bring complementary dishes. Less frequently, pig
roasts are held. In earlier times, a suckling was used, but, because
sucklings are difficult to obtain, pig roasts today are centered around a
young adult pig, either quartered and grilled or roasted whole in a hole
in the ground. Also frog legs, turtle, squirrel, rabbit, or even dove may
serve as the principal meat for such get-togethers. Occasionally, a "varmint"
dinner will be hosted—indeed, a few Kentucky governors have hosted
such affairs. "Varmint" dinners serve such wild game as the above and
also less desirable game like 'possum and groundhog (both considered
poor people's food).

Wild game is usually prepared in much the same way as fried chicken
(although turtle may be served in a turtle soup)—that is, soaked in salt
water, coated with meal and/or flour, quickly browned in hot grease, and
then cooked through slowly over low heat. Game prepared this way,
especially rabbit and squirrel, has also been a traditional breakfast dish,
for many Bluegrass Kentuckians enjoy almost any kind of meat for
breakfast as long as it is fried—even hog brains scrambled with eggs.

BURGOO AND BARBECUE

The precise origin of burgoo—like that of bourbon—is obscure. It is
variously credited to the Indians, who used a variety of vegetables and
wild meats in their soups, to Virginia—supposedly burgoo is derived
from Brunswick stew—to France, because a version of burgoo, resembling oatmeal porridge, was purportedly served to crews on French
sailing vessels, or even to the Bluegrass itself. As mentioned previously,
pioneer families and early Bluegrass taverns and inns often maintained a
continuously cooking stew pot, to which various vegetables and meats

were added from time to time. No matter its ancestry, burgoo is today a traditional Kentucky dish.* "Burgoo," as Squire Coleman notes, "is to Kentucky what Creole Gumbo is to Louisiana or Clam Chowder to New England." A thick, highly spiced soup containing all kinds of vegetables, burgoo was originally stewed with whatever wild game was available; a popular mixture in pioneer days contained buffalo meat, venison, elk, bear, and turkey. Burgoo ingredients were always something of a mystery, since almost anything edible might be dropped into the pot—including fighting cocks. Alvin Harlow retells this anecdote:

Hardin, the Frankfort chef, has a houseboat on the Kentucky River, and confesses to an interest in cockfighting. Once, he and about fifteen of his friends, most of them owners of birds, attended a cocking main near Lexington, and when it was over, ten or twelve of their champions had died a Spartan's death. Having the chicken ingredient already on hand, Hardin suggested preparing a mess of burgoo on his boat. "We calculated," says he, "that that was the most expensive burgoo ever made. The chicken alone, counting the value of the birds and the bets we lost on them, figured up to more than $500."

Burgoo has been used to attract and feed large crowds of people, whether for a pioneer house raising or log roll, a political gathering, a farm or horse sale, a picnic, a convention, or a racing event. Indeed, Tom Clark says burgoo experts claim that "there is no such thing as a little burgoo; ... only by cooking in huge quantities can the delicacy of such proportions as 1,800 pounds of potatoes to ½ pound of curry powder be maintained." Burgoo chefs have cooked for as many as 200,000 people at one time, providing 30,000 gallons "of the delection;" and one chef owned a colossal burgoo kettle capable of holding 700 gallons.

Secret Recipes   Exact recipes for burgoo can today be found in cookbooks, but good cooks, including the so-called Burgoo Kings of years past—men renowned for their ability to create superb burgoo—remain flexible and even secretive in their choice of ingredients. These may include beef, pork, chicken, lamb, veal, and wild game—all often barbecued—parsley, potatoes, cabbage, green and red peppers, carrots,

---

*Some maintain that, historically, Bluegrass cuisine has been influenced by French recipes, which were obtained by gentrywomen who sent away for them when the Marquis de Lafayette visited the Region in 1825; hosts and hostesses wanted to impress him and serve him familiar dishes, and some or parts of these dishes were adopted and adapted by local cooks; indeed, the name Fayette County itself honors the Marquis. Also, Bourbon countians are quick to point out that their county's name derives from France's House of Bourbon; the Region's ties to New Orleans have been noted; and burgoo chef Gus Jaubert (discussed below) was of French extraction.

onions, tomatoes, corn, lima or butter beans, navy beans, celery, green or split peas, okra, turnips, green beans, garlic, apples, various spices, and perhaps a little whiskey or wine added for zest. However, the best burgoo chefs guard their cooking secrets: "This ain't all we use; we put in a few other little things, but that's a secret." For best results, this concoction is traditionally cooked outdoors in iron kettles, over a hickory-wood fire. Cooking continues for a day or two, during which the burgoo is continuously stirred. The longer it cooks the better the flavor is thought to be. Custom demands that burgoo be served in tin cups, and it is claimed that its taste is impaired if any other dish or vessel is used.

For more than forty years—from the post Civil War era well into the twentieth century—the Region's chief burgoo chef was Gus Jaubert, who cooked for John Hunt Morgan during the War. According to legend, Jaubert invented the first burgoo—using crow as the main ingredient, all other meat supplies being nonexistent—when Morgan requested a hearty meal for his men. In another version, Jaubert—called Wango Jobier— used blackbirds in his stew. Other accounts says Morgan's soldiers foraged for wild game to put into the stew, with no mention of birds of any sort. Whatever the main ingredient, the meal, it is said, was so delicious that the officers ate nearly all of it, leaving little for their men. Jaubert supposedly had a cleft palate (perhaps this was the folk explanation for his French accent) and when he was asked what he called his concoction, he replied "Bur stoo." This is certainly a colorful story, but it appears to be a misguided attempt at folk etymology. Of course, Jaubert did not create the first burgoo; as early as 1830 burgoo was mentioned in Lexington newspapers, and during the antebellum era numerous accounts exist of burgoo being served at large public gatherings.

After Jaubert's death, Colonel James T. Looney became the Region's top burgoo maker, especially in demand at political gatherings. So delicious was Looney's special brand of burgoo that, after it was eaten by 7,000 people attending a charity race at Colonel E. R. Bradley's private track, Bradley proclaimed: "Jim, you're the Burgoo King. . . . That's the greatest eating in the world! I'm going to name a colt after you." Bradley kept his promise and christened a colt "Burgoo King;" it won the 1932 Derby. (One wonders if Bradley would have bestowed such an honor upon Looney if burgoo had not begun with the letter B—the initial letter in the names of *all* horses in Bradley's stable.)

Looney also loved to cook burgoo for out-of-state visitors, most of whom relished it, though some were befuddled over its ingredients. Alvin Harlow describes one of these incidents:

When a delegation of Philadelphians came over in 1892 to help celebrate the State's centenary anniversary and were told at Lexington that they were to be

Alben Barkley (Vice President, 1949–1953), on left, with ladle, and chef Looney, behind Barkley, holding hat in right hand, at a political burgoo meeting in Jessamine County, 1944 (Photo courtesy of Transylvania University Library)

given "a burgoo," they hadn't the faintest notion what it meant. In the small hours of the night, as they lay in the old Phoenix Hotel, a peacock, which for some reason was being kept in a rear courtyard, screamed raucously, and one guest, awakened by it, nudged his bedfellow and said, "That must be that burgoo."

Barbecue   Today burgoo continues to be served in the Bluegrass at large outdoor public gatherings, such as at Keeneland or the Kentucky Horse Park, or for Derby Day and various civic club celebrations. Often it is served in conjunction with various barbecued meats (in the Bluegrass, pork is preferred, in Western Kentucky, mutton). Indeed, as noted above, the meat used to make burgoo is often first barbecued, thus the two—burgoo and barbecue—are a natural combination. (It is possible that the term "burgoo" derives from a folk etymological process that combined "barbecue" with "goo"—the soupy mixture of barbecue remnants; thus "barbecue goo" became "burgoo.") The annual Kentucky Colonel Barbecue, held the first Sunday after the Derby, serves both smoked ribs and burgoo, as well as country ham with red-eye gray, Bibb lettuce, strawberries, cheese grits, and Derby Pie. The annual Iroquois Hunt picnic at Grimes Mill also often includes both burgoo and barbecue. Large public barbecues may have antedated burgoo in the Bluegrass, since notices of military and Fourth of July barbecues appeared in newspapers of the early 1800s. Not all early barbecues were public, of course, but it was difficult to keep them private. People who were not invited sometimes took their revenge by stealing food or playing pranks on guests, such as horridly trimming the manes and tails of their horses. Some probably gate-crashed like the young man described in this anonymous limerick:

> There was a young man so benighted
> Who never knew when he was slighted.
> He'd go to a party
> And eat just as hearty
> As if he'd been really invited.

The grandest of public affairs for which burgoo and barbecues have been served, however, are the elaborate, all-day political barbecues.

The Political Barbecue   Described by William Davis as Kentucky's most exciting form of entertainment, public or private, the political barbecue combines a camp meeting atmosphere—political handshaking and backslapping and speech making—with mountains of food and drink. The last two ingredients are probably the most notable. Indeed, one observer quipped that the cooks were far more important than the candidates. "Democracy disappeared before the dictatorship of the chef, whose word was unquestioned law," writes Davis.

Political barbecues have enjoyed a long history in the Bluegrass. One such affair has been eloquently described by Thomas Allen:

The barbecue was the great event of the campaign. It was held . . . in a woods pasture . . . near town. . . . A long trench was dug, the full length of which was now a bed of live coals, and across this trench poles were placed at intervals, some to support great iron kettles and others the divers kinds of meats to be roasted—muttons and shoats and beeves. In the kettles, green corn, tomatoes, potatoes, red peppers, chickens and squirrels bobbed up and down in the bubbling water, intermingling their rich juices, the hot vapors filling the air, and sending off a sweet savor. . . .

A dozen negroes . . . turned and basted the roasts, and stirred the burgoo. Negro women . . . spread cotton cloths on the rude tables, and distributed along the whole length of them loaves of bread, cakes, pies, pickles, and jellies. In addition . . . there was a great hogshead of whiskey toddy, with numberless bright, new tin cups which did double duty as goblets for the liquor and as soup plates for the burgoo. . . .

The crowd was prodigious. And the noise! The talking, the hallooing, the quips and the quirks, the neighing of the horses. . . . First the burgoo and the various roasts and eatables, with liberal potations from the hogshead of toddy, and then came the speeches.

As Tom Clark comments: "If Kentucky politics is 'the damnedest,'...many of the sins are traceable historically to a languishing electorate gorged on burgoo and raw whiskey."

DESSERTS

To soothe the palate after the potent combination of burgoo and bourbon, Bluegrass cooks have created a delectable array of desserts, often structured around locally grown fruits: apples, blackberries, peaches, plums, mulberries, pears, cherries, gooseberries, strawberries, and rhubarb (also called "pie plant" or "blushing celery"). Other desserts consist of rich mixtures of eggs, milk or cream, and sweeteners, or combine such a mixture with a fruit. For sweeteners early cooks most often used honey, Southern cane sugar, or sorghum (sorghum, which served as a flavoring as well as a sweetener, was measured by the number of "blurps" it made while flowing from the jug). Recipes brought from Virginia often called for brandy as a flavoring, but less affluent families substituted apple jack or raisin jack, or other fruit and berry syrups or jams.

Pies and Cobblers   Fruit cobblers and pies, utilizing most of the above mentioned fruits, have always been Bluegrass favorites. Frontier cooks even used cornmeal for pie dough when wheat flour was unavailable. Supreme among cobblers is blackberry cobbler; blackberries grow wild in the Bluegrass and were one of the few fruits available to the earliest settlers, so this luscious dessert has a long history. Blackberries and nearly all other fruits are also used to make jellies, jams, and preserves—all wonderful on biscuits and cornbread—and blackberry jam is the usual choice for making jam cake—probably the favorite Christmas cake in the Bluegrass. Apples, fresh or dried, are another particularly favored fruit and are frequently eaten in pies, dumplings, and cobblers. Although drying machines are available, a number of dry-apple devotees maintain that folk methods of drying produce a more flavorful apple. Thinly sliced apples are spread on a cloth, which is placed on the ground or on the roof of a house or shed or on a similar flat surface, and covered to protect from flies and bees; the apples are allowed to lie in the sun for about three days, then stored. Another ingenious folk technique for drying fruit is simply to lay old-fashioned window screens with fruit on them across the front and back seats of an abandoned car sitting in a field; when the windows are rolled up, the car becomes a solar oven.

A delicious dessert using dried apples is fried or half-moon pie. Rolled-out dough is draped over a saucer and one half of it covered with dried apples which have been soaked overnight and then cooked; the other half of the dough is flipped over the apples, the edges pinched together with fingers, and the excess dough trimmed with a knife. The pies are then fried in hot grease. Dried peaches also make delicious fried pies, but drying peaches is no longer as popular as it was in the past. Peaches were mashed, combined with sugar, rolled out in thin sections, and sun-dried until they resembled leather, and were appropriately called peach leather.

Custards and Puddings   A versatile Bluegrass dessert is custard. It can be boiled, baked, or molded, and can be eaten either alone or in combination with leftover cake or biscuits, as in Poor Man's Pudding, which combines leftover bread with custard and spices. More elegant— though not well known in contemporary times—are tipsy cake and trifle, created by pouring custard over wine-soaked cake. The Keeneland Clubhouse's Brandy and Rum Custard, another form of custard, makes an excellent ending to a burgoo lunch, as does Kentucky Bourbon Bread Pudding with warm bourbon sauce, a specialty of The Mansion at Griffin Gate, the boyhood home of Squire Coleman and now an upscale restaurant. Woodford Pudding—a recipe for which first appeared in *Houskeeping in the Bluegrass*, published by the ladies of the Paris Presbyterian Church in 1875—adds blackberry jam and flour to the custard mixture and may be topped with meringue or bourbon sauce or cream with a little sugar and vanilla added. Banana pudding, the subject of numerous recipes, is currently popular, but has a relatively short history in the Bluegrass, since bananas, which must be imported into the United States, were a rare luxury in the past; nevertheless, once bananas were obtained, cooks used them in puddings and as puddinglike fillings for cakes. Thus, the local pudding tradition was adapted to include a nonnative fruit.

Both custard pie—also called egg pie—and chess pie are popular Bluegrass desserts, the latter being the traditional dessert for the Iroquois Hunt picnic. At one time, while the men were vigorously arguing the relative merits of various mint julep preparations, the ladies were deliberating whether chess pie was authentic without a spoonful of cornmeal. A close cousin of chess pie is Derby Pie—a custard pie considerably enriched with chocolate chips, nuts, and a bit of Kentucky bourbon. Derby Pie is one of the few desserts unique to the Bluegrass—although, to be exact, Derby Pie was first made in 1954 at the Melrose Inn in Oldham County (where this writer was among the very first to taste it), and Kern's Kitchen of Louisville presently holds rights to the name, which it has successfully protected in court against other piemakers. Kern's refuses even to write down its Derby Pie recipe and steadfastly bars visitors from the kitchen when it is being prepared. Nevertheless, slightly varying recipes of the pie have proliferated, and it is popular in the Inner Bluegrass.

Other pies traditionally served in the Bluegrass, although certainly not unique to the area, include: pumpkin (the dessert eaten at the first Christmas celebration in Louisville in 1778 was pumpkin pie); black bottom; rhubarb; transparent; vinegar (originally a substitute for lemon pie when lemons were not available); green tomato (a Kentucky specialty); damson plum; sweet potato (somewhat like pumpkin but available earlier); mincemeat (original mincemeat was made with real minced beef, apples, raisins, and whiskey); buttermilk (another Kentucky specialty)—and its variant, buttermilk bourbon pie; and pecan.

Pecans are also used in an old favorite, pecan balls, which are actually vanilla ice cream balls rolled in chopped pecans and served with hot fudge or hot butterscotch sauce. Such sauces, and especially those served over various kinds of puddings, frequently contain a generous dollop of bourbon ("¼ cup . . . or more to taste," says one recipe), butter, and cream or double cream. The availability of rich creams, plus lots of fruits, combined with a climate of short, mild winters and long, warm summers, have also made homemade ice cream a Bluegrass favorite, on special occasions perhaps accompanied by a piece of cake.

Cakes   Long a part of Kentucky's heritage, cakes have often reflected the ingenuity of early Bluegrass cooks and their ability to make do. For example, pork cakes, also called Kentucky Poor Man's Cake, used hog lard for shortening and omitted butter, milk, and eggs. Both jam cake, with its traditional caramel icing, and applesauce cake are based on the older spice cake, and Kentucky Black Cake is a traditional molasses and spice cake with fruits and nuts added. Kentucky's fruit cakes, of which Kentucky Black Cake is one, would not be complete without the addition of bourbon, and pecan cake not only contains a bit of whiskey, but often it is also wrapped in a bourbon-soaked cloth after baking. Along with jam cake, which also may contain bourbon, all of these are cakes traditionally prepared for Christmas and other holidays and special occasions. Even cooks who shun the use of liquor at any other time will often add bourbon to their Christmas cakes; one informant, who is now in her seventies, remembers that her mother, who was a member of the WCTU and a strict teetotaler, nevertheless added whiskey to her cakes and sauces.

Perhaps the most glamorous of Bluegrass cakes is Kentucky Pecan Bourbon cake, a scrumptious mixture of butter, eggs, flour, sugar, pecans, and bottled-in-bond bourbon. According to the grapevine, the recipe for this delight was coaxed from a famous New York maitre d' of the early 1920s by a Frankfort matron, who crossed his palm with a lot of silver. Other cakes traditional to the Bluegrass include Mary Todd's White Cake (created by a Lexington caterer to honor Lafayette's visit to the city in 1825, the recipe was later given to the Todd family and became one of Lincoln's favorites), pound cake, buttermilk cake, Scripture Cake (so-called because all ingredients are named in *The Holy Bible*), and angel food; as nutritionist Shirley Snarr has noted, "In the days when most Kentuckians raised their own food the dozen eggs required for an angel food cake were a low-cost ingredient." (Perhaps this explains a Christmas eggnog recipe, which calls for 12 eggs, 1 quart of cream, 1 quart of milk, and 1 quart of bourbon.) One Bourbon County bride cake contained, among other ingredients, "the whites of two dozen eggs, two cupfuls of butter, five cupfuls of sugar, seven cupfuls of flour, . . . [and a] half cupful of whisky." Such cakes are not, of course, unique to the Bluegrass. In fact, there are only two sweets unique to the Region—Derby Pie and bourbon balls.

Candies   A delectable candy concoction of powdered sugar, butter (*not* margarine), bourbon, and pecans dipped into and coated with chocolate, bourbon balls are a simple yet elegant candy. Today they are made commercially by Rebecca-Ruth Candy, Inc., founded in 1919 by Rebecca Gooch and Ruth Hanly, two schoolteachers from Frankfort, who worked part-time at candy making. When Prohibition forced the old Frankfort Hotel to close its barroom, a friend offered the ladies the use of the bar facilities, which included a marble bar, ideal for candy making, and they went into the business full-time. The idea for bourbon balls was not conceived until 1936 when another friend happened to remark that "the two best tastes in the world were a sip of Bourbon and Mrs. Booe's [Ruth Hanly's married name] mint candy," and Rebecca-Ruth Bourbon Kentucky Colonels were born. The Kentucky Colonel consists of a fondant center soaked with bourbon, surrounded by pecan halves, and coated with dark chocolate. So generous was the allotment of bourbon— Rebecca-Ruth bourbon balls contain 2-3 percent alcohol—that for years, unbeknown to its makers, the shipping of Kentucky Colonels outside Kentucky was a Federal offense. Fortunately, the law was changed in 1986. Even when sugar was rationed during World War II, customers so loved the Colonels that some saved their personal sugar rations for Mrs. Booe to make the candy for them. The combination of bourbon and chocolate was too perfect to remain a monopoly, however, and today bourbon balls of some type are made by numerous other Bluegrass cooks and candy makers.

Another traditional Bluegrass candy, probably Mrs. Booe's second most famous confection, although not unique with her, is cream candy. Even today in some country and neighborhood stores, jars or baskets of cream candy, each piece homemade and carefully wrapped in wax paper, sit on the counter, often with a brief description of the ingredients and perhaps its maker. A confection called candy pudding—a fondant mixed with a "pudding" of coconut, pecans, and candied cherries, shaped into a loaf, and then covered with melted unsweetened chocolate—is also traditional, as are an assortment of other, less unusual candies such as peanut brittle, taffy, and divinity.

HOSPITALITY

Considering all the above delicacies, perhaps it is small wonder that Bluegrass Kentuckians have been accused, as Clark McMeekin says, of "putting the hospital in hospitality." McMeekin elaborates further:

Admittedly, a round of ladies' luncheons in the Bluegrass state, replete with such famous dishes as cucumbers broiled in cream and butter, brandied sweet potatoes, huge fluffy chicken croquettes enriched with calves' brains and double cream (that float off the plate, but leave a grease spot in the air), cobblers, hot biscuits, spoon bread, bourbon balls, *et al*, presents a challenge either in self-control or endurance.

At times a Kentuckian's reputation for hospitality can come into conflict with a natural reticence to share an heirloom recipe. The story is told, for instance, of a charming Lexington bride and her new husband who, while visiting a Louisville judge, tasted his cook's delicious transparent pie and asked for the recipe. The judge said no, but not wanting to seem inhospitable, assured the bride that, if she ever wanted to serve the pie, he would be happy to have his cook make some for her; she had only to name the day and time. This she did. On the appointed evening, her guests arrived, and they sat down to the meal, but the promised dessert still had not come. As the meal progressed, the bride became more and more uneasy. Then, just as the salad plates were cleared away, the judge's cook, in apron and red bandanna, arrived from Louisville, holding a huge silver platter of her prize transparent pies. The judge kept his promise—and his recipe.

Get-Togethers   Not only do Kentuckians pride themselves on their hospitality, but they also tend to be a gregarious people who, James Lane Allen notes, love "the swarm."

The very motto of the State ["United We Stand, Divided We Fall"] is a declaration of good-fellowship, and the seal of the Commonwealth the act of shaking hands. . . . The Kentuckian must be one of many; must assert himself, not through the solitary exercise of his intellect, but the senses; must see men about him who are fat, grip his friend, hear cordial, hearty conversation, realize the play of his emotions. . . . Hence his fondness for large gatherings: open-air assemblies of the democratic sort—great agricultural fairs, race-courses, political meetings, barbecues and burgoos . . . where no one is pushed to the wall, or reduced to a seat and to silence, where all may move about at will, seek and be sought, make and receive impressions. Quiet masses of people in-doors absorb him less. He is not fond of lectures, does not build splendid theatres or expend lavishly for opera, is almost of Puritan excellence in the virtue of church-going, which in the country is attended with neighborly reunions.

Of course, the occasions for such gatherings invariably include the sharing of good food. In addition to the tradition of family reunions, some held for as long as seventy-five years, one of the most important such gatherings in the religiously oriented Bluegrass, is the congregational dinner, or as it was known in years past, dinner-on-the-ground. (The black version of this, which is still a viable tradition in places, is called a basket dinner.) This was a glorious repast in which church members would gather together bearing huge baskets of fried chicken, salads, desserts, etc., and picnic on the ground (literally, or today meaning on the church "grounds"). Some of these affairs were covered-dish meals where everyone shared everything; others were simply communal picnics where each family brought its own food. These dinner-on-the-ground picnics are thought to have provided the impetus for the invention of the stack (many-layered) cake—for generations a favorite sweet. The best way to transport a number of cakes in the large hampers was to stack them on top of each other and hold them together with a filling—in the Bluegrass usually stewed apples, applesauce, or apple butter—between the layers. Another stackable combination, appearing in a nineteenth-century Bluegrass cookbook, is gingerbread layers filled with applesauce. Sometimes pies are also stacked. Usually a recipe similar to chess or transparent pie is followed, although the filling is shallower and cooked a little stiffer than usual. Both stack cakes and pies can be topped with icing or whipped cream. In more modern times, dinners-on-the-ground have become potluck-in-the-church-basement, as modern air-conditioning and heating have made inside dinners more comfortable in the summer and possible in the winter. However, the gathering and sharing remains intact.

Food is also presented to a new preacher to welcome him to his church or to send off a missionary, to congratulate newlyweds or new parents, and so on. In years past such presents of food were called a pound party or simply poundings (each person would supposedly give a pound of food). Food dishes are taken as a gesture of sympathy to families in which a death has occurred; one such speciality is Funeral Cake—an easily made pound cake.

Coffee Clubs   Nearly every Bluegrass town has at least one eating place where males, and a few working females, meet every morning, often six or seven days of the week. It could be an old-fashioned drugstore with a snack bar or a family eatery, but more often today a fast-food franchise. The customers drink untold amounts of coffee (a few people actually eat breakfast), joke and gossip, read newspapers, debate local, regional, state, national, and even international topics, sometimes play checkers, cards, or other table games, and generally see and be seen. They stroke each other's egos and assure themselves that they are popular and important, and that their opinions and talents are respected, and that their town, region, and state is the envy of all others.

Most of these gathering places are populated by "regulars," in attendance for many years. For instance, at Grider's Drugstore in Danville, a group has met together so long they have earned the respectful epithet "the Old Goats Club." Dating to the 1950s, the group got its name from a waitress who used to return the teasing from male coffee drinkers, who called her "Nanny," by calling them "Old Goats." When one of the old goats falls ill, the club sends him a card covered with coffee stains from each of the member's cups, along with signatures and a personal greeting. Today the club even issues membership cards to its regulars, which indicate rank in the club—buck, billy, kid, or doe. Many of these informal groups are integral parts of the community, aptly illustrated by the activities of the Old Goats Club, which regularly engages in philanthropic projects. Consequently, they are recognized and respected; when a member of the Old Goats Club, for instance, was traveling in Europe and sent the club a card simply addressed "Old Goats Club," it was delivered without a question—and the population of Boyle County is over 25,000.

So many regulars drink coffee at a Winchester restaurant that each has a coffee cup bearing his name, the displayed cups covering nearly half of one wall. The same is true of the Blue Ribbon Deli in Harrodsburg, where regulars' hand-decorated cups hang from pegs on the wall. Regulars at many such gathering places represent a cross section of Bluegrass socioeconomic classes—business people, lawyers, doctors and other professionals, as well as working classes all meet at the Harrodsburg and Winchester restaurants, and horsemen and other gentry can be found alongside grooms and other working classes in a favorite Paris eatery— but the classes nonetheless usually sit at separate tables. In some Bluegrass towns different classes have their own, separate informal gathering places; in one town, for example, there is a virtual stratification: businessmen, and retired well-to-do farmers and other old-timers meet at one restaurant; working farmers, construction workers and other

"Regulars" at the Blue Ribbon Deli coffee club in Harrodsburg (Note individualized, hand-decorated cups on wall in background.) (Photo by author)

skilled laborers meet at another; and common laborers meet at a local pool room and redneck bar.

Tailgating   Ranking along with religious affiliations and kinship ties in the affections of Bluegrass Kentuckians is the love of sports, and on a college level, this means UK—"Big Blue"—sports. Many out-of-state sport fans are aware of the university's basketball tradition but, locally, UK football is also quite popular—this despite the fact that the football Wildcats have not had a spectacular season for years. This relative lack of success on the football field has not dampened the ardor of many fans, thousands of whom have established a new way of getting together, called tailgating. Driving multiequipped vans, RV's, jeeps, or station wagons (from the tailgate of which the term probably derived), fans meet on the grass and gravel parking area next to the stadium, three or four hours before game time, and "rev up" for the game. "You've got to go early to park, so why not enjoy the wait for the game to start?" explains one fan. Some tailgaters turn the gathering into a family picnic, taking favorite picnic foods; indeed, some families have more than a twenty-year tradition of tailgating before UK football games. Other tailgaters join with friends and acquaintances and make the party a potluck meal. Some even prepare foods while waiting for the game to start. A menu for such a tailgate picnic, appearing in a fall issue of the Lexington *Herald-Leader*, suggested some traditional Bluegrass food but in somewhat altered states: a beer-cheese-and-beef-broth soup; a well-dressed ham and cheese sandwich on a French loaf; a roasted new potato and green bean salad; and apple tarts.

Modern Modifications   This tailgate picnic menu is an apt example of how popular and elite culture have changed traditional Bluegrass cuisine. Certain traditional foods, such as corn and green beans, remain popular but are at times prepared in new ways, and these, over time, have themselves become traditional. Mrs. Alma Stapleton, who cooks for parties held at Paris' historic Duncan Tavern, laments that, in place of the more traditional corn pudding, "Everyone who steps in this front door thinks they have to have corn soufflé," a fluffier variant containing more eggs and milk. Pioneer food favorites have also been combined to create newer dishes, such as the Hot Brown. Technically a sandwich, but in reality a hearty entree, the Hot Brown is thinly sliced turkey (though ham can be substituted or used in addition) layered on toast over which a rich cheese sauce has been poured, and topped with tomato slices, bacon strips, and more cheese, and baked. The original Hot Brown, created in the late 1920s at the Brown Hotel in Louisville, is now a popular, traditional dish in the Bluegrass.

Some traditional foods have become less popular. Mrs. Stapleton relates the story of a Southern lady who was hosting a party at the tavern and wanted ham and sweet potatoes on the menu. When advised that sweet potatoes were no longer as popular in the Bluegrass as they once were, the lady from the South was thoroughly surprised: "Why, Miss Alma, I didn't know there was anyone who didn't like sweet potatoes." Conversely, other traditional foods, such as beef, have become more popular. Bluegrass Kentuckians have always liked beef, of course, and the area has been famous for its fine herds of cattle, but they were more expensive to raise than hogs and their meat not so easily preserved, thus beef was eaten more rarely. Today, however, probably as much beef is consumed in the Bluegrass as elsewhere in the country, and one particular cut of steak, the porterhouse, originated here. It was created and named by a Midway restaurant owner, Nathaniel Porter, who had previously maintained a tollgate house at Nugents Cross Roads on the Frankfort Pike, the same building which had once served as the Offutt-Cole Tavern.

Because of the pop-culture, fast-food, worldwide restaurant chain called Kentucky Fried Chicken, the Commonwealth has become identified with that dish, and a lot of fried chicken is indeed eaten in the Bluegrass. Curiously, however, the "Kentucky fried rat" legend is not frequently told in the Region. In this story a woman customer orders fried chicken—some tales say it is "extra crispy"—at a fast-food restaurant. As she is eating it in a darkened car, she complains to her husband or boyfriend that it tastes funny; when he finally turns on the light, they discover a tail (and sometimes little legs) hanging out of the piece of "batter-fried chicken." A subtype of this legend is a Winchester tale about the town's locally produced and quite popular soft drink, Ale-8. According to this story, a worker in the plant accidentally cuts off a finger, which is later discovered by a customer at the bottom of a bottle of Ale-8. Typical of such fictional folktales, the worker is never identified, though many local people have supposedly "heard about" the incident. Notwithstanding such stories, both Ale-8 and Kentucky Fried Chicken continue to be quite popular in the Bluegrass, though many maintain that their home-cooked fried chicken is much superior to anything "the Colonel" serves up. Indeed, chicken prepared in any number of ways—not just fried—is a favorite meat of the Region. Probably the most traditional is chicken croquettes, preferably prepared with generous amounts of butter and cream, and less elegant but equally delicious is chicken and dumplings. Recipes that feature chicken breast with Kentucky ham stuffing are also popular as are other combinations of chicken and country ham, both traditional Bluegrass favorites.

A Conservative Diversity   In general, Bluegrass Kentuckians have perhaps been more reluctant than people in many other regions to relinquish their traditional food habits. In the early 1940s, for example, when shrimp was first placed on the Duncan Tavern menu, people refused to eat them, calling them crawdads. Previously the only seafood enjoyed in the Bluegrass were oysters (shipped packed in barrels of ice covered in sawdust on paddlewheelers from New Orleans), used usually in stew or scalloped or served creamed over toast or shells or put in cornbread dressing, often for holidays or special occasions. However, under the unremitting assault of popular culture and elite culture—in the form of fast-food restaurants, mass media commercials, dietary prohibitions for medical reasons, etc.—plus the increasing multiethnic diversity of the Region, traditional eating customs are changing. Indeed, perhaps most Kentuckians have little choice in the matter. As one sprightly lady in her eighties says, describing the recipes in the above-mentioned *Housekeeping in the Bluegrass*, "All the recipes are on such a big scale and call for so much cream and butter and eggs and liquor and so on that nobody but a millionaire could afford 'em, and these delicate modern stomachs couldn't digest 'em."

Desserts seem to be particularly affected, since these are the dishes with which women most often experiment, changing ingredients to lower calories, using prepackaged mixes to save time, swapping recipes with friends or cutting new ones from newspapers or magazines, etc. Changes can be seen, however, in all areas of Bluegrass cooking. For example, margarine and vegetable oils are replacing butter and lard and Crisco; baking and broiling and microwaving are replacing frying and all-day stewing; Dream Whip and 2 percent milk are replacing whipped cream and whole milk; fast-food restaurants and microwave dishes are replacing the elaborate family meal, which consisted of numerous dishes requiring hours to prepare.

However, one feels that many such changes are necessities of convenience, or of health, not of preference, and when Central Kentuckians get together to celebrate, old customs die hard, as exemplified in a newspaper description of a family reunion: "When it is time to eat, plates are piled high with fried chicken [and mashed potatoes with butter], green beans and ham, corn pudding—and little dabs of potato salad out on the edge of the plate, lapping over the lone carrot stick picked up as a gesture toward lower cholesterol." Though no Regionwide survey has been undertaken, it is perhaps safe to say that, when it comes to cooking, most Bluegrass residents would agree that the "old ways"—country cooking—are best.

Catering to these "old ways" are innumerable small town eateries, some of which serve "family style"—that is, large bowls of vegetables, meats, breads, salads, etc., are set on the tables and the customers help themselves. Some of the best of the more expensive restaurants in the Bluegrass also prefer country cooking: Lexington's Campbell House Inn (known for its delicious Hot Browns and spoon bread) and Merrick Inn, named after the famous Thoroughbred, Merrick (its Limestone Bibb lettuce salad with cucumber dressing is a house specialty); Harrodsburg's Beaumont Inn (fried "yellow-legged" chicken, carefully aged country ham, corn pudding, cornbread, and chess pie are menu standards); and Shakertown (featuring "family style" service, vegetables and fruits from its own garden, and a unique lemon pie made out of paper-thin lemon slices). In addition, there exist several more modestly decorated and priced establishments, which serve traditional Bluegrass dishes: Hall's on the River at Boonesborough (in addition to beer cheese and lamb and turkey fries, also features fried chicken livers with cream gravy); Nicholasville's Jessamine Inn (whose home-style food "could have come from Grandma's kitchen"); and, in Lexington, Roger's, Smitty's, and Greenlee's—all offering, among other traditional Bluegrass specialities, lamb fries with cream gravy. Although such restaurants are popular-culture establishments, they nonetheless cater to people who appreciate "country" or "down home" cuisine.

"Down home," in fact, in its fullest and finest folklife connotations, aptly epitomizes what most residents of Kentucky's Bluegrass feel about this unique sociocultural Region. It is hoped that in these pages an appreciation of that "down home" way of life has been created, but the reader should realize that there is much much more to Bluegrass Kentuckians than can be savored in one "bite" from their sumptuous folk traditions.

During the pioneer era the Bluegrass seemed uniquely capable of realizing the Jeffersonian ideal of an agrarian society. For a while, especially before the Civil War, the Region appeared to be developing in accord with Jefferson's tenets. Today, however, were it not for the gentleman and other farms in the area, that initial agrarian way of life would hardly be discernible. The situation as outlined by Tom Clark in 1968 is even worse today:

The bulldozer, the fiercest varmint ever to exist in Kentucky, has gnawed its way deep into the bowels of the state's soil and has made an even deeper gash into its way of life. A frog pond today becomes a subdivision or a shopping center tomorrow. The rolling Bluegrass meadowland spreading out from the very door of James Lane Allen's secluded home in Lexington has been transformed into a warren of monotonous look-alike red-brick houses, winding streets, shopping centers, and traffic snarls. Where once fields of tall hemp, golden tobacco, and rich meadows inhabited by placid sheep, horses, and cattle sustained a civilization, chain stores, funeral homes, filling stations, and apartment houses with their accompanying traffic and confusion now clutter the landscape. On the smiling land where Henry Clay... operated a rich Bluegrass farm... there are now miles of asphalt ribbons and urban subdivisions.... Since 1940 the state has lost almost 100,000 farms.... Steadily the number of farms shrinks, and the average acreage goes up.... This is one of Kentucky's most serious breaks with the past. Its people built a good part of their tradition on that comfortable society which flourished in the countryside. Its monuments are the remains of commodious old homes which have outlived their time. Roofs and porches sag, chimneys have crumbled down below gable peaks, yards are weed-grown, and once elegant windows have lost their glass, and tufts of hay often stick out of windows to mark their final desecration. Mounting blocks are buried beneath debris, driveways are obliterated, and the old gate pillars stand nodding in neglect or have tumbled over in final surrender.... If Kentucky is being physically eroded by the mad push of suburbia, the individual suffers also. The old individualism is being replaced by a rather blank kind of social and communal conformity, and the spirit of what was once a hardheaded old agrarian state is rapidly falling into a pattern of national sameness.

Although Richard L. Troutman observes that the Inner "Bluegrass country was never a poor man's frontier," and that "no man in the ante-bellum Bluegrass was considered well-to-do unless he owned at least 500 acres of land," today postage-stamp-size lots with houses of cookie-

cutter sameness dot the landscape and encroach even upon the large
gentleman farms. Moreover, commercial development is today an omnipresent threat to the beauty and history of the Bluegrass. Just twenty
years after Clark's observations, a 1988 master's thesis in cultural geography noted that much of the Bluegrass landscape is being visually polluted
with what scholars call "kitsch"—mass-produced objects and structures
designed to attract an anonymous public with "quaintness, cuteness,
[and] artificiality, [resulting] in mediocrity and 'phoniness,' rather than
excellence and honesty." Even more tragic is the fact that to create these
innumerable kitsch objects on the Bluegrass landscape, more and more
of the Region's old traditional artifacts are destroyed. It is ironic that
Lexington has created Equifestival to help preserve the Region's uniqueness,
but simultaneously permits more and more of the "grazing park" land to
be paved over by commercial developers; and at the same time, the
University has sacrificed its Coldstream Farm to industrial uses; and the
decision to widen Paris Pike and tear down the old stone fences appears
to be the fait accompli in these destructive drives for "progress."

Are we seriously intent on becoming a Region of fast-food facades
and ersatz, glitzy veneers? Or will we eventually learn to cherish and
preserve our irreplaceable folk cultural heritage, such as the stone fences
of the Bluegrass? As we have done with various endangered animal
species, perhaps we should make illegal the destruction of various aspects
of our surviving heritage, thus preserving our past from what has proved
to be the gravest threat to everything on this planet—ourselves.

Moreover, in the process of destroying our historical artifacts for
supposed "progress," and in our efforts to emulate transient lifestyles
advertised through the media, we often lose our own individuality as
well, and youth are particularly vulnerable; Kentucky journalist M. B.
Morton's trenchant observations about Kentucky of the 1930s are even
more appropriate for today's Kentuckians:

Kentucky is not so much a political unit as a soul, an achievement in character. . . . We
should say *was*; for Kentucky, in this day and age, is suffering from the great
leveling process which is going on all over America. Individuality, folkways are
disappearing. . . . Our younger generation . . . study to be like the people who
walk the streets of New York and Chicago as is physically and psychologically
possible; God knows why!

In 1991, Dr. Mary Wharton observes that Bluegrass horse farms now
number only about 1,000, which is 400 fewer than just ten years ago, and
her assessment is dismal:

The way we are going, we are making this region just like every other, without its
own individuality. Tourists are not going to come to see industrial parks and
subdivisions.

Today, Kentuckian Wendell Berry is perhaps the most profound voice crying out against the destruction of both our historical and environmental heritage, and, like Clark, Morton, and Wharton, he also sees it as the loss of a decent way of life; yet, in the face of rampant urbanization, Berry has hope.

With the urbanization of the country so nearly complete, it may seem futile to the point of madness to pursue an ethic and a way of life based upon devotion to a place and devotion to the land. And yet I do pursue such an ethic and such a way of life, for I believe they hold the only possibility, not just for a decent life, but for survival. And the two concerns—decency and survival—are *not* separate, but are intimately related.

As these writers note, all regions of the country face continuing attacks on their cultural heritage. The Bluegrass has always been subject to outside influences, and yet has remained culturally unique. Historically, Kentuckians have always been stubborn individualists and have always taken pride in who and what they are. These qualities may still serve to preserve an agrarian way of life cherished for generations. In the process Kentuckians would retain their unique cultural characteristics through an identification with their most precious heritage—what poets call a sense of place and belonging—the land. Today, for example, one sees more and more bumper stickers on Bluegrass cars that proudly proclaim a truth most urban and urbane Americans too easily forget: "Farming is *Everybody's* Bread and Butter." Moreover, historical preservation is increasingly becoming a central concern when planning new developments. The Bluegrass is beginning to realize that it is a unique cultural Region, one the world has admired and envied for generations. Let us hope that our traditional Bluegrass way of life will be preserved for future generations to appreciate; for, as folklife scholars are quick to state, nothing less than the whole of the past is needed to understand the present, and to comprehend fully who we are.

BIBLIOGRAPHIC NOTES

INTRODUCTION

Data for this study have been obtained primarily by fieldwork among people from all socioeconomic levels in the Region. Since I have lived in and studied the Bluegrass for nearly twenty years, considerable data also derive from personal experiences and insights. Too, I have consulted publications and materials of all sorts, at local libraries and historical societies, universities and colleges, and at the Kentucky Historical Society. In addition, a few examples are included from fieldwork projects conducted by my students over the last sixteen years and from a recent survey conducted by the Kentucky River Folklife Project.

Any number of works discuss the geography/geology of the Bluegrass, and its cultural geography. Especially beneficial is Karl B. Raitz, *The Kentucky Bluegrass: A Regional Profile and Guide*, University of North Carolina Studies in Geography No. 14 (Chapel Hill: University of North Carolina Press, 1980), used throughout this study. See also Darrell Haug Davis, "The Geography of the Blue Grass Region of Kentucky," *Kentucky Geological Survey Series* 23 (1927) 6; Lloyd G. Lee, *A Brief History of Kentucky and Its Counties* (Berea: Kentucke Imprints, 1981), 2–3; and Leonard S. Wilson, "Land Use Patterns of the Inner Bluegrass," *Economic Geography*, 17 (1941): 287–96. Joseph R. Schwendeman, *Geography of Kentucky* (Norman, Oklahoma: Harlow, 1974), 16–32, provides a simplified concise geological overview. A wealth of settlement era information is in Nancy O'Malley, *Stockading Up: A Study of Pioneer Stations in the Inner Bluegrass Region of Kentucky* (Frankfort: Kentucky Heritage Council, 1987), 1. Recent essays that endeavor to illustrate "regional consciousness," a regional "state of mind," "a regional sense of self," and "a region's collective self-concept" are in Barbara Allen and Thomas J. Schlereth, eds., *Sense of Place: American Regional Cultures* (Lexington: University Press of Kentucky, 1990), 170 et passim.

My previous discussions of folk, popular, and elite culture are in *Dulcimer Maker: The Craft of Homer Ledford* (Lexington: University Press of Kentucky, 1984), 2–3, 113–22, and *Kentucky Folklore* (Lexington: University Press of Kentucky, 1989), 9–12. See also Jan Harold Brunvand, *The Study of American Folklore* (New York: Norton, 1986), 4–6. The Yoder quote is from his seminal article "The Folklife Studies Movement," *Pennsylvania Folklife* 13 (July 1963) 3: 43; see also, Allen and Schlereth, passim, and Suzi Jones, "Regionalization: A Rhetorical Strategy," *Journal of the Folklore Institute* 13 (1976): 105–20, which echoes Yoder's work. A concise summary of Bluegrass music, with bibliography, is Neil Rosenberg, "Bluegrass," *Encyclopedia of Southern Culture*, edited by Charles Reagan Wilson and William Ferris (Chapel Hill: University of North Carolina Press, 1989), 993–95.

Thomas D. Clark is the most perceptive, and perhaps prolific, Kentucky historian, and I owe much to his works; present quotes are from his *Agrarian Kentucky* (Lexington: University Press of Kentucky, 1977) 2, and *Kentucky: Land of Contrast* (New York: Harper & Row, 1968), 165. A number of popular historians have recorded folkloric data about Kentuckians; perhaps the two best are Clark McMeekin, *Old*

Kentucky Country (New York: Duell, Sloan & Pearce, 1957), 10, and Alvin F. Harlow, *"Weep No More, My Lady"* (New York: McGraw-Hill, 1942) 17, 33, 59.

The Lexington *Herald–Leader* often carries articles on any number of topics discussed in this study, as in Gil Russell, "Commentary," January 21, 1990, B-5; and in one of the paper's advertising pamphlets, 4, 18. The Jansen quote is from "Who'll Bid Twenty?" *Kentucky Folklore Record* 2 (1956) 4: 113.

CHAPTER 1

Chinn's remark is widely quoted, as in Eslie Asbury, *Horse Sense and Humor in Kentucky* (Lexington: The Thoroughbred Press, 1981), 184–85. The Smith quote is from his essay, "Near to Heaven," in *Bluegrass Cavalcade*, edited by Thomas D. Clark, (Lexington: University of Kentucky Press, 1956), 40–41, an invaluable collection of essays used throughout this study, such as the quote from Ulric Bell, "That Particular 'It'," 49–52, and the Warner essay, "An Orthodox and a Moral Region," 37. Many valuable folkloric insights and quotes are recorded in Bradley Smith, *The Horse and the Blue Grass Country* (Garden City, N. Y.: Doubleday, 1960). The Eldorado, "garden," and other romantic quotes are in W. R. Jillson, *Tales of the Dark and Bloody Ground* (Louisville: C. T. Dearing, 1930), 33–52; Robert M. Rennick, *Kentucky Place Names* (Lexington: University Press of Kentucky, 1984), 182; Otis K. Rice, *Frontier Kentucky* (Lexington: University Press of Kentucky, 1975), 20, 75; John Filson, *Discovery, Settlement and Present State of Kentucky* (Wilmington: James Adams, 1784); Lewis Collins, *Historical Sketches of Kentucky* (Cincinnati: J. A. & U. P. James, 1847), 153–54, 553; Mary Newton Standard, *Colonial Virginia*, (Philadelphia: Lippincott, 1917), 15; *Irish Pioneers in Kentucky*, edited by Michael I. O'Brien, (New York: n.p., n.d.), 2; and scattered throughout articles in *Bluegrass Cavalcade*; Tom Clark's comments, *Land of Contrast*, 3, 72–82, place these in proper perspective, and "Memoirs of Captain Buford Allen Tracy: A Scrap of Clark County History," (manuscript in my possession) reveals the hardships of frontier life.

A version of the cane legend is recorded in Edna Talbot Whitley, "Footnotes to Local History," *The Kentuckian–Citizen*, Paris, October 23, 1957, and I have heard it often; cane in the Bluegrass is also discussed in Whitley, "Footnotes," August 16, 1957; and in Bettye Lee Mastin, *Lexington, 1779* (Lexington: Lexington-Fayette County Historical Commission, 1979), 15; in Bill Cunningham, *Kentucky's Clark* (Kuttawa, Ky.: McClanahan, 1987), 19–20; and a modern discussion is in James O. Luken, "Canebrakes: Preserving Kentucky's Native Vegetation," *Kentucky Living* 43 (October 1989): 10–11.

Clark's comments are in *Agrarian Kentucky*, 2–4; the Civil War study is cited in William Henry Perrin, *History of Bourbon, Scott, Harrison, and Nicholas Counties, Kentucky* (Chicago: O. L. Baskin, 1882), 13, an early, uneven work, but with much valuable data; and Warner's and Bell's chauvinistic remarks, and the "geologists-Bluegrass girl" legend are in *Bluegrass Cavalcade* 37, 50–51. Geological data are from a personal correspondence with Dr. Don Hutcheson of the Kentucky Geological Survey.

The folk belief that true "blue" grass is found only in the Bluegrass Region is often stated, as in Ingalls' remarks and in Perrin, 14–15, and Collins, 155. Good scholarly articles on bluegrass are J. S. McHargue, "Kentucky Bluegrass—Whence Did It Come?" *Transactions of the Kentucky Academy of Science* 2 (1926): 179–90, and Kentucky Department of Agriculture ditto handout, "Kentucky Bluegrass . . . and Its Role in the Rich Agricultural Heritage of the State," 1971, 2–3. See also Raitz, 107; J. Winston Coleman, Jr., *Kentucky: A Pictorial History* (Lexington: University Press of Kentucky, 1971), 101; and the booklet *Historical Scrapbook of Bourbon County, Kentucky*, published in celebration of the 150th anniversary of the founding of Hopewell (Paris), September 1939.

Early historians provide many discussions of the naming of Kentucky, and of Native Americans' views of the Bluegrass, and their conflicts with white hunters and settlers; e.g., see Mann Butler, *A History of the Commonwealth of Kentucky* (Berea: Oscar Rucker, 1968, reprint of the 1834 edition), 15, 34, 132, 136, et passim; Robert Spencer Cotterill, *History of Pioneer Kentucky* (Cincinnati: Johnson & Hardin, 1917), 27–28, 32, 64–65, 95, 208, et passim; Hedges, Draper MSS, 11cc, 298, No. 9, 47, 49; Jonathan W. VanCleve, "Colonel Robert Patterson," in *American Pioneer* (Cincinnati: Logan Historical Society, n.d.) II: 344; and, Joseph Dodderidge, *Notes on the Settlement and Indian Wars of the Western Parts of Virginia and Pennsylvania, 1763–1783* (Albany: Joel Munsell, 1876) passim; see also, Thomas D. Clark, *A History of Kentucky* (Lexington: John Bradford Press, 1950), 32, et passim; A. Goff Bedford, *Land of Our Fathers: History of Clark County, Kentucky*, Vol. I (privately published, 1958), 129–44; Cunningham, 19–20, 66–67; Clark, *Land of Contrast*, 11–12; McMeekin, 29; and O'Malley, passim. I have heard the Frankfort place-name legend many times, and my students report it regularly; it is noted in Carl E. Kramer, *Capital on the Kentucky* (Frankfort: Historic Frankfort, Inc., 1986), 18.

Legends of the origin of bluegrass are numerous, and many writers have noted them. See, for instance, McHargue; Perrin, 11; Bedford, 15–18, 54–55; Tracy memoirs, 21–22; Sam McElwain, "Bluegrass and Its Origin," unidentified newspaper clipping in Kentucky State Historical Society Archives; and Beckner's "Eskippakithiki: The Last Indian Town in Kentucky," *Filson Club History Quarterly* 6 (October 1932) 4: 355–82, and in the same journal his "John Findley: the First Pathfinder of Kentucky" 43 (July 1969) 3: 206–15; see also, Rennick, 148–49; Collins, 182; and "Clark County Chronicles," Winchester *Sun*, October 25, 1923, and November 1, 1923.

Boone legends are uncountable; ones noted here are in Bedford, 1, 17–18, 21; Clark, *Land of Contrast*, 13; and "Clark County Chronicles," Winchester *Sun*, September 20, 1923; Marshall W. Fishwick casts Boone as the American Moses in "Daniel Boone and the Pattern of the Western Hero," *Filson Club History Quarterly* 27 (January 1953) 1: 119. The Bluegrass folk hero Logan is discussed in Charles Gano Talbert, *Benjamin Logan, Kentucky Frontiersman* (Lexington: University of Kentucky Press, 1962); see also, George Morgan Chinn, *Kentucky Settlement and Statehood, 1750–1800* (Frankfort: Kentucky Historical Society, 1975), 151–62; Cotterill, 116; and James H. Perkins, *Annals of the West* (Pittsburgh: W. S. Haven, 1857), 254–56. A good summary of early Bluegrass demographics is Thomas L. Purvis, "The Ethnic Descent of Kentucky's Early Population . . . 1790–1820," *Kentucky Historical Society Register* 80 (Summer 1982) 3: 260–61.

CHAPTER 2

The "Boone singing" legend and similar data are noted in Cotterill, 26–28, 55, 152–53; Clark, *A History*, 31; and Clark, *Land of Contrast*, 14. The Henderson quote is in Cotterill, 94–95; see also Robert A. Powell, *Sketches of the Kentucky Bluegrass Area* (Lexington: Kentucky Images, 1981) 21, 24–25, a popular but interesting treatment of historical Kentucky. Everman, a trained historian, provides excellent documented data in *The History of Bourbon County, 1785–1865* (Paris, Ky.: Bourbon Press, 1977), 1; and the excellent overview of settlers is from Raitz, 6–7. Other comments and statistics on early immigration are from Carolyn Murray Wooley, *The Founding of Lexington: 1775–1776* (Lexington: Lexington–Fayette County Historic Commission, 1975), 3–6, et passim; John D. Wright, Jr., *Lexington: Heart of the Bluegrass* (Lexington: Lexington–Fayette County Historic Commission, 1982), 17–18; Bernard Mayo, "Goshen of the Western World," in *Bluegrass Cavalcade*, 17; Perkins, 306, et passim; Coleman, 24; Chinn, 209–27; Cotterill, 238, 243–45; Rice, 111, 118–19; Asbury, 60; and McMeekin, 5, 62, 81, 88.

The Ashe and Hamilton, and similar, stereotypes are discussed in Clark, *Land of Contrast*, 77–80; McMeekin, 8, 13–15, 82–83; Asbury, 9–10; Cotterill, 64–65; Cunningham, 73–74; the Townsend quote is from Elizabeth M. Simpson, *Bluegrass Houses and Their Traditions* (Lexington: Transylvania Press, 1932), 1; and the Allen and Shaler chauvinistic sketch is from "Bluegrass Kentuckians," in *Bluegrass Cavalcade*, 57. Clark's observations about Bluegrass farmers and Clay are taken from *Land of Contrast*, 38–39, and *Agrarian Kentucky*, 47; other observations on rural life are from McMeekin, 13, 32; and Tracy 19–21. The early trait of individuality was noted by many, as in Cotterill, 214–18; and James G. Leyburn, *Frontier Folkways* (New Haven: Yale University Press, 1935) 189, 191, sees pioneers as "self-seeking." The braggart stereotype and other characteristics are discussed in McMeekin 57, 92–93, 98; Coleman, 44, 167; Clark, *A History*, 72–73; Mayo in *Bluegrass Cavalcade*, 18; Cunningham, 26–27, 32–34; and Clark, *Land of Contrast*, 70–72, 80. Clark's "Introduction," to *Bluegrass Cavalcade*, xi–xii, discusses general Bluegrass traits, including the "first," "best," etc., syndrome. The county orientation, hospitality, and apparently contradictive traits, are discussed in McMeekin, 9, 122; Cunningham, 42–44; Clark, *Land of Contrast*, 71; J. Winston Coleman, Jr. *Sketches of Kentucky's Past* (Lexington: Winburn Press, 1979), 174; Dove Hamilton Smith, "Remember When," *The State Journal*, Frankfort, April 9, 1976, 12; Nathaniel C. Hughes, Jr., *Kentucky Memories of Uncle Sam Williams* (Chattanooga: privately printed, 1978), 41, et passim; and in the diary of Jefferson T. Craig, covering the dates November 1853 to May 1856, in the Scott County Public Library, are numerous entries discussing frequent uninvited visitations.

Some pertinent data on slavery in the Bluegrass is from *Kentucky's Black Heritage* (Frankfort: Kentucky Commission on Human Rights, 1971), 3, 5, 6, 8, 10, 12–26, et passim; Cotterill, 120, 245; Whitley, "Footnotes to Local History," 23, et passim; Federal Writers' Project, *Lexington and the Bluegrass Country* (Lexington: Commercial Printing, 1938), 19; J. Winston Coleman, Jr., *Slavery Times in Kentucky* (Chapel Hill: University of North Carolina Press, 1940), 3, 145, et passim, a reliable source from which one can also gain insights about the folk aspects of slavery; as one also can from the Jefferson Craig diary (e.g., see entries under October 7 and 13 and November 1) and the rare papers in Mary E. Wharton and Ellen F. Williams, eds., *Peach Leather and Rebel Gray: Diary and Letters of a Confederate Housewife*, (Lexington: Helicon Co.,

1986), 3, 33, 152, et passim. The data and quote about black servants and other roles is from Coleman, *Sketches*, 174–75, 184, 186–87; and local historian Ann Bevins' invaluable unpublished study for the Commonwealth, "Black History Statement of Historic Context and Property Types Listing, Scott County, Kentucky," dated May 31, 1989, 1, 3, 5–7, 9, et passim, which contains a wealth of data on blacks. The Lion of White Hall legends are widely known and frequently noted, as in Clark, *Land of Contrast*, 112–15, and Coleman, *Sketches*, 184; and a recording of a speech about Clay's abolitionist activities is widely circulated in the Bluegrass; for other abolitionist data, see Asa Earl Martin, *The Anti-Slavery Movement in Kentucky Prior to 1850* (Louisville: Standard Printing, 1918), and Coleman, *Slavery*, passim. "Some Kentuckians stubbornly resisted blacks' efforts to vote," Louisville *Courier-Journal*, Monday, September 14, 1987, A–6, discusses those folk shenanigans; see also, Bedford, 409; J. Winston Coleman, Jr., "Lexington As Seen By Travellers, 1810–1835," *Filson Club History Quarterly* 29 (July 1955) 3: 272; and William H. Townsend, *Lincoln and the Bluegrass* (Lexington: University of Kentucky Press, 1955) passim for discussions of other ill treatment of blacks. Other sources of legends about blacks and treatment of them are in Clark, *Land of Contrast*, 109–15; "Clark County Chronicles," Winchester *Sun*, March 4, and August 5, 1981; Williams, *Kentucky Memories*, 75–77; Coleman, *Sketches*, 187; and Bedford, 126.

The definitive work on hemp farming in the Bluegrass, including its folk aspects and the role of blacks is James F. Hopkins, *A History of the Hemp Industry in Kentucky* (Lexington: University of Kentucky Press, 1951), 4, 215, et passim. Other data on hemp farming are in Coleman, *Sketches*, 186; and in James Lane Allen, *The Reign of Law: A Tale of the Kentucky Hemp Fields* (New York: Macmillan, 1900), 3–23, a romantic, literary history, but nonetheless valuable.

Scholarship documenting the contributions of the Irish and especially the Scotch-Irish to the settling of the Kentucky frontier is abundant; see, for example, *The Scotch-Irish in America*, Proceedings of the Scotch-Irish Congress, Columbia, Tenn., May 8–11, 1889 (Cincinnati: Robert Clark, 1889), 128; W. D. Weatherford, *Pioneers of Destiny* (Birmingham: Vulcan, 1955), 52; O'Brien, 12, 17, 31–33, 41–43, 48; and, Wooley, 9, 14, 18. The Ann McGinty reference is in O'Brien, 43. For background concerning early Irish and Scotch-Irish immigrants, consult Carl Wittke, *The Irish in America* (Baton Rouge: Louisiana State University Press, 1956), vi–vii; Henry Jones Ford, *The Scotch-Irish in America* (New York: Peter Smith, 1941), 521–23; Kerby A. Miller, *Emigrants and Exiles: Ireland and the Irish Exodus to North America* (New York: Oxford University Press, 1985), 20, 103, 137, 139–41, 147, 152–57, 160–61, 165, 170, 194, 203, 291, 297; and William C. Lehmann, *Scottish and Scotch-Irish Contributions to Early American Life and Culture* (Port Washington, N. Y.: Kennikat Press, 1978), 5, 36, 45. Miller perceptively and meticulously analyzes the reluctance of Catholic Irish to emigrate; see especially Chapter 3. The quote describing shared folk characteristics of the Irish and Scotch-Irish is also from Miller, p. 111, as is the estimate of Ulster lineage settlers on the trans-Appalachain frontier, p. 161, and the message from the Ulster-American in Kentucky, p. 203. Negative stereotypes attributed to Irish and Scotch-Irish are documented in Wittke, vii; Lehman, 39–41; *Scotch-Irish in America*, 95; and, Charles A. Hanna, *The Scotch-Irish* (New York: G. P. Putnam's Sons, 1902), 2, 60, 63. The flow of immigrants through Cumberland Gap is described by Ford, 181, 192, 199, 212, 260–90, 379–80; Hanna, 2, 37, 44, 46, 60; and, Lehmann, 33–41, 185.

Folk stereotypes and stories, as well as written references about the Bluegrass Kentucky Colonel and his way of life are legion, as in McMeekin, 14. Data on Coleman as a more realistic figure of the typical landed gentry Bluegrass Colonel are from Clement Eaton, "Kentucky Colonel—New Vintage," *The Collected Writings of J. Winston Coleman, Jr.*, edited by J. Winston Coleman, Jr. (Lexington: Winburn Press, 1969), 73–78, and in the Thompson and Mastin articles and the Hamilton "Introduction" in the same work, pp. 12–13, 17, 19, 21, 23, 28, 91, 95.

Stereotypical notions about the effects of bluegrass upon Bluegrass livestock are likewise legion, as in Perrin, 14, who also cites yield statistics; and Clark, *Land of Contrast*, 171–72. Data about the first folk fair are from Wright, 68; Perrin, 64; and Wharton and Williams, "Introduction;" see also, Whitley, "Footnotes," August 8, 1958, whose 1816 date for the Sandersville fair and 1818 date for the formation of an Agricultural Society conflict with the other published dates.

The "two Kentucky's" discussion is from Clark, *Agrarian Kentucky* 42; Cunningham, 70; Doris Osborne, "Floyd Teachers Reply...," and Michael D. Hogg, "East of Winchester: Where One 'Falls over the Edge'," Lexington *Herald–Leader*, January 7, 1990, F–3, and March 3, 1991, F–2; see also Bedford, 2–3. The 1834 visitor's description is quoted in Eugene L. Schwab, ed., *Travels in the Old South: Selected from Periodicals of the Times* Vol. 1 (Lexington: University Press of Kentucky, 1973), 266–67; see also, Raitz, 19.

CHAPTER 3

I am deeply indebted to Karl Raitz and Carolyn Murray Wooley and their research on Bluegrass rock fences; much of the discussion on rock fences, especially the step-by-step construction methods, is paraphrased or quoted from their unpublished research paper, "Rock Fences of the Bluegrass," done as part of a grant from the Kentucky Heritage Council, June 1989; other data are from my own research. Other rock fence sources are Mary E. Wharton and Edward L. Bowen, *The Horse World of the Bluegrass* (Lexington: John Bradford Press, 1980), 12, 105–109, and from Dr. Wharton's comments on a panel discussion on "Newsmakers" on WKYT-TV, Lexington, March 25, 1990; Federal Writers' Project, 2; Raitz, *Kentucky Bluegrass*, 129, 133, 138; Coleman, *Pictorial*, 236; Warren Roberts, "Folk Crafts," *Folklore and Folklife*, edited by Richard Dorson (Chicago: University of Chicago Press, 1972), 246; Thomas A. Knight and Nancy Lewis Greene, *Country Estates of the Blue Grass* (Lexington: Henry Clay Press, 1973 reprint of 1904 edition), 160, et passim; and, Richard S. and Patricia S. DeCamp, *The Bluegrass of Kentucky* (Lexington: Rayburn Press, 1985), 52; see also, Charles H. Stone, "Good Fences Make Good Neighbors," in *A Barn Well Filled*, edited by Kent Hollingsworth (Lexington: The Blood–Horse Publishers, 1971), 48–51.

Rail fences are mentioned in Lee, 30; and William E. Railey, *History of Woodford County* (Versailles, Ky.: Woodford Improvement League, 1968, reprint of 1938 edition), 6. Photos and other aspects of rail fences are in Allen, *Reign of Law*, 56; Knight and Greene, 196, 199; and, 140th Anniversary edition of *Kentuckian-Citizen* (Paris, Ky.) 1948. The halloween prank was reported by Jim Cherry in *Forkland Heritage: Its People Past and Present 1793–1988*, 55.

Most Bluegrass counties had "stray pens" or, as Scott County called theirs in 1792, "stray pound," and other log and stone structures. See Ann Bolton Bevins, *History of Scott County as Told by Selected Buildings* (Georgetown: privately printed, 1989), 10; B. O. Gaines, *History of Scott County* (Georgetown, Ky.: Frye Printing reprint of 1904 edition, 1961) Vol. II, 10; A. Goff Bedford, *The Proud Land: A History of Clark*

County, Vol. 2 (Mt. Sterling, Ky.: privately printed, 1983), 300–302, 519; Everman, 25, 29.

Data about blacks and Irish and German immigrants and their role in rock fence construction are from Raitz and Wooley, 19–21; Everman, 64–68; Whitley, "Footnotes," May 23, 1958; Wittke, 31, 125–26, 147; Bedford, *Proud Land*, 8–11, 289; Railey, 7; Collins, 555; Kramer, 118–19; Don Edwards, "Bourbon County, 'Canaan of the West,'" Lexington *Herald– Leader*, February 26, 1978; Nettie Henry Glenn, *Early Frankfort, Kentucky* (privately printed, 1986) 229–31; and from a fieldwork interview with Mr. Lafe Taylor of Lexington's Irishtown, April 18, 1990. The activities of "old Fitz," were noted by Gaines, Vol. 1, 119.

Most of the information on the traditional four-plank Bluegrass fences and gates is from fieldwork with Mr. John Sosby, general manager, Claiborne Farm, Mr. Robert Alexander, general manager, Darby Dan Farm, and their employees, from Calumet Farm employees, and from interviews with fencing and gate contractors. See also, Bradley Smith, 85; Wharton and Williams, 30, 109–11; Raitz, *Kentucky Bluegrass*, 125, 132. Raitz's invaluable study "Gentleman Farms in Kentucky's Inner Bluegrass: A Problem in Mapping," *Southeastern Geographer* 15 (May 1975) 1: 41, is also used elsewhere in this work.

CHAPTER 4

Data on early log architecture are from Rexford Newcomb, *Architecture in Old Kentucky* (Urbana: University of Illinois Press, 1953), 7; and Wharton and Bowen, 111; Clay Lancaster, *Ante Bellum Houses of the Bluegrass* (Lexington: University of Kentucky Press, 1961), 1–10; Henry Glassie, "The Types of the Southern Mountain Cabin," in Brunvand, 338–70; Lee, 30; Railey, 6; Everman, 28; Bedford, *Proud Land*, 7–8; Lehmann, 56–57; *Survey of Historic Sites in Kentucky: Clark County* (Frankfort: Kentucky Heritage Commission, 1979), 12; William Lynwood Montell and Michael Lynn Morse, *Kentucky Folk Architecture* (Lexington: University of Kentucky Press, 1976), 8–11, et passim; and, Reuben Gold Thwaites, ed., *Early Western Travels, 1748–1846* (vol. 5 of *Bradbury's Travels in the Interior of America*) (Cleveland: Arthur H. Clark, 1904), 282–84. Lancaster's sketches are in Wooley, *Founding of Lexington*, 12, 16, 24; see also, Lancaster, 2–4, and Wharton and Bowen, 113.

Much is written about Harrodsburg and other early settlements, and the springs in the Region. Max Charleston, a Fellow at Oxford, "proved" in simulated "legal, courtroom" format that Harrodsburg was the oldest Kentucky town and presented his scholarly findings in a paper, "The Oldest Town in Kentucky: 1774," read in Harrodsburg October 2, 1929; see also, O'Malley, passim; Lee, 14, 187, 444; J. Winston Coleman, Jr., *The Springs of Kentucky* (Lexington: Winburn Press, 1955); Maude Ward Lafferty, *The Lure of Kentucky* (Louisville: Standard Printing, 1939) 45, 96–97, 278–82; George Morgan Chinn, *Kentucky Settlement and Statehood, 1750–1800* (Frankfort: Kentucky Historical Society, 1975), 81–107; Willard Rouse Jillson, *Harrod's Old Fort* (Frankfort: Kentucky Historical Society, 1929); George W. Ranck, *Boonesborough* (Louisville: Morton, 1901); J. Winston Coleman, Jr., *Historic Kentucky* (Lexington: Henry Clay Press, 1967), 61, 69, 175; *Survey of Historic Sites in Kentucky: Jessamine County* (Frankfort: Kentucky Heritage Commission, 1979), 3–5; Ann Bolton Bevins, *The Royal Springs of Georgetown, Kentucky* (Georgetown: Frye Printing, 1970); Mary

Stephenson, "Old Graham Springs at Harrodsburg, Kentucky," *Kentucky Historical Society Register* 12 (1914): 27–35; Neal O. Hammon, "The Legend of Daniel Boone's Cabin at Harrodsburg," *Filson Club History Quarterly* 48 (July 1974) 3: 241–52; Mastin, 85; Gaines, Vol. 1, 49, Vol. 2, 15–17, 136–37; Collins, 446, 504–5; Bevins, *History*, 6–7, 32–33, 284; Newcomb, 32–36, 42; *Clark County Survey*, 4–5, 99–100; Lancaster, 2–3; Wooley, 25–27; and Thwaites, 282–83.

Flowers around early log houses are mentioned in Mary Willis Renick Woodson, "My Recollections of Frankfort," clipping in Kentucky Historical Society Archives; Allen M. Trout, *Greetings from Old Kentucky* (Louisville: Courier–Journal, 1947), 28–29; and Montell and Morse, 50–51. The "hospitality house" is noted in McMeekin, 9–10. See also Martha Graham Purcell, *Stories of Old Kentucky* (New York: American Book Co., 1915), 39; Standard, 118; Glassie, 341–43; Montell and Morse, 42, et passim; and Bevins, *History*, 13–14, 36, for aspects of log cabin life and legends. Other aspects of log cabins, including construction, are found in Montell and Morse, 9–11, 46, et passim; Lancaster, 2; Everman, 6; Lee, 26; *Clark County Survey*, 12; Collins, 162–64; Perkins, 343–45; Bedford, *Proud Land*, 7–8; Marie Thompson Daviess, *History of Mercer and Boyle Counties* (Harrodsburg: Harrodsburg Herald, 1924), 15–16; and Willard Rouse Jillson, *Early Frankfort and Franklin County* (Louisville: Standard Printing, 1936), 61–63, which describes the first log cabin in Frankfort.

Various aspects of log houses are discussed in Lehmann, 56; Glassie, 342, 361–62, et passim; Lancaster, 2–10; Montell and Morse, 8–46; *Clark County Survey*, 12–14; Newcomb, 2, 7, 14–37, et passim; Coleman, *Historic Kentucky*, 166, 196; Fred Kniffen and Henry Glassie, "Building in Wood in the Eastern United States," *Geographical Review* 56 (January 1966) 52–53, 55, 57, et passim; Railey, 306–07; Cunningham, 47; Ranck, 105–6, 181; Miller, 165; Kathryn Owen, *Old Homes and Landmarks of Clark County, Kentucky* (Lexington: Thoroughbred Press, 1967), 18; and Bevins, *History*, 6, 10, 33, and 62; p. 20 has a description and photo of the log house-animal shelter; and a photo of a detached kitchen and breezeway is in Coleman, *Slavery Times*, facing p. 66.

Double pen, and two-story single-pen log houses are noted by Montell and Morse, 18–19, 23, 30–32; Lancaster, 4–6; *Clark County Survey*, 12–14; Bevins, *History*, 15–16, 24–25, 39, 45, et passim; and, Walter E. Langsam and Gus Johnson, *Historic Architecture of Bourbon County, Kentucky* (Paris, Ky.: Historic Paris-Bourbon Co., Inc., 1985), 14–15, et passim.

Data on the saddlebag and dogtrot are drawn from fieldwork and also Langsam and Johnson, 14–15; Montell and Morse, 18, 20–22, 24–26; *Clark County Survey*, 14; Lancaster, 14–15, 158; Bevins, *History*, 17–18, 59; Newcomb, 31–32; Jessica Foy, "Saddlebag House," *Encyclopedia of Southern Culture*, 519; Whitley, "Footnotes," January 24, 1958; and, Mary C. Oppel, "Paradise Lost..." *Filson Club History Quarterly* 56 (April 1984) 2: 204.

Kniffen's seminal article on the I-house is "Folk Housing: Key to Diffusion," *Annals of Association of American Geographers* 55 (1965), 549–77. General characteristics and Bluegrass examples of I-houses are discussed in *Clark County Survey*, 15–29; Montell and Morse, 32–40; Langsam and Johnson, 17, 90, 105, 153, 180; DeCamp, 68–69; Coleman, *Historic Kentucky*, 150; *Jessamine County Survey*, 10–26; Bevins, *History*, 98, 105–7; and, Lancaster, 16–17, 30–33. Robards and his infamous I-house is discussed in Bruce Strother, "Negro Culture in Lexington, Kentucky," M. A. thesis, University of Kentucky, 1939, 15, 20; and, Coleman, *Slavery Times*, 157–71 (a photo is opposite p. 162). The hall-and-parlor/central-passage discussion draws on Bevins, *History*, 84; Montell and Morse, 28–30, 89; *Clark County Survey*, 13; *Jessamine County Survey*, 10–16; and Newcomb, 38.

The discussion of slave quarters, the transition from log houses to nonfolk forms, and the appearance of sawmills and frame and brick houses, and the effect of language upon architecture, is enhanced by Coleman, "Lexington . . . Travellers," 267–68, 272; J. Winston Coleman, Jr., *Lexington's First City Directory* (Lexington: Winburn Press, 1953), 3; Coleman, *Sketches*, 187–88 (photos of slave cabins); Langsam and Johnson, 211; Kramer, 41–42; Ann Bevins, "Black History Statement of Historic Context . . . , Scott County, Kentucky, 1774–1918" (unpublished report prepared for the Kentucky Heritage Council, 1989), 2–3, 12, et passim, an invaluable study, used elsewhere in this present work; Coleman, *Slavery Times*, 21–28, 51–54, 76–77 (and see photos of slave quarters facing p. 50, and of detached kitchen, p. 56); *Jessamine County Survey*, 4, 10–16; Kniffen and Glassie, 42, 44–45; Wright, 9; Coleman, *Historic Kentucky*, 105, 185; Coleman, *Sketches*, 67–73; Samuel M. Wilson, "Pioneer Kentucky in its Ethnological Aspects," *Kentucky Historical Society Register* 31 (October 1933) 97: 29; Purvis, 263–64; McMeekin, 4; Richard Pillsbury, "Cultural Landscape: The Upland South," *Encyclopedia of Southern Culture*, 539; *Clark County Survey*, 3, 5, 15, 19–22; Wharton and Bowen, 11; Lancaster, 11–14, 19–20; Bevins, *History*, 4, 84, 86, 108; Montell and Morse, 42; Frances Jewell McVey and Robert Berry Jewell, *Uncle Will of Wildwood: Nineteenth Century Life in the Bluegrass* (Lexington: University Press of Kentucky, 1974), 50; Langsam and Johnson, 17; Raitz, *Kentucky Bluegrass*, 107; and Newcomb, 1–2, 16, 37–38.

The gentry's custom of naming their estates and the legends associated with them are widely noted, as in Coleman, *Slavery Times*, 173–75, 305–306; DeCamp, 14, 42–44, 70–71, 96, 162–63, et passim; McMeekin, 12–13; Mary Ida Williams, *Living in Kentucky* (privately printed, 1962), 75–78; Simpson, 17–20, 30, et passim; Coleman, *Sketches*, 13–20, et passim; Everman, 65–66; Raitz, *Kentucky Bluegrass*, 130; Bradley Smith, 111, 114; Strother, 13; Wharton and Bowen, 181, et passim; Newcomb, 41, 44–46, 67–68; Langsam and Johnson, 17; *Jessamine County Survey*, 54–55, 60–61. Some data about Liberty Hall are from student projects; and I have personally heard all of these tales.

The discussion of Georgian, Federal, and other nonfolk styles and the Bluegrass recycling custom of enclosing an older log house within a newer form draws upon *Jessamine County Survey*, 10–30; *Clark County Survey*, 19–33; Langsam and Johnson, 17–26; Bevins, *History*, passim; Newcomb, 41–71; DeCamp, 70–71; Coleman, *Historic Kentucky*, 140, 150–51; Bedford, *Proud Land*, 518–19; Raitz, *Kentucky Bluegrass*, 106; and, Lancaster, 16–17.

Carolyn Murray Wooley's definitive work on Bluegrass stone houses is not yet published, but a prelude is her article "Kentucky's Early Stone Houses," *Antiques* 105 (March 1974): 593. Other Bluegrass stone houses of note, Kentucky "marble," and legends about houses are discussed in Newcomb, 7–8; Owen, 15; DeCamp, 26–27, 32–33, 88, 90, 116–17; Lancaster, 15–18; Bevins, *History*, 38, 62, 66, 76, 78; *Clark County Survey*, 15–17; Langsam and Johnson, 15–16, 82, 94–95; *Jessamine County Survey*, 6–8; Coleman, *Historic Kentucky*, 53, 80, 82, 130, 185; Powell, 110; and *Historic Woodford County, Kentucky*, pamphlet. The Clay and Dora legend and others are retold by William H. Townsend, *Hundred Proof* (Lexington: University of Kentucky Press, 1964), 118–37; Coleman's summary of antebellum gentry life is from *Slavery Times*, 15–47.

CHAPTER 5

The definitive work on urban Bluegrass freedmen and their residential patterns has yet to be written, so sources are sketchy; two clear exceptions are the invaluable study of rural Bluegrass black settlement patterns by Peter C. Smith and Karl B. Raitz, "Negro Hamlets and Agricultural Estates in Kentucky's Inner Bluegrass," *Geographical Review* 64 (1974): 225–26, et passim; and, Bevins' excellent "Black History," 9–11, 14–18, 19–26, et passim, both used elsewhere in this present work. Also helpful are J. Winston Coleman, Jr., *Lexington During the Civil War* (Lexington: Commercial Printing, 1938), 46–49; Coleman, *Slavery Times*, passim; Herbert A. Thomas, Jr., "Victims of Circumstance: Negroes in a Southern Town, 1865–1880," *Kentucky Historical Society Register* 71 (July 1973) 3: 253–71; Lowell H. Harrison, *The Civil War in Kentucky* (Lexington: University Press of Kentucky, 1975), 89–97, 102–110; John Kellogg, "Negro Urban Clusters in the Postbellum South," *Geographical Review* 67 (July 1977) 3: 313; Thomas D. Clark, "Southern Common Folk After the Civil War," *South Atlantic Quarterly* 44 (April 1945) 2: 141–43; Clark, *History*, 261, 348–52; Clark, *Land of Contrast*, 114–15; Hambleton Tapp and James C. Klotter, *Kentucky: Decades of Discord, 1865–1900* (Frankfort: Kentucky Historical Society, 1977), 5–10, 61–62, 90–94, 283–85, 377–78, 382–83; Bedford, 83; *Clark County Survey*, 5; Everman, 64–68, 104–13; *Federal Writers' Project*, 5–6; Gaines, Vol. 2, 118–19; Glenn, 199–200; Kramer, 114–15; Railey, 5–6; and, Wharton and Williams, 73, 94, 127–28, 135–50. Some oral history data are from interviews with Mr. Charles Hicks, and Ms. Nawanta Jenkins.

The postbellum shift to "Victorian" and other "stylish" houses, and criticism of them, is discussed in Bevins, *History*, 4; Bevins, "Black History," 21–26, et passim; *Clark County Survey*, 5, et passim; Tapp and Klotter, 283–85; and Clark, *History*, 261.

The shotgun house has been well documented; see either of two articles by John Vlach, "Shotgun Houses," *Natural History* 86 (February 1977): 50–57, or "The Shotgun House: An African Architectural Legacy," in *Common Places: Readings in American Vernacular Architecture*, edited by Dell Upton and John Vlach (Athens: University of Georgia Press, 1986), 58–78; and, M. B. Newton, Jr., "Shotgun House," *Encyclopedia of Southern Culture*, 519–20. The Frankfort, Georgetown, and Lexington examples are noted in Kramer, 181, Bevins, "Black History," 19, et passim, and Raitz, *Kentucky Bluegrass*, 58, 146–47. Some data are from my fieldwork.

General descriptions of the T-plan, bungalow, and pyramidal vernacular forms are provided in the *Encyclopedia of Southern Culture*, 496–97, 517, 521–22, 538; and Bluegrass examples, as well as the railroads' influence, are discussed in *Clark County Survey*, 103–4, 111–12.

In addition to interview data from Jimmy Fox, Betty Smith, and others who wish to remain anonymous, and from personal experience, the discussion of the "wrong side of" town/tracks in Winchester, Frankfort's Craw, and other similar Bluegrass areas profits from Glenn 27–28, 130–33, 187; Kramer, 179, 181–82, 327, 342, 365–68; Thomas D. Clark, "Agriculture: Rural Life: Folk Culture," *Encyclopedia of Southern Culture*, 8; Helen Price Stacey, "The Beauty of Frankfort at Christmastime," *Re-Discover Kentucky*, December 15, 1972; *Clark County Survey*, 3, 6–7; *Federal Writers' Project* 25–26; and, Kentucky River Folklife Survey #KR0033LC.TAP, August 4, 1989.

Data about Lexington's Pralltown and Irishtown and other ethnic neighborhoods are from fieldwork with Ms. Nawanta Jenkins, Mr. Lafe Taylor, Ms. Geneva Spickard, Ms. Dede Kalbfleisch, and others who wish to remain anonymous, and a telephone conversation with Don Edwards on the *Herald– Leader* staff. Other information is from *North University Small Area Plan* (Lexington: Lexington-Fayette Urban County Division of Planning, 1983), 12, 31; *Pralltown Development Study* (Lexington: Lexington-Fayette Urban County Government, 1975), 2–3, 14; *Irishtown, Davistown, South Hill Neighborhood Study* (Lexington: City-County Planning Commision, 1971), 9–11, 47; Jacqueline Duke, "New Housing Brings Heartache in Irishtown," Lexington *Herald–Leader*, December 20, 1983, 1; Joe Woestendiek, "Valley of Neglect," Lexington *Leader* supplement, December 19, 1980; "Description of the Manchester Center Area," and C. Frank Dunn, "The Town of Manchester," unpublished manuscripts in the library of the Manchester Center in Irishtown; Raitz, *Kentucky Bluegrass*, 58; and, *Federal Writers' Project*, 25–26.

In addition to my own fieldwork, descriptions of the black rural hamlets and postbellum estates are taken from Smith and Raitz, 218–34; Clark, *History*, 350–52; *Federal Writers' Project*, 119; Raitz, *Kentucky Bluegrass*, 100–108; Harold M. Rose, "The All-Negro Town...," *Geographical Review* 55 (1965): 362–81; Knight and Greene, 7–8; and Schwabb, 292–303.

Tenancy in the South is well-documented, as in Tapp and Klotter, 296–99; Clark, *History*, 351; and in two articles in *Encyclopedia of Southern Culture*, "Tenant Farmers," by David E. Conrad, 1412–13, and "Sharecropping and Tenancy," by Paul E. Mertz, 29–31. The tenant house is discussed in Montell and Morse, 26–28; and noted in Raitz, *Kentucky Bluegrass*, 105–107.

CHAPTER 6

Considerable data are from my own fieldwork on various sorts of farms and rural trailer patterns in the Region, but much of the discussion of Bluegrass gentleman farms and baby farms is either quoted or paraphrased from Raitz's invaluable survey, noted above. Other data are from Coleman, *Sketches*, 171; Raitz, *Kentucky Bluegrass*, 9–10, 56, 97; Bradley Smith, 136, et passim; "Trailer Transformation," Lexington *Herald–Leader*, December 15, 1989, E-2; Sue Wahlgren, "British are Hungry for Details of Queen's Visits to Bluegrass," Lexington *Herald–Leader*, December 3, 1989, K-2; Wharton and Bowen, 106, 109–10, 192, 237, et passim; and student project by Teddi Baker, December 1989.

In addition to my own fieldwork data, the discussion of Bluegrass rural outbuildings draws upon Mary Wharton, "Barns in the Bluegrass Scene," *Lexington As It Was* (Lexington: Lexington-Fayette County Historic Commission, 1981), 28–33; Wharton and Bowen, 113, 115, 126, 137–42; Wright, 204–5; Richard Pillsbury, "Cultural Landscape," *Encyclopedia of Southern Culture*, 536; Eric Sloane, *An Age of Barns* (New York: Funk & Wagnalls, 1966), 80; Montell and Morse, 52–86; Bevins, *History*, 4, 10, 13, 21–22, 24, 37, 81–82; *Clark County Survey*, 34, 47, 53, 69–70, 81–82, 86, 88–89, 93–94; DeCamp, 14, 16, 18, 25–26, 28, 64, 92; Langsam and Johnson, 29–30; Coleman, *Historic Kentucky*, 80, 91; Owen, 26; Newcomb, 71; and *Jessamine County Survey*, 94–95.

CHAPTER 7

The early history of mill construction, as well as photographs of both extant and destroyed mills, is documented in Bedford, *Proud Land*, 12–13; Bevins,, *History*, 260–64; Everman, 9–10, 38–40; Whitley, "Footnotes," January 10, 1958, January 24, 1958, January 31, 1958, February 7, 1958, June 20, 1958; Coleman, *Historic Kentucky*, 104, 110–11, 194; Newcomb, 8, 40; Powell, 48, 64; Wharton, 128; DeCamp, 32; Bettie L. Kerr, *Lexington: A Century in Photographs* (Lexington: Lexington-Fayette County Historic Commission, 1984), 230; *Jessamine County Survey*, 4, 163; Clark, *Land of Contrast*, 86; and Owen, 60. Examples of meal sacks, a rare nineteenth century steam mill, and other folk artifacts can be seen at the Forkland Heritage Festival. The mill as a social center is described in Bedford, *Proud Land*, 12, 109; "Clark County Chronicles," Winchester *Sun*, April 5, 1923; Coleman, *Historic Kentucky*, 194; and Whitley, "Footnotes," February 7, 1958, from which is drawn the description of everyday mill atmosphere. The destruction of most Bluegrass mills, and the preservation of the Weisenberger Mill, is discussed in Bevins, *History*, 262–65; Owen, 15; Powell, 64; Raitz, *Kentucky Bluegrass*, 108; and Whitley, "Footnotes," January 24, 1958.

The romantic days of the stagecoach, and the social significance of early inns and taverns, are addressed in J. Winston Coleman, Jr., *Stage-Coach Days in the Bluegrass* (Berea, Ky.: Kentucke Imprints, 1976), especially 57–60, 63, 182, 184, 195; Perrin, 191; Newcomb, 37; Kramer, 92–93; Powell, 126; Williams, 22; Bedford, *Proud Land*, 128–30; *Federal Writers' Project*, 90; Coleman, *Historic Kentucky*, 177; Langsam and Johnson, 244–45; Newcomb, 73–74; and Powell, 120. The Jillson quote is from Kramer, 62. An advertisement pamphlet by Julia S. Ardery, *Visit Duncan Tavern and Anne Duncan House* (n. p., n. d.), contains pertinent information about Duncan Tavern; Grayson Tavern is also detailed in a tourist pamphlet, *Discover Historic Danville* (Danville: Danville-Boyle County Historical Society, n. d.); see also Powell, 116. Mai Flournoy VanArsdall in a mimeographed manuscript, "Morgan Row—History," examines that Harrodsburg tavern; see also Coleman, *Stage-Coach Days*, 187–88. Postlethwait's is described in Coleman, *Stage-Coach Days*, 180; Newcomb, 18; Raitz, *Kentucky Bluegrass*, 81; Charles R. Staples, *The History of Pioneer Lexington, 1779–1806* (Lexington: Lexington-Fayette County Historic Commission, 1939), 34–35; *Federal Writers' Project*, 25–26; and John D. Wright, Jr., "Histories of Lexington," *Lexington—As It Was* (Lexington: Paddock Publishing, 1981), 63, 86. The three country taverns—Johnston's, Offutt-Cole, and Colby—are discussed in Bedford, *Proud Land*, 145–46, 522; Coleman, *Historic Kentucky*, 55, 73, 138; Coleman, *Stage-Coach Days*, 184–85; Lee, 184; Powell, 32, 80–81, 128; Railey, 65–66, and see Offutt-Cole photo and caption between pp. 32 and 33; Langsam and Johnson, 45–46; DeCamp, 76–77; *Historic Woodford County, Kentucky* (Versailles: Woodford County Historical Society, n. d.), pamphlet; and Offutt-Cole Tavern Kentucky Historical Highway Marker. Additional information concerning the Colby Tavern was obtained from an interview with its present owner, Mrs. Laurel Garrett.

Early Bluegrass churches are described in Bevins, *History*, 268; Bedford, *Land of Our Fathers*, 247–55; Clark, *Land of Contrast*, 42–49, 51; Coleman, *Historic Kentucky*, 99; Newcomb, 35, 73; and Powell, 58. Information about the Cane Ridge Meeting House and the Barton Stone religious movement was acquired though personal interview of Rev. Franklin McGuire, curator at Cane Ridge, and from informational material provided by him; see also: Newcomb, 36; James B. Finley, "Awful Beyond

Description," *Bluegrass Cavalcade*, 289–91, and editor Clark's comments, 286–89; William L. Hiemstra, "Early Frontier Revivalism in Kentucky," *Register of Kentucky Historical Society* 59 (April 1961): 138–45; Harry Harrison Kroll, *Bluegrass, Belles, and Bourbon* (South Brunswick and New York: A. S. Barnes, 1967), 46–48; and Coleman, *Sketches*, 203–205. For information concerning the Old Stone Meeting House, see: Carol Marie Cropper, "State's Oldest Active Church Still Has a Faithful Congregation," Lexington *Herald–Leader* October 26, 1980, B-1; *Clark County Survey*, 34–35; Owen, 16; James H. French, personal correspondence; Bedford, 207–208; and Coleman, *Historic Kentucky*, 33. Other early stone churches and Old Mud are discussed in Coleman, *Historic Kentucky*, 39, 44–45, 76, 97, 154; DeCamp, 53; *Jessamine County Survey*, 85; Langsam and Johnson, 61; Wharton and Bowen, 222; Newcomb, 9, 37–38; and "Old Mud Meeting House is Unique," *Historic Boyle and Mercer Counties*, 28. Shaker customs and resultant architecture have been well documented; e.g., see Rexford Newcomb, "Introduction," *Old Kentucky Architecture* (New York: Bonanza Books, 1940); Newcomb, *Architecture in Old Kentucky*, 102–5; *Historic Boyle and Mercer Counties*, 7, 19; "Shaker Architecture," public service videotape presentation made for Kentucky Educational Television; "This is Pleasant Hill: A Brief History with Index," mimeographed pamphlet, 1973, 3–4; James C. Thomas, "Shaker Architecture in Kentucky," *Filson Club History Quarterly* 53 (January 1979): 29–32; Coleman, *Pictorial History*, 69–70; and data from student fieldwork project, Kathy Richards, December 1989. Data on storefront churches were drawn primarily from my own fieldwork and a student project by Sherry Gann, April 1987. For comments on Bluegrass attitudes toward religion see McMeekin, 145; Asbury, 34; and *Federal Writers' Project*, 6.

CHAPTER 8

In addition to my own fieldwork over the years, and more recently with Mr. Sosby and Mr. Alexander, managers of Claiborne and Darby Dan farms, respectively, and employees of Calumet farm, the discussion of the Bluegrass horse world draws upon Raitz, *Kentucky Bluegrass*, 93, et passim; Bradley Smith, 19–29, 97–110, et passim; Wharton and Bowen, 70–96, et passim; Dan White, *Kentucky Bred* (Dallas: Mountain Lion, 1986), 69, 76–80, et passim; Joe H. Palmer, *This Was Racing* (Lexington: Henry Clay Press, 1973), 250–52, et passim; Peter Willett, *Makers of the Modern Thoroughbred* (Lexington: University Press of Kentucky, 1986) passim; Tom Biracree and Wendy Insinger, *The Complete Book of Thoroughbred Horse Racing* (Garden City: Doubleday & Co., 1982), 8–15, et passim; and, James Lane Allen, *The Blue-Grass Region of Kentucky* (New York: Harper & Brothers, 1892), 93, 115, et passim. The desert oasis story is from memory, as I have heard it often; and the printed version of the Clark County horse-swapping legend is in Lawrence S. Thompson, *Kentucky Tradition* (Hamden, Conn.: Shoe String Press, 1956), 44–45. Boone quotes are from Coleman, *Sketches*, 232, 241, and Glenn, 26, records the treatment of horse thieves in Frankfort.

History, figures, and quotes about early Bluegrass horse activities and about the famous stallion Lexington are drawn from Timothy Flint, *History and Geography of the Mississippi Valley*, Vol. 1 (Cincinnati: E. H. Flint, 1833), 355; F. A. Michaux, *Travels to the Westward of the Allegheny Mountains* (London: J. Mawman, 1805), 231–40; Thomas D. Clark, *The Rampaging Frontier* (Bloomington: Indiana University Press,

1939), 226–27; Kent Hollingsworth, *The Kentucky Thoroughbred* (Lexington: University Press of Kentucky, 1985), 13–17, 24–32; Sara Shallenberger Brown, "The Kentucky Thoroughbred," *Filson Club History Quarterly* 25 (January 1951) 1: 11; Palmer, 160; Tapp and Klotter, 103–4; and Wharton and Bowen, 10–17, 27–30.

The quote about modern horse farms is from the excellent study (pp. 35, 46) by Raitz of Bluegrass gentleman farms, cited previously, and used throughout this present discussion. Bowen's comments are in Wharton and Bowen, 143–64; see also, White, 12–13, 15. Some data also are from the Keeneland Association Library and the Lexington Chamber of Commerce, and fieldwork.

Comments, data, and legends about early Bluegrass street races are taken from McMeekin, 58–59; Bradley Smith, 19, 28–29, 62; Thompson, 46; J. Winston Coleman, Jr., *The Squire's Sketches of Lexington* (Lexington: Henry Clay Press, 1972), 22; Coleman, *Sketches*, 232; Newcomb, 49; Hollingsworth, 15–19; Brown, 9; Tapp and Klotter, 105; and, Wharton and Bowen, 16–17.

Historical data concerning the Jockey Club, the Kentucky Association, the Williams track, Chittlin' Switch, Keeneland, Henry Clay's involvement, and early equestrian folk paintings are derived from Wright, 41, 68; Clark, *Agrarian Kentucky*, 31; Hollingsworth, 22, 158; Richard Laverne Troutman, "Henry Clay and His 'Ashland' Estate," *Filson Club History Quarterly* 30 (April 1956) 2: 167; Coleman, *Squire's Sketches*, 23, 27, 34, 87; Coleman, *Sketches*, 177–83, 232–38; Newcomb, 49; Ann Bevins, "Lesson in History," Lexington *Leader*, October 30, 1962; Bradley Smith, 49–55, 62, 64; Wharton and Bowen, 16–22, 40–42, 50, 53–56; Bettie L. Kerr, *Lexington: A Century in Photographs* (Lexington: Lexington-Fayette County Historic Commission, 1984), 14, 167, 219; *The American Turf* (New York: The Historical Society, 1898), 455; Palmer, 165, 194; and William Butt and William Strode, eds., *Keeneland: A Half-Century of Racing* (Louisville: Harmony House, 1986), 25, 92–93. Some information, including the anecdote about Keeneland's black section, comes from fieldwork.

The folklore of racing is vast, and especially legends and trickster tales are in wide oral circulation; I have personally heard all those represented here, but they also are often recorded in print. The Dare Devil story is in *The Kentucky Gazette*, March 5, 1905, and is also noted in Thompson, 45–46. Billy Reed's moving version of the Graustark legend is taken from Butt and Strode, 67. Tom R. Underwood and John I. Day, *Call Me Horse* (New York: Coward-McCann, 1946), 86, record a version of the "mare dropping her foal" story that is set in Montana, illustrating a typical characteristic of such stories, indeed *all* folklore, to migrate in variants; see also, Clark, *Rampaging*, 229–30. Tales about Colonel Chinn are prolific; the printed version of the "moving the post" trickster tale/legend is taken from Jack Lohman and Arnold Kirkpatrick, *Successful Thoroughbred Investment in a Changing Market* (Lexington: Thoroughbred Publishers, 1984), 46–47, an excellent, practical, and thorough work, used elsewhere in this study; for another printed version of the Chinn story and for Chinn's quoted comments see Bradley Smith, 144–45. See also: Eslie Asbury, "Kentucky Wit and Humor," *Filson Club History Quarterly* 55 (January 1981) 1: 32; and, Kent Hollingsworth, *The Archjockey of Canterbury and Other Tales* (Lexington: The Blood-Horse, 1986), 298–304, for other Chinn comments and for the historically accurate details surrounding the Chinn legend. The "veranda" trickster/stereotype anecdote is from Palmer, 177–78; and the "financial rewards" anecdotes are from fieldwork and from Don Edwards, Lexington *Herald–Leader*, September 12, 1988, B-1.

Fieldwork provided most data about the folk shenanigans, mascots, superstitions, the "duck reward" and other customs, and the legends about Will Harbut and Man

O' War; but some are also noted in Bradley Smith, 58, 61, 90, 139–40, 144; Wharton and Bowen, 55, 191–93; Kerr, 218; Underwood and Day, 20; and "Biggest Hoss in Wuld," Lexington *Herald*, November 2, 1947. The Harbut quote is from Thompson, 42–43. Big Red's life, including his birthday party, is outlined in Page Cooper and Roger L. Treat, *Man O' War* (New York: Julian Messner, Inc., 1950), 154, et passim.

Though stories about Man O' War's funeral are still told in the Bluegrass, the details are from "Man O' War Is Embalmed," Louisville *Courier–Journal*, December 2, 1947; "Man O' War to Lie in State..." Lexington *Leader*, November 2, 1947; Ed Ashford, "Great Horse Buried..." Lexington *Herald*, November 5, 1947; Kyle Vance, "2,000 See Man O' War Rites..." *Courier-Journal*, November 5, 1947; and "Man O' War Will Be Interred Today," *Courier-Journal*, November 4, 1947.

Fieldwork data is used for much of the discussion of black and Irish handlers and jockeys, but other information is provided by Wittke, 25; Biracree and Insinger, 125; and, Knight and Greene passim. Strother, 75–90, Bradley Smith, 154, and Wright, 152–53, discuss the Bluegrass folk hero Isaac Murphy, and Strother provides data on Brown-Dick. Comments about Hispanic jockeys are from fieldwork, from Lohman and Kirkpatrick, 63, and from a TV interview with Randy Romero, WLEX-TV, April 21, 1990.

In addition to fieldwork, Standardbred, Saddlebred, horse show, and Red Mile data, as well as printed versions of the Nancy Hanks legend are derived from Coleman, *Sketches*, 236; Coleman, *Squire's Sketches*, 75, 88; Wharton and Bowen, 22, 70, 74–76, 78–79, 88–89; Wright, 129, 180; Bradley Smith, 99, 101–2; Kerr, 31, 47; and Thompson, 47–48, who also provides the Nancy Hanks spin-off legend set at Hialeah, which again illustrates the wide range of oral folk tradition. Folk "tricks of the trade" at the trots are detailed in a 1981 student project by Laura Williams, and some data, such as the "Fuzzy-Wuzzy" anecdote, are from fieldwork. The smoking scandal and other anecdotes and data, and quotes about absentee-owners and the gentry's carriages, are taken from Joe Jordan, *The Blue Grass Horse Country* (Lexington: Transylvania Press, 1940), 131–32; Gerald Carson, *The Polite Americans* (New York: William Morrow, 1966), 230; Bradley Smith, 64; Wharton and Bowen, 31, 35, 72–78; McMeekin, 136; Lohman and Kirkpatrick, 76; White, 167–68; Hester P. Wilson, *An Escape from Reality* (New York: Exposition Press, 1963), 10–11; and Coleman, *Sketches*, 174. The discussion of buggy racing, etc., draws on fieldwork interviews with Jane Stafford, Alma Stapleton, and others, and is supplemented by Kerr, 112, Harlow, 299, Jim Warren, "Tuned Up," Lexington *Herald–Leader*, February 18, 1990, and by student projects and personal fieldwork.

CHAPTER 9

Most data about traditional horse-farm procedures derive from personal fieldwork over the years, and more recently with Mr. Sosby and Mr. Alexander and their employees, of Claiborne Farm and Darby Dan Farm, respectively, and with Calumet farm employees, and other horse people. The discussion also draws upon the following secondary sources: Lohman and Kirkpatrick, 103–10, 113–22, 185–99, et passim; Biracree and Insinger, 5, 47, 60–61, 65–69, 74–75, 82, 94–103, et passim; White, 7, 15–24, 89–94, 101–24, et passim; Bradley Smith, passim; Wharton and Bowen, 219, et passim; Palmer, 15, et passim; Thomas Kiernan, *The Secretariat Factor*

(Garden City: Doubleday, 1979), 30–32, 57, 68–69, 97–99, et passim; Hollingsworth, *Thoroughbred*, passim; and, Willett, 223, et passim. Allen's, "The Genealogical Landscape and the Southern Sense of Place," in Allen and Schlereth, 152–63, perceptively outlines Kentucky genealogy/culture ties.

The passage about the use of "Mane N' Tail" by women as a hair conditioner is from Catherine Chriss, "Product for Horses' Tails Going Straight to Kentuckians' Heads," Lexington *Herald-Leader*, November 23, 1989, E-1, 8; and fieldwork data on the popular culture exploitation of folk veterinary treatments is supplemented by Lyndel Meikle, "The Scrap Pile," *American Farrier's Journal* 15 (December 1989) 7: 10–12; see also, White, 128, 132. Contemporary fieldwork data about farriers was supplemented with historical data from Brent Mershon, "Neighbors at Work," Winchester *Sun*, November 29, 1989, 1; Lucille S. Davis, "Old Photo Stirs Memories of Blacksmith Shop in Midway," Woodford *Sun*, August 2, 1984; Mrs. Charles Nave, "Blacksmith Shop in Midway Was Active into the 1950s," Woodford *Sun*, August 9, 1984; "Time Was When Blacksmith Shops Were Familiar Sight," Lexington *Herald*, April 8, 1980, D-6; and, Lorena Wise, "Remember When," *Frankfort State Journal*, June 16, 1976, 27.

The "white stocking" rhyme is from memory, and Biracree and Insinger, 75, record another version. Data about John Henry are from fieldwork and from the Kentucky Horse Park; but Hollingsworth, *Thoroughbred*, 167–83, Lohman and Kirkpatrick, 24–26, and White, 23–24, also provide information on this superb gelding.

There are many folk subterfuges at the sales and the quote about them, and the trickster tale about the inebriated greenhorn is from Palmer, 256–59; see also White, 15–23, et passim. The Jansen quote and excerpts are from his "Who'll Bid Twenty" article cited in the Introduction; and Biracree and Insinger, 90–91, White, 29–38, and Bradley Smith, 42, provide other information on sales, auctions, and auctioneers.

The traditional naming of Thoroughbreds and stories about that process are topics of great interest in the Bluegrass, and in addition to fieldwork the discussion draws upon Biracree and Insinger, 118–19; Lohman and Kirkpatrick, 53–54; Palmer, 21, 27–29; Underwood and Day, 26; and Wharton and Bowen, 172–74. The specious Nancy Hanks legend is recorded in "Naming of Nancy Hanks," *Paris Kentuckian-Citizen, 140th Anniversary Edition* (1948), 4, 8, and has also been in oral circulation. Breaking and training data are from fieldwork and student projects, but White, 108–24, et passim also provides a good discussion of the process; and he notes the Thoroughbreds' disposition at death.

The following supplemented fieldwork data about traditional horse cemeteries: Ray Hemphill, "Marble and Memories," *The Blood-Horse*, January 3, 1981, 52–54; Judi Joseph, "Horse Cemeteries," Lexington *Herald–Leader*, May 4, 1980; Frank T. Phelps, "No Public Cemeteries for Horses," Lexington *Leader*, April 4, 1968; "Horse Cemeteries," Lexington *Herald*, October 16, 1962, 16; Don Edwards, "Horse Laugh," Lexington *Herald–Leader*, March 15, 1984; Wharton and Bowen, passim; and the Keeneland Association Library. The Morgan/Black Bess legend may be the most widely circulated story in the Bluegrass; I have heard it many times. In addition to field data, the following historic accounts provide the quotes and otherwise supplement the discussion: Burton Milward, "The Unveiling of the Morgan Statue," *Lexington As It Was*, 53–56, and Townsend, 102–7.

CHAPTER 10

Tales of wagering and games of chance, and of legendary gamblers in the early Bluegrass can be found in Bradley Smith, 30–31, 55, 62, 144–46, 154; Clark, *Land of Contrast*, 80; Thompson, 51–59; Wright, 40–41; Bedford, *The Proud Land*, 505; Whitley, "Footnotes," March 22, 1957; James I. Robertson, Jr., "Revelry and Religion in Frontier Kentucky," *Register of the Kentucky Historical Society* 79 (1981): 363, and VanArsdall, 1, 7. The delightful relationship between Parrish and his church is revealed in Joe H. Palmer, "The Finger of Providence," *Bluegrass Cavalcade*, 120–23. Data concerning "handbooks" and modern-day bookmaking were drawn from personal interviews with, among others, Nawanta Jenkins, Blanche Kercheval, Sue Wahlgren, and Owen Williams; field research at Darby Dan and Claiborne farms; and a student project by Jeff Rogers, April 1990. See also Wharton and Bowen, 163.

CHAPTER 11

Iroquois huntsman Patrick Murphy provided much of the information and materials utilized in this discussion, and I also attended the annual Blessing of the Hounds, November 1989. In addition, an article by Linda S. Henson and Richard A. Smithers, "The Blessing of the Hounds," *Rural Kentuckian* 42 (1988): 8–11, 17–18, provided pertinent data. Thompson includes a chapter on fox hunting from which was drawn the story of James Campbell and the tall tales about foxes; see especially pp. 64–65, 165. The attribution of fine foxhounds to the Bluegrass limestone is found in Roger D. Williams, *Horse and Hound* (Lexington: privately printed by author, 1905), 138–39; the place-name legend is from *Jessamine County, Kentucky, 1798–1973 Souvenir Book* (n.d., n.p.), 32. The eloquent tribute to the foxhound is found in Bradley Smith, 110; see also p. 106. Other sources include Richard S. and Patricia S. DeCamp, *The Bluegrass of Kentucky* (Lexington: The Rayburn Press, 1985), 32; Kerr, 230; Wharton and Bowen, 134–35; Asbury, "Kentucky Wit and Humor," 38; *The Complete Guide to Kentucky Horse Country* (Louisville: Classic Publishers, 1981), 72, 73, 75; Peter Winants, "The Great American Foxhound Match," *The Chronicle of the Horse* 52 (September 1989): 3–6; student project by J. C. Gaines, December 1989; "Annual Roster of the Organized Hunts of America 1989–1990," *The Chronicle of the Horse*, 41, 43, 56.

CHAPTER 12

Comments on early Bluegrass hunting traditions, including the Boone/ Audubon legend were provided by Mann Butler, "Details of Frontier Life," *Kentucky Historical Society Register* 62 (July 1964) 3: 206–29; Cotterill, 94–95, 238–39; Collins, 51; Thompson, 137–38; and, John James Audubon, "The Management of the Rifle," in

Bluegrass Cavalcade, 258–62. The Mike Fink legends are noted in Thompson, 2–3, 135–37. Chinn, 333–36; Thompson, 4, 52; Harlow, 98; and student projects and fieldwork provide data about the long rifle and Kentuckians' modern use of it; see also, the four "muzzleloader" articles by Art Lander, Jr. in the Lexington *Herald–Leader*, October 14, 1990, C-12.

Arthur K. Moore, *The Frontier Mind: A Cultural Analysis of the Kentucky Frontiersman* (Lexington: University of Kentucky Press, 1957), 54–56, 70–71, 82, 107, 200–202, 223; and, Lehmann, 125–26, support the discussion about the romanticizing of hunting traditions. The Clay legends, sometimes still told in the Region, are recorded in William C. Davis, "'Taking the Stump': Campaigning in Old-Time Kentucky," *Kentucky Historical Society Register* (Autumn 1982): 378; Robb Sagendorph, *Robb's Cabinet of Curiosities* (Dublin, N. H.: Yankee, Inc., n. d.), 24; Carson, *Polite Americans*, 120–21; and Coleman, *Sketches*, 20. An excellent discussion of turtle hunting and consumption as folk activities is in Simon J. Bronner, *Grasping Things* (Lexington: University Press of Kentucky, 1986), 160–78.

Ganderpulling, bearbaiting, and cockfighting are discussed in David F. Hawke, *Everyday Life in Early America* (New York: Harper & Row, 1988), 98–99; Thompson, 48–50, 147; Coleman, *Sketches*, 60–61; Dora Peel Haines, *Life on a Kentucky Stock Farm* (New York: Hobson Book Press, 1947), 87–88; Thomas D. Clark, "The Sign of the Cockpit," in *Bluegrass Cavalcade*, 265–69; and, "Commentary," Lexington *Herald–Leader*, April 1, 1990, B-5; some data are from fieldwork and student projects.

Clay Smith and modern hunting, fishing, etc., traditions and the laws that impact them are discussed in articles by Art Lander, Jr., in the Lexington *Herald–Leader*, November 26, 1989, B-12; and October 21, 1990, C-16; and, in the same paper, an article by Jamie Lucke, "Hunters, Activists Square Off," October 7, 1990, C-1; and in a 6:00 p. m. newscast on WKYT-TV, September 20, 1990; considerable data from fieldwork.

CHAPTER 13

Providing an overview of the penchant for violence and homicide in the Bluegrass is Robert M. Ireland, "Homicide in Nineteenth Century Kentucky," *Kentucky Historical Society Register* 81 (1893): 134–53. J. Winston Coleman, Jr. wrote more specifically about the "code of honor" both in his books and in various articles; see, for example, "The Code Duello," *Filson Club History Quarterly* 30 (April 1956): 126–27; "The Code of Honor in Kentucky," in *Lexington—As It Was*, 46–51; and *Sketches*, 39–46. Carson devoted an entire chapter, "Murder at Ten Paces," to the practice of dueling in his book *The Polite Americans*, 114–28. Other authors who discuss Bluegrass dueling and the proliferation of weapons on the Kentucky frontier are Clark, *Land of Contrast*, 80; Wright, 57–58; Chinn, 358, 601; Townsend, 118–37; Staples, 145; Bradley Smith, 94; Robertson, 357–58, 364; McMeekin, 100; Harlow, 106–8, 181; Bedford, *Proud Land*, 509; Kroll, 21; and Tapp and Klotter, 402–4.

CHAPTER 14

Discussions concerning the origin and history of bourbon, and its uses on the Bluegrass frontier, can be found in Gerald Carson, *The Social History of Bourbon* (Lexington: University Press of Kentucky, 1963), 10, 24–25, 28, 32, 33–49, 53, 55, 71–93, 245; Kroll, 24–26, 36, 55, 61, 96–98, 143; Marie Campbell, "This Hosesome Beverage," in *Kentucky Hospitality: A 200-Year Tradition*, edited by Dorothea C. Cooper (Louisville: Kentucky Federation of Women's Clubs, 1976), 132–35; Bernard Mayo, "Goshen of the Western World," in *Bluegrass Cavalcade*, 20; Clark, *Land of Contrast*, 184–85; Everman, 36–37; Langsam and Johnson, 38; Thompson, 34–35; Bradley Smith, 147–48; Coleman, *Squire's Sketches*, 20; Lehmann, 187; and Glenn, 210. See also: Ireland, *County*, 1; "U. S. S. Kentucky Christened with Bourbon," Lexington *Herald–Leader*, August 12, 1990, C-7; "High Bridge," mimeographed sheet in Kentucky Historical Society Archives; and "Fish Might Thrive on 'Whiskey Leavings'," Lexington *Herald–Leader*, January 20, 1991, E-1.

The probably fortuitous discoveries of using corn for whiskey distillation and of then aging it in charred barrels, as well as associated legends, are described in Carson, *Social History*, 26–29, 36–37, 40; Clark, *Land of Contrast*, 50, 184–85; Kroll, 26; and Lawrence S. Thompson, "Whiskey in Kentucky Folk Belief," *Kentucky Folklore Record* 20 (1974): 35. Contemporary data on the craft of the master distiller is from fieldwork with master distiller Booker Noe of Jim Beam Distillery, and tape logs from Kentucky River Folklife Project, Teresa Hollingsworth fieldworker; see also Kroll, 54, 155.

Many tales are told about Kentuckians' legendary love of their native brew; see, e.g., Asbury, "Kentucky Wit and Humor," 37–38; Carson, *Social History*, 56; Mayo, 14, 22; Robertson, 355, 357; Thompson, *Kentucky Tradition*, 33, 38; Kroll, 155; Clark, *Rampaging*, 188; and promotional materials from Heaven Hill Distillery. Stories of Bluegrass politicians and their love of bourbon are innumerable; see, e.g., Carson, *Social History*, 47, 55, 58, 212; and Kroll, 147–48, 150, 155–56. The role of whiskey in Bluegrass folk politicking is further described in Thomas N. Allen, "The 4th of July," in *Bluegrass Cavalcade*, 201–9; Carson, *Social History*, 55–56; Clark, *Agrarian Kentucky*, 115; Ireland, *County*, 14; William Littell, "Too Much Spirit," in *Bluegrass Cavalcade*, 186–91; and Robertson, 365–66. The status of moonshining and bootlegging in the modern Bluegrass derives from my own research and common knowledge; see also: Carson, *Social History*, 89; Kroll, 147; David W. Maurer, *Kentucky Moonshine* (Lexington: University Press of Kentucky, 1974), xv, xvii; Bradley Smith, 148; Wright, 169–70; and Thompson, *Kentucky Tradition*, 39.

The effects of Prohibition upon the family distilling business and its product is described in Carson, *Social History*, 33–34, 57; Kroll, 79, 123; Thompson, *Kentucky Tradition*, 32, 38; and by Jim Beam's master distiller, Booker Noe. Various reasons have been offered for the shift by distilleries away from the Inner Bluegrass counties; see, e.g., Carson, *Social History*, 83, 89; Kroll, 21, 79, 143, 146; Wright, 169; and promotional materials from Heaven Hill Distillery. Most of the information concerning the Jim Beam Distillery and the Beam dynasty is drawn from an interview with Booker Noe; see also: Carson, *Social History*, 34, 43, 79; Kroll, 61–76; materials in the Oscar Goetz Museum of Whiskey History, Bardstown. Endeavors by the whiskey industry to promote its product by evoking age and tradition are apparent in its promotional materials and merchandizing tactics; see also Carson, *Social History*, 34, 53, 84, and Kroll, 213, 215. Information about the remaining influences of tradition upon the industry, as well as the Japanese factor, is drawn from Carson, *Social History*, 43, 223–24; Kroll, 40, 41, 83, 210; Wild Turkey, Ancient Age, and Seagrams tape logs from the Kentucky River Folklife Project; Noe interview; and Heaven Hill, Jim Beam, and Wild Turkey promotional materials. Heaven Hill and Maker's Mark Distilleries are discussed in Kroll, 15, 29–34, 35–37, 55–63; Bruce Allar, "The Little Distillery That Could," *Sky* 17 (May 1988) 5: 105–6; and in their promotional materials. In addition to fieldwork data, the mint julep discussion derives from Carson, *Social History*, 214–15; Thompson, *Kentucky Tradition*, 31–32; *Kentucky Hospitality*, 139; Bradley Smith, 149–50; White, 176; Clark, *Land of Contrast*, 192–93; J. Soule Smith, "Zenith of Man's Pleasure," in *Bluegrass Cavalcade*, 270–71; and Heaven Hill promotional materials.

CHAPTER 15

The lament concerning the popularity of tobacco appeared in "Clark County Chronicles," Winchester *Sun*, January 14, 1981; see also Kramer, 185, and Wright, 148. The boast and descriptions of the "filthy practice" of tobacco chewing can be found in Carson, *Social History*, 51; Clark, *Rampaging*, 104; Robertson, 357; and Harlow, 53. *Jessamine Souvenir Book*, p. 33, is the source of the place-name legend. Early Kentuckians' preference for chewing rather than smoking is explained in W. F. Axton, *Tobacco and Kentucky* (Lexington: University Press of Kentucky, 1975), 58–60, and Melvin G. Herndon, *William Tatham and the Culture of Tobacco* (Coral Gables: University of Miami Press, 1969), 413. Introduction of White Burley is documented by numerous sources, including Axton, 68–70; Herndon, 404, 409; Kerr, 170, 231; Kramer, 184–85; and Wright, 148, 198. Contemporary data concerning tobacco farming and auctioneering are primarily drawn from my own fieldwork and tape logs of the Kentucky River Folklife Project, LuAnne Cervelli and Jennifer Ramsay, fieldworkers. See also: Raitz, *Kentucky Bluegrass*, 114–16; Axton, 123–24, 127; Charles S. Guthrie, "Tobacco: Cash Crop of the Cumberland Valley," *Kentucky Folklore Record* 14 (1968): 39–41; Herndon, 437–38; Don Kendall, "Number of Farms Growing Tobacco Declines Rapidly," Owensboro *Messenger–Inquirer*, June 23, 1990, 6-A; McMeekin, 126; Raymond Jahn, ed., *Tobacco Dictionary* (New York: Philosophical Library, 1954); and Hensley C. Woodbridge, "Eleven Kentucky Tobacco Words," *Kentucky Folklore Record* 3 (1957): 59–65. Beliefs concerning tobacco and smoking are enumerated in Lawrence S. Thompson, "Some Notes on the Folklore of Tobacco and Smoking," *Kentucky Folklore Record* 10 (1964): 43–46. In addition to oral fieldwork versions, the "horse eating tobacco" legend is recorded by Don Edwards, "Smoking Fires up Passions in Kentucky," Lexington *Herald–Leader*, February 22, 1991, C-1.

CHAPTER 16

Perhaps the most valuable source for the early history of Bluegrass foodways are the articles contained within *Kentucky Hospitality*, a compilation of brief, mainly historical, papers by various scholars and contributers, plus traditional recipes; see particularly Otis Rice, "The Foods of Pioneer Kentucky," 20–28; Marcia Cebulska, "The Pioneer Kitchen," 29–35; R. Gerald Alvey, "Folk Beliefs About Food and Eating in Kentucky," 11–19; and comments preceeding salad recipes by Jay Anderson, 164–65, and introducing dessert recipes by Shirley Snarr, 190–95. The description of Colonel Whitley's breakfast is from the same book, Burton Milward, "Elegant Dining in Kentucky," 51. The parched corn/Native American data are from a graduate student project by Kathy Dickison, December 1990. Other pertinent information can be found in Janet Alm Anderson, *A Taste of Kentucky* (Lexington: University Press of Kentucky, 1986), 1–3; *Food For Thought: An Ethnic Cookbook* (Lexington: Fayette County Human Rights Commission, 1976); Clark, *Land of Contrast*, 242; Thompson, *Kentucky Tradition*, 123–30; and Everman, 5. A concise description of southern foodways can be found in the *Encyclopedia of Southern Culture*, 614–15.

As is much of the information concerning Bluegrass foodways, the data on lamb fries are drawn from my own research and knowledge of the area. The popularity of pork is attested by various sources; see, for example, Marion Flexner's classic cookbook, first published in 1949, *Out of Kentucky Kitchens* (Lexington: University Press of Kentucky, 1989), 132; McMeekin, 140; Collins, 451; and Asbury, *Horse Sense*, 177. The delightful description of Johnnie Furlong's is from Bradley Smith, 152–53. Both Flexner, 130, and Clark, *Bluegrass Cavalcade*, 278–79, proclaim the superiority of Kentucky ham; and its place in Bluegrass culture and history is heralded by Asbury, *Horse Sense*, 181, and Harlow, 282, and in the charming tale about General Harrison's visit to the Bluegrass recounted by M. C. Darnell in the typed manuscript, "Historic Bellepoint," 2–3. Recipes for the selection and preparation of Kentucky hams, and the red-eye gravy which often accompanies them, are myriad; see, for example, Flexner, 130–31; Janet Anderson, 9; Kroll, 36; and a recent cookbook which includes, among many others, favorite recipes of various Bluegrass horse farms, *Bluegrass Winners: A Cookbook* (Lexington: The Garden Club of Lexington, 1985), 142. The defender of ham gravy is Allan Trout, "Abundant Life," in *Bluegrass Cavalcade*, 279–80.

Much of the discussion concerning biscuits is drawn from my own fieldwork data; see also *Bluegrass Winners*, 37, 45; Harlow, 278; and *Kentucky Hospitality*, 117, for recipe. The importance of corn and cornbread in the life of early Bluegrass Kentuckians is documented in Janet Anderson, 3; Rice, 25; and Bradley Smith, 26. Various kinds of cornbread, and their traditional preparations, are detailed in Jay Anderson's introduction to "Breads" in *Kentucky Hospitality*, 110–11, and subsequent recipes 112–15; Rice, 23–24; Cebulska, 31; *Bluegrass Winners*, 269.

The traditionality of all-day cooking of beans and greens and other vegetables by both black and white cooks is verified by my own fieldwork; see also Margaret Allen Averill, "'Good Old Days' Had Good Cooks, Too," *Frankfort State Journal*, January 4, 1976. The remainder of the discussion concerning vegetables also draws from my own fieldwork data. The history of Bibb lettuce is entertainingly recounted in Jack Clowes, "Kentucky Burgoo," Harrodsburg *Herald*, December 11, 1969, 6; see also Flexner, 172, and Jay Anderson, 165. Traditional menus of some horse farms are from my fieldwork, but are also detailed in *Bluegrass Winners*, 19, 39, 79, 87, et passim.

The fishing legend of Daniel Boone is from "Clark County Chronicles," Winchester *Sun*, June 24, 1981, 18. Fish and game fries, and complementary dishes, pig roasts and varmint dinners, are described in *Bluegrass Winners*, 31, 100; Flexner, 30; Kentucky River Folklife Project tape logs, Teresa Hollingsworth, fieldworker; and John Ed Pearce, "Franklin: Kentucky's Capital County," *Courier-Journal Magazine*, January 8, 1978, 13. For ruminations concerning the origin and history of burgoo, consult Thomas D. Clark, "An Air of Mystery," in *Bluegrass Cavalcade*, 276–78; Davis, 375; Flexner, 54–56; Marion Brown, *Southern Cookbook* (Chapel Hill: University of North Carolina Press, 1968), 65; *Bluegrass Winners*, 124; Janet Anderson, 21; *Kentucky Hospitality*, 2, 54, 181, 186–87; Wright, 41; Rice, 22; Paul Atkinson, *Kentucky: Land of Legend and Lore* (Cincinnati: Kalko Productions, 1962), 10; Coleman, *Sketches*, 160–64; Thompson, *Kentucky Tradition*, 127–28; Clark, *Agrarian Kentucky*, 116; McMeekin, 66; White, 176; and Whitley, "Footnotes," July 10, 1959. The stories of Hardin, the Frankfort chef and cockfighter, and of the visiting Philadelphians, as well as other references to burgoo, can be found in Harlow, 289–92. The eloquent description of a political barbecue belongs to Thomas N. Allen, "The 4th of July," in *Bluegrass Cavalcade*, 202–3; see also McMeekin, 66; Davis, 374–75; and Clark, "Air of Mystery," 278.

For an overview of traditional desserts, see Snarr, 190–97. In addition, consult: Charles Patteson with Craig Emerson, *Charles Patteson's Kentucky Cooking* (New York: Harper & Row, 1988), passim—a good source not only for desserts but many traditional items of Kentucky cuisine; Flexner, 182, 194, 198–99, 210, 219–20, 237, 257–58; Marty Godbey, *Dining in Historic Kentucky* (Kuttawa, Ky.: McClanahan Publishing House, 1985), 63–64; Harlow, 274–75; and *Bluegrass Winners*, 287. The origin and preparation of Derby Pie is in Kevin Osbourn, "Kern's Kitchen Wins Trademark Suit," Lexington *Herald–Leader*, March 15, 1990, B-5. Bourbon balls are discussed in *Kentucky Hospitality*, 268–73, Heaven Hill Distillery promotional materials, and Susan Stone, "A Sweet Kentucky Tradition," *Kentucky Living* 45 (1991): 8–10.

The delicious dishes consumed at Bluegrass ladies' luncheons is provided by McMeekin, 61, and the transparent pie story is recounted in Flexner, 219. The quote about "the swarm" is taken from James Lane Allen, "County Court Day," in *Bluegrass Region*, 89–125. The discussion of dinner-on-the-ground and other similar get-togethers, such as family reunions, which feature the sharing of food, is drawn from my own fieldwork data plus the following sources: *Kentucky Hospitality*, 194, 238–39, 248, 266; Flexner, 219; McMeekin, 141; and Judi Joseph, "Shropshire Clan Turns Reunions into an Art Form," and "Of Family Gatherings and Potato Salad," Lexington *Herald–Leader*, August 29, 1990, FA-2. The tailgate picnic has also been featured in two articles: Leo Demski, "Fans, Baked Beans and Sun Part of Tailgating," *Kentucky Kernel*, September 4, 1990, 1, 7; Julee Rosso and Sheila Lukins, "A Tailgate Picnic Anyone Can Tackle," *Parade*, September 23, 1990, 10, 12.

Recipes and brief discussions of the Hot Brown can be found in Flexner, 31–32, and *Kentucky Hospitality*, 101; the origin of the porterhouse steak is identified in Raitz, *Kentucky Bluegrass*, 111. The words of the "sprightly lady in her eighties" were quoted from Harlow, 275; see Joseph, "Of Family Gatherings," for the description of a typical family reunion. Restaurants serving traditional foods are described in Godbey, 59, 60, 76, and in local Bluegrass newspapers, especially the "Weekender" section of the Lexington *Herald–Leader*. The author has also conducted considerable fieldwork on this subject!

AFTERWORD

Tom Clark's comments and "bulldozer" quote are from *Land of Contrast*, 280–90; the Bluegrass as no "poor man's" land observation is from Richard L. Troutman, "The Physical Setting of the Bluegrass Planter," *Kentucky Historical Society Register* 66 (October 1968) 4: 368, 370. The Bluegrass "kitsch" quote comes from a perceptive study by a former student of mine and Karl Raitz: Dorn Van Dommelen, "The Mobilization of Place," unpublished M. A. thesis, University of Kentucky, 1988, 38; Morton's comments are from his *Kentuckians Are Different* (Louisville: Standard Press, 1938), 42; Berry's views are from his *A Continuous Harmony: Essays Cultural and Agricultural* (New York: Harcourt Brace Jovanovich, 1975), 70, et passim; and, Dr. Wharton's comments are recorded in Beverly Fortune, "Steel Magnolia," Lexington *Herald–Leader*, October 20, 1991, K–1.